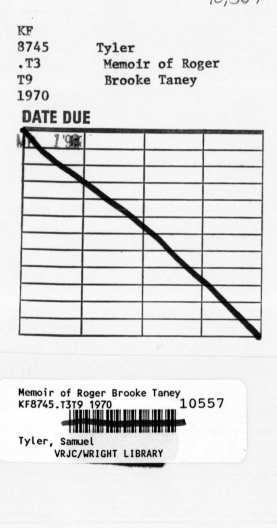

Memoir of Roger Brooke Taney

MEMOIR OF
Roger Brooke Taney

By Samuel Tyler

DA CAPO PRESS · NEW YORK · 1970

A Da Capo Press Reprint Edition

This Da Capo Press edition of Samuel Tyler's *Memoir of Roger Brooke Taney* is an unabridged republication of the first edition published in Baltimore in 1872.

Library of Congress Catalog Card Number 78-87703

SBN 306-71688-7

Published by Da Capo Press
A Division of Plenum Publishing Corporation
227 West 17th Street
New York, N.Y. 10011

Manufactured in the United States of America

Memoir of Roger Brooke Taney

ever & truly
your friend
R. B. Taney

MEMOIR

OF

Roger Brooke Taney, LL.D.

BY SAMUEL TYLER, LL.D.

OF THE MARYLAND BAR.

Qui nihil in vitâ nisi laudandum, aut fecit, aut dixit, aut sensit.

BALTIMORE:
PUBLISHED BY JOHN MURPHY & CO.
182 BALTIMORE STREET.
1872.

JOHN MURPHY & CO.,
PRINTERS AND PUBLISHERS,
BALTIMORE.

TO THE

Hon. Richard H. Marshall,

AND

Hon. James M. Coale,

OF THE FREDERICK BAR.

GENTLEMEN:

BECAUSE OF OUR FRIENDSHIP RUNNING THROUGH SO MANY YEARS, AND THE FACT THAT YOU HAVE SIGNALIZED YOUR VENERATION FOR THE MEMORY OF CHIEF JUSTICE TANEY, BY ERECTING, WITH THE PERMISSION OF HIS FAMILY, A MONUMENT OVER HIS GRAVE, I INSCRIBE THIS MEMOIR TO YOU. YOURS, FAITHFULLY,

SAMUEL TYLER.

MAY, 1872.
FREDERICK CITY,
MARYLAND

vii

PREFACE.

ABOUT two years before the death of Chief-Justice Taney,* in a conversation with him on the Lives of the Chief Justices of England, by Lord Campbell, he expressed a wish that I would write his life. It was accordingly agreed between us that I would do so; though I was fully aware of the difficulty and the delicacy of the undertaking. And how, almost entirely, I have had to rely upon my own resources for the materials of the life, will appear by the following letters from Mr. Campbell, the son-in-law of the Chief Justice, and a distinguished member of the Baltimore Bar.

BALTIMORE, November 4, 1864.

My Dear Sir:

I this morning received your favor of the 3d. It gives me and the family great satisfaction to learn that you intend writing the Chief Justice's life, and have been for some time making collections with that view. I shall be very happy to contribute any information to you which I possess. I do not know whether you have ever seen Van Santvoord's Lives of the American Chief Justices. The volume was published by Scribner, of New York, in 1854. Many of the facts in it, and particularly those relating to his English ancestors, were communicated to the author by me, *ex relatione* of the Chief Justice. Van Santvoord says that the name Taney is of Welsh extraction, but I think that a mistake. There is a church known as Taney in Ireland, and I think in the county Dublin; and the name appears in the Rolls of Letters Patent and Closed in the years 1203 and 1221, published by the English Record Commission. I have a copy of a pedigree of the Brookes beginning in 1602 and ending in 1717. It records the aspect of the Planets at the time of the births of several of the children. If you think it would be worth while, I will send you a copy. I will also send Van Santvoord's book, if you have not got it.

Great men have often simple tastes, and the Chief Justice was no exception. He was passionately fond of flowers, and always thought well of one who liked them.

Yours, very truly,   J. MASON CAMPBELL.

SAMUEL TYLER, ESQ., Frederick City, Md.

* Taney is pronounced *Tawny.*

ix

BALTIMORE, November 29, 1864.

MY DEAR SIR:

I received your letter of the 26th, and to-day send you the Lives of the Chief Justices.

The Chief Justice kept no copies of the letters he wrote, and, with very few exceptions, destroyed all he received. I have not yet examined his private papers, of which he left very few, but have no idea that any which he did leave would be of any service to his biographer. The Supplement which he wrote to the Dred Scott case was copied by Mr. William J. Stone of Washington, and sent to Bishop Hopkins, to be used by him in his then forthcoming work on Slavery. He made no use of it that I am aware, and would no doubt return it to Mr. Stone on his application.

I will send you a copy of the Brooke pedigree, and I will also send you a copy of a protest which he addressed to Secretary Chase, against the taxation of the salaries of the Judges of the Supreme Court. Although the other Judges did not unite with him in it, it received their approbation so far, at least, that they directed it to be recorded on the minutes of the Court. I shall bear in mind the necessity of furnishing you with everything available for your work, which I am glad to know is in such fit hands.

Yours, very truly,   J. MASON CAMPBELL.

SAMUEL TYLER, ESQ.

With the small aid furnished by Mr. Campbell, my long intimacy with the Chief Justice enabled me to inquire at the proper sources for the information which I have given in the Memoir. It is all perfectly authentic. I spared no pains in verifying everything. To vindicate one who had been so misrepresented, so hated, even after he had gone to his grave, has necessarily imposed upon his biographer the duty of dealing somewhat harshly with his political enemies. I have forborne to speak of some public men, who deserve censure, because I feel that I have sufficiently vindicated the character of the Chief Justice without doing so.

> Get but the truth once uttered, and 'tis like
> A star new born, that drops into its place,
> And which, once circling in its placid round,
> Not all the tumult of the earth can shake.

NOTE. — The engraved likeness of the Chief Justice, in this volume, is a perfect representation of him in his eighty-fifth year. It was thought best to represent him as a private citizen, as he appeared every day.

CONTENTS.

CHAPTER I.

xi

CHAPTER II.

LIFE IN FREDERICK. — A. D. 1801–1823.

Description of Frederick — The business of the place — The refined society — Thomas Johnson, upon whose nomination General Washington was
chosen Commander-in-Chief of the American forces — The kind of law business in Frederick — His diligence as a student — His studies miscellaneous —
A candidate, on the Federal ticket, for the Legislature — Is defeated — Marries
Miss Key, the sister of the author of "The Star-Spangled Banner" — The
romantic residence where Miss Key was born — The charming mode of life on
Maryland Plantations — Happily married — He affiliated with society in all
its relations — Trustee of the Academy — Director of a Bank — His punctuality
in the discharge of duties — His festive relaxations qn the shady banks of the
Monocacy — Fond of excursions on horseback — In the summer at Arcadia, the
residence of Mr. Shaaf — Mrs. Taney participates in his love of nature — Counsel for General Wilkinson — Refuses to receive a fee for defending the General —
The war of 1812 — Against the declaration of war — After war is declared, sup-
ports it with zeal — Denounced by a portion of the Federal party — Alienated
from Mr. Thomas — Their reconciliation at the death-bed of Mr. Thomas — The
history of the origin of "Star-Spangled Banner" — Nominated for a seat in the
House of Representatives — Is defeated — His spirit of toleration of difference
of opinion — Elected to the Senate of Maryland — Serves with distinction — An
amusing anecdote of Mr. Martin and Mr. Taney — Mr. Martin, Mr. Taney, and
Mr. Shaaf in a great ejectment cause — Defends the Rev. Mr. Gruber charged
with attempting to incite slaves to insurrection — His speech — The impartiality
of the administration of law in Maryland — A Marylander murdered in Pennsylvania in attempting to recover by law his fugitive slave — A gentleman murdered by his slaves in Frederick County — The slaves receive a fair trial at law —
Mr. Taney attains such eminence, that he argues causes, from every county in
the State, in the Court of Appeals — His training as a lawyer — His skill and
manner in the trial of causes — Always advises amicable adjustment of disputes — His marked deference to the Bench and courtesy to the Bar — Anec-
dotes of Mr. Ross and Mr. Palmer — His character as a lawyer, by Mr. Schley
of Baltimore — The death of William Pinkney — Mr. Randolph's speech in the
Senate of the United States on the occasion — Chief-Justice Marshall's opinion
of Mr. Pinkney — Mr. Walter Jones's opinion — The last days of Mr. Martin —
The grave of Mr. Taney's mother, at Frederick — His pious devotions — Request that he shall be buried by the side of his mother, whenever he dies.

CHAPTER III.

LIFE IN BALTIMORE. — A. D. 1823–1836.

Takes up his residence in Baltimore — The origin and character of the
Federal Government — The history of its working — The origin and history
of the two great political parties traced through every administration down
to the election of General Jackson — The policy and principles of the two parties — Many of the great statesmen as they appeared as actors on the politi-

CHAPTER IV.

Judicial Life. — A. D. 1836–1856.

CHAPTER V.

JUDICIAL LIFE. — A. D. 1856–1860.

CHAPTER VI.

JUDICIAL LIFE. — A. D. 1860–1864.

CHAPTER VII.

PRIVATE LIFE.

APPENDIX.

MEMOIR

OF

ROGER BROOKE TANEY, LL.D.

CHAPTER I.

EARLY LIFE AND EDUCATION.

(Written by Mr. Taney himself.)

A. D. 1777 — 1801.

I BEGIN this account of my life at Old Point Comfort, Virginia, on the 16th of September, 1854. It is late to begin it, for, if I live until to-morrow, I shall be seventy-seven years and six months old. I may not live to finish it, and, if finished, it may not be thought worthy of publication. Of that, however, my executors must judge.

The work is undertaken without much deliberation. Ten days ago, I had never thought of it. But I received at that time Mr. Van Santvoord's Lives of the Chief Justices of the U. States, and among them is a sketch of my own. The work is full of interest, and obviously prepared with much labor and industry.

My life is, therefore, to form a part of the history

17

of the country. The high offices I have filled, and the stirring and eventful political scenes in which I was engaged before I received the appointment I now hold, and in which my position compelled me to take a prominent part, may naturally create a desire to know more about me than can be found in Mr. Van Santvoord's life. Yet I am sensible that he has written it in the kindest spirit, and has used every means in his power to obtain information from those whom he supposed might be able to give it.

The truth is, that scarcely any one living could do much more than Mr. Van Santvoord has done. I have survived all my early associates and companions, and most of those also with whom I was acting in maturer life. At the moment I am writing, the names of dear and valued friends who are now in their graves come crowding on my memory, and I begin this work in sadness and sorrow.

But if there is any curiosity to know more about me than Mr. Van Santvoord narrates, it cannot be gratified, unless I write my own biography. Indeed, upon thinking the matter over, I have come to the conclusion that, if the public should be indifferent and careless as to my life and character, the work may derive some interest from its connection with men and things as they existed in the generation which has now passed away. I belong to that generation, and lived and acted in it and with it. And the history of my life is necessarily associated with the manners, habits, pursuits, and characters of those with whom I lived and acted.

I am sensible of the delicacy of this undertaking. An autobiography is hardly ever impartial, and I cannot hope that I am free from the general infirmity of self-love. But I will try to write my own life as if it were that of a third person.

My situation at Old Point Comfort is some inducement to begin the work at this time.

The labors of the last term of the Supreme Court impaired my health seriously, and I have spent the summer with my family at this place for the benefit of the sea-air and salt-water bathing. It will be six weeks more before my official duties require me to return home. While I remain here, I am free from the calls of business. And to one whose life has been spent in the active concerns of life, and whose mind has been constantly exercised, a long-continued state of perfect idleness, without books, cannot be good for the mind or the body. And an hour or two every day passed in recalling to memory times gone by, and putting down my recollections, will afford me an agreeable occupation without fatigue, useful, perhaps, to the mind and the body. Constant thought about one's health, and watching its changes, is not a very pleasant occupation, nor the best way of restoring it.

But to begin my task. I have no family papers or

memoranda with me. The life must, therefore, be written altogether from memory.

I was born on the 17th of March, 1777, in Calvert County, in the State of Maryland. My father, Michael Taney, owned a good landed estate, on which he always resided, and slaves. His property was sufficient to enable him to live comfortably, and to educate his children. His plantation was situated on the banks of the Patuxent River, about twenty miles from its mouth, where the river is more than two miles broad, and navigable for vessels of the largest size. The British fleet anchored opposite to his house during the War of 1812, in the expedition against the city of Washington.

The situation, for all social purposes, was a very retired one. It was bounded, as I have said, on one side by the river, and on another by a deep tide-water creek, called Battel Creek, which runs into the country for several miles at a right angle to the river. The families which we visited by land were several miles distant from us, and our chief social intercourse was, in boats across the river or the creek, with families who resided on the opposite shores.

My forefathers, on my father's side, were among the early emigrants to Maryland, and had owned and lived upon this estate for many generations before I was born. We have no family record showing the precise time of their coming to Maryland, or the country from which they migrated. They were Roman Catholics. After the accession of William and Mary to the throne of England, the severe penal laws of that country against Roman Catholics were introduced into Maryland; and, among others, every Roman Catholic was prohibited from teaching a school in the province. Parents were naturally unwilling to send their children to a school where their religion would be scoffed at, and the children subjected to humiliation and insult. The education of Roman Catholics, therefore, whose parents could not afford to send them abroad, was generally nothing more than their parents could teach, with occasional aid secretly given by the priest.

It was, consequently, usually confined to reading, writing, and a little arithmetic, just enough to enable them to transact their ordinary business, as planters, without inconvenience. The children, whose fortunes would afford it, were sent to France to be educated. And my father was accordingly sent to the English Jesuits' college at St. Omer's, and removed with it to Bruges when it was expelled from St. Omer's. He had finished his education, and returned home, some years before the commencement of the American Revolution, and his father being dead, he took possession of his estate, and married my mother, Monica Brooke, about the year 1770.

My mother was the daughter of Roger Brooke, who owned a large landed estate on Battel Creek, directly opposite to that which belonged to my father. He was lineally descended from Robert Brooke, who left a written memorandum of his family, and of the time of his settlement in Maryland, which has been preserved by his descendants. It is in the following words:

"Robert Brooke was born at London, 3d June, 1602, being Thursday, between 10 and 11 of the clock in the forenoon, being Corpus Christi Day.

"Mary Baker, born at Battel in Sussex.

"Robert Brooke and Mary Baker intermarried 1627, the 25th of February, being St. Matthias' Day and Shrove Monday.

"1. Baker Brooke, eldest son to Robert and Mary Brooke, was born at Battel, November the 16th, being Sunday, at half hour past 9 o'clock in the morning, being new moon the night before, and was baptized the 2d day of December following, his Uncle Thomas Brooke, and his Grandfather Baker, his Godfathers, and his Aunt Foster, wife to Mr. Robert Foster, his Godmother, 1628.

"2. Mary Brooke, eldest daughter to Robert Brooke and Mary his wife, was born 1630, at Battel, the 19th day of February, being Saturday, between 2 and 3 of the clock in the afternoon, the moon being new the next day, and was baptized the Sunday following, her Godfather Mr. Thomas Foster, of Battel, and her Godmothers her Grandmother Baker and her Cousin Heath.

" 3. Thomas Brooke, second son to Robert Brooke and Mary his wife, was born at Battel, 1632, the 23d day of June, being Saturday, a quarter of an hour past 2 o'clock in the morning, and was baptized the 3d day of July following, his Godfathers Mr. Christopher Dow Dean, of Battel, and Mr. Thomas Bryan, of Battel, his Godmother Mrs. Eliza Foster, wife to Mr. Goddard Foster.

" 4. Barbara Brooke, second daughter to Robert Brooke and Mary his wife, born at Whickham.

" May the 11th, 1635, Robert Brooke (aforementioned) was married to Mary, second daughter to Roger Mainwaring, Doctor of Divinity and Dean of Worcester, which Mary was born at St. Giles-in-the-Fields, London.

" 1. Charles Brooke, eldest son of Robert Brooke and Mary his wife, was born at St. Giles-in-the-Fields, Middlesex, 3d April, 1636, between 11 and 12 o'clock in the forenoon, being Sunday, and was baptized the day following, his Grandfather, the Bishop of St. David's, and his Uncle Townley, his Godfathers, and his Aunt Stedney his Godmother, under ♃ Jupiter 3 min.

" 2. Roger Brooke was born the 20th September, 1637, at Bretnock College, between 11 and 12 o'clock at night, it being Wednesday, and was baptized the following day, his Godfathers the Bishop of St. David's and his Uncle Stevens, and his Aunt Sarah Mainwaring his Godmother, ♃ under Jupiter.

"3. Robert Brooke was born at London, in St. Brides' Parish, April 21st, 1639, half an hour before 1 of the clock in the morning, it being Sunday and new moon two days after, his Godfather my Cousin Thomas Foster (♃ under Jupiter), son to Serecant Foster and my Cousin William Brooke, and his Godmother my sister Elizabeth.

"4. John Brooke, born at Battel, the 20th September, 1640, being Sunday, between 1 and 2 o'clock in the afternoon, his Godfather William Jackson, D. P., and his Godmother Mrs. Jackson.

"5. Mary Brooke was born at Battel the 14th day of April, being Thursday, 1642, after 1 o'clock in the morning, the moon being in the last quarter the Tuesday before, her Godfather Mr. Jackson, and her Godmother old Mrs. Beneford.

"6. William Brooke, born at Battel the 1st day of December, 1643, between 11 and 12 o'clock at night, the moon being new in the morning at 5, and baptized the same day, his Godfather Mr. March and his Godmother Mrs. Pound.

"7. Ann Brooke, born at Bretnock, 22d January, 1645, between 5 and 6 of the clock at night, being Thursday, her Godfather the Bishop of St. David's, his Deputy her Uncle Henry Mellyne, her Godmothers Mrs. Mary Mainwaring and Mrs. Jones, ♀ under Venus.

"8. Francis Brooke, born at Horwett in Hantshire,

the 30th May, 1648, being Tuesday, between 11 and 12 o'clock at noon, D under Luna.

"The before-named Robert Brooke, Esquire, arrived out of England in Maryland the 29th day of June, 1650, in the 48th year of his age, with his wife and ten children. He was the first that did seat the Patuxent, about twenty miles up the river at Dela-brook, and had one son there, born in 1651, called Basil, who died the same day. In 1652 he removed to Brooke Place, being right against Delabrook; and on the 28th of November, 1655, between 3 and 4 o'clock in the afternoon, had two children Eliza and Henry, twins. He departed this world the 20th day of July, and lieth buried at Brooke Place Manor; and his wife, Mary Brooke, departed this life the 29th November, 1663."

I give this memorandum in full, not merely to show his family and the time of his immigration, but as a curious historical fact, showing how deeply the delusions of astrology at that time influenced the minds of intelligent men. For the precision of his entry as to the times of the birth of his children, and the position of the planets at the moment, are evidently noted in this memorandum to enable an astrologer to foretell their fortunes.

I speak of Robert Brooke as a man of intelligence because the offices he held show that he was so considered by his contemporaries. For soon after his arrival he was appointed by Lord Baltimore Commander of Charles County, and was chosen by the commissioners, appointed by Cromwell for the reducing the Plantations, Governor of Maryland. He, as well as my father's ancestors, originally settled in St. Mary's County, on the banks of the Patuxent, nearly opposite to their Calvert dwellings; and within my recollection some of their descendants were still residing on the same places.

I do not know what was the religion of Robert Brooke, but my grandfather Roger Brooke was a Roman Catholic; and, for the reasons I have stated, my mother's education, as far as mere matter of human learning was concerned, was a very limited one. But her judgment was sound, and she had knowledge and qualities far higher and better than mere human learning can give. She was pious, gentle, and affectionate, retiring and domestic in her tastes. I never in my life heard her say an angry or unkind word to any of her children or servants, nor speak ill of any one. When any of us or the servants about the house who were under her immediate control (all of whom were slaves) committed a fault, her reproof was gentle and affectionate. If any of the plantation-servants committed faults, and were about to be punished, they came to her to intercede for them; and she never failed to use her influence in their behalf, nor did she ever hear of a case of distress within her reach, that she did not endeavor to relieve it. I remember and feel the effect of her teaching to this hour.

So much for my parents and parentage. My parents both lived to an advanced age. They had several children, — four sons and three daughters. I was the third child and the second son.

The Revolution had removed all difficulty in our education upon the score of religion. For the constitution established by the State of Maryland in 1776 placed all persons professing the Christian religion on an equal footing. But the situation in which we lived was, as I have said, a retired one; and there was no school within ten miles of us except one, which was distant three miles, kept in a log-cabin by a well-disposed but ignorant old man, who professed to teach reading, writing, and arithmetic as far as the rule of three. The reading and writing, as may well be supposed, were poor enough; but, for want of a better, I was sent to it, when not more than eight years of age, with my elder brother and sister. We walked every day to and from the school when the weather was good, and when it was unfavorable we stayed at home. Our attendance, therefore, was not very regular. My father had no taste for teaching, and did not very often assist us in our lessons. He was fond of reading, and I believe read every work he could obtain in the then scant libraries of the country. But he soon wearied with the lessons of children, and became impatient if we did not learn as fast as he thought we should. He took far more pleasure in teaching my elder brother and myself how to ride and swim, and to fish, and to row and sail in the summer, and to skate and to shoot ducks and wild geese in the winter. I cannot remember the time when I could not ride on horseback, and but faintly remember my first efforts at swimming.

With all these disadvantages we however got along in due time as far as our humble teacher could carry us. Our only school-books were Dillworth's spelling-book and the Bible; and these, I believe, were the only books our teacher had ever read. I remember yet the pleasure I felt when I was able to read and understand the fable of the boys and the frogs, and the wagoner praying to Hercules, etc., etc., in the spelling-book, and admired the wretched wood-cuts with which it was embellished. As for the Bible, it was used merely as a book to teach us how to spell words and pronounce them. Our teacher professed to belong to the Episcopal Church; but the nearest church was ten miles distant, and as he was poor, and his two horses were worked hard in cultivating a few acres of poor land which he owned, and were not, from their appearance, very well fed, I doubt whether he went to church more than once or twice a year, if so often. He was, however, a kind man, upright and conscientious, and faithfully performed his duty to the best of his power. How he happened to obtain the little learning he had, I do not know. For at the time of which I am speaking, I believe the one-half of the men in the county, of his humble rank in life, could not write their own names. But it must be recollected that this was soon after the conclusion of the Revolutionary War, and the men of whom I am speaking had grown up under the English Government. And the parents in our neighborhood, who could not read themselves, eagerly sent their children to this school. It had generally about thirty scholars, — which was a large number considering its retired situation and the sparse population about it.

The only exciting event which occurred while I was at this school was barring-out the school-master. I mention it to show the usages and the habits of the times in the part of the State in which my family lived. It was the custom of the school to have a fortnight's holiday at Christmas; and the day it was to commence was always announced by the school-master a week beforehand. The object of barring him out was to compel him to begin the holidays some days sooner. But it was not so much for the purpose of gaining a few more days of idleness, as for the pleasure and excitement of the feat. And, strange as it may appear at this day, the parents of the scholars all knew of the plan, and were always ready to advise as to the best mode of defence, and encouraged the children to fight bravely and conquer the master, if he should prove obstinate and break in.

The barring-out to which I was a party, was carefully planned among the boys some days before it was executed. It was the custom of the school-master to give us a recess every day from twelve o'clock until one, to give us an opportunity of eating our dinners, (which we all brought with us,) and for recreation. This hour was technically called in the school, playtime, during which the teacher always went to his own house, distant a few hundred yards, for his own dinner, and never returned to the school-house until playtime was over. When the hour was out, he soon appeared at the door and shouted with a loud voice, " Come to books," and, upon this signal, it was the duty of the scholars to hasten to their places. The boys determined that on the appointed day the barring-out should take place at playtime. Accordingly, as soon as the recess commenced, and the school-master was out of hearing, the benches were heaped against the door, and the window nailed up, and a strong fire made, to prevent him from ascending the low roof of the cabin and coming down the chimney; and after eating our frugal dinners, we awaited with some anxiety his return. The girls who belonged to the school were of course excluded from the garrison.

He returned at the usual hour, and appeared sur-

prised when he found the door closed against him.
He ordered us to open it. We refused unless he
would agree that the holidays should commence on
that day. He seemed offended, and threatened us;
and after trying to force the door by his own strength,
and failing, he took a rail from a fence at hand and
began striking the door with considerable force, as if
he was determined to break in. We began to think
there would be a real fight. But after thumping the
door for some time, and trying the window, and threatening to keep us confined there all the ensuing night
unless we surrendered, he finally yielded to our demands, and we unbarred the door and let him in.
After some good-natured conversation on both sides,
we took leave of him in our usual respectful manner,
calling him " Master," as was the usage of the time,
and returned to our homes in triumph.

But I doubt whether he intended to do more than
he supposed to be necessary for the purpose of showing that he did not connive in our attempt to gain an
addition to the customary holiday, by which he would,
in truth, profit as well as ourselves. For the school-
house belonged to him, and any injury done to it
would have been his own loss; and, moreover, he
knew very well that if he broke in, and any of the
scholars were injured in the fight, it would be resented
by the parents and injure his school; yet it sometimes happened in the country that the master of the

school lost his temper, and a serious fight ensued. Our master, however, was a good-natured man, and saw the folly of such a conflict, when he must have been sure that the scholars were abetted by their parents. As for my part of the business, then a child of eight or nine years of age, I had very little in forming the plan, and should have been of very little service if it had come to blows. But every boy on such occasions was expected to be present to share the fortunes of his comrades, unless excused on the score of sickness or near relationship to the master. This was to show that it was the united action of the school, and not of a part only, and to prevent favoritism after the holidays, if the master should take offence at what was done. And any boy, however small, would have lost caste with his fellows if he had absented himself, unless his absence was previously sanctioned by them. Upon the occasion of which I am speaking, there were several small boys present as well as myself; but there were several well-grown lads in the school, well advanced in their teens, who would have been able to manage the master if he had proved obstinate and forced his way in.

When it was found useless to send us longer to this school, my elder brother and myself were placed at a grammar-school in the county, about ten miles off, which was kept by a man by the name of Hunter, and in which the pupils never exceeded a certain number: I think twenty. He was a Scotchman, and had been, on his arrival in this country, employed as tutor in the family of one of the wealthy gentlemen of the county. He had the reputation of being an accomplished classical scholar; and his school, which had been established some years before I went to it, enjoyed a high reputation. The pupils all boarded in his house. Here I began the study of the Latin grammar. But I had made very little progress before the school was broken up. We had not been there more than two or three months before the conduct of the teacher struck the scholars as much altered and strange. He absented himself more than usual from the school, was observed to be often talking to himself as he walked about the grounds, and was often absent and odd when hearing our lessons. And one day, soon after the scholars had assembled, he came in and dismissed us, telling us to go home. He gave no reason for what he did; but we supposed he found himself too sick to attend to the school, and supposed we should all return again in a short time. But it turned out that his mind had become disordered, and he was drowned in the Patuxent River a few weeks afterwards. It was said that he fancied himself a disembodied spirit, and that he could walk on or through water without danger, and was drowned in attempting to walk across the river where, in the channel, it was deep enough to float large ships.

After this disappointment, my father determined to employ a private tutor for his own family, who should reside in the house. It was the only way in which he could educate his daughters, and, indeed, it was the usual way at that time in the county we lived in, where the family was large and the parent could afford the expense of a tutor. Besides, it was no part of my father's plan to give my elder brother a classical education. He was, at that period of his life, strongly imbued with the English notion of perpetuating the family estate in the eldest son. And he gave us all to understand, as early as we were capable of understanding it, that his landed estate would go to my elder brother; and that his younger sons would have a liberal education and the means of studying a profession, and, after that, we must rely on ourselves for support. And carrying out this plan, which proved to be an unfortunate one for my elder brother, he designed to give him nothing more than a good English education, that would fit him for the business of a landed gentleman cultivating his own estate, and qualify him to associate upon equal terms, as to education and information, with the gentlemen of the county. All this would be accomplished by a private tutor. Accordingly one was engaged. He was an Irishman, who, I believe, was a ripe scholar, and who was certainly an amiable and accomplished man in his disposition and manners. But he died of consumption before his first year was out. The second was an American, a native of the State, who was a good English scholar, but whose knowledge of Latin was very slender, and who was altogether ignorant of Greek. He remained with us a year, and at the end of that time a third was engaged, David English, who afterwards edited a paper in George Town, and was for many years employed as an officer in one of the banks of that place. He was, I believe, a native of New Jersey, and had graduated at Princeton, and was in every respect a fortunate selection; for he was undoubtedly an accomplished scholar, and seemed to take pleasure in teaching us, and was altogether an agreeable inmate in the family. At the end of the year he advised my father to send me at once to college, and encouraged him to do so by the very favorable accounts he gave of my progress. His advice was followed; and I went to Dickinson College, Carlisle, when I was little more than fifteen years of age. I recall with pleasure now the unwearied attention and kindness of my old preceptor when I was under his care. He died a few years ago at an advanced age; and it is pleasant to remember the interest he took in my fortunes as long as he lived. He was residing in George Town, retired from business, when I was appointed Chief Justice of the Supreme Court. I had not seen him for a great many years. But as soon as I went to Washington to take my seat on the bench, he came to see me, and we met one another full of old recollections and mutual kindness. And day after day I have seen him take his seat on a bench outside of the bar in front of the court, without any business to bring him there or any interest in the case under argument, but solely, as it seemed to me, for the pleasure of seeing his old pupil presiding in that court. I was sensibly touched by these tokens of enduring interest in my fortunes, and never failed to go up to him and converse with him for a few moments, whenever I saw him in court, unless the engagements of the court made it impracticable.

My father was induced to select Dickinson College from the circumstance that two young men, a few years older than myself, were already there, with whose families he was intimately acquainted, and who gave very favorable accounts of the institution. It certainly deserved it while Dr. Nisbet was at its head, and the other departments were in the hands in which I found them.

I went in company with one of the young gentlemen of whom I have spoken, when he returned after the spring vacation in 1792. It was no small undertaking, however, in that day, to get from the lower part of Calvert County to Carlisle. We embarked on board one of the schooners employed in transporting produce and goods between the Patuxent River and Baltimore, and, owing to unfavorable winds, it was a week before we reached our port of destination; and, as there was no stage or any other public conveyance between Baltimore and Carlisle, we were obliged to stay at an inn until we could find a wagon returning to Carlisle, and not too heavily laden to take our trunks and allow us occasionally to ride in it. This we at length accomplished, and in that way proceeded to Carlisle, and arrived safely, making the whole journey from our homes in about a fortnight. And what made the whole journey more unpleasant was that we were obliged to take, in specie, money enough to pay our expenses until the next vacation. The money was necessarily placed in our trunks, and they were often much exposed in an open wagon in a public wagon-yard, while the wagoner and ourselves were somewhere else. But, in truth, we were not very anxious on that score, for a robbery in that day was hardly to be thought of as among the hazards of travel. But times are greatly changed in that respect, although certainly much improved as to travelling itself. I remained at college until the fall of 1795, when I graduated, and received the diploma of Bachelor of Arts. The difficulties of the journey were so great that I went home but twice, and, upon both occasions, walked from Carlisle to Baltimore with one of my school-companions, performing the journey in a little over two days. We came to Owing's Mill, within twelve miles of Baltimore, on the evening of the second day. The distance from Carlisle to Baltimore was then said to be eighty-five miles. But estimated distances are often overstated, and in this instance the true distance may be less.

I have not a great deal to say of my college life. It was, taken altogether, a pleasant one. None of us boarded in the college, but at different private boarding-houses about town,— for the present edifice was not then erected, and the building used was a small and shabby one, fronting on a dirty alley, but with a large open lot in the rear, where we often amused ourselves with playing bandy. After the first six months I boarded with James McCormick, the professor of mathematics. There were generally eight of us in the house, which were as many as it could accommodate. Mr. McCormick and his wife were as kind to us as if they had been our parents. He was unwearied in his attentions to us in our studies, full of patience and good-nature, and sometimes seemed distressed when, upon examining a pupil, he found him not quite as learned as he was himself.

I took a letter from my father to Dr. Nisbet, asking him to stand in the place of a guardian to me on account of my youth and distance from home and friends, and the retirement and seclusion in which I had so far been educated. He cheerfully took upon himself the duty, and invited me to visit him often. I did so. And many a pleasant evening have I spent at his house. He did not worry or fatigue me by grave and solemn lectures and admonitions. But although his conversation was always intended, as I afterwards saw, for my benefit and instruction, yet it did not seem so at the time. It was cheerful and animated, full of anecdote and of classical allusions, and seasoned with lively and playful wit. The class under his immediate instruction always became warmly and affectionately attached to him; yet, if he saw conduct that merited reproof, his sarcasm was sometimes bitter, and cut deep at the time. But I never saw it used towards a pupil unless he deserved it.

In my visits in the evening I always met Mrs. Nisbet, who was far advanced in life, but in good health. She, as well as Dr. Nisbet, took an interest in me from my youth and the manner in which I had been placed under his care; and she never failed, when she had an opportunity, to give me a regular course of motherly instruction and advice. I always listened to her with feelings of real respect. But, unfortunately, her dialect was so broadly Scotch, that I never understood the half of what she said, and could do nothing therefore but bow in assent. Perhaps I may sometimes have given this sign when she was putting a question that I ought to have answered "No," if I had exactly understood what she was saying.

Dr. Nisbet's share of the college duties was Ethics, Logic, Metaphysics, and Criticism. His mode of instruction was by lectures written out and read to the class slowly, so that we might write it down; yet it required a pretty good penman and fixed attention to keep up with him; and with all my efforts, I was sensible that his idea was not always expressed with perfect accuracy in my copy. But it was always sufficiently full to enable me to recall the substance of what he had said, when, in order to impress it upon my mind, I read it over. In addition to these lectures, there was a compendium of each science, in the form of question and answer, which each of the class was required to copy. It was a good-sized octavo volume closely written. But although the answers were written out by him, yet he always showed most pleasure when the pupil gave the answer in different words from those in the book, even if the answer was not strictly exact and scientific. He would, on such occasions, go over what the student had said, comment kindly upon it, and say how far it was correct, and in what respect it was not full enough or diffuse. His object was to teach the pupil to think, to reason, to form an opinion, and not to depend merely upon memory, and repeat what had been written for him without, perhaps, exactly understanding what he was talking about. He undoubtedly succeeded in fastening our attention upon the subject on which he was lecturing, and induced us to think upon it and discuss it, and form opinions for ourselves. These opinions were, of course, greatly influenced by what he had said. But there was one subject upon which the class was unanimously opposed to him. In his lectures on Ethics, he, of course, introduced the laws of nations, and the moral principles upon which they should be governed. And political questions, and the different forms of government existing in different nations, were therefore within the scope of his lectures. Upon these subjects he was decidedly anti-Republican. He had no faith in our institutions, and did not believe in their stability, or in their capacity to protect the rights of person or property against the impulses of popular passion, which combinations of designing men might continue to excite. These opinions were monstrous heresies in our eyes. But we heard them with good humor, and without offending him by any mark of disapprobation in his presence. We supposed they were the necessary consequence of his birth and education in Scotland. Yet many, I believe a majority of the class, would not write down those portions of his lectures; and, if the opinions had been expressed by any other professor, the class would probably have openly rebelled. Dr. Robert Davidson, the Vice-Principal, was not so popular.' Indeed, he was disliked by the students generally, and some of them took no pains to conceal it. Yet he was not harsh or ill-natured in his intercourse with us. But he was formal and solemn and precise, and, in short, was always the pedagogue in school and out of school. He lectured on History, Natural Philosophy, and Geography. He had written a rhyming geography, which, as well as I remember, contained about fifty printed pages, printed in octavo, and was an enumeration of the countries and nations of the world, and the principal rivers, mountains, and cities in each of them.

This little book we were all required to buy, and to commit to memory, and repeat to him in lessons. It filled our minds with names of places and general descriptions, without giving us any definite idea of their position on the globe, or their relation to one another; and, as may well be supposed, some of the lines and rhymes were harsh and uncouth enough to be the subject of ridicule. But he was very vain of it, and always showed his displeasure if any one was not master of the lesson, and could not repeat it readily, word for word, as he had written it. And what rendered the whole thing more absurd in the eyes of the students, he had composed what he called an acrostic upon his own name, by way of introduction, and this he required us to commit to memory, and to repeat to him with the rest of the book. Nothing lessens the respect of young men for a teacher more than a display of vanity, and they are always prompt in seeing it and amusing themselves with it. And nothing, I think, impaired the respect of the class for Dr. Davidson more than his acrostic; especially as he required us to commit it to memory as part of our lessons in geography. It was so often and habitually repeated among us in derision that, although I have not thought of it for forty or fifty years, yet, in recalling the scenes of my college life, I find I can still repeat all of it but the last four lines. I give what I remember, from which the reader may judge of the whole performance, and of the literary character and taste of the professor:

> " Round the globe now to rove, and its surface survey,
> Oh, youth of America, hasten away;
> Bid adieu for awhile to the toys you desire,
> Earth's beauties to view, and its wonders admire;
> Refuse not instruction, improve well your time,
> They are happy in age who are wise in their prime.
> Delighted we'll pass seas, continents, through,
> And isles without number, the old and the new;
> Vast oceans and seas, too, shall have their due praise,
> Including the rivers, the lakes, and the bays."
> *   *   *   *   *   *   *

The rest has dropped from my memory. The only remaining professor in the college, when I entered it, was Charles Huston, and his province was to teach the Latin and Greek languages. There was no teacher of French or any other modern language, nor was there any teacher of the English grammar. We were expected to make ourselves masters of it by the study in the Greek and Latin, and reading the best authors in the English language. I completed my studies of the Latin and Greek under Mr. Huston.

He was studying law at the time he was teaching in
the college, and resigned when the class to which I
belonged became the senior class. He remained in
Carlisle a year or more afterwards in order to complete his legal studies. I need not speak of his character and capacity; for he afterwards became one of
the first jurists in the country, and was for many
years one of the Judges of the Supreme Court of
Pennsylvania. He was an accomplished Latin and
Greek scholar, and happy in his mode of instruction.
And when he saw that a boy was disposed to study,
his manner to him was that of a companion and
friend, aiding him in his difficulties. The whole
school under his care were much attached to him.

Under these professors I studied the different
branches of science which I have enumerated. I
studied closely, was always well prepared in my lessons, and, while I gladly joined my companions in
their athletic sports and amusements, I yet found time
to read a great deal beyond the books we were required to study. And as my course of reading was
selected by myself, and governed by the impulse or
taste of the moment, it was rather desultory, and some
of it not wisely selected. It was perhaps fortunate
for me, when I entered college, that I was not far
enough advanced to be placed in the junior class, but
yet farther advanced than the next class below it;
for I found there a youth about my own age, who had

just entered before me, and was in the same situation
in this respect with myself. His name was John
Lyon, and his family lived within a mile or two of
Carlisle. We were both, in the first instance, placed
in the inferior class. But as we had read, before we
entered the college, the books which that class were
studying, and they would not for six months reach
the point we had attained, Mr. Huston saw that we
had almost nothing to do, and would be idle and
unemployed for the greater part of our time, if we
were held back and confined to the duties of that
class. Perhaps, too, he formed a favorable opinion
of our capacity and disposition to study. And he
proposed to put us in a class by ourselves, and give
us an opportunity, by close application, to overtake
the junior class, so as to be ready to enter with
them the senior, and to graduate with them. We
gladly accepted his proposition. My classmate was a
youth of fine genius, and, at that time, a close student.
We were, perhaps, both a little flattered by the good
opinion of our teacher which this arrangement indicated, and we were anxious not to disappoint him. We
studied hard, helped one another, and found ourselves
gaining on the class before us. We got over the
ground they had passed in less time than they had
done. And when we were examined with them, preparatory to our admission to the senior class, we were,
by no means, the worst scholars. Our professor was

evidently pleased with the vigor and success with which we had pressed forward; was always ready to aid us, and, after he resigned and remained in Carlisle studying law, he kept up his intercourse with us, and always treated us with marked kindness.

Mr. Lyon afterwards studied law, but died while quite a young man. Our relation to one another in the school had made us intimate and attached friends, and I sincerely deplored his death. If he had lived, he was undoubtedly capable of attaining a high and leading position at the bar.

The time of examination and of conferring diplomas must always be an anxious and exciting one to the students; and every circumstance connected with it is most commonly so deeply impressed upon the memory that it is never forgotten. They come back to my memory freshly at this day, although they took place fifty-nine years ago.

The examination was public. It was generally attended by most of the trustees, or visitors who were in town, and sometimes by other gentlemen of literary taste who took an interest in the success of such institutions. When the examination was over, and the professors had decided who were entitled to the degree of Bachelor of Arts, another day, about three or four weeks distant, was fixed on, when the Commencement was to be held with more ceremony, and speeches made by some of the graduates, and diplomas con-

ferred.   Our class consisted of about twenty or thirty,
I think : but I have no catalogue before me ; none
were rejected, although there were certainly some very
indifferent scholars among us.   Those who desired
to return home as soon as the examination was over,
without waiting for the public Commencement, were
always permitted to do so by the professors ; and those
who remained were not all required to deliver speeches.
In a large class it would take up too much time, and
weary the audience.   Each of those who intended to
speak had a subject selected for him by Dr. Nisbet,
and with it what was called a skeleton, that is, brief
notes of the manner in which it might be handled ;
the skeleton generally covering about half a page of
small letter-paper closely written.   There were two
honors conferred.   The first was the Salutatory oration
in Latin, the second the Valedictory.   What I am
inclined to think was a peculiarity in that college,
these honors were not conferred by the professors or
trustees, but were left to the decision of the graduates.
In other words, the students were to elect the persons
on whom these honors should be conferred ; and the
election was made by ballot.

These elections naturally created much interest ;
yet, in the class to which I belonged, they were conducted with perfect good humor and kind feelings.
But they were more animated and exciting than usual
upon this occasion, because it was uncertain who

would be designated until all the ballots were counted.
This difficulty arose from the following circumstances.
There were two societies among the students, each of
which had existed for many years, — the "Belles-Lettres," and the "Philosophical." There was always a
rivalship between the two societies for the graduating
honors; and, as they were conferred by the class without any interposition by the professors, if one of the
societies had a majority of the whole class, it generally
took the two honors to itself, much to the mortification of its rival. But it often happened that neither
society had this majority, and the selection depended
upon the votes of outsiders, who belonged to neither
society, and who voted according to their individual
preferences. There was, moreover, sometimes a contest in the society itself. Both of these difficulties
arose on this occasion. The two societies were about
equal in numbers, and there were three or four of the
class who belonged to neither, and upon whose votes
the election depended. And in the Belles-Lettres
Society, to which I belonged, there was a serious
division among ourselves as to both honors. It was
rumored among us that there was a like difficulty in
the Philosophical Society. But whether the rumor
was well founded or not, I do not know, as it was the
duty of the members of each to keep secret what
passed in it. And the impression among us, as to the
division in the rival society, arose from expressions

inadvertently dropped in conversation, or something accidentally overheard.

Be this as it may, there was much difficulty in our society both as to the first and second honor. The selection of the candidates was to be made by the majority of the society, and the minority were considered as bound in honor to support them in the election by the class. My friends in the society nominated me to deliver the Valedictory. My principal opponent was Henry Williams, of Pennsylvania, who afterwards became a distinguished clergyman of the Presbyterian Church. He was a man of fine talents, a good scholar, very much respected by the class, and we regarded him as an eloquent speaker. The contest was a very animated one, and both of the candidates not a little anxious. I was selected by a majority of the society, and became its candidate for the honor. Why I was selected in preference to Mr. Williams, I can hardly now say. He was several years older than myself, and his mind more matured, and would very probably have performed the duty better. But he entered college in the senior class, and came there, it was understood, merely to obtain a diploma in order to qualify him to become a minister of the church to which he belonged. His age (for he had arrived at the age of manhood before he came among us) and his pursuits and destination prevented him from mingling as much as I did among the students, and partaking in their amusements and athletic exercises. Besides, I had been much longer in the college, and much longer associated with the society to which we belonged. And as I now look back to what may be called my first entrance into public life in this little republic, the " Belles-Lettres Society," I am persuaded that the strong attachments which boys of good feelings form to one another, when they have been long daily companions in study and in play, must have contributed quite as much to the earnestness displayed in my behalf as any supposed superior fitness on my part. Mr. Williams and his friends faithfully supported the nomination at the election by the class.

This election, as I have said, was doubtful until the ballots were counted. The outsiders kept their intentions to themselves. But I succeeded by a close vote; I think a majority of two only. This result was mainly due to my classmate John Lyon, who, I found afterwards, had not only voted for me, but taken an interest in my behalf among those who were not members of either society. We, however, lost our candidate for the Salutatory oration. Mr. McConaughy, the nominee of the Philosophical Society, was selected, and delivered the oration. He was a very fine scholar, and worthy of the honor conferred upon him. He was amiable and kind in his disposition, and modest and retiring in his habits. He, like Mr. Williams, became a minister of the Presbyterian Church. I met him often afterwards, and we renewed our college friendship; and I had the pleasure of voting for him as the Principal of the Frederick Academy, of this State, when I resided in that town, and was a trustee of the school.

It may well be supposed that I was much gratified by my success. It could not, I suppose, be otherwise with a boy between eighteen and nineteen years of age, to whom the college was as yet his world, and whose name, by this election, was inscribed upon its record as one of its honored sons; but, as most commonly happens to successful ambition in a wider world, I soon found that success had brought with it troubles and anxieties to which I had before been a stranger.

I had to write an oration, which, from its character, would be more likely to attract attention and provoke criticism than any other in the class. It was to be submitted to Dr. Nisbet before it was delivered, and I knew and felt the great superiority of his judgment and taste, and feared he might find it all wrong. It was to be delivered in the presence of a large and highly intelligent audience of ladies and gentlemen, who always attended the college Commencement; and I was unaccustomed to composition. For in the Belles-Lettres Society our exercises consisted of debating a question agreed on, or of delivering an oration selected from some speech and committed to

memory, or in reciting passages from a poem or play.
The manual labor of writing was always unpleasant
to me ; and, although some of the members of the
society occasionally wrote out their speeches and read
them in the debate, and sometimes read an essay upon
some subject selected by themselves, yet I never had
done so. My speeches in the debate were always
made from very brief notes, unintelligible and unmeaning to everybody but myself — consisting of the
heads and order of the argument I intended to offer,
each head containing only a few words to recall to
my memory the point I meant to urge. And when I
sat down to write this valedictory oration, I had never
written a paragraph of my own composition, except
familiar and unstudied letters to my family.

This oration cost me much trouble and anxiety.
I took great pains with it, and perhaps should have
done better if I had taken less. I remember well
that my greatest difficulty was how to begin it; and
the first two or three sentences gave me nearly as
much trouble as all the rest of it put together. I am
quite sure that I spent hours upon them, and wrote
them over at least a dozen times. However, the speech
was worked out at last, and submitted to Dr. Nisbet;
and I was much relieved when he returned it to me
with only one or two slight verbal alterations.

But now came my severest trial. The Commencement was held in a large Presbyterian church, in

which Dr. Nisbet and Dr. Davidson preached alternately. A large platform of unplaned plank was erected in this church in front of the pulpit, and touching it, and on a level with its floor. From this platform the graduate spoke, without even, I think, a single rail on which he could rest his hand while speaking. In front of him was a crowded audience of ladies and gentlemen; behind him, on the right, sat the professors and trustees in the segment of the circle; and on the left, in like order, sat the graduates who were to speak after him; and in the pulpit, concealed from public view, sat some fellow-student, with the oration in his hand, to prompt the speaker if his memory should fail him. I evidently could not have been very vain of my oration, for I never called on my prompter for it, and have never seen it since it was delivered, nor do I know what became of it. I sat on this platform, while oration after oration was spoken, awaiting my turn, thinking over what I had to say, and trying to muster up courage enough to speak it with composure. But I was sadly frightened, and trembled in every limb, and my voice was husky and unmanageable. I was sensible of all this, much mortified by it; and my feeling of mortification made matters worse. Fortunately, my speech had been so well committed to memory, that I went through without the aid of the prompter. But the pathos of leave-taking from the professors and my classmates, which had been so carefully worked out in the written oration, was, I doubt not, spoiled by the embarrassment under which it was delivered.

Perhaps it may be thought that the honor of speaking the Valedictory, in the manner in which the task was executed, was hardly worth the pain and mortification which it brought with it. Philosophically considered, this is true; for I might have gone home, after my examination, without further labors, or trials, or mortifications.

And as a mere calculation of interest, my college honor was of no consequence in my future pursuits. I doubt whether a dozen persons out of my own family connection, in the new world upon which I was afterwards to enter, even knew that this mark of distinction had been awarded to me. Yet, in the little world of a college, it is as much valued, and as much the object of ambition, as the high offices of government in the great political world. And I confess that I would, at that time, have endured much more than I did rather than not have obtained it. Such is ambition in the little world and the great, and so early do our teachers and instructors plant it in our hearts. I do not say that it is wrong. For when it is properly regulated, and directed to proper objects, it often leads the possessor to great personal sacrifices for the benefit of others. But I doubt whether it promotes often his own happiness, however successful he may be.

Having graduated, I returned home to my family. This was in the fall of 1795. I remained at home during the ensuing winter, which was idly spent in the amusements of the country. My father kept a pack of hounds, and was fond of fox-hunting. It was the custom to invite some other gentleman, who also kept fox-hounds, to come with his pack on a particular day, and they hunted with the two packs united. Other gentlemen, who were known to be fond of the sport, were also invited, so as to make a party of eight or ten persons, and sometimes more. The hunting usually lasted a week. The party always rose before day, breakfasted by candle-light, — most commonly on spareribs (or bacon) and hominy, — drank pretty freely of eggnog, and then mounted and were in the cover, where they expected to find a fox, before sunrise. The foxes in the country were mostly the red, and, of course, there was much hard riding over rough ground, and the chase apt to be a long one. We rarely returned home until late in the day; and the evening was spent in gay conversation on the events and mishaps of the day, and in arrangements for the hunt of the morrow, or in playing whist for moderate stakes. There was certainly nothing like drunkenness or gambling at these parties. I myself never played. By the end of the week the hunters and dogs were pretty well tired, and the party separated. But before they parted, a time was always fixed when my father was to bring his dogs to his friend's house, or they were to meet by invitation at the house of some other gentleman of the party, where another week would be passed in like manner; and these meetings, with intervals of about a fortnight or three weeks, were kept up until the end of the season. I joined in all of them; and when not so engaged, my father, with my elder brother and myself, hunted with his own dogs when the weather was fit.

It was an idle winter, and a very different one from my winters at college. It was intended, I presume, to give me a season of relaxation and amusement before I entered on the study of the law; and I liked it and enjoyed it greatly. For although my health was not robust, and eggnog was very apt to give me a headache, yet, in the excitement of the morning, I forgot the fatigues of the preceding day, and rode as hard as anybody, and followed the hounds with as much eagerness. By the end of the winter I was a confirmed fox-hunter. But by this time I began to feel tired of this idle life, and impatient to begin the study of the law. It was the profession my father had always desired me to follow, and which I myself preferred. Accordingly, in the spring of 1796, I went to Annapolis, to read law in the office of Jeremiah Townley Chase, who was, at that time, one of the Judges of the General Court of Maryland. This Court had original jurisdiction in all civil cases,

throughout the State of Maryland, where the matter
in dispute exceeded £1 Maryland currency, ($2.66⅔),
and in criminal cases of the higher grade. It sat
twice a year at Annapolis for the Western Shore, and
twice at Easton for the Eastern Shore; and jurors
from every county of the respective Shores were summoned to attend it. This Court was abolished in
1805, and courts sitting in the several counties substituted in its place. It may now perhaps, at this
day, be a matter of surprise that it was continued so
long; for it was exceedingly inconvenient to the
suitors who resided in the distant counties to attend
it, and the costs of bringing witnesses to Annapolis
and Easton, and keeping them there sometimes for
weeks together, was oppressive, and often ruinous to the
parties. There were no railroads or steamboats at that
time, and stages were almost in their infancy in Maryland; and such as had been established were as rough
as a road-wagon, and found only between the principal towns, and running then only once or twice
a week. Almost everybody came on horseback to
Annapolis, except those coming from Baltimore.
But the Court was maintained by the confidence the
people entertained in the ability and impartiality of
the tribunal, and their fear that, if a change was
made, and courts for each county constituted in its
place, that injustice, and not justice, would be brought
to their doors. They would have been shocked be-

yond measure in that day, at the idea of trying a case, civil or criminal, out of doors, or in the newspapers, before it was tried in Court, or while it was under trial, or after it had been there decided. Young America was not then born.

The Court consisted of three judges, always selected from the eminent men of the bar; the jurors from each county were taken from the most respectable and intelligent class of society; and, generally speaking, the jury who tried the cause probably never heard of it before they were empanelled, and had no knowledge whatever of the parties, except what they gathered from the testimony. There was every security, therefore, for an impartial trial. The extent of its jurisdiction, and the importance of the cases tried in it, brought together, at its sessions, all that were eminent or distinguished at the bar on either of the Shores for which it was sitting.

The sessions at Annapolis were of course the most important, from the great population, extent of territory, and commercial character of the Western Shore. Several of the most eminent lawyers in the State resided in the city. From the character of the Judges of the General Court, of the bar who attended it, and the business transacted in it, Annapolis was considered as the place, of all others in the State, where a man should study law, if he expected to attain eminence in his profession. There were generally between

twenty and thirty students from different parts of
the State while I was there, some in our office, some
in another. It was there I first saw the distinguished
men of whom I shall hereafter speak.

Everything I saw, when this Court was in session,
was calculated to stimulate my ambition. I determined not to go into society until I had completed
my studies, and I adhered to that determination. In
the midst of the highly-polished and educated society
for which that city was at that time distinguished, I
never visited in any family, and respectfully declined
the kind and hospitable invitations I received. I
associated only with the students, and studied closely.
I have for weeks together read law twelve hours in
the twenty-four. But I am convinced that this was
mistaken diligence, and that I should have profited
more if I had read law four or five hours, and spent
some more hours in thinking it over, and considering
the principle it established, and the cases to which it
might be applied. And I am satisfied, also, that it
would have been much better for me, if I had occasionally mixed in the society of ladies, and of gentlemen older than the students. My thoughts would
often have been more cheerful, and my mind refreshed
for renewed study, and I should have acquired more
ease and self-possession in conversation with men eminent for their talents and position, and learned from
them many things which law-books do not teach. I

suffered much and often from this want of composure,
and from the consciousness of embarrassment, when I
emerged from my seclusion and came into the social
and business world.

My reading in the office of a judge, instead of a
practising lawyer, had some advantages; but, upon
the whole, was, I think, a disadvantage to me. It is
true it gave me more time for uninterrupted study,
but it gave me no instruction in the ordinary routine
of practice, nor any information as to the forms and
manner of pleading further than I could gather it
from the books. In the office of a lawyer in full
practice, the attention of the student is daily called to
such matters, and he is employed in drawing declarations and pleas, special and general, until the usual
forms become familiar to his mind, and he learns, by
actual practice in the office, the cases in which they
should be respectively used, and what averments are
material, and what are not. The want of this practical knowledge and experience was a serious inconvenience to me. And for some time after I commenced
practice, I did not venture to draw the most ordinary
form of a declaration or plea without a precedent
before me; and, if the cause of action required a
declaration varying in any degree from the ordinary
money counts, or the defence required a special plea,
I found it necessary to examine the principles of
pleading which applied to it, and endeavored to find

a precedent for a case of precisely that character; nor was it so easy, in that day, for an inexperienced young lawyer to satisfy himself upon a question of special pleading. Chitty had not made his appearance, and you were obliged to look for the rule in Comyn's Digest, or Bacon's Abridgment, or Viner's Abridgment, and the cases to which they referred; and I have sometimes gone back to Lilly's Entries and Doctrina Placitandi in searching for a precedent.

Although this deficiency gave me so much trouble, it, perhaps, in the end made me a better pleader; for the consciousness of my want of knowledge, and that I had no office-experience to rely on, made me study the subject the more carefully, whenever a case was likely to present a question of pleading; for in that day strict and nice technical pleading was the pride of the bar, and I might almost say of the Court. And every disputed suit was a trial of skill in pleading between the counsel, and a victory achieved in that mode was much more valued than one obtained on the merits of the case.

Some of the students, of whom I was one, formed a debating society; but the questions discussed were rarely law questions. The object was to prepare ourselves for the bar, by the practice of oral arguments among ourselves. We had no moot court. My preceptor, Mr. Chase, did not encourage them, and in this he agreed, I believe, with the leaders of the bar

in Annapolis in whose offices there were students.
He thought that discussions of law questions by
students were apt to give them the habit of speaking
upon questions which they did not understand, or
of which they had but an imperfect and superficial
knowledge — that its tendency, therefore, was to accus-
tom them to make loose arguments, and to lay down
principles without the proper qualifications. He advised me to attend regularly the sittings of the General Court, to observe how the eminent men at that
bar examined the witnesses and brought out their
case, and raised and argued the questions of law, and
afterwards to write a report of it for my own use. He
thought that listening to such men, and making a
note of the arguments of counsel and the decisions
of the Court, and reading the cases referred to, would
be of more service to me than attempting to argue
such points myself, or listening to the arguments of
my fellow-students in a moot court or debating society. I followed his advice, and reported a good
many cases; but upon looking at them after I came
to the bar, and upon maturer experience, I threw
them into the fire. They satisfied me, when I read
them, that no one was fit for a reporter who was not
an accomplished lawyer. As I found that my report,
after all I had listened to, did not fully and with legal
precision bring out the points, I am inclined to think
that arguments upon them in a moot court would not

have tended to an increase or advance of legal knowledge, and that Mr. Chase was right. No one improves his own knowledge or capacity for argument by habitually speaking upon subjects which he does not fully understand, or by listening to those who speak under like circumstances. The danger is that he will bring the habit with him to the bar, and he will find it there a very bad habit. He will sometimes find that it would have been better to have been silent than to have spoken. All the lawyers of Maryland who have risen to eminence and leadership were trained in the manner described and advised by Mr. Chase.

I have always deemed it a fortunate circumstance that William Carmichael, of the Eastern Shore of this State, came to Annapolis to read law while I was there. We became intimate friends, and roomed together for a year. We read in different offices; but we read the same books, and at the same time, and every night we talked over the reading of the day, and the principle of law it established, and the distinctions and qualifications to which they were subject. We did not talk for victory, but for mutual information, and neither of us felt or was entitled to feel any superiority of genius or information over the other. He afterwards became eminent at the bar; but inheriting, by the death of his father, a large landed estate, and attached to a country life, he gradually withdrew himself from the profession, and finally, while he was yet in the prime of life, abandoned it altogether, and devoted himself to the pursuits of agriculture. He died a few months ago. The friendship formed between us when students continued unbroken and undiminished to the hour of his death; and I could not write my biography without recording our early associations, nor can I introduce his name without expressing the cordial friendship I entertained for him. He was a frank, manly, high-minded gentleman.

The first session of the General Court, after I went to Annapolis, made a strong impression upon me. The three judges, wearing scarlet cloaks, sat in chairs placed on an elevated platform; and all the distinguished lawyers of Maryland were assembled at the bar. I was familiar with their names and standing; for many of my fox-hunting friends in Calvert County, with whom I had spent the preceding winter, had been jurors to the General Court, and, knowing that I intended to study law, they frequently talked to me about the great lawyers they had seen and heard at Annapolis. There I saw Luther Martin, Philip Barton Key, John Thompson Mason, John Johnson, Arthur Shaaff, James Winchester, and others who were highly respectable, but not so distinguished. Pinkney was abroad, having been appointed a commissioner under the British treaty, and Harper had not then taken up his residence in Maryland. I looked with deep interest upon the array of talent and learning which I saw before me, and hoped (perhaps in candor I ought to say believed) that the day would come that I might occupy the like position in the profession. There certainly was about me, at that time, no want of ambition for legal eminence, not so much for the emoluments it would bring, as for the high rank and social position which were in that day attached to it.

In the enumeration of the great men of the bar, I have placed Luther Martin first. He was not only much older than any of the other gentlemen, but he was the acknowledged and undisputed head of the profession in Maryland. He was so in the eye of the public, he was so admitted by the bar. Nobody disputed it with him until Mr. Pinkney returned from Europe. Yet I confess, when I first heard Mr. Martin, I was disappointed; and, if I had followed the dictates of my own inexperience and unformed judgment, I should have awarded a higher place to some others. Mr. Martin's habits, however, had at that time become bad. He often appeared in Court evidently intoxicated, and, perhaps, was not free from the influence of stimulants when I first heard him. His dress was a compound of the fine and the coarse, and appeared never to have felt the brush. He wore ruffles at the wrists, richly edged with lace, — although

every other person had long before abandoned them, —
and these ruffles, conspicuously broad, were dabbled
and soiled, and showed that they had not been changed
for a day or more. His voice was not musical, and
when much excited it cracked. His argument was
full of digressions and irrelevant or unimportant
matter, and his points were mixed up together and
argued without order, with much repetition, and his
speech was consequently unreasonably long. He was
an accomplished scholar, and wrote with classical correctness and great strength. But in his speech (and
what I say of this speech may be said of his speeches
generally) he seemed to delight in using vulgarisms
which were never heard except among the colored
servants or the ignorant and uneducated whites. For
example, I have heard him say he *cotch* him, instead of *caught* him, and he *sot* down, instead of *sat*
down, and many other words and phrases not much
better. He seemed to take pleasure in showing his
utter disregard of good taste and refinement in his
dress and language and his mode of argument. He
was as coarse and unseemly at a dinner-table, in his
manner of eating, as he was in everything.

But with all these defects, he was a profound lawyer.
He never missed the strong points of his case; and,
although much might generally have been better
omitted, everybody who listened to him would agree
that nothing could be added, but, unfortunately for

him, he was not always listened to. He introduced
so much extraneous matter, or dwelt so long on unimportant points, that the attention was apt to be
fatigued and withdrawn, and the logic and force of
his argument lost upon the Court or the jury. But
these very defects arose in some measure from the
fulness of his legal knowledge. He had an iron
memory, and forgot nothing that he had read ; and he
had read a great deal on every branch of the law, and
took pleasure in showing it when his case did not require it. His associates at the bar had, as I have said,
great respect for his legal learning. Many years after
I came to the bar, I remember on one occasion, when
I was engaged in an important case on the same side
with Mr. Shaaff, and Mr. Martin was opposed to us,
Mr. Shaaff and myself went over the case together
very carefully ; and when we had done with the examination, he said, I think the case is with us, and I see
nothing in it to be afraid of; but I am always afraid
of Martin. Yet Mr. Shaaff ranked then with the
foremost men in Maryland, was resolute and firm in
his opinions, and would, I am sure, have felt no apprehension of being taken by surprise by any other
member of the bar.

Mr. Martin was Attorney-General of Maryland in
the war of the Revolution, and continued so for a
great many years. He did not resign until long after
I had entered upon the practice. His prosecutions

were always conducted with great fairness to the accused, and the attention of the jury called to the evidence which might operate in his favor as well as that against him. Nor was any attempt made to take from it by argument the weight to which it was justly entitled. He was strong in his attachments, and ready to make any sacrifice for his friends. This was proved by the zeal with which he defended Mr. Chase when he was impeached by the House of Representatives of the United States, and still more in the time he devoted, and the money he spent, in defence of Colonel Burr. In both of these cases he was a volunteer.

He certainly received, and would have taken, no fee in the impeachment case; and I doubt whether he received any from Colonel Burr. He became one of his securities for his appearance to answer the charge of misdemeanor after his acquittal for treason. After that recognizance was forfeited, Mr. Martin was harassed with proceedings against him to recover the amount. How it ended, and whether Mr. Martin paid it out of his own means or not, I do not know; but if it was in the end paid by Colonel Burr, no fee, however liberal, could have remunerated him for his sacrifices in behalf of his friend, whom he persisted in believing, in spite of evidence, to be an innocent and persecuted man, and a pure patriot; for the case withdrew him from all other practice, and the cases in the Maryland Courts, in which he was engaged, were tried in his absence by others. He was kind to young members of the profession, and liberal, and indeed profuse, in his charities, and easily imposed upon by unworthy objects. Indeed his unfortunate habits made him reckless in money matters; and after a long life of severe labor and large profits, when late in life he was struck with paralysis, which impaired his intellect and rendered him incapable of business, he was found to be utterly penniless, and dependent upon charity for support. And the only good thing I know of Colonel Burr is, that, soon after this happened, he took Mr. Martin to his house and provided for his wants, and took care of him until his death.

When William Pinkney returned from England, and resumed the practice, the reign of Martin was at an end. Mr. Pinkney had distinguished himself from his first appearance in Court, and, although still a young man when he accepted the appointment of Commissioner under the British treaty, he was already in the foremost rank of the profession; and when he had returned, and had been heard in some important and difficult cases, his supremacy was universally acknowledged. He was a perfect contrast to Martin. He was very attentive to his dress, indeed more so than was thought suitable for his age and station. It approached to dandyism, if it did not reach it. He was always dressed in the extreme of the newest fashion, and, for some time after his return, took notes at the bar and spoke with gloves on nice enough to wear in a ball-room. His style was metaphorical, but by no means turgid. And, although on some occasions I thought it too ornate, and his metaphors too gorgeous for a legal argument, yet it was impossible not to listen to them with pleasure. They were always introduced at the right time and the right place, and seemed to grow out of the subject of which he was speaking, and to illustrate it. He was fastidiously correct in his language, in its grammatical arrangement, in the graceful flow and harmony of the sentences, and in the correct and exact pronunciation of every word; and I have seen him writhe as if in pain when he was listening to Martin speaking in his slovenly way, in broken sentences, using the most indefensible vulgarisms, and sometimes mispronouncing his words. Mr. Martin seemed indifferent to everything else, provided he impressed upon the Court the idea he wished to convey, while Mr. Pinkney was as attentive to the graceful and ornamental as he was to the logic of his argument; and, while it was often a labor to listen to Martin, it was impossible not to listen to Pinkney, and to follow him from the beginning to the end of his argument. His arguments were syllogisms, and his points clearly stated and carefully kept separate in the discussion. He came to every case fully prepared, with his argument and authorities arranged; and no temptation could induce him to speak in a case, great or small, unless he had time to prepare for it; and he argued every one as carefully as if his reputation depended upon that speech; while Martin would plunge into a case when he had not even read the record, relying on the fulness and readiness of his own mind; and, if he found unexpected difficulties, would waste a day in a rambling, pointless, and wearisome speech against time, in order to gain a night to look into the case.

I have heard almost all the great advocates of the United States, both of the past and present generation, but I have seen none equal to Pinkney. He was a profound lawyer in every department of the science, as well as a powerful and eloquent debater. He always saw the strongest point in his case, and he put forth his whole strength to support it, and enforced it by analogies from other branches of the law. He never withdrew the attention of the Court from this point by associating with it more questionable propositions obviously untenable. He seemed to regard such arguments as evidence of a want of legal knowledge in the speaker; and when replying to them, he took particular pleasure in assailing the weaker points, and dwelling upon them in a tone and manner that sometimes made the adversary ashamed

of them, and sometimes provoked his resentment.
There was, however, one defect in his mode of speaking. His voice and manner and intonations did
not appear to be natural, but artificial and studied.
There were at intervals sudden and loud outbreaks
of vehemence with impassioned gesticulation, which
neither the subject matter nor the language actually
spoken seemed to call for or justify. This want of
naturalness in tone and manner was unpleasant to
those who heard him for the first time, and impaired
the effect of his oratory until you became accustomed
to it, and forgot it in attending to the argument. But
a man who, at the age of fifty, spoke in amber-colored
doeskin gloves, could hardly be expected to have a
taste for simple and natural elocution. His manner
was dressed up, — overdressed like his person.

I remember a conversation among some of us, one
evening (after we had been listening to Pinkney), in
which Mr. Johnson (father of Reverdy Johnson),
whom I have before mentioned as one of the leaders
of the bar, remarked that those who were not accustomed to hear Pinkney, and had not heard him in a
great variety of cases, would not estimate him as
highly as he deserved, and would be apt to think we
had overrated him — that he would leave nothing behind him to compare with the living proofs of greatness which he was daily exhibiting.

The latter part of the remark is undoubtedly true.

He wrote nothing worthy of his living fame. His diplomatic correspondence, when published, disappointed those who admired him as a speaker; and he gained no laurels in the discussion with Mr. Canning. He may have been sensible that writing was not his forte. But he was not apt to doubt his power in anything, and whatever may have been the reason, he never wrote out one of his speeches. He delivered two arguments in Congress upon Constitutional questions, which are yet remembered, and which were regarded at the time as among the ablest and most brilliant ever delivered in those halls. One of them was in the House of Representatives on the Treaty-making power, and the other in the Senate upon the famous Missouri question. Reporting for the newspapers in that day was a very different thing from what it is now, and the newspaper reports of these speeches are utter failures; yet he could not be prevailed upon to write them out. The truth is he was not a man for the closet. He needed the excitement of the forum, and there was unrivalled.

Besides, I doubt very much whether he set much value on posthumous fame, as compared with the present enjoyment. He loved honors and distinction, and contended for them, and maintained them after they were acquired, with unwearied energy. But I incline to think he sought and loved them chiefly for the present pleasure they gave him. He was epicurean and self-indulgent in his tastes and habits; and, although far advanced in life, he was evidently ambitious to have the reputation of high fashion and *ton*, and to be listened to and received as its leader. I am inclined to think he would not have bartered a present enjoyment for a niche in the temple of Fame. He was willing to toil for the former, but made no effort to leave any memorial of his greatness behind him.

The strong impression he made upon those who were accustomed to hear him, may, I think, be discovered in the language and style of the opinions delivered in the Courts at that period. It will be found, upon looking into them, that in many of the cases argued by him the language of the opinion is more ornate and embellished than usual at other seasons. I speak of opinions delivered in the Supreme Court as well as in the State Courts. And the remark applies even to some of the opinions of the late Chief Justice, whose style at other times is not less remarkable for its simplicity and judicial calmness than for its perspicuity and force. Mr. Pinkney's speeches must have been much admired, or his ornamented style would not have been imitated.

I have spoken more particularly of Martin and Pinkney on account of the pre-eminence they respectively held at the Maryland bar among the lawyers of the last generation. It is not my purpose to give a particular description of the others whom I have named, or to compare them with one another. It was my good fortune to commence the practice of the law when they were all yet in the prime of life, and to become familiarly acquainted with all of them, and to be engaged in the practice in the same Courts. They were all gentlemen of high attainments, courteous and kind in their intercourse with each other, and of unblemished honor. They have now all passed away; and I can truly say, when the recollection of them has come back freshly to my memory, that each one of them would have been eminent at any bar or in any Court of justice.

I return to the history of my own life. I remained in Mr. Chase's office studying closely for three years, and in the spring of 1799 was admitted to the bar. I had, by practice in our debating societies, become capable of speaking before my companions without any feeling of embarrassment; but I remembered what I had passed through in my Valedictory oration, which was the only speech I had made in public, and I feared that I should break down in my first essay at the bar. I could not write out a speech in a Court of original jurisdiction, and depend upon my memory to speak it; for I could not know precisely what the evidence would be, or what points might arise. I knew I must be able to think and exercise the power of reasoning while I was speaking, and while I was conscious that every one was looking at me and listening to me.

I selected, therefore, a very humble forum for my first effort. The Mayor's Court of Annapolis had then jurisdiction of certain minor offences committed within the precincts of the city, and a grand and petit jury, composed of citizens of the town, were regularly summoned to attend at the stated terms of the Court. I knew the mayor, who was a good-natured old gentleman and had never studied law; and I was quite sure that I knew more law, and had more capacity, also, than the mayor or any of the aldermen who sat with him. Gabriel Duvall, who was then a Judge of the General Court, and afterwards a Judge of the Supreme Court of the United States, was the Recorder; but he did not regularly attend the Court, and came in only occasionally when the mayor and aldermen wished his aid in a case of difficulty. The case I had selected for my first trial was the defence of a man indicted for an assault and battery, in which very little mischief had been done to either party, and I had no suspicion that Judge Duvall, for whom I had the highest respect, would think it worth his while to preside at the trial. I thought if I ever could speak without confusion in any Court of justice, I should be able to do so before the Court and jury I expected to meet. One of my fellow-students, who, like myself, was about to commence the practice, was associated with me in the defence; and just as we had empanelled the jury, and felt quite brave, and men of some consequence in the presence of those around us, to our utter dismay in walked Recorder Duvall, with his grave face and dignified deportment, and took his seat on the bench.

I do not know whether my associate or myself was the more frightened. We had both been accustomed to see him administering justice in the General Court, and listening to the first lawyers of the State, and we thought he would hardly, in his own mind, fail to contrast our efforts with theirs. There was no drawing back, however, for the jury was empanelled, and the examination of witnesses about to begin. I think he saw our embarrassment, for his manner was kind and encouraging.

The case turned out to be a very good one for a speech. As almost always happens when a fight takes place in an excited crowd, there was much contradictory testimony, and it was difficult to say whether our client committed the assault or struck in self-defence.

I watched the testimony carefully as it was given in, turning in my own mind the use that might be made of it. I took no notes, for my hand shook so that I could not have written a word legibly if my life had depended on it; and when I rose to speak, I was obliged to fold my arms over my breast, pressing them firmly against my body; and my knees trembled under me so much that I was obliged to press my

limbs against the table before me to keep me steady
on my feet; yet, under all these disadvantages, I determined to struggle for composure and calmness of
mind, and by a strong effort of the will I managed
to keep possession of the reasoning faculties, and made
a pretty good argument in the case, but in a tremu-
lous and sometimes discordant voice, and inferior to
what I could have made under more auspicious circumstances. A verdict in favor of my client hardly
consoled me for the timidity I had displayed and the
want of physical firmness, which seemed, I thought, to
be little better than absolute cowardice.

This morbid sensibility, of which I am speaking,
has, upon many occasions throughout my professional
life, given me deep pain and mortification. It was the
struggle of my life to keep it down ; but, long as that
professional life was, I was never able entirely to conquer it. And although I had been some years in the
practice when I made my first speech in the Court of
Appeals of Maryland, and many more when I first
appeared in the Supreme Court of the United States,
I felt it on each of these occasions nearly as much as
when I tried the case in the Mayor's Court. Even in
the Courts in which I was familiar, and where I had
risen to the first rank of the profession, and tried
almost every case of importance, I have sometimes
felt it at the beginning of a term, although I had so
mastered it that nobody perceived it but myself. It

depended in a great degree on the state of my health; but I never knew whether it would harass me or not until I rose to speak; and it is chiefly on account of the consciousness of this weakness, that I have uniformly refused to make a Fourth-of-July oration, or to speak upon any of those occasions where an orator of the day is a part of the ceremony; and, perhaps, have refused sometimes where those who requested me to make the speech regarded my refusal as disobliging and unkind.

Indeed, this morbid sensibility was so painful to me, in the first years of my practice, that I am not sure that I should not have abandoned it, if I had been rich enough to have lived without it; but, as things were, I never for a moment thought of engaging in any other pursuit. I knew that my father and family had formed high hopes of my future eminence, and that a good deal of money had been spent on my education. So I determined from the first to march forward in the path I had chosen, and, whatever it might cost me, to speak on every occasion, professional or political, when my duty required it. A firm and resolute will can do a great deal, yet I knew in many instances I fell far short of what I was capable of performing, had I been perfectly calm and self-possessed.

The source of this misfortune was my delicate health. It was infirm from my earliest recollection;

my system was put out of order by slight exposure; and I could not go through the excitement and mental exertion of a Court, which lasted two or three weeks, without feeling, at the end of it, that my strength was impaired and I needed repose.

With the burden of this constitutional weakness upon me, I entered on the practice of the law; and, soon after my speech in the Mayor's Court at Annapolis, I returned to Calvert County, where my father desired I should commence the practice, attending also the Courts in the adjoining counties. It was not a very desirable theatre for a lawyer, for the counties were small and the population agricultural, so that there were but few controversies of much moment, and a lawyer, confined to those counties, even in full practice, could hope for little more than a mere support.

But my father had ulterior objects in wishing me to settle in Calvert. His frequent election to the House of Delegates of Maryland had given him a taste for public life, and an ambition for political eminence. He looked upon distinction in the profession of the law as a stepping-stone to political power. He had formed a higher opinion of my capacity than I had myself, and higher than I deserved. And he supposed I could more readily make my way into public life from that part of the State than from any other, and might then select a more suitable theatre for the practice of the law.

Acting upon this principle, soon after I returned to the county he proposed to me to become a candidate for the House of Delegates. I was, at that time, sufficiently imbued with political ambition to be quite willing to go at once into public life, and was, perhaps, not a little flattered at the idea of becoming a member of the General Assembly at the age of twenty-two years; for while I was reading law at Annapolis, I had seen every year some of the most distinguished men of the State members of that body, and had often listened to the debates, and estimated highly the honor for which my father desired me to become a candidate. I was afraid, however, that I could not be elected, and told him so; for I had been absent from the county, with short intervals, from my boyhood, and was personally known to very few of its inhabitants. I was unwilling to begin my political career with a defeat. He, however, thought there was no danger of that, and upon a conference with some of his friends, they agreed with him, and I was announced as a candidate. The election proved to be a very contested one. There were five candidates, and only four could be elected, and each candidate had active personal friends. Parties in the affairs of the general Government had already been formed, and almost everybody had taken his side. My family and friends generally were Federalists, and so was I. But at the time of which I am speaking, it was not thought expedient, or right in principle, to carry these party divisions and conflicts into the concerns of the State, and the election of the candidate depended on his personal weight and supposed fitness for the station, and the influence of friends who took an interest in him. Nothing, therefore, was said as to whether the candidate was a Federalist or Republican,—which were the party names of that day,—but whether he was better qualified for the place than his competitor. The whole county voted at the court-house, and the election lasted four days. The votes were *viva voce*, and the sheriff held the election, and when the polls were closed, and the votes added up, he proclaimed in a loud voice the names of those who were chosen. The candidates, during the election, sat on a raised bench immediately behind the sheriff, so that each of them could see and be seen by every voter. It was an exciting scene to an inexperienced young man like myself. When a voter came up, every candidate began to solicit his vote, and press his own name upon him ; and, as many of the voters cared very little about the candidates, except the particular favorite he came to support, I think it very likely that the skilful in these struggles sometimes obtained votes that would otherwise have been given to another. These scenes were occasionally enlivened by sallies of wit between the voter and the candidate, and sometimes the voter gave a pretty hard hit to a can-

didate whom he happened to dislike.   But, however
hard the hit, the candidate was obliged to take it in
good humor, and treat it as a joke.   I made no great
figure in this part of the contest, for I was not experienced in it, nor hardened to it, and knew very
few of the voters even by name.   Some of my friends
saw my deficiency, and often stood near me and spoke
for me.

These four days were days of no small anxiety to
me, — the poll-books being open before us and the
voting *viva voce*, and we were always aware of the exact
number of votes that each candidate had received,
and the ebbs and flows in his prospects, as his friends
or the friends of other candidates came in.   The
election was closer than my friends had anticipated;
and I felt relieved when the polls were closed, and I
saw that I was elected.   I need not say that I was
gratified, greatly gratified, at the result; yet I was not
over-elated, for I saw plainly enough that I did not
owe my election to the speeches I had made during
the canvass, but to the energetic and active support
of a few personal and popular friends, who had determined to carry me through.   Under the influence of
these feelings, when the successful candidates had been
proclaimed to a crowded court-house, I very modestly
returned thanks in a brief speech.   It must, I think,
have been pretty well done for the occasion, for it was
received with loud hurrahs, and I was immediately

placed in a chair, raised upon the shoulders of the
crowd, and marched in triumph about the court-
house green. The other successful candidates were
also cheered. But it was manifest that my friends were
most numerous and far more elated. I was the only
one accustomed to public speaking, and the only one
who made a speech. And they seemed to think they
had achieved a triumph, in electing a man who had
shown himself capable of supporting the interests of
his constituents on the floor of the House of Delegates.

The session of the Assembly to which I was elected
began on the first Monday of November, 1799. It is
not my purpose to give a history of the proceedings
of the session. Some very interesting questions came
before it, and, among others, the law authorizing a
canal between the Chesapeake and Delaware Bays,
which has now become such an important channel of
trade. This law was strongly opposed by the Baltimore interest, and brought out a great deal of discussion, and was carried through with much difficulty. I
took an active part in favor of it, and a fair share in
the other business of the House, and felt, before the
close of the session, that I was listened to with respect
and attention.

General Washington died while the Legislature was
still in session. The news reached Annapolis in the
evening, and the next morning, when the House met,

almost every countenance looked sad, and nothing else was spoken of. Immediately after the Houses were organized, the Senate sent down a message to the House of Delegates, proposing to pay appropriate honors. Charles Carroll, of Carrollton, and John Eager Howard, two of the most distinguished men in Maryland, were appointed by the Senate to bring the message; and I never witnessed a more impressive scene. The two honored Senators with their gray locks stood at the bar of the House with the tears rolling down their cheeks. The Speaker and members rose to receive them, and stood while the message was delivered. It was no empty formal pageant. It was the outward sign of the grief within, and few were present who did not shed tears on the occasion. My eyes, I am sure, were not dry.

This session was certainly of much advantage to me in my future life. The discussions, in which I took part, enabled me to speak with less sense of embarrassment, and to diminish the morbid sensibility which I had before experienced on such occasions. It also brought me into familiar association with the most distinguished men of the State in debate, and in the conduct of public affairs, and gave me more confidence in myself. I laid aside my solitary habits and mixed freely in the society of the place, which, at that period, was always gay during the session of the General Assembly, and highly cultivated and refined. Yet

I cannot say that I was always at ease in it. In my lonely and retired student's life I had not acquired a talent for that light and playful conversation which usually prevails at such assemblies, and I felt more at home in the business scenes of the House of Delegates than in the gayer scenes of the drawing-room. Besides, my vision was unfortunately defective. I could not recognize the face of a man or woman unless I had seen it frequently, or there was something striking about it. And I felt awkward and uncomfortable on entering a room, from the consciousness of this defect, and the apprehension that I might pass without notice some lady or gentleman whom I had been introduced to, and whom, of course, I desired to treat with respect.

This imperfection of vision is a most unfortunate infirmity for a man in public life, who must unavoidably become acquainted with a multitude of people whose good-will he desires to preserve. And there is no readier way to lose it than to pass, without a sign of recognition, one to whom perhaps you were introduced the day before, and familiarly conversed with. Yet I have no doubt this has happened to me hundreds of times in the streets of Baltimore and Washington; and that I have passed, without knowing them, men for whom I entertained a real respect and regard, and whom I should at all times have been glad to meet, and meet as friends, if I had known who they

were. I can now read ordinary print, or write, by the
light of a single candle; but I sometimes pass my
own children in the street without knowing them until
they speak to me.

I returned to Calvert after the session ended. I had
gained a standing in the State and in the county
which seemed to leave no doubt of my re-election;
and I was to be a candidate, of course. The first part
of the summer was passed idly. There was very little
professional business to occupy me, and I read very
little law, and not a great deal of anything else. What
I did read was chiefly belles-lettres or political and
historical writings. I mixed but little in the society
of the county, and returned again very much to my
retired domestic life, spending my time with my own
family. Indeed, I have always loved the country and
country scenes too much to study, except in the long
nights of winter. When the weather permitted, I
was always out, wandering on the shore of the river
or in the woods, much of the time alone, occupied
with my own meditations, or sitting often for hours
together under the shade, and looking almost listlessly
at the prospect before me. There was always a love
of the romantic about me, and my thoughts and imag-
inings when alone were more frequently in that direction than in the real business of life. When I did
work in earnest, my chief business was to make myself familiar with the interests of the State, in order

that I might qualify myself for taking a leading part
at the next session.

But about the middle of the summer a new political
question arose which blighted all these plans. It was
seen that the next election was not (like the former)
to turn upon the personal popularity of the candidate.
A question as to the mode of choosing Electors of
President was started, upon which the whole State
became agitated, and the election of the candidate in
every county was supported, or opposed, according to
his opinions on this question. Tickets on each side
were brought out, upon which the two parties respectively rallied.

The question arose in this way. At the previous
elections of President and Vice-President, the Electors,
both in Maryland and Virginia, were chosen by districts. This mode was adopted upon the principle
that the rights of the minority as well as the majority
were to be respected and protected; and that when
the people of the State were divided in opinion, the
electoral body ought to represent it as it was, as far as
practicable, and not merely speak the opinion of the
majority. Upon this mode of voting, although the
great majority of the Legislature which passed the
law dividing the State into districts belonged to
the Federal party, it was well known that two or
three of the districts would choose Electors favorable
to Mr. Jefferson. One district, as well as I recollect,

had, at the former election, voted for Mr. Adams; and it was confidently believed that at the ensuing election two or three districts would vote in like manner. About the end of the session of the Legislature, the contest between Mr. Adams and Mr. Jefferson had become more animated; and it was understood by both parties that the election would be very close, and probably decided by two or three votes. In this state of affairs, the Legislature of Virginia passed a law requiring the Electors to be chosen by a general ticket; thus securing to Mr. Jefferson, past dispute, the entire vote of that State, and depriving Mr. Adams of the two or three votes upon which his friends had confidently counted. When this fact came to the knowledge of the Maryland Federalists, they determined, if possible, to counteract it, and, as Maryland was a federal State, to give to Mr. Adams the entire vote.

The Maryland Legislature had adjourned, and the district law could not be altered without calling an extra session of the Legislature. This would have subjected the State to an expense which could hardly be justified in a mere party question relating exclusively to the general Government. If it had been called, and a general ticket substituted for the district system, I do not know how it would have resulted. I think it would have been very doubtful; for, although a great majority of the counties were in favor of Mr. Adams, the vote of Baltimore City was very large, and the numerical majority in favor of Mr. Jefferson a heavy one.

The leaders of the party, however, I believe, were very confident that they could carry the State by a general ticket. I was too young and too little accustomed to electioneering calculations and tactics to have any opinion about the matter; but, judging from subsequent counts, I think the leaders of the party in Maryland were always too sanguine, and that, in this instance, a general ticket would have gone against them. But, however that may be, a general ticket in the then state of public feeling was out of the question. The political power of the State was in the hands of the counties, and the population of the counties was agricultural. They were very jealous of the growing influence of Baltimore, and unwilling to give the commercial interest any increase of power, fearing it would be used in a manner that might prove injurious to the landed interest. And if a Legislature composed of a majority of Federalists, had passed a law by which the majority in the counties might be overwhelmed by a sweeping majority in town, they would have been inevitably ruined in the counties, and lost all influence in the State Government. We now elect our Governor by general ticket; but, at the time of which I am speaking, nothing could have induced the counties to consent to it.

Under these circumstances, the gentlemen who were

at the head of the Federal party determined to put it to the people, at the approaching election, to say whether the Legislature should not elect the Electors, so as to secure the entire vote for Mr. Adams, and in that manner counteract the movement in Virginia. In this way it was put to the people as organized in the State Government, and not to the numerical majority.

Who first suggested this plan, I do not know. It was brought before the public in a pamphlet signed "A Bystander," which was avowedly written by Robert Goodloe Harper. He had become a resident of Baltimore only a few months before, and hence the signature he adopted. Although he had but recently come among us, he was well known to the people of the State from the distinguished rank he had held in Congress as a Representative from South Carolina; and he was personally and intimately acquainted with most, if not all, of the Maryland statesmen who at that time took the lead in public affairs. I take for granted he consulted them, and received their approbation before he acted. I, of course, was too young, and had too little influence in the State, to make it necessary to send to Calvert to consult me. Indeed, I was not personally acquainted with Mr. Harper at that time, and his pamphlet, which I received through the post-office, was the first intimation of the contemplated movement. It was sent to many gentlemen of the county, and soon became a subject of conversation. The pamphlet was written with all the force and eloquence for which Mr. Harper was distinguished in public life and at the bar. It convinced me; and I at once openly took ground in favor of the measure. Some of the Federalists objected to it; and it was, of course, vehemently attacked by the friends of Mr. Jefferson. But the great body of Federalists throughout the State supported the proposed change, and adverse tickets were formed in Calvert and in every other county upon that issue. But the relative merits of Mr. Adams and Mr. Jefferson were also necessarily involved in the controversy, and votes for one ticket or the other were, in many instances, undoubtedly influenced by the voters' preferences for the Presidential candidate.

The ground constantly pressed in opposition to the plan was that it took away the rights of the people. And I am satisfied that some men, who wished for the election of Mr. Adams, voted against a legislative choice of Electors on that ground. For myself, I did not see the force of this objection. So far as the voter was concerned, his intention would be as fully carried out by Electors chosen by the Legislature as by an Elector voted for immediately. His vote for the Electors, or for members of the Legislature, designated the person whom he wished to be President; and his share of the sovereign power was equally exercised, whether he accomplished his object by voting immediately for the President preferred, or appointing an agent or several agents to execute his wishes.

I was the only speaker on the Federal ticket, and supported and defended the legislative choice of Electors upon these grounds and those herein-before stated. During the canvass, I addressed three or four meetings of the people, and we went into the election very confident of success. To our surprise, we were beaten. It was a close vote, so close that we elected one of our candidates. But I was among the defeated; and when the news came in from the other counties, we found that many of them, upon which we confidently counted, had gone against us, and that the Federalists, who were two to one in the House of Delegates of 1799, were in a minority in that of 1800. The majority against us was a large one, and the power of the State passed from the hands of the Federalists, and was in the hands of the Republican party.

The unpopularity of Mr. Adams no doubt contributed greatly to this result. The Federalists of Maryland had lost confidence in him. The letter of General Hamilton, which was published on the eve of our election, increased their dissatisfaction with Mr. Adams, and he was supported from necessity, in order to prevent the general Government from falling into the hands of the opposing party. Indeed, I heard many who voted for him say they felt no great anxiety about his election ; that they took him in preference to Mr. Jefferson, but should care very little if he was defeated.   When we knew that such opinions prevailed extensively in the party, and the only object of the proposed measure was to secure the election of Mr. Adams, I think we were over-sanguine in looking so confidently for success.

My father and myself, as may be supposed, were sufficiently mortified at this defeat.   It put an end to any prospect of immediate political elevation.   And as it never had been intended that Calvert should be my permanent place of residence, there was no object to be gained by continuing there any longer.   As I have said, there was not business enough in the county to make the profession of the law worth pursuing, and any hopes of political distinction must be postponed to a future day.   We expected, to be sure, that the Federalists would soon recover their lost power in the county and the State.   But I was not willing (nor did he wish that I should) to remain there another year, doing nothing to advance me in my profession, but wasting my time in small contests for county ascendency.

As I was not in public life, it was desirable that I should at once select a place for my permanent residence and the pursuit of my profession.   We had many consultations upon the subject.   He suggested Baltimore.   But I had scarcely any personal acquaintances there, and I feared I should be lost in a large city, without any friends to give me an opportunity of coming forward. I therefore proposed Frederick. My inducement for selecting Frederick was that, next to Annapolis and Baltimore, it was, with a view to profit, the best point of practice in the State. The two lawyers who had been for years at the head of the profession in that place were John Thomson Mason and Arthur Shaaff. The former had recently retired from practice, and the latter removed to Annapolis; and the bar was a young one, most of the members being but a few years older than myself. Besides, I had at Annapolis formed friendships with some young men near my own age who resided in Frederick. And I felt that I should not there be as lonely and without friends, on my first arrival, as I should have been in Baltimore.

My father yielded to these considerations, and in March, 1801, I took up my residence there, and appeared in Court and made my first speech. It was a volunteer speech: Mr. Shaaff, who still practised in Frederick, having invited me to take part in one of his cases, in order to give me an opportunity of appearing before the public.

Thus far Mr. Taney wrote his own life, but no farther.

CHAPTER II.

FREDERICK, now usually called Frederick City, where Mr. Taney had taken up his residence, is the seat of justice in Frederick County, and contained, at that time, about three thousand inhabitants. It is situated in a valley remarkable for fertility, salubrity, and picturesque scenery. On the east, at a distance of eight miles, the Linganore hills, with their gentle slopes, are seen stretching from north to south. On the west, at a distance of three miles, is the Catoctin Mountain, with its woody sides and undulating summits, running parallel with the Linganore hills. At the north, the valley seems closed by the converging mountain and hills, and at the south stands the Sugar Loaf Mountain, with its solitary summit in the blue distance. Not many miles from the town, in all directions, were fine country - seats, owned and occupied by wealthy farmers. The society of the town and the neighborhood was intellectual, refined, and hospitable.

The business of the place was, for that early period, very considerable. During the Revolutionary War, there sprang up in the neighborhood a variety of

96

manufactures. Even powder and cannon were manufactured there. In the town, and throughout the
county, there were tanneries and flour-mills. The
manufacture of hats and shoes, and saddles and har-
ness, and carriages, wagons, ploughs, and all kinds of
farming-implements, constituted a large business in
the town. Coopering of casks and barrels was also a
profitable employment. There were also in the neighborhood a manufactory of glass, and works for smelt-
ing and casting iron. Here and there throughout the
county were distilleries for making whiskey and fat-
tening hogs. Horses and cattle of all kinds were
raised for sale. Books, as well as newspapers, were
printed in the town. So, too, there were looms for
weaving coarse cloths, and potteries for making earth-
enware. Dry-good stores, groceries, and hardware
stores abounded; and banks and money-lenders gave
life to business. As Frederick was situated on the
Cumberland Road, the great highway from Baltimore
and Washington to the West, it was always enlivened
by stage-coaches and by wagons, and the entry and
exit of travellers. During the early history of the
State, and until 1776, Frederick County embraced
what are now Montgomery and Washington and
Alleghany Counties, and a part of Carroll; and Frederick was the county town. It continued to be the
great western town of the State. Not only were
lawyers attracted to it, but also physicians who had

received a European education. Among the lawyers who resided there at the time, and for many years previous, was Thomas Johnson — on whose nomination, the 15th of June, 1775, as a delegate from Maryland to the Continental Congress, General Washington was chosen commander-in-chief of the American forces; and who was the first Governor of Maryland after the Declaration of Independence; and to whom President Washington offered, first a seat on the bench of the Supreme Court of the United States, which was accepted, but was resigned after a service of two years, and afterwards, the Secretaryship of State, which was declined. He stood in the first rank of Maryland lawyers, but was now retired from practice. Being born in the same county with Mr. Taney, and an intimate friend of his father, he often went to his office and advised him in matters of his profession, and talked of the men and events of the Revolution. His conversations made so much impression on the mind of Mr. Taney that often, in the last years of his life, he narrated some of them to me, in regard to the men of that period, especially Mr. Madison.

Such was the professional field where Mr. Taney now appeared. In the transactions of such various business as I have described, there was much need of the aid of lawyers for direction, as well as conducting lawsuits that inevitably arise out of the disputes of business. And as at that early day the boundaries and the titles to estates were unsettled, a very lucrative practice in actions of ejectment and of trespass had sprung up; and lawyers practised in other counties than the one in which they resided. Besides the County Courts, the Court of Chancery and the Court of Appeals were open to Mr. Taney. The bar of Frederick was an able one; and the leading lawyers of other bars practised there.

I studied law at Frederick under Mr. John Nelson, afterwards Attorney-General of the United States, and one of the ablest of American lawyers, and from him, and others of Mr. Taney's contemporaries at the Frederick bar, I learned, during the earlier years of my practice at that bar, the history of his professional career during his residence at the place. I learned, too, from all classes of citizens of the town, and of the county, their estimate of him, and how he appeared to them in all his relations, professional and private. What I shall now relate will therefore be upon the testimony of those with whom he lived and acted, confirmed by indisputable facts.

From his first appearance at Frederick, Mr. Taney was a diligent student. Law was his chief study; but he devoted much time to the study of history and of letters. The notes which he took of Dr. Nisbet's lectures at Dickinson College, mentioned by himself in the first chapter of this memoir, were very full and very accurate. They were preserved in bound manuscript volumes, which I have examined with some care, and they might be published as good treatises on the respective subjects. The notes on moral philosophy cover two hundred and forty-eight closely written pages. Those on the dead languages and classical education, and the character of the principal classic authors, beginning with Homer and ending with Seneca, cover one hundred and twelve pages. Those on criticism cover two hundred and ninety-six pages, and those on logic, one hundred and seventy-eight pages. Upon these foundations, laid in his collegiate studies, he now built with untiring zeal. He not only studied thoughts, but he studied words and style with uncommon care. He cultivated a simple and severe taste.

In 1803, Mr. Taney became a candidate on the Federal ticket for the House of Delegates. He canvassed the county, and made a deep impression by his speeches. But at this early period in Mr. Jefferson's administration, Frederick County was very decidedly Republican, and he was defeated.

Though it was only in the fifth year of his residence in Frederick, Mr. Taney had acquired such a position at the bar, and his practice was so lucrative, that he was about to be married. Francis Scott Key, afterwards, as we shall see, the author of "The Star-Spangled Banner," was Mr. Taney's fellow law-student at Annapolis. Mr. Key and a sister were the only

children of their parents. Mr. Taney had met Miss
Key in Annapolis, and her beauty and bright mind
and womanly graces won his heart. Mr. Key was
practising law in Frederick when Mr. Taney went
there, but had lately removed to George Town, District
of Columbia. John Ross Key, the father of
Miss Key, was a lieutenant in the first artillery
which went to Boston from Maryland at the outbreak
of the Revolutionary War, owned a large estate in
Frederick County, where Miss Key was born and was
now living with her parents. The mansion was of
brick, with centre and wings and long porches. It
was situated amidst a large lawn, shaded by trees, and
an extensive terraced garden adorned with shrubbery
and flowers. Near by flowed Pipe Creek, through a
dense woods. A copious spring of purest water, where
young people loved to retire, and sit under the sheltering
oaks in summer, was at the foot of the hill. A
meadow of waving grass spread out towards the Catoctin
Mountain, which could be seen at sunset curtained
in clouds of crimson and gold. It was at this happy
home that Mr. Taney was, the seventh day of January,
1806, married to Anne Phebe Charlton Key. For
years afterwards Mr. Taney and Mr. Key, and their
families, met annually at this parental home, to enjoy
together all those pleasures which belong to family re-
unions. At evening, when the labors of the farm
were over, the negroes were summoned to prayers

with the family, which were usually conducted by Francis Scott Key when he was there, and by his mother when he was away. After prayers, almost every night, as was common on plantations in Maryland, music and dancing might be heard at the quarters of the negroes, who are a mirth-loving people.

No man was ever more happily married than Mr. Taney. And the happy circumstances of this period shed a benign influence over his studious and contemplative life, and nurtured that bland suavity of manner which so distinguished him, while they made the home circle the sphere of his happiness.

Mr. Taney did not stand on the outskirts of society, connected with it only by professional relations. He was affiliated with society in all relations, and was scrupulously faithful in discharging every duty. He was, for years, a director in the Frederick County Bank, and hardly ever missed a meeting of the board of directors. He was also a Visitor of the Frederick Academy, a State institution of some note; and as I have been, for many years, the President of the Board of Visitors, and know how seldom Visitors are punctual at meetings, as a matter of biographical curiosity, I wrote to the present Principal of the Academy, and received the following answer:

FREDERICK CITY, MARYLAND,
March 1, 1871.

MY DEAR SIR:—In the minutes of the Board of Visitors I find the following: "Oct. 30, 1802. The chairman informed the Board that Mr. Wm. Campbell, heretofore appointed a Visitor, declined serving; whereupon the Visitors proceeded to fill the vacancy, and Roger Brooke Taney was appointed."

"February 1, 1822. Roger B. Taney having resigned his seat at the Board, Dr. William Tyler was elected to fill the vacancy."

It thus appears that Judge Taney was a member of the Board for twenty years. I have gone over the minutes for all those years, and find that, with one or two exceptions, he was never absent from the meetings of the Visitors—an example worthy of imitation.

Yours truly,   J. S. BONSALL.

SAMUEL TYLER, ESQ.

Though, during his life in Frederick, Mr. Taney was strict in his religious observances, he was, nevertheless, fond of festive relaxations. It was common for gentlemen to dine together, the Fourth of July, under the shade of the beach-trees on the banks of the Monocacy River, which flows between wooded banks two miles from Frederick. Some of his companions, who lived until a few years ago, have often narrated to me how much he contributed to the pleasure of such occasions. As Mr. Taney was, like all southern Marylanders, a good horseman, he took much pleasure in horseback excursions in the country, when professional duties required him to go into the country to try cases before juries upon view. In these excursions, the picturesque aspects of the Catoctin Mountain had become so familiar to him, that when, in after years, he would speak of them, his descriptions were so accurate, that they seemed as if frescoed on his memory. In the summer Mr. Taney would sometimes retire, with his family, a few miles from Frederick to Arcadia, the country-seat of the eminent lawyer Arthur Shaaff, a bachelor, and a cousin of Mrs. Taney, to recruit the exhausted energies of his body, and refresh his overtasked mind in the serenities of the country. In all his love of nature, Mrs. Taney participated with the romantic ardor of a woman, who, like her brother, was inspired, by the beauties of nature, with "thoughts that voluntary move harmonious numbers."

In 1811, General Wilkinson, then Commander-in-Chief of the United States Army, was tried on a series of charges before a military court convened at Frederick. He was a Marylander by birth, and knew the professional reputation of Mr. Taney. He selected Mr. Taney and John Hanson Thomas, of whom I shall have occasion to speak presently, as his counsel. General Wilkinson labored under much public odium. He was suspected of having been an accomplice of Aaron Burr in his supposed treasonable enterprise; and to cover his guilt had turned State's evidence against him upon his trial at Richmond. Conduct so flagitious as his was supposed to have been, could not but make the community, in which he was tried, feel that his counsel shared some of his infamy in defending him.   This feeling, though wholly unwarrantable, ignoring as it does the duty of a lawyer, is, nevertheless, more or less ever entertained, as all lawyers know who have been engaged in the defence of unpopular culprits.   Mr. Taney labored for several months, with singular zeal and ability, against Walter Jones, of Washington City, the Judge Advocate, the subtlest of the most casuistic of lawyers.   General Wilkinson was acquitted, and his sword restored to him.   Both Mr. Taney and Mr. Thomas had shared in the general suspicion of Wilkinson's treachery to Burr; and, because of their conviction of the injustice they had done him, refused to receive a fee for their professional services, communicating the fact to him, and begging him to acquiesce in their course, as it would gratify their feelings.   This manifestation of a high sense of honor, and desire to atone for an unintentional wrong, was a pre-eminent trait in the character of Mr. Taney.

In the terrible struggle between the nations of Europe to preserve their independence and their institutions, which originated in the French Revolution, England, in her extremity, claimed that every man of British birth was her subject by an inextinguishable allegiance, and that she had a right to his services as a soldier in the wars in which she was engaged. Acting upon this doctrine, she assumed the right, and acted upon it, to board our ships upon the ocean and seize any man of British birth, whether he claimed to be an American citizen, and was such by our laws of naturalization, or not, and to carry him off and impress him into her service.   A claim so abhorrent to American notions of allegiance, and so defiant of the protection which international law extends over the watery highways of nations, making the ships of every nation as inviolable as its territory, could not but awaken intense resentment in the United States, where the enmity of the Revolutionary War still burnt in the national breast.   So persistent was the British Government in her claim of search and impressment, and she was guilty of so many provocations, that the United States, in June, 1812, declared war against Great Britain.

From the outbreak of the French Revolution, which became a struggle of democracy to extirpate aristocracy and monarchy, not only from France but from all Europe, two parties were formed in the United States in regard to the contest.   The Republican party sympathized with France, and the Federal party sympathized with England.   Mr. Jefferson, when in France, had become inoculated with the radical philosophy of that country, and infected with its political doctrines.   And though, when he became President of the United States, he maintained the neutrality in the European wars which Washington had originated, his predilection for France and antipathy to England still animated both himself and his party. And the Federal party was animated by predilection for England and antipathy to France. When, therefore, the Republican party, which was now in possession of the Federal Government, proposed war against Great Britain, the Federal party opposed it, both from party feeling and from considerations of prudence, and to a great extent from sectional interest in commerce which would be broken up by war. Mr. Taney was of the Federal party, and shared in its opposition to a declaration of war; but, as soon as war was declared, he gave his support to the Government; and so did most of the Federalists of Maryland. Mr. Taney, and the Federalists in Frederick County who followed his lead in supporting the Government, were nicknamed, by the other wing of his party, Coodies, and he, because of his great influence, was called King Coody. John Hanson Thomas, an able lawyer of the Frederick bar, was the leader of the other wing of the Federal party. Such was the bitterness of feeling between the two wings of the party, and such was the estrangement between Mr. Thomas and Mr. Taney, that it was not until Mr. Thomas was on his death-bed that he could forgive Mr. Taney for his course. But now that all rivalry between them must cease, and the memories of their early friendship and the great qualities of Mr. Taney came before his magnanimous soul, he felt that their old friendship must be restored.   He sent for Mr. Taney, who hastened to the bedside of his rival, and gave him a greeting so generous and so tender that their reconciliation was consecrated by mutual tears. Mr. Thomas died May, 1815, and few followed him to the grave in deeper sorrow, or with more sincere admiration for his high qualities, than Mr. Taney.

The spirit which animated Mr. Taney and the Federalists in Maryland who acted with him in the War of 1812, is manifested in "The Star-Spangled Banner," and the circumstances in which it was written.   It was the song of Maryland Federalism, which became the song of the nation because of its patriotism and its origin in the midst of battle.   Never did a national song have so glorious a birth.   It was written by a Maryland Federalist while on board of a cartel-ship, as he witnessed the fruitless attack upon Fort McHenry, and the flag of his country still waving in triumph.   The song will live in the American heart until the stars fall from the national flag, or are absorbed in one imperial star, which has quenched the glory of the States.   In a letter to Charles Howard, of Baltimore, who married the eldest daughter of Mr. Key, the author of the song, Mr. Taney has given the history of its origin.   The letter was intended only as a family memorial.

WASHINGTON, D. C., March 12, 1856.

MY DEAR SIR : — I promised some time ago to give you an account of the incidents in the life of Mr. F. S. Key which led him to write "The Star-Spangled Banner," and of the circumstances under which it was written. The song has become a national one, and will, I think, from its great merit, continue to be so, especially in Maryland ; and everything that concerns its author must be a matter of interest to his children and descendants. And I proceed to fulfil my promise with the more pleasure, because, while the song shows his genius and taste as a poet, the incidents connected with it, and the circumstances under which it was written, will show his character and worth as a man. The scene he describes, and the warm spirit of patriotism which breathes in the song, were not the offspring of mere fancy or poetic imagination. He describes what he actually saw. And he tells us what he felt while witnessing the conflict, and what he felt when the battle was over and the victory won by his countrymen. Every word came warm from his heart, and for that reason, even more than for its poetical merit, it never fails to find a response in the hearts of those who listen to it.

You will remember that in 1814, when the song was written, I resided in Frederick and Mr. Key in George Town. You will also recollect that soon after the British troops retired from Washington, a squadron of the enemy's ships made their way up the Potomac, and appeared before Alexandria, which was compelled to capitulate ; and the squadron remained there some days, plundering the town of tobacco and whatever else they wanted. It was rumored and believed in Frederick, that a marauding attack of the same character would be made on Washington and George Town before the ships left the river. Mr. Key's family was in George Town. He would not, and indeed could not, with honor, leave the place while it was threatened by the enemy; for he was a volunteer in the Light Artillery, commanded by Major Peter, which was composed of citizens of the District of Columbia, who had uniformed themselves and offered their services to the Government, and who had been employed in active service from the time the British fleet appeared in the Patuxent preparatory to the movement upon Washington. And Mrs. Key refused to leave home while Mr. Key was thus daily exposed to danger. Believing, as we did, that an attack would probably be made on George Town, we became very anxious about the situation of his family. For if the attack was made, Mr. Key would be with the troops engaged in the defence; and as it was impossible to foresee what would be the issue of the conflict, his family, by remaining in George Town, might be placed in great and useless peril. When I speak of *we*, I mean Mr. Key's father and mother and Mrs. Taney and myself. But it was agreed among us that I should go to George Town and try to persuade Mrs. Key to come away with her children, and stay with me or with Mr. Key's father until the danger was over. When I reached George Town, I found the English ships still at Alexandria, and a body of militia encamped in Washington, which had been assembled to defend the city.   But it was then believed, from information received, that no attack would be made by the enemy on Washington or George Town; and preparations were making, on our part, to annoy them by batteries on shore, when they descended the river. The knowledge of the preparations probably hastened their departure; and the second or third day after my arrival, the ships were seen moving down the Potomac.

On the evening of the day that the enemy disappeared, Mr. Richard West arrived at Mr. Key's, and told him that after the British army passed through Upper Marlbro on their return to their ships, and had encamped some miles below the town, a detachment was sent back, which entered Dr. Beanes's house about midnight, compelled him to rise from his bed, and hurried him off to the British camp, hardly allowing him time to put his clothes on; that he was treated with great harshness, and closely guarded; and that as soon as his friends were apprised of his situation, they hastened to the head-quarters of the English army to solicit his release; but it was peremptorily refused, and they were not even permitted to see him; and that he had been carried as a prisoner on board the fleet. And finding their own efforts unavailing, and alarmed for his safety, his friends in and about Marlbro thought it advisable that Mr. West should hasten to George Town, and request Mr. Key to obtain the sanction of the Government to his going on board the admiral's ship, under a flag of truce, and endeavoring to procure the release of Dr. Beanes before the fleet sailed.   It was then lying at the mouth of the Potomac, and its destination was not at that time known with certainty. Dr. Beanes, as perhaps you know, was the leading physician in Upper Marlbro, and an accomplished scholar and gentleman. He was highly respected by all who knew him; was the family physician of Mr. West, and the intimate friend of Mr. Key. He occupied one of the best houses in Upper Marlbro, and lived very handsomely; and his house was selected for the quarters of Admiral Cockburn, and some of the principal officers of the army, when the British troops encamped at Marlbro on their march to Washington. These officers were, of course, furnished with everything that the house could offer; and they, in return, treated him with much courtesy, and placed guards around his grounds and out-houses, to prevent depredations by their troops.

But on the return of the army to the ships, after the main body had passed through the town, stragglers, who had left the ranks to plunder, or from some other motive, made their appearance from time to time, singly or in small squads; and Dr. Beanes put himself at the head of a small body of citizens to pursue and make prisoners of them. Information of this proceeding was, by some means or other, conveyed to the English camp; and the detachment of which I have spoken was sent back to release the prisoners and seize Dr. Beanes. They did not seem to regard him, and certainly did not treat him, as a prisoner of war, but as one who had deceived, and broken his faith to them.

Mr. Key readily agreed to undertake the mission in his favor, and the President promptly gave his sanction to it. Orders were immediately issued to the vessel usually employed as a cartel, in the communications with the fleet in the Chesapeake, to be made ready without delay ; and Mr. John S. Skinner, who was agent for the Government for flags of truce and exchange of prisoners, and who was well known as such to the officers of the fleet, was directed to accompany Mr. Key. And as soon as the arrangements were made, he hastened to Baltimore, where the vessel was to embark ; and Mrs. Key and the children went with me to Frederick, and thence to his father's on Pipe Creek, where she remained until he returned.

We heard nothing from him until the enemy retreated from Baltimore, which, as well as I can now recollect, was a week or ten days after he left us ; and we were becoming uneasy about him, when, to our great joy, he made his appearance at my house, on his way to join his family.

He told me that he found the British fleet at the mouth of the Potomac, preparing for the expedition against Baltimore. He was courteously received by Admiral Cochrane and the officers of the army, as well as of the navy. But when he made known his business, his application was received so coldly that he feared it would fail. General Ross and Admiral Cockburn — who accompanied the expedition to Washington — particularly the latter, spoke of Dr. Beanes in very harsh terms, and seemed at first not disposed to release him. It however happened, fortunately, that Mr. Skinner carried letters from the wounded British officers left at Bladensburg; and in these letters to their friends on board the fleet they

all spoke of the humanity and kindness with which
they had been treated after they had fallen into our
hands.   And after a good deal of conversation, and
strong representations from Mr. Key as to the character and standing of Dr. Beanes, and of the deep
interest which the community in which he lived took
in his fate, General Ross said that Dr. Beanes deserved much more punishment than he had received ;
but that he felt himself bound to make a return for
the kindness which had been shown to his wounded
officers, whom he had been compelled to leave at
Bladensburg, and upon that ground, and that only, he
would release him.   But Mr. Key was at the same
time informed that neither he, nor any one else, would
be permitted to leave the fleet for some days, and
must be detained until the attack on Baltimore, which
was then about to be made, was over.   But he was
assured that they would make him and Mr. Skinner
as comfortable as possible while they detained them.
Admiral Cochrane, with whom they dined on the day
of their arrival, apologized for not accommodating
them in his own ship, saying that it was crowded
already with officers of the army; but that they would
be well taken care of in the frigate *Surprise*, commanded by his son, Sir Thomas Cochrane.   And to
this frigate, they were accordingly transferred.

Mr. Key had an interview with Dr. Beanes before
General Ross consented to release him.   I do not recollect whether he was on board of the admiral's ship,
or the *Surprise*, but I believe it was the former.   He
found him in the forward part of the ship, among the
sailors and soldiers ; he had not had a change of clothes

from the time he was seized; was constantly treated with indignity by those around him, and no officer would speak to him. He was treated as a culprit, and not as a prisoner of war. And this harsh and humiliating treatment continued until he was placed on board of the cartel.

Something must have passed, when the officers were quartered at his house on the march to Washington, which, in the judgment of General Ross, bound him not to take up arms against the English forces until the troops had re-embarked. It is impossible, on any other grounds, to account for the manner in which he was spoken of and treated. But whatever General Ross and the other officers might have thought, I am quite sure that Dr. Beanes did not think he was in any way pledged to abstain from active hostilities against the public enemy. And when he made prisoners of the stragglers, he did not consider himself as a prisoner on parole, nor suppose himself to be violating any obligation he had incurred. For he was a gentleman of untainted character and a nice sense of honor, and incapable of doing anything that could have justified such treatment. Mr. Key imputed the ill usage he received to the influence of Admiral Cockburn, who, it is still remembered, while he commanded in the Chesapeake, carried on hostilities in a vindictive temper, assailing and plundering defenceless villages, or countenancing such proceedings by those under his command.

Mr. Key and Mr. Skinner continued on board of the *Surprise*, where they were very kindly treated by Sir Thomas Cochrane, until the fleet reached the

Patapsco, and preparations were making for landing
the troops. Admiral Cochrane then shifted his flag
to the frigate, in order that he might be able to move
farther up the river and superintend in person the
attack by water on the fort; and Mr. Key and Mr.
Skinner were then sent on board their own vessel,
with a guard of sailors or marines, to prevent them
from landing. They were permitted to take Dr.
Beanes with them; and they thought themselves fortunate in being anchored in a position which enabled
them to see distinctly the flag of Fort McHenry from
the deck of the vessel. He proceeded then, with
much animation, to describe the scene on the night
of the bombardment. He and Mr. Skinner remained
on deck during the night, watching every shell from
the moment it was fired until it fell, listening with
breathless interest to hear if an explosion followed.
While the bombardment continued, it was sufficient
proof that the fort had not surrendered. But it suddenly ceased some time before day, and, as they had
no communication with any of the enemy's ships,
they did not know whether the fort had surrendered
or the attack had been abandoned. They paced the
deck for the residue of the night in painful suspense,
watching with intense anxiety for the return of day,
and looking every few minutes at their watches to see
how long they must wait for it; and as soon as it
dawned, and before it was light enough to see objects
at a distance, their glasses were turned to the fort, uncertain whether they should see the Stars and Stripes or
the flag of the enemy. At length the light came, and
they saw that " our flag was still there." And, as the

day advanced, they discovered, from the movements of the boats between the shore and the fleet, that the troops had been roughly handled, and that many wounded men were carried to the ships. At length he was informed that the attack on Baltimore had failed, and the British army was re-embarking, and that he and Mr. Skinner and Dr. Beanes would be permitted to leave them, and go where they pleased, as soon as the troops were on board and the fleet ready to sail.

He then told me that, under the excitement of the time, he had written the song, and handed me a printed copy of "The Star-Spangled Banner." When I had read it, and expressed my admiration, I asked him how he found time, in the scenes he had been passing through, to compose such a song? He said he commenced it on the deck of their vessel, in the fervor of the moment, when he saw the enemy hastily retreating to their ships, and looked at the flag he had watched for so anxiously as the morning opened; that he had written some lines, or brief notes, that would aid him in calling them to mind, upon the back of a letter which he happened to have in his pocket; and for some of the lines, as he proceeded, he was obliged to rely altogether on his memory; and that he finished it in the boat on his way to the shore, and wrote it out, as it now stands, at the hotel on the night he reached Baltimore, and immediately after he arrived. He said that, on the next morning, he took it to Judge Nicholson, to ask him what he thought of it; that he was so much pleased with it that he immediately sent it to a printer, and directed copies to be struck off in hand-

bill form; and that he, Mr. Key, believed it to have
been favorably received by the Baltimore public.

Judge Nicholson and Mr. Key, you know, were
nearly connected by marriage, Mrs. Key and Mrs.
Nicholson being sisters. The Judge was a man of
cultivated taste; had, at one time, been distinguished
among the leading men in Congress, and was, at the
period of which I am speaking, the Chief Justice of the
Baltimore-Court, and one of the Judges of the Court of
Appeals of Maryland. Notwithstanding his judicial
character, which exempted him from military service,
he accepted the command of a volunteer company of
artillery; and when the enemy approached, and an
attack on the fort was expected, he and his company
offered their services to the Government to assist in
the defence. They were accepted, and formed a part
of the garrison during the bombardment. The Judge
had been relieved from duty, and returned to his
family, only the night before Mr. Key showed him
his song; and you may easily imagine the feelings
with which, at such a moment, he read it and gave it
to the public. It was, no doubt, as Mr. Key modestly
expressed it, favorably received. In less than an hour
after it was placed in the hands of the printer, it was
all over town, and hailed with enthusiasm, and took
its place at once as a national song.

I have made this account of "The Star-Spangled
Banner" longer than I intended, and find that I have
introduced incidents and persons outside of the subject
I originally contemplated. But I have felt a melancholy pleasure in recalling events connected in any
degree with the life of one with whom I was so long

and so closely united in friendship and affection, and whom I so much admired for his brilliant genius, and loved for his many virtues.   I am sure, however, that neither you, nor any of his children or descendants, will think the account I have given too long.

With great regard, dear sir,

Your friend truly,

R. B. TANEY.

CHARLES HOWARD, ESQ.

Besides the historical interest of this letter, it illustrates the warm affection Mr. Taney had for his friends.   No man ever had a warmer heart.   Mr. Howard, to whom the letter is written, is a son of Col. John Eager Howard, who was so distinguished at the battle of the Cowpens, and other hard conflicts of the Revolutionary War.

While the division in the Federal party produced by the war was at its height, Mr. Taney was nominated by his friends for a seat in the House of Representatives of the United States; and, notwithstanding the great strength of the Republican party in the congressional district, he was defeated by only three hundred majority.

Mr. Taney was of a most vehement and passionate nature, which, though under the most perfect control, gave great decisiveness to his opinions on all subjects, and on none more than on politics.   But such was his consideration for opinions differing from his own, that no one ever felt his judgment disparaged by Mr. Taney's dissent. It was not long, therefore, before the Federalists, whose opinions in regard to the War of 1812, differed from his, affiliated with him with the sincerity of their old party relations. In 1816 he was, with the approbation of all, elected a member of the State Senate. By the Constitution of the State at that time, and ever since 1776, the Senate consisted of fifteen members, whose term of service was five years. They were selected by a college of electors, composed of two members chosen in each county by the people, and one from each of the cities Baltimore and Annapolis. Mr. Taney was one of the electors from Frederick County. As the Electoral College could choose Senators from their own members as well as from the State at large, they chose Mr. Taney. Though preferring professional life, he yet yielded to the wishes of his friends, and served out his term in the Senate to the great benefit of the State. The period is marked by some of the most important legislation in regard to the courts, of law, of equity, the orphans' courts, and all tribunals that administer law. Many of the statutes were drawn by him, and all others, probably, received his aid. The mode of electing the Senate by electors sworn to select men most distinguished for their wisdom, talents, and virtues, and their term of service for five years, constituted the Senate such a body, that Mr. Taney always talked of his service in it with singular pleasure. Upon several occasions the integrity and firmness of the Senate withstood the unwise course of the more popular branch. Before the adoption of the Constitution of the United States, Samuel Chase proposed, in the House of Delegates of Maryland, the issue of paper money, and the House approved it; but the Senate, under the lead of Thomas Stone and Charles Carroll, of Carrollton, rejected the bill. General Washington, in a letter to Thomas Stone, approved the action of the Senate. Dugald Stewart, in his Lectures on Political Science, edited by Sir William Hamilton, and for the first time not long since published, bears testimony to the signal excellence of the Maryland Constitution of 1776.

Mr. Taney lived before the introduction of codes permitting lawyers to state causes of action and defences, without any regard to the rules of common law pleading, which, wherever introduced, have made a Babel of the court-room. When he came to the bar, Maryland lawyers were especially distinguished for their knowledge of the science, and their skill in the practice, of special pleading. Without such knowledge and skill, it was impossible to attain even a respectable position at the bar. And, owing to the peculiar organization and practice of the Land Office, in a proprietory government like that of Maryland, and the manner in which original grants of land were made, the boundaries of estates had become very uncertain, and, consequently, in suits involving title, extensive re-surveys had to be made to ascertain boundaries. Out of this grew up, under the direction of technical lawyers and judges, the most subtle principles and the most complex forms of pleading in actions of ejectment known to the history of administrative justice. Luther Martin had been a forerunner in this form of pleading; and Mr. Taney learned from him, in cases in which they were employed together as counsel, the mystery of plots and their function in actions of ejectment. In a suit of great magnitude, as to the interests involved, in which he was employed with Mr. Martin, he had to study the case and prepare for trial without Mr. Martin's aid. The case was in Washington County Court at Hagerstown; and he and Mr. Martin started from Frederick, the evening before the day set for the trial, in a stage-coach, to be at Court in time. The distance is twenty-six miles. At every relay of horses, which was every five miles, Mr. Martin drank at the tavern — whiskey when he could get it, and when he could not, he drank ale, and when he could get neither, he drank buttermilk. On their arrival at Hagerstown, they took supper; and Mr. Taney told Mr. Martin that, after he had smoked a cigar and rested, he would come to his room and go over the case with him. At eleven o'clock he went to Mr. Martin's room, and found him, with his hat on and one boot and all his clothes, lying across the bed, asleep from his various potations on the road and what he had taken since his arrival. He tried, by words, to awaken the slumbering jurist, but, finding them unavailing, he dared not use other means, though he knew, from Mr. Martin's habits, that, when once awakened, there would not be a cloud or a shadow over his legal reason. Though much disturbed, but not daunted, he retired to his room and studied the case until nearly day; as Mr. Shaaff, who, in legal technicalities was a match even for Mr. Martin, was an opposing counsel. At the opening of the Court Mr. Taney was in his seat, fearing that Mr. Martin would not be in Court, as he found his door locked when he called for him before leaving the hotel. But just as the case was called, in walked Mr. Martin; and in none of his forensic efforts did he excel his skill in the management of this cause. A chief point in the case was a spring of water, that had been located to determine the boundary in dispute. Mr. Taney told me that Mr. Shaaff showed the most extraordinary ingenuity in bringing before the jury evidences of the change that the location of the spring might have undergone, from its topographical relations and physical causes; but that Mr. Martin met it all with the same sort of sagacity; and that from the trial he, a comparatively young man, got a new insight into ejectment causes.

At the March Term, 1819, in Frederick County

Court, Mr. Taney was counsel for the defence in a cause which throws light over his whole subsequent life, enabling men to form a just estimate of his conduct in regard to a matter about which the most erroneous opinions have been entertained.

Because, by the public law of Europe, the right to property, by Christian white men, in pagan African negroes was recognized, and African slave-labor was available and the trade in slaves profitable, in the American colonies, African slaves were, at an early period, introduced into Maryland. Marylanders were, therefore, from the beginning, born with negro slavery before their eyes as a lawful institution. Neither the public nor the private conscience revolted at an institution which, because of the inferiority of the negro, seemed natural to those familiar with it from their birth. In every one of the colonies it was recognized as lawful. The New England colonies were the importers, and the Southern colonies the purchasers, in a traffic that was profitable to both parties. Slave-labor became the only labor in the Southern colonies; and therefore slavery became incorporated in the whole fabric of society. The slaves rocked the cradle and dug the graves of their masters; and the masters, from the birth to the death of the slaves, in sickness and health, sheltered and protected them. Out of this mutual dependence and association grew a mutual regard and kindness. My ancestors, for two centuries, were slave-holders on a plantation in Maryland, where I was born; and often in that neighborhood have I seen slaves shed as sorrowful and affectionate tears at the funerals of members of the white family as their own kindred did. In the working of society, moved by its changed opinions and its passions and prejudices, it was inevitable that an institution like African slavery would sooner or later perish: but that, by no means, justifies condemnation of it, either as an evil, or a crime, or a sin, while it lasted. For a long period, if not through its whole duration, the relation of master and slave was best for both races, and especially for the negro, as it raised him from pagan barbarism to a phase of Christian civilization. In the divine decrees by which nations are marshalled in the grand procession of the human races, negroes have performed their part as slaves in the march of the United States towards their destiny; it remains for the future to reveal what part they will perform as citizens under a Government and institutions formed solely by white men and for white men only.

As legislation did not originate the relation of master and slave, there was not even any recognition of it by statute in Maryland until 1663, when a statute was passed regulating it.

While slaves were in every house in Maryland, and could murder the whites by poison in their food, or by fire, or by open violence, a Mr. Jacob Gruber, a minister of good standing in the Methodist Church, preached, at a camp-meeting in Washington County, to about three thousand persons, of whom four hundred were negroes. After addressing the audience generally, he addressed to them such words as these: "But are there not slaves in our country? do not sweat and blood and tears say there are? The voice of my brother crieth blood. Is it not a reproach to a man to hold articles of liberty and independence in one hand and a bloody whip in the other, while a negro stands and trembles before him, with his back cut and bleeding?"

"We Pennsylvanians think it strange, and it seems curious, to read the prints or newspapers, from some States, and find — *For sale, a plantation, a house and lot, horses, cows, sheep, and hogs; also, a number of negroes — men, women, and children — some very valuable ones; also, a pew in such and such a church.* In this inhuman traffic and cruel trade the most tender ties are torn asunder, the nearest connections broken."

What aggravated Mr. Gruber's conduct was that he came over from Pennsylvania, and in his harangue threw a slur upon Maryland in contrast with the elevated civilization of his own State.

For preaching this sermon, Mr. Gruber was indicted by the grand jury of Washington County, as intending thereby, unlawfully and maliciously, to incite the slaves who heard him to insurrection and rebellion

for the disturbance of the peace of the State.   The
case was, at Mr. Gruber's request, removed to Frederick County Court, and Mr. Taney appeared as his
principal counsel.

Mr. Taney opened the case to the jury, on the part
of Mr. Gruber, and the following extracts from his
opening statement will show the grounds upon which
he rested the defence of his client.   These grounds he
elaborated and enforced with all his power in his argument before the jury, which was not reported as the
other parts of the trial were.

"The statement," said Mr. Taney, "made by the District Attorney has informed the jury of the interesting principles involved in the trial pending before
you.   It is, indeed, an important case, in which the
community, as well as the accused, has a deep interest.
The prosecution is without precedent in the judicial
proceedings of Maryland; and as the jury are judges
of the law as well as the fact, it becomes my duty
not only to state the evidence we are about to offer,
but to show you the grounds on which we mean to
rest the defence.

" I need not tell you that, by the liberal and happy
institutions of this State, the rights of conscience and
the freedom of speech are fully protected.   No man
can be prosecuted for preaching the articles of his religious creed; unless, indeed, his doctrine is immoral,
and calculated to disturb the peace and order of society.

And subjects of national policy may at all times be freely and fully discussed, in the pulpit or elsewhere, without limitation or restraint. Therefore, the reverend gentleman, whose cause I am now advocating, cannot be liable to prosecution, in any form of proceeding, for the sermon mentioned by the District Attorney, unless his doctrines were immoral and calculated to disturb the peace and order of society. The sermon, in itself, could in no other way be an offence against the laws. If his doctrines were not immoral, if the principles he maintained were not contrary to the peace and good order of society, he had an undoubted right to preach them, and to clothe them in such language, and enforce them by such facts and arguments, as to him seemed proper. It would be nothing to the purpose to say that he offended or that he alarmed some or all of his hearers. Their feelings, or their fears, would not alter the character of his doctrine, or take from him a right secured to him by the Constitution and laws of the State.

"But, in this case, he is not accused of preaching immoral or dangerous doctrine. It is not the charge contained in the indictment. The preaching of such a sermon is not laid as the offence. He is accused of an attempt to excite insubordination and insurrection among our slaves; and the intention of the preacher is the essence of the crime. On this indictment, no matter what doctrines he preached, no matter what language he used, yet his doctrines or his language could not amount to the crime now charged against him.   They could be evidence, I admit, to show his intention; but they would be nothing more than evidence, and could not constitute the offence itself. . . .

"You have already been told that Mr. Gruber is a minister of the Methodist Episcopal Church.   It is well known that the gradual and peaceable abolition of slavery in these States is one of the objects which the Methodist society has steadily in view. No slave-holder is allowed to be a minister of that Church.   Their preachers are accustomed, in their sermons, to speak of the injustice and oppressions of slavery.   The opinions of Mr. Gruber on the subject no one could doubt; and if any slave-holder believed it dangerous to himself, his family, or the community, to suffer his slaves to learn that all slavery is unjust and oppressive, and persuade himself that they would not, of themselves, be able to make the discovery, it was in his power to prevent them from attending the assemblies where such doctrines were likely to be preached.   Mr. Gruber did not go to the slaves : they came to him.   They could not have come, if their masters had chosen to prevent them. . . .

"Mr. Gruber feels that it is due to his own character, to the station which he fills, to the respectable society of Christians in which he is a minister of the gospel, not only to defend himself from this prosecution, but

also to avow, and to vindicate here, the principles which
he maintained in his sermon.   There is no law which
forbids us to speak of slavery as we think of it.   Any
man has a right to publish his opinions on that subject whenever he pleases.   It is a subject of national
concern, and may, at all times, be freely discussed.
Mr. Gruber did quote the language of our great act of
national independence, and insisted on the principles
contained in that venerated instrument.   He did rebuke those masters, who, in the exercise of power, are
deaf to the calls of humanity; and he warned them
of the evils they might bring upon themselves.   He
did speak with abhorrence of those reptiles who live
by trading in human flesh, and enrich themselves by
tearing the husband from the wife, the infant from
the bosom of the mother; and this, I am instructed,
was the head and front of his offending.   Shall I content myself with saying he had a right to say this?
that there is no law to punish him?   So far is he
from being the object of punishment in any form of
proceeding, that we are prepared to maintain the same
principles, and to use, if necessary, the same language
here, in the temple of justice and in the presence of
those who are the ministers of the law.   A hard necessity, indeed, compels us to endure the evil of slavery
for a time.   It was imposed upon us by another nation
while we were yet in a state of colonial vassalage.   It
cannot be easily or suddenly removed.   Yet, while it

continues, it is a blot on our national character; and every real lover of freedom confidently hopes that it will effectually, though it must be gradually, wiped away, and earnestly looks for the means by which this necessary object may be best attained."

Upon such grounds did Mr. Taney rest the defence before a slave-holding jury and before slave-holding judges. The jury retired, and in a few minutes brought in a verdict of *not guilty.* And a report of the trial was immediately published in Frederick, with a letter from Mr. Gruber, in which, among other severe things, he says: " I hope, while I keep my senses, I shall consider *involuntary perpetual slavery* miserable injustice; a system of *robbery and theft.*"

A good many years after this trial, Mr. James Kennedy, from the neighborhood in which the sermon had been preached, in the exercise of a right guaranteed to him by the Constitution of the United States, went to Pennsylvania, to bring back his runaway slave under the provisions of the fugitive slave law, and was murdered in the streets of Lancaster by a mob encouraged, if not instigated, by an eminent minister of the Methodist Church. I mention this fact only to signalize the case of Gruber as a rare example of administrative justice against the prejudices and the fears of a community. And while Mr. Taney lived in Frederick, a Mr. Owings, a farmer, was murdered in a brutal manner by several of his negro men, and his body thrown into a well for concealment. The murderers were committed to the county jail, and received as fair a trial, according to the common forms of law, as the highest citizen in the State would have done. There was no attempt at mob violence. Such was the influence of Mr. Taney, and other eminent lawyers on the bench and at the bar, in advocating obedience to the law of the land, that the people of that community never attempt to substitute violence for law and murder for an execution by law after a fair trial. They have learned that nothing so much as an impartial administration of law gives vigor and elevation to the moral life of a community.

Such was Mr. Taney's reputation, at this period, that he argued appeals from every county on the Western Shore of Maryland, as may be seen in the reports of the cases. And when we see him, in 1821, taken into the case of Brown *vs.* Kennedy, 5 Harris & Johnson, 195, with Mr. Harper, against Pinkney and Winder and Williams — as the case involved riparian rights founded on the original proprietary title to lands reclaimed from the navigable waters of Maryland, — we can understand that his reputation must have been great, or he would not have been called from Frederick to try the case. It is worthy of note, that, among the authorities cited by Messrs. Harper and Taney, in their brief, is the opinion of Daniel Dulany. The opinions of this great Maryland lawyer

had almost as much weight in courts in Maryland, and
hardly less with the crown lawyers of England,
than the opinions of the great Roman jurists, that
were made authority by edict of the Emperor, had in
Roman Courts.   This was due, in some degree, to the
fact that there were no reports of Maryland decisions
until 1809 : 1 Harris & McHenry.   In that volume,
the opinions of Daniel Dulany are published along
with the decisions of the General Court and the Court
of Appeals.   The high reputation of this great lawyer
stimulated the ambition of the Maryland bar, while
his opinions were models of legal discussion for their
imitation.

When Mr. Taney came to the bar, and during his
life in Frederick, the old law treatises, like Coke upon
Littleton, had not been superseded by Indexes, and
Digests, and Treatises, which supply thoughts without
cultivating the power of thinking.   The *Entries*,
Brooke, and Coke, and Levincz, and Rastall had not
yet made their *exits*.   He had studied law in the old
way, beginning with the fundamental law of estates
and tenures, and pursuing the derivative branches in
logical succession, and the collateral subjects in due
order, considering the grounds and reasons of everything as he proceeded, thereby acquiring a knowledge of principles that rule in all departments of the
science, and knowing, thereby, what is in harmony
with those principles and what not.   All his after

reading at once distributed itself at the various parts of the system of jurisprudence where it belonged.   He became a thoroughly read and a thoroughly trained lawyer.   Pleading and evidence and the rules of practice, he had thoroughly mastered.   Though technical, as every great lawyer must be, he was not narrow and confined to precedents, but was of large and original speculation, always searching for principles and applying them by his great practical sagacity, through settled forms, which, from his familiarity with them, he knew were adapted to apply principles to every possible combination of circumstances.   He was trained at the great Olympic of the early period of administrative justice in Maryland.   He acquired the strength and the skill of the great lawyers with whom he wrestled.   But he was too original a man to imitate any of them.   He rose to eminence at the bar as one marked by extreme individuality.

Though the General Court, where all the great lawyers met, that had original jurisdiction over the whole State, was abolished soon after Mr. Taney came to the bar, yet the excellent judicial system which took its place was hardly less fitted to raise up great lawyers.   The State was divided into six judicial districts, each embracing three or more counties, according to population and extent of territory.   For each district there were a chief judge and two associates, who resided in the district, and held a court, at fixed terms in each county, called a County Court. The chief judges of each district constituted the Court of Appeals; and all judges held their places during good behavior. By this constitution of the judiciary, all cases of importance were tried, in the first instance, before a judge of the highest tribunal; and the chief judge always brought down the latest decisions of the Court of Appeals before they had been reported; and the judges of the Court of Appeals were kept familiar with practice by sitting in *nisi prius* trials. Mr. Taney, therefore, from the first, argued causes before judges learned in the law and trained in its technicalities. In trying cases before juries presided over by such judges, prayers and bills of exceptions were used with consummate skill, and by no one with more tact than Mr. Taney. As able as he was in discussing questions of law raised by the pleadings, because of his order and terse and perspicacious diction and perfect knowledge of law, he rose, perhaps, to still greater superiority in discussing the side questions raised by prayers and bills of exceptions; and when he got before the jury, he kept the facts so completely within the issues presented by the pleadings that he made the evidence tell with all its force in proof of his points. With singular alacrity, he would so group and collate the facts as to impart to the one on which his argument turned an exaggerated significance, from the unexpected relations it was shown to have to the other facts. And he would sometimes embody the whole pith of his argument in a single terse sentence, that would fix itself, like an arrow of truth, in the hearts of the jury. In defending a person charged with an assault, who, though first assailed, had so used his privilege of self-defence as to make himself the aggressor by the heavy blows he had dealt, he said, "Gentlemen of the jury, if a man have a head like a post, you must hammer him like a post." As he progressed in his argument, every absurdity would vanish that might, at first, have hidden the strength of his side of the case. And when the morality of a transaction came into view, his lofty sentiments of honor, his magnanimity and scorn of sharp dealing and trick, delivered with such earnest sincerity of manner and in such persuasive tones, led a jury captive. He was a master in conducting a cause before a court and jury.

It was Mr. Taney's habit to advise his clients to settle their disputes amicably, in all cases where he thought it could be effected. In 1813 there was a notorious dispute between George Graff and Richard Lee Head, partners in business at Frederick. They had published each other in the newspapers. The matter was referred to Mr. Taney by both parties as their counsel. With the aid of a common friend of the parties, the whole difficulty was amicably arranged. In his written opinion, closing the controversy, Mr.

Taney said, "There is nothing in the settlement that can impeach the integrity or impair the reputation of either of you. My opinion was not given on the ground that one has right and the other has wrong on his side. Your differences had placed the partnership property in a very perplexing situation to both of you; and the settlement was made, not by arbitration, but by the agreement of yourselves in all the material points, on the principle of the mutual advantage to be derived from mutual concession." By such delicate treatment of the feelings of both parties, he made those, who had been mutual enemies, mutual friends.

No man's professional life was more marked by deference to the bench, respect for the jury, and courtesy towards his professional brethren. Mr. William Ross, of Lancaster, Pennsylvania, married a lady of Frederick, and settled there to practice law in 1805. In speaking to me, when I was a mere youth at the bar, he told me that, soon after he began practice at Frederick, he was employed in an eject-ment cause in which Mr. Taney was opposing counsel; that, when the case stood on the docket for trial, and he was asked by the Court if he was ready for trial, and answered yes, Mr. Taney said, in a whisper, that his locations were all wrong; and that, if he went to trial, he must lose his case, whether the right was with him or not. Thereupon Mr. Ross had his case continued.   Mr. Ross, who was himself the soul of honor, never forgot this courtesy, and told it once before the Court of Appeals of Maryland, to shame a lawyer who had been guilty of sharp practice in the case before the Court.   And Joseph M. Palmer, whose name appears so often in the reports of cases in the Court of Appeals of Maryland, told me that not long after he came from Connecticut, in 1817, to Frederick, a client of Mr. Taney's mentioned his case to him, and that he expressed his opinion as to the law of the case. The client told Mr. Taney what the *Yankee lawyer*, as he called him, had said.   Mr. Taney saw the force of Mr. Palmer's view, which differed from the one he held, and at once sent for Mr. Palmer, and employed him in the case to help him forward in his profession. His kindness to the young members of the bar was a distinguishing feature in his professional life.   Mr. William Price, a late member of the Baltimore bar, who had been engaged in many cases as junior counsel with Mr. Taney, while he practised in Frederick, thus spoke of him : " But few men of his eminence have ever displayed so much kindness to the younger members of the profession.   Often have I left his room after midnight, having gone through the authorities and settled the points to be made at the trial, and always believed that I was a better lawyer for the interview ; for he never kept back from his younger associate a single thought that occurred to his mind during the investigation. In a case of difficulty, he would tarry to explain the law, and usually made it so plain that no man could well fail to understand it. After our labors were finished, he would invite me to remain and talk with him; for, although his dignity was a part of his nature, yet he was one of the most genial persons I ever knew."

The professional character of Mr. Taney at this period of his life has been well drawn in outline by Mr. William Schley, an eminent lawyer of the Baltimore bar.

"I knew Mr. Taney from my early childhood. For many years he resided in my native town — now Frederick City. As a boy, as a youth, and afterwards, as a student of law, I heard him very often, in causes of magnitude in the Court of Frederick; and his arguments and his manner made a deep impression upon me. He sought no aid from rules of rhetoric, none from the supposed graces of elocution. I do not remember to have heard him, at any time, make a single quotation from any of the poets. Yet his language was always chaste and classical, and his eloquence undoubtedly was great — sometimes persuasive and gentle, sometimes impetuous and overwhelming. He spoke, when excited, from the feelings of his heart, and, as his heart was right, he spoke with prodigious effect. And yet, perhaps above all other attributes, his exalted private character gave him, with the honest, right-minded juries of Frederick County, an extent of success which even his great abilities as an advocate would not have enabled him otherwise to secure. He had acquired, and he ever retained it, in an eminent degree, the confidence and respect of that community. The people knew that he was sincere and honest; they knew that he was a composer of strifes and controversies, whenever the opportunity was afforded, and that he never promoted any; and they also knew that, whilst he was earnest, strenuous, and indefatigable in his efforts to secure for his clients their full rights, yet he never sought to gain from the other party any unjust advantage. He was an open and fair practitioner. He never entrapped the opposing counsel by any of the manœuvres of an artful attorney; and he contemned, above all things, the low tricks of a pettifogger. In taking exception to the adverse rulings of the Court, he never cloaked a point, but presented it, fairly and distinctly, for adjudication by the Court."

It was now the year 1823. Great casualties had befallen the bar of Maryland. Mr. Pinkney, the greatest forensic character who has ever appeared in the American Courts, was dead. He died representing Maryland in the Senate of the United States. His death was announced to the House of Representatives by Mr. Randolph, of Virginia. The published debates give this account of it: "Mr. Randolph rose to announce to the House an event which he hoped would put an end, at least for this day, to all further jar or collision, here or elsewhere, among the members of this body.   Yes, for this one day, at least, let us say, as our first mother said to our first father —

'While yet we live, — scarce one short hour, perhaps, —
Between us two let there be peace.'

" I rise to announce to the House the not unlooked for death of a man who filled the first place in the public estimation, in the first profession in that estimation, in this or in any other country.   We have been talking of General Jackson, and a greater than he is not here, but gone forever.   I allude, sir, to the boast of Maryland and the pride of the United States — the pride of us all, but more particularly the pride and ornament of the profession of which you, Mr. Speaker [Mr. Philip P. Barbour], are a member, and an eminent one."

When I was a student of law, Judge John Scott, an eminent lawyer of Virginia, told me, that soon after the death of Mr. Pinkney, Chief-Justice Marshall remarked to him, at Richmond, in the presence of that eminent lawyer Walter Jones, that Mr. Pinkney was the greatest man he had ever seen in a Court of justice, and that Mr. Jones responded, Yes; no such man has ever appeared in any country more than once in a century.   Mr. Pinkney had no political aspirations. He seems never to have even thought of the Presidency.

Luther Martin was now a wreck.   His vast learning was hidden in the oblivious darkness of an extinguished intellect.   And so generous, and withal so improvident, had been this great lawyer, that after all the great professional harvests he had reaped, the Legislature of Maryland, in February, 1822, passed the foling joint resolution: "*Resolved*, That each and every practitioner of law in this State shall be and he is hereby compelled, from and after the passage of this resolution, to obtain from the Clerk of the County Court in which he may practise, a license to authorize him so to practise, for which he shall pay annually, on and before the first day of June, the sum of five dollars; which said sum is to be deposited by the Clerk of the County Court, from which he may procure such license, in the treasury of the Western Shore or Eastern Shore, as the case may be, subject to the order of Thomas Hall and William H. Winder, Esqrs., who are hereby appointed trustees for the application of the proceeds raised by virtue of this resolution to the use of Luther Martin: Provided that nothing herein contained shall be taken to compel a practitioner of law to obtain a license in more than one Court, to be annually renewed, under penalty of being suspended from the bar at which he may practise. And provided, that this resolution shall cease to be valid at the death of the said Luther Martin."   This is a sad and instructive memorial in the public archives of Maryland.   I recall it for the warning it gives to men in the arduous toils of the practice of law.

As Martin and Pinkney had left a large opening at the Baltimore bar, the high reputation of Mr. Taney at once suggested to all that there was now a call to him to place himself at the head of the leading bar in the State.   Therefore it was, that with all his love of Frederick, both duty and professional ambition constrained him to leave it.   His mother, whom he loved with singular devotion, had left her home in Calvert County, during the War of 1812, and taken refuge from the ravages of the British, under her son's roof, and continued to live with him until her death in 1814.   She was buried in the little graveyard back of a little chapel, then the only place of Roman Catholic worship in Frederick.   Before his departure from Frederick, Mr. Taney made an arrangement with a particular friend, William Murdock Beall, a much younger man than himself, for his own burial by the side of his mother, no matter when and where his death should occur.   It was in this little chapel, with its twilight stillness, that Mr. Taney, for many years, could be seen every morning, in sunshine and in rain, during his residence in Frederick, at his religious devotions.   Under its shadow, his filial piety made him select his grave.

CHAPTER III.

A. D. 1823—1836.

AS Mr. Taney will be seen occupying high posts in the Federal Government at important political crises, it is necessary, before sketching his life in Baltimore, to take a view of the nature and the working of the Federal Government, in order to judge of the wisdom and the patriotism of his conduct in those positions. Unless we have before our minds the nature of the Federal Government, and the tendency of its working disclosed in our political history, we cannot judge of the acts of the functionaries who are employed in its administration. It is by the nature of the Government that the legitimate policy of its administration must be determined. The two great parties which have striven for the control of the Government, were formed, as we shall see, because of their opposite views of the powers of Government granted by the Constitution, and of the opposite policy upon which they respectively sought to administer the Government. Mr. Taney's conduct, as an officer of the Federal Government, must be judged by his view of the Federal Constitution and his judgment of the ten-

144

dency in the working of the Government. And whether his view of the Constitution, and his judgment of the tendency in the working of the Government, be true or not, can only be tested by the history of the country down to the present time.

In order to judge of the nature of the Federal Government, we must recur to its origin.

So little inclined were the American colonies to form a political union, that it was only to defend their respective liberties against a common enemy that they formed a confederation. As soon as the pressure of the war with England was withdrawn by peace, the colonies, then independent States, were dissatisfied with the confederation, because of its inefficiency, and determined to form a more perfect union. Accordingly, a convention of delegates, appointed by the several States, each acting for itself, met in Philadelphia, in 1787, and framed a Federal Constitution, which was submitted to the several States for ratification, on condition, when ratified by nine States, it should be binding between the nine. After a thorough discussion of its merits and demerits, the Constitution was adopted by eleven States; and the other two finally came into the Union, and the Federal Constitution became a constitutional compact between the thirteen States.

It was in accordance with the laws that regulate the progress of society, that the Federal Government then formed was one of only delegated powers. When independent States form a common government, it is always federative in its character. The individuality of the States is never merged; even though, in the working of the Government, the States finally become absorbed by the irresistible forces of centralization.

Of all the great Governments which have appeared in the progress of society, our Federal Government is the only one which has been framed by political architects. The leagues of States in ancient times were not Governments. Neither were those in modern times. They answered a temporary purpose. The most memorable Government of ancient times, the Roman, rather grew than was built. The organizing hands of statesmen, from time to time, only adapted it to the changes in society by incorporating into it new provisions. And the most celebrated Government of modern times, and the most glorious in achieving the great ends of political institutions, that of England, — though from *Magna Charta* downwards it shows, from time to time, the hands of master-builders, — is, nevertheless, rather a growth than a product of human wisdom. But the Government of the United States, from its very foundations, is the work of political architects. The State Governments were framed first by the statesmen of the several States. Then came the great work of forming a common Government for all the States. And never before, in the history of nations, as if ordered by Providence to meet the experiment of a great republic, did such an assembly of wise statesmen meet for any purpose. The great men were the sons of the separate colonies, educated to the great work by their separate fostering care. No monarchy, no empire, no great centralized State, in the long history of man striving after security for person and property, has ever nurtured at her bosom such sons. Their profound and comprehensive views of government, their transcendent powers as writers, their surpassing eloquence, constitute them the greatest assembly that, in the order of Providence, has ever been called together for the accomplishment of a great purpose in the progress of society. The great statesmen, born of the separate colonies, conscious of their own greatness, though reared in such small, isolated, communities, felt that the separate States must be preserved to rear up, by their separate special influences, great men in after times to administer the general Government which they had ordained and established. And the political instincts of the peoples of the several States, serving them in the stead of a well-reasoned political creed, would have rejected any constitution that abolished the sovereignty of the States.

The polity, accordingly, established by the Constitution of the United States, while it embraces all the powers relating to foreign relations, has the grant of only general powers relating to the internal interests

of the country, leaving to the several States large
reserved political rights.

It was inevitable, in the working of such a Government, that two great political parties should spring up
—one construing the Constitution so as to claim the
largest powers for the Government, and the other construing it so as to limit the powers to those expressly
granted. In the Federal convention that framed the
Constitution, and in the separate conventions of the
several States that ratified and adopted it, there were
two great opposing parties—the Federal and the anti-
Federal. The first was for establishing a centralized
Government, and the latter was for reserving the sovereignty of the States. The same parties, as we shall
see, appeared as soon as the Government went into
operation, each striving, by construction, to make the
Government what each wished to make it in the convention which framed it. One retains its name,
Federal, while the other assumes the name Republican.

It was on the 4th of March, 1789, that the Government of the United States went into operation,
though General Washington was not inaugurated as
President until the 30th of April.

General Washington appointed to his Cabinet the
two leading minds of the country—Alexander Hamilton as Secretary of the Treasury, and Thomas Jefferson as Secretary of State. These two statesmen

became, as we shall see the fathers of the two great opposing political parties which have, down to the present time, divided the people of the United States.

Alexander Hamilton had no faith in the capacity of the people for self-government. He believed, in great sincerity, that they must be governed for their own good, in spite of themselves. Early bred to arms, and knowing the importance of supreme authority in military affairs, he had formed an exaggerated estimate of the importance of executive authority in civil administration. He was, in fact, a sincere and avowed monarchist. From the first, he had hoped that a centralized general Government would be established, and had no confidence in the success of the federative one that was established by the Constitution of the United States; he therefore considered the Constitution as only a temporary bond of union, a mere transitional form in the progress of events towards a centralized Government; and believed, with perfect sincerity, that it was the duty of statesmen, in administering the Government, to interpolate into the Constitution, by construction, such powers as would gradually build up a central authority, in which the reserved sovereignty of the States would be ignored and finally abolished. With this political faith honestly entertained,—for he belonged to the school of Machiavelli,—he, as the head of the Treasury department, strove at once to begirt and strengthen the new

Government with the moneyed power of the country organized under the control of the Federal executive. He thought that the people could only be governed by corruption, as it is called in politics, or self-interest, as it is called in philosophy. He repudiated ideas altogether in politics as unpractical and absurd. Governing, therefore, solely by state craft, he succeeded in inducing Congress to establish a funded system and a national bank. These were the means by which he began the work of centralization.

The latitudinarian construction of the Constitution, by which Hamilton persuaded Congress to establish a national bank, was opposed by a doctrine of strict construction denying the power to establish a bank, put forth at the time by Jefferson, as Secretary of State, and enforced by Madison in the House of Representatives by irrefutable argument. General Washington yielded, rather than acceded, to the view of Hamilton. It was not Hamilton's imperial policy that influenced Washington, but the expediency of the juncture of a new Government founded on the ruins of one that had been declared perpetual, and yet had perished without any attempt to uphold it.

With the establishment of the bank, in 1791, the two old parties reappeared in the politics of the country — the Federal party with its old name, and the anti-Federal party with the name Republican. Hamilton was the leader of the first, and Jefferson was the leader of the last.

Under the countenance of Washington, the Federal party grew so strong that it elected as his successor to the Presidency John Adams, who was only a little less of a monarchist than Hamilton. Such was the genius of Hamilton and his rational control over the minds of the leading men of the Federal party, that, though not of the Cabinet of Adams, he controlled his administration, making the Federal party almost ignore him. Hamilton was the soul of his party. The leading men thought his thoughts and spoke his words, and the very acts of Congress were his. To carry out his centralizing policy of making everything yield to Federal authority, the Alien and Sedition laws were passed by Congress, which struck at personal freedom of speech. From the passage of these laws began the struggle of the States against Federal usurpation, under color of construing the Constitution. The State of Virginia, by a series of resolutions passed by her Legislature in 1798, condemning the Alien and Sedition laws, called on the other States to co-operate with her in arresting Federal usurpation. These resolutions were prepared by Madison, who was a member of the Legislature. And when the other States sent in answers hostile to the resolutions, as most of them did, he, as the chairman of a committee, made a report of extraordinary ability, defining the character of the Government which had been established by the Constitution, of which he was the chief architect. By these resolutions and this report, the doctrine of State-rights was declared.* It was proclaimed that ours is a Government of divided powers, and that the States are sovereign in their sphere; and that it is their right and their duty to interpose between the Federal Government and a violated Constitution. Kentucky passed similar resolutions drawn by Jefferson.

Taking the resolutions of Virginia and of Kentucky as their political creed, the Republican party organized itself amidst the dissatisfaction created by the Alien and Sedition laws, and, in 1800, elected Jefferson President in opposition to Adams. The landed interest everywhere was for the Republican or State-rights party. The mercantile and moneyed power were with the Federal or centralizing party. Jefferson was re-elected in 1804. Jefferson was a man of the most commanding genius, and was at the same time a great political manager ; so that he organized a party held together by a great principle underlying the Constitution, and determining the character of the polity embodied in it.

The Republican party was so strong as to defy all opposition. It elected Madison President in 1808, and re-elected him in 1812. So, too, in a regular line of Republican presidents, it elected Monroe President in 1816, and re-elected him in 1820. The Federal party had ceased to influence the Federal administration at all; and had, in fact, become so odious to the country, because of its course in the War of 1812, that it was almost extinguished.

It was fortunate for the success of our institutions, that the Government fell so soon into the hands of the strict constructionists, and continued in their hands for twenty-four years. For, notwithstanding Jefferson, Madison, and Monroe were strict constructionists, the Federal Government in its working, during their administrations, encroached upon the reserved rights of the States. Jefferson, without any constitutional authority, as he admitted, purchased Louisiana, justifying it upon State necessity. And Madison, though he had shown by conclusive argument, on the floor of Congress, that the Federal Government had no power to charter a bank, yet yielded to the mischief of the paper currency issued by the State banks during the War of 1812, and agreed to charter another to correct the mischief, as he supposed it would. Madison can only be justified upon the principle of interpretation of the Federal party, which construes the Constitution by facts and considerations extrinsic to the Constitution. The words "necessary and proper" which are applied by the Constitution to the merely incidental powers which are given by an express grant like the substantive powers, in order to make the substantive powers a limitation upon the incidental powers, are made to vary in their import by the exigencies of Government which are brought about by the abuses of the Government itself, and not by the inevitable course of events.

It was perhaps also fortunate for the success of the Government, that these three successive Presidents were, like Washington, from Virginia, who presented a constellation of greater men than any other State, and therefore gave more respectability to the Government, and obtained for it more confidence from the country. And it was no small thing, that these three Presidents had been great actors in the Revolution with Washington, and, being of the same State, shared his prestige.

But a stage in the politics of the country had arrived, when though it was none the less important that the principles of the Virginia school of politicians should be carried out in the administration of the Government, the Government should not be in the hands of a President who was a Virginian.

From the beginning, the theory of the Constitution had been wholly disregarded by the country in the mode of electing the President and Vice-President. By the Constitution, the people are only to choose electors, to whose superior intelligence the choice of President and Vice-President is confided. But the electors have been deprived of their constitutional function of choice, and have been made to pledge themselves to give their votes for a particular person who has been nominated, by a caucus or a convention, as a party candidate.

During the administration of Monroe, as the Federal party had practically ceased to exist, the Republican party as an organization had fallen to pieces. Therefore it was that, in 1824, upon the expiration of Monroe's second term, there were four candidates, all professing to be Republicans — Adams, Clay, Crawford, and Jackson.

Such was the state of politics when Mr. Taney began his professional life in Baltimore. It was an important crisis in the history of the country. A new era had, in fact, begun. The candidates for the Presidency were all of one party, and neither were they, like their predecessors, great actors in the Revolution.

The War of 1812 had terminated without accomplishing the purpose for which it was declared. The Republican party, who brought on the war, believed that the failure of the war was due in part to the New England States under the influence of the Federalists. Though these States did not oppose the war with arms, they did so with arguments and remonstrances, and refusal to vote supplies. And the hostility to the war culminated in the Hartford Convention, whose purpose was prevented from being developed by the sudden termination of the war. The existence of such a convention at such a time made the Government and the Republican party suspect it of treasonable purposes. In this suspicion no one participated more than Monroe, who was elected President,

as we have seen, in the fall of 1816. General
Jackson, who, by his victory at New Orleans, had
elevated himself above all other military leaders, had
become a person of extraordinary influence over
public opinion. Feeling, as he did, that the great purpose of Monroe's administration should be to remedy
the evils and the weakness of the country that had
been made manifest during the war, he, as a personal
as well as a political friend of Monroe, undertook to
advise him in regard to the formation of his Cabinet.
Though a Republican of the Virginia school, his
patriotism and his political forecast led him to see the
importance of breaking up those sectional party differences, which had made the New England States
seem enemies, in time of war, to their Government.
He discriminated between the Federalists who opposed
the war before it was declared, but supported it afterwards, and those who continued to oppose it. He
wished Monroe to adopt this view in forming his
Cabinet or ministry. In a letter dated 23d October,
1816, he says, " Everything depends on the selection of your ministry. In every selection, party
and party feeling should be avoided. Now is the time
to exterminate the monster called party spirit. . . . The
chief magistrate of a great and powerful nation should
never indulge in party feelings." Monroe could not
bring himself to disregard party in forming his
Cabinet. In answer, 14th November, 1816, to Gen-

eral Jackson, he said, "That some of the leaders of
the Federal party entertained principles unfriendly to
our system of Government, I have been thoroughly
convinced; and that they meant to work a change in
it, by taking advantage of favorable circumstances, I
am equally satisfied. . . . You saw the height to which
the opposition was carried in the late war; the embarrassment it gave to the Government, the aid it gave to
the enemy. . . . It is under such circumstances that the
election of a successor to Mr. Madison has taken place,
and that a new administration is to commence its
service." To this General Jackson replied, 6th January, 1817, "I have read with satisfaction that part
of your letter on the rise, progress, and policy of the
Federalists. It is, in my opinion, a just exposition. I
am free to declare, had I commanded the military department where the Hartford Convention met, if it
had been the last act of my life, I should have punished the three principal leaders of that party. I am
certain an independent court - martial would have
condemned them under the second section of the act
establishing rules and regulations for the government
of the army of the United States. These kind of
men, although called Federalists, are really monarch-
ists, and traitors to the constituted authorities. But
I am of opinion that there are men called Federalists
that are honest and virtuous, and really attached to
our Government; and although they differ in many

respects and opinions with the Republicans, still they will risk everything in its defence. It is therefore a favorite adage with me, that *the tree is best known by its fruit.*" General Jackson, upon these views, recommended Col. Drayton, a Southern Federalist, for Secretary of War; but Monroe appointed Mr. Calhoun, a Southern Republican.

This correspondence was published, for the first time, in the year 1824, to promote the election of General Jackson to the Presidency. It brought to his support many Maryland Federalists, and among them Mr. Taney; though of course other reasons concurred to induce Maryland Federalists to support the election of General Jackson. Mr. Taney has left on record these remarks on the course of the Maryland Federalists after the War of 1812: "When the war was over, the Federal party, as it existed before, was dissolved by the events of the war. This is not the place to show why it was dissolved. But it may not be improper to say, so far as Maryland is concerned, that during the war the deepest dissatisfaction was felt by the greater number of the prominent Federalists of the State with the conduct of the Eastern Federalists. For while the enemy was in the midst of us assailing our cities, and burning our houses, and plundering our property, and the citizens of the State, without distinction of party, were putting forth their whole strength and blending in its defence, those with whom the Maryland Federalists had been associated as political friends in the Eastern States, and whom they had regarded and treated as the leaders of the party, were holding the Hartford Convention, talking about disunion, conferring with one another in secret conclave; demanding from us, one of the Southern States, a surrender of a portion of the political weight secured to us by the Constitution; making this demand, too, in the hour of our distress, when the enemy was upon us. They were moreover using every exertion in their power to destroy the credit and cripple the resources of the general Government, feeble as it then was, and leaving us to defend ourselves as well as we could by our own resources.

"It will readily be imagined that after this the Federalists of Maryland would hardly desire to continue the party association, and continue the lead in hands who appeared to be not only indifferent to the sufferings of our citizens, but ready to take advantage of the peril in which the State was placed, to extort from it the surrender of a portion of its legitimate power. We thought it time that the party connection should be dissolved.

"There was no general concert of action between the members of the old Federal party, in relation to the general Government, after the close of the war. Mr. Monroe was elected without opposition. Nor was there any organized opposition to him during his ad-

ministration.   Indeed, some of the Federalists of the
Eastern States, who had been most prominent and
active in the reprehensible proceedings which I have
just mentioned, seemed anxious to enroll themselves
under his banner, and to be recognized as his political
friends."

Entertaining such views, Mr. Taney entered the
party supporting General Jackson; but only from a
sense of duty as a good citizen, and not with political
aspirations.   His only aim in life was professional.
To his career in Baltimore as a lawyer, I will now
turn; to recur to his political life when it becomes
important.

Mr. Taney was, at this time, the leading lawyer at
the Baltimore bar.   Mr. Wirt, who was several years
older than Mr. Taney, did not take up his residence
in Baltimore until 1829, after he had retired from the
office of Attorney-General of the United States.   But
he had so much practice at the Baltimore bar long
before, that I count him as one of its members when
Mr. Taney began to practise in Baltimore.   Between these great lawyers there was mutual friendly
regard.   They did not feel towards each other as
rivals, but as colleagues in the great work of administering justice.   The following extract from a letter
written by Mr. Wirt to Mrs. Wirt, while it relates
an amusing anecdote, shows the kind feelings of Mr.
Wirt towards Mr. Taney.   The letter is dated Octo-

ber 30th, 1825. "I dined yesterday with the Duke of Saxe-Weimar, at Mr. Oliver's. He is about a head taller than myself, with a nose *retroussé*, and features a good deal like ——, but with a sallow complexion and dark hair; no redundant fat, but brawny, muscular, and of herculean strength. He is about thirty-five years old, and looks like a Russian, or one of those gigantic Cossacks. I dare say he makes a magnificent figure in uniform. He speaks English tolerably well; yet he has the apparent dulness of apprehension which always accompanies a defective knowledge of a language, and renders it rather up-hill work to talk with him. He sat between Mr. Oliver and Mr. Barney, neither of whom seemed to be able to find him in talk. Taney, who you know is a pious Roman Catholic, as well as a most amiable gentleman, said, 'Come, Mr. Barney, Mr. Wirt and I sit side by side quite enough in Court; let me change places with you:' his object being to amuse the Duke. The change was made, and Taney and the Duke got into a side-talk. The Duke was soon observed to speak with a most 'saracenical and vandalic' fury, and, as I was afterwards informed, was pronouncing a philippic against the Roman Catholic religion, which he blamed for all the political conspiracies in Europe. Taney took the occasion to tell him that he was a Roman Catholic. This produced some embarrassment, but the Duke got over it. Taney changed the subject to the war, in which the Duke had figured, — particularly at Waterloo — and unluckily asked the Duke about Blucher. Now Blucher, it seems, had on some occasion gone into the Duke's territories, and was exacting contributions from his subjects, which the Duke hearing of, he had put him in prison. So here was a new *contre-temps;* and as there was a general pause at the table, I attempted to relieve it by asking the Duke another question, which contributed to increase the difficulty. I dare say he wished himself amongst the wild boars of the forest of Westphalia."

Mr. Wirt's prestige was, at this time, far greater than that of Mr. Taney, except in the State of Maryland, to which Mr. Taney's reputation was confined.

Mr. Taney was now employed in most of the important cases in the Court of Appeals of Maryland. The cases embrace every variety of judicial controversy, as the Court has appellate jurisdiction in all cases of equity as well as of law. In 1826, we find him, with Wirt, Jones, and Magruder, arguing the great case of Ringgold *vs.* Ringgold, (1 Harris & Gill, R. 11.) In this case the important relation of trustee and *cestui que trust,* in every aspect and every phase of obligation and reciprocal right and duty under the most varied circumstances, was thoroughly discussed under all the light of learning belonging to the doctrine of trusts. And the case is marked by the precision with which the controversy and the relief is kept within the pleadings.

We find Mr. Taney engaged, in this same year, with Mr. Wirt as counsel for the State of Maryland in a case in the Supreme Court of the United States. The following letter from Mr. Wirt, in regard to the case, shows the free and amiable spirit in which he corresponded with Mr. Taney.

WASHINGTON, March 30, 1826.

DEAR SIR:—I enclosed to Mr. Culbreth, in both our names, a copy of the opinion of the Court in the L'd Baltimore case as soon as the copy could be procured, — which was the day after the Court rose; and wrote him a short letter, as polite as possible, saying not one word on the subject of fees, which I thought would be rather unseemly on *our* part (for I spoke in both our names) towards the sovereign State of Maryland, our liege mother. But the old lady is maintaining rather an unnatural silence on her part; for I have not received a single word in reply, not even in the form of thanks, for our *great* and *successful* exertions — for, as nobody else will praise us, why should not we praise ourselves? Governor Kent has been here until within a few days back; and perhaps his absence has occasioned Mr. Culbreth's silence. But we will be patient for a fortnight or so, when I hope to find you in Baltimore.

Yours truly,   WM. WIRT.

ROGER B. TANEY, ESQ.

In 1827, upon the unanimous recommendation of the Baltimore bar, Mr. Taney was appointed Attorney-General of Maryland. The appointment was made by Governor Kent, who was a warm supporter of the administration of Mr. Adams, while Mr. Taney was well known as a Jackson Republican. I have often heard Mr. Taney say that he had never desired to hold any office but that of Attorney-General of Maryland.

As Attorney-General, Mr. Taney had the appointment of deputy attorneys for the State in the several judicial districts. In these appointments, while he showed his regard for the public interests, he manifested his personal friendship for those who stood in need of aid in their struggles at the beginning of professional life. In the judicial district embracing Frederick County, he appointed James Dixon, who had come from Pennsylvania and studied law in the office of Mr. Taney at Frederick. Mr. Dixon was of humble birth, little education, no friendly influences to help him forward in his profession. Mr. Taney knew his great natural abilities. And never did any man fill any office with faculties more exactly suited to its duties, or perform the duties more faithfully. It so happened, that several murders of a most flagitious character were perpetrated within Mr. Dixon's district, which rested for proof solely upon circumstantial evidence. One of these trials, and the most remarkable of them all, I heard just as I began the study of law. It was The State *vs.* Markley. In no case of State trials either in England or America, that I have read,

is there such a combination of strange circumstances
pointing out the murderer.   I can never forget the
force of argument by which the facts were combined
into evidence of guilt, and the transcendent eloquence
of appeals to the feelings of the jury, by which this
case was prosecuted to conviction.   Mr. Dixon was
beyond all question the ablest criminal lawyer I have
ever heard in Court.   He owed all his success in
life to Mr. Taney; and never did any one show more
gratitude to a benefactor.   There is nothing which
evinces more convincingly the high nobility of Mr.
Taney's nature than to see him, through his whole
career, as he stepped from altitude to altitude of personal success, extending, whenever occasion offered, a
helping hand to all classes of persons struggling
amidst the hopes and the fears of life.

The doctrine of the law founded on the Statutes of
Limitations was so confused, in regard to what the suit
should be based upon, so as to escape the provisions
of the statute, where an acknowledgment of the debt
had been made, after the period of limitation had
occurred, that it became important to the business of
the State that the doctrine should be settled by the
Court of Appeals.   With this view, the case of Oliver
vs. Gray was argued at the June Term, 1827, by Mr.
Taney.   The very comprehensive and elaborate opinion
of the Court indicates, by its accurate analysis of the
question, the thoroughness with which it had been

discussed at the bar.   The case is reported 1 Harris &
Gill, 204.   In the same volume of Harris & Gill, 324,
the case of the Union Bank *vs.* Ridgley exhibits the
skill of Mr. Taney as a special pleader.

Mr. Taney was at this time employed in many cases
of maritime law and marine insurance, where he
showed that he had mastered these branches of jurisprudence, though he had lately come from an inland
town to a commercial city.

It is out of the scope of my purpose to notice the
cases in detail of Mr. Taney's practice.   His professional labors were at this time very diversified and
very arduous.   He worked by day and by night.
Professional duties and his home circle occupied his
whole time.   Not a moment was spent in fashionable
life.   He looked at the world from the point of duty,
and his whole course was directed accordingly.   Yet
he walked in the straight and steep path with unchang-
ing cheerfulness, greeting with singular cordiality
every one he met.

Now begins a new era in Mr. Taney's life.   He is
forced into the world of ambition against all his tastes
and his strongest judgment in regard to true happiness.

General Jackson had been elected President of the
United States, and was inaugurated the 4th of March,
1829.   It turned out that, because of difficulties
between some of the members of his Cabinet, all of

the members resigned their posts. There were now, in secret, so many aspirants to succeed General Jackson in the Presidency, that it was very important that his new Cabinet should be composed, as far as possible, of persons who would be zealous in co-operating to make his administration successful. The formation of the Cabinet was, in fact, a matter of deep concern to General Jackson. He, of course, consulted with his personal friends on the subject, and was glad to receive their suggestions in regard to persons whom they might think fitted for his constitutional advisers. Hence it was that Dr. William Jones, of Washington City, who was born in Montgomery County, State of Maryland, in a conversation with General Jackson, said, "I know a man who will suit for Attorney-General." "Who is he?" said the General. "Roger B. Taney, of the Baltimore bar. He is now the leading lawyer of Maryland, and a zealous friend of your administration. I learned his character while I studied medicine with your friend Dr. William Tyler, of Frederick, where Mr. Taney then resided. He was a Federalist, but after war was declared in 1812, gave it his hearty support." From this information given by Dr. Jones, the appointment of Mr. Taney assumed so much importance that Mr. Francis S. Key, Mr. Taney's brother-in-law, who knew Mr. Taney's aversion to political life, wrote him the following letter:

GEORGE TOWN, D. C., June 14, 1831.

MY DEAR TANEY : — I had some talk with Berrien
in our journey, and found that he expected he was to
resign, but thought he was willing (if the President
was so) to remain.   He inquired what was thought
and said upon the subject.   I told him that some inferred, from the President's letters, that he contemplated an entire change; others thought there was
nothing in the affair to require it, and that, as to him,
it was not necessary nor desirable, and that it would
gratify some of the General's friends if he could be
retained; and I told him that was your opinion, and
that you thought it desirable to the party that he
should continue in the Cabinet.

He intimated that he apprehended Van Buren
would have required that he should be included in the
arrangement, and he asked who had been talked of as
the successor.   I told him I thought Buchanan would
be more apt to be named than any others who were
spoken of; that you had been mentioned, but that I
did not believe the appointment would be offered to
you.   He asked whether you would take it, and I told
him it was possible that you might, if you saw a prospect of things going on well.   In the course of the
conversation, I told him that he saw Green was trying
to put the late confusion on the ground of Mrs. Eaton's
affair; and that I thought if he was continued, it
would be plain that that matter had not occasioned the
change of the Cabinet; and that I thought it desirable
that such a proof should be given that the difference
arose from no such cause.

As we came on, he mentioned the prospect of set-
tling matters with Georgia and the Indians; that he
had been urged to go to the Indian country, and was
assured that an arrangement could be made satisfactory to both parties and greatly to the credit of the
Government; and that he believed he could now so
arrange it in two or three months.

I thought a good deal of this on getting here, and
determined I would see Barry, and perhaps Livingston,
and see if anything could be done about it.   I have
seen Livingston.   Barry was not at home.   And I
also saw Woodbury.   I told them I thought if Berrien
could be retained, it would have a good effect upon the
affairs of the party, both as to its bearing upon the
Indian and the Eaton question.   They both expressed
their wish that it could be so, but doubted whether
they could say anything on the subject unless consulted with.   Livingston seemed to take it up with
most earnestness, but wished me to see Barry.   I called
again, but could not see him — that was this morning,
and of course after what occurred last night, of which
I will presently tell you.

I told Livingston that I had talked with some of
the President's friends on the subject, and mentioned
you.   He said that you had been talked of for the
place.   I told him you had heard so, but would prefer,
I believed, Berrien's being continued, and thought it
would be better.

Upon getting home, I found a note from the President, requesting me to call out and see him; and I
went, of course, though it was almost nine o'clock.

He said he wanted to tell me confidentially that he

wished to offer you the place of Attorney-General;
and he wanted to know if it would be acceptable to
you.   I told him that some of your friends had told
you that the appointment would be probably offered
to you, and that I had conversed with you recently
upon the subject; that I believed you would prefer his
continuing Berrien, thinking such a thing would be
conducive to the success of the administration and
gratifying to his friends, some of whom thought it
would be advantageous to keep Berrien in the Cabinet.
He said at once that was entirely out of the question;
that he would have been glad to retain Berrien; that
he thought highly of him, and had still the kindest
feelings towards him; but that it was a necessary part
of the arrangement he had been compelled to make,
and was understood as such, and that he could not go
back from it.   He was very decisive.   I told him
that, of course, we, who could not know the circumstances fully under which he had been placed, could
not have known whether he could consistently keep
Mr. Berrien; but that looking only to what would
benefit the cause sustained by the administration, you
had thought it desirable to keep Mr. Berrien, if he
could do so with propriety.   As to your accepting the
place, I would immediately write and get your views.
I believed you would accept, because I thought you
would feel it a duty.   He said it would give pleasure
to his heart to understand that you would; that he
would feel gratified to have you in his counsels; that
your doctrines upon the leading constitutional questions he knew to be sound; and your standing in the
Supreme Court he well knew from Baldwin and

others.   He requested I would write and let him know your answer as soon as possible.

This, of course, you understand is to be kept entirely to yourself; and you are now to make up your mind (if you have not already done so) as quick as you can, that the Cabinet may be filled and matters become settled.

You will get this to-morrow evening, and can let me hear from you by the mail of Thursday.

I do not think you ought to have any hesitation in accepting.   I believe it is one of the instances in which the General has acted from his own impulses, and that you will find yourself, both as to him and his Cabinet, acting with men who know and value you, and with whom you will have the influence you ought to have, and which you can do something efficient with. As to your business, you can be as much in Baltimore as you would find necessary or desirable, with the understanding that you would come over whenever wanted.   This would only be when you were wanted at a meeting of the Cabinet, or anything important. On ordinary occasions, and applications for opinions from the Departments, they could send you the papers to Baltimore, and you could reply from there.   As to the Supreme Court, it would of course suit you entirely, and the increase in your business there would make up well for lesser matters.

I shall therefore look for a letter on Thursday; and tell me when I must come on, as I am very busy here.

   With love to Uncle and Aunt M.,
                              Yours truly,
                                      F. S. Key.

P. S. I think the President said Berrien was to send in his resignation to-day.

This letter was sent to Annapolis, where Mr. Taney was attending the Court of Appeals. I have not been able to procure Mr. Taney's answer, which was in accordance with the wishes of General Jackson, as the following reply from Mr. Key shows:

George Town, D. C., June 16, 1831.

My Dear Taney: — I am writing this at the post-office, as the mail is closing. I have seen the President. He expressed great pleasure at your determination. Barry was there, with whom I had also some talk. He is much gratified. He said it need not interfere at all with your affairs in Baltimore; that it seemed to him you need not even change your residence, if you did not wish it. The President said in reply, to what I said about your engagements in the Court of Appeals, that that would have presented no difficulty in any event, but that, as it was, Mr. Berrien wished to continue a little while to get the business of the office brought up; and that when he was ready he would say so, and he would inform you; that he did not wish you to let it interfere with your business, and did not suppose it would in any material degree. Both Barry and the President speak of the parting with Berrien as being quite friendly on both sides.   Yours affectionately,

F. S. Key.

P. S. There is a son of Caldwell's who is Berrien's clerk: you must continue him.

Mr. Taney was still at Annapolis.   On the 21st of June, 1831, Mr. Livingston, the Secretary of State, wrote to him as follows:

DEPARTMENT OF STATE, June 21, 1831.

SIR:—I have great satisfaction in obeying the President's instructions to inform you that he has this day appointed you Attorney-General of the United States, and to ask your acceptance of the office.

Mr. Berrien will be employed for a few days in arranging the business of the office in order to transfer it to you, should you signify your acceptance, in which case your commission will be made out, ready to be delivered when you shall find it convenient to come on and assume the duties of the office.

I have the honor to be, with great respect,

Your most obedient servant,

EDW. LIVINGSTON.

ROGER B. TANEY, ESQ.

Mr. Taney's answer to Mr. Livingston's letter was as follows:

ANNAPOLIS, June 24, 1831.

SIR:—I had the honor of receiving by the last mail your letter of the 21st inst., informing me that I have been appointed by the President, Attorney-General of the United States.   I accept the appointment, and pray you to convey to the President my respectful acknowledgments for this distinguished mark of his confidence.

The Court of Appeals of this State is now in

session, and I cannot leave it before the end of the
Term, without doing injustice to several persons who
rely on me to argue their cases.   Under such circumstances, I hope that my presence at Washington can
be dispensed with until I have fulfilled my engagements here ; and as soon as I have done so, I shall be
prepared to enter upon the duties of the office to which
the President has been pleased to appoint me.

I have the honor to be, with the highest respect,

Your most obedient servant,

ROGER BROOKE TANEY.

The Hon. EDWARD LIVINGSTON,

Washington.

Mr. Taney had now become a member of General
Jackson's Cabinet.   In order to judge of his wisdom
as a counsellor of the President, it is necessary to
recur to the political issues that were involved in the
election which made General Jackson President.

At the Presidential election of 1824, when Adams,
Clay, Crawford, and Jackson were candidates, Jackson
received 99 votes, Adams 84, and Crawford 41, and
Clay a less number.   As neither candidate had a
majority of all the electoral votes, the election was, by
the Constitution, referred to the House of Representatives to choose a President from the three candidates
who had received the largest number of electoral
votes.   The representatives vote by States, each
State having one vote.   Mr. Clay threw his influence
in favor of Adams, and elected him President.   Mr.

Clay was made Secretary of State. The friends of General Jackson immediately charged that there was a corrupt bargain between Adams and Clay, by which the latter had sold his influence for the Secretaryship of State. And to enhance the feeling of the country against these two honest statesmen, it was contended that it was the duty of Clay to give his influence to Jackson, who had the highest number of votes. This doctrine would strip the House of Representatives of its independent choice when the Electoral College had failed to elect a President. This false doctrine and the false charge of corruption were used with great effect against the administration of Adams, and rendered his chances of re-election less and less every day.

But a great political issue had been presented by Adams, in his inaugural address. The views presented by him were eminently Federal. And Clay, who became the soul of his administration, had fallen in with the doctrines of Alexander Hamilton, and by a scheme of a high tariff, and internal improvements by the Federal Government, and the influence of the moneyed power organized through the United States Bank, was striving to introduce the centralizing policy in the administration of the Government which had been rejected in the beginning of the century. Mr. Clay even advocated the right to construct roads through the States by Federal authority. This Alexander Hamilton had not advocated, because he was too familiar with public law, and had too much intellectual pride, to contend that a Government, which has not the right of eminent domain, can condemn to public use the private lands of the people, as a Government must do that undertakes to construct roads over a territory. The Adams and Clay wing of the Republican party, conscious of their Federal proclivities, called themselves *National* Republicans.

With such a policy was Adams put before the American people, in 1828, for re-election, and was beaten by General Jackson by a vote of 178 to 83. During Jackson's administration, the battle of 1800 was to be fought over in the political cycle which had brought forward old questions to be discussed anew. And we shall see that it was fought over by the Federal party led by Clay, and the Democratic party represented by Jackson as President. And it was the most gigantic contest since the formation of the Federal Government. The great men of the Revolution were not the combatants; but they were men who had been brought up under the tuition of the men of the Revolution, and had striven to rise to their intellectual standard. They appreciated the grandeur of our system of government, and had a patriotic anticipation of a glorious destiny for the United States in the history of nations. Both parties had the good of the country in view: it would be puerile to say otherwise.

It was at such a crisis in the progress of the

American people, in relation to the character and the policy of their Government, that Mr. Taney was called by General Jackson into his Cabinet, in 1831. And we shall see it was upon Mr. Taney, in the final struggle of the administration with its powerful enemies, that the blows fell the heaviest, and were returned by him with such power that the Democratic policy triumphed, and the organ of the money power, the great instrument of centralization, was trodden upon until it utterly perished.

General Jackson's inaugural address, on the 4th of March, 1829, was merely a general declaration — as all such addresses are — of the political principles by which the administration would be guided. It left to time and events the qualification of these general views by the acts of the Government as exigencies might occur. It was a general chart of the principles upon which he had been elected. One serious objection urged against the election of General Jackson, and enforced with all the vehement power of Mr. Clay's eloquence, was, that he was a military chieftain, and therefore prone to put the civil power beneath the military. This was a strong point. For so abhorrent is military rule to all the race of the English-speaking people, that Mr. Adams had, in his inaugural address as President, on the 4th of March, 1825, signalized by a specific declaration the importance of keeping the military subordinate to the civil authority. Therefore it was that General Jackson, in his inaugural, said, "considering standing armies as dangerous to free government, in time of peace, I shall not seek to enlarge our present establishment, nor disregard that salutary lesson of political experience which teaches that the military should be held subordinate to the civil power." He also repudiated the Federal doctrine, that a national debt is a national blessing, in these words : " Under every aspect in which it can be considered, it would appear that advantage must result from the observance of a strict and faithful economy. This I shall aim at the more anxiously, both because it will facilitate the extinguishment of the national debt, — the unnecessary duration of which is incompatible with real independence, — and because it will counteract that tendency to public and private profligacy which a profuse expenditure of money by the Government is but too apt to engender." And that most wicked, because the most fatal to liberty, of all the possible acts of the Federal Government — the interference in elections — is thus rebuked: "The recent demonstration of public sentiment inscribes on the list of executive duties, in characters too legible to be overlooked, the task of reform ; which requires, particularly, the correction of those abuses that have brought the patronage of the Federal Government into conflict with the freedom of elections."

On the 8th of December, 1829, General Jackson

delivered his first annual message to Congress, which was the first practical step in his administration.   He declared his views of the Bank of the United States in these words : " The charter of the Bank of the United States expires in 1836, and its stockholders will most probably apply for a renewal of their privileges.   In order to avoid the evils resulting from precipitancy in a measure involving such important principles and such pecuniary interests, I feel that I cannot, in justice to the parties interested, too soon present it to the deliberate consideration of the Legislature and the people.   But the constitutionality and the expediency of the law creating the bank are well questioned by a large portion of our fellow-citizens ; and it must be admitted by all that it has failed in the great end of establishing a uniform and sound currency."   This sentence contains a proclamation of hostility to the great organ of the money power of the country, which had been established by Alexander Hamilton as the instrument of his centralizing policy.   The nation was at once notified that the decentralizing policy of Jefferson would be restored in the working of the Government.   The Maysville Road bill had been vetoed, just as Madison and Monroe had vetoed similar bills proposing to make internal improvements by the Federal Government.   And General Jackson had, on the 13th of April, 1830, at the celebration, in Washington, of the birthday of Jefferson, given the celebrated toast, "The Federal union : it must be preserved !" to make issue upon the doctrine of nullification, which had been broached by Mr. Hayne, of South Carolina, in the Senate of the United States, as a legitimate basis for resisting the collection of the revenue of the United States.

It was to assist General Jackson in maintaining the principles and the policy avowed in his inaugural, his messages, and his toast, that Mr. Taney consented to become a member of his Cabinet.

General Jackson had, by the measures of his administration, clearly developed his decentralizing policy. He was opposed to the renewal of the national bank charter, to the continuance of the high protective policy, and to internal improvements by the Federal Government—the three great measures of the American system which Mr. Clay advocated. He now, in 1832, becomes a candidate for re-election to the Presidency. Mr. Clay becomes the opposing candidate.

It was now, in the winter of 1832, that the Bank of the United States petitioned Congress to pass a bill renewing its charter. It well knew that Congress would pass such a bill, and that General Jackson would have to veto it, or recede from his policy of opposition to the bank. It was a defiance to General Jackson on the eve of the Presidential election. It felt mighty in its power of corruption. The bill renewing the charter was passed by Congress, and sent to the President for his approval. Mr. Taney was in Annapolis, at the Court of Appeals, and had already, the 27th of June, 1832, written to General Jackson, giving his reasons why the bill, if it was passed, should be vetoed. The General now calls him to Washington, and Mr. Taney aids in preparing a message vetoing the bill, which was sent to Congress; and the bill was thereby defeated. Mr. Taney was the only member of the Cabinet who favored the veto.

General Jackson now put himself upon the country for re-election, making a definite issue between the centralizing policy of Mr. Clay and his own decentralizing policy. It was a momentous crisis in the working of the Government.

The bank was fully prepared for the contest. Its loans had been sown broadcast over the country. In the year immediately preceding its petition for a renewal of its charter, that is, from the 30th of December, 1830, to the 30th of December, 1831, it had increased its loans and discounts from $42,402,304.$\frac{24}{100}$ up to $63,026,652.$\frac{23}{100}$. And while its petition was actually pending in Congress, it added, before the 1st of May, 1832, $7,401,617.$\frac{79}{100}$ more to the sum last mentioned, making the whole amount $70,428,270.$\frac{72}{100}$. This was an increase of $28,025,766.$\frac{48}{100}$ in the short space of twenty-six months, being an extension of sixty-six per cent. on its previous loans. The State

banks did likewise: so that the money power, led by
the great fiscal agent of the Government, was fairly
in the field, exerting its mighty influence in the election against General Jackson. The old hero and his
Attorney-General, relying upon the intelligence and
the patriotism of the people, stood fast by the policy
which they believed to be that which could alone save
the country from utter corruption. The struggle was
fierce, malignant, and desperate. It was a struggle
between the Constitution and the money power —
whether the Government was to conform to the provisions of the one or the behests of the other.

The defeat of Mr. Clay, and the consequent condemnation of his policy, was overwhelming. He received only forty-nine votes out of two hundred and
eighty-eight.

After a declaration so emphatic by the people, in
favor of his policy, General Jackson could but carry
it out in his second term. And there was no measure
more distinctly embraced in his policy than the re-
duction of the tariff. Yet South Carolina, possessed
by a spirit of waywardness, had voted neither for Mr.
Clay nor General Jackson, but threw away her vote
on Mr. Floyd, of Virginia; and now determined not
to wait for relief from the burden of the tariff by any
measure of General Jackson's administration, but to
throw off the burden herself. This course of South
Carolina was presented, by General Jackson, to Con-

gress, in his next annual message, in these words: "It is my painful duty to state that in one quarter of the United States opposition to the revenue laws has risen to a height which threatens to thwart their execution, if not to endanger the integrity of the Union. Whatever obstructions may be thrown in the way of the judicial authorities of the general Government, it is hoped they will be able, peaceably, to overcome them by the prudence of their own officers and the patriotism of the people. But should this reasonable reliance on the moderation and good sense of all portions of our fellow-citizens be disappointed, it is believed that the laws themselves are fully adequate to the suppression of such attempts as may be immediately made. Should the exigency arise, rendering the execution of the existing laws impracticable, from any cause whatever, prompt notice of it will be given to Congress, with the suggestion of such views and measures as may be deemed necessary."

The fiscal function of a Government consists of taxation and disbursement. If the revenue system be such as to impose the taxes upon one section of the country and disburse them in another, it operates great injustice. The revenue system of the United States has, from the beginning, done this to a considerable degree. Madison, as soon as the first Congress under the Constitution met, introduced a bill laying duties upon imposts, and another levying a tax upon tonnage. In defending the provisions and the policy of the bills, he admitted that they would operate more heavily upon the Southern States than upon the Northern, and appealed to the patriotism of the South to bear the burden, for the sake of the compensation made by the advantages afforded by the Federal Union. With this unavoidable evil of a revenue system operating upon States of such opposite interests as those of the North and the South, the perverse ingenuity of the statesmen who favored a high protective tariff, led them to think that the market opened to the South, by the manufacturing interest built up at the North by the tariff, equalized entirely the burden of the revenue between the Southern and Northern States. Upon this doctrine, tariff after tariff was enacted by Congress, until a bill was passed in 1828, not so much to raise revenue as to encourage manufactures, and to construct internal improvements by the Federal Government. This scheme of policy was called the "American system."

The perennial sentiment of State-rights, that is so obtrusive in American politics when States either at the North or the South or the West consider themselves oppressed by the measures of the Federal Government, became so extravagant at the South, that Southern statesmen, by an ingenuity as perverse as that of the advocates of the protective policy, convinced themselves that, by the tariff act of 1828, the whole revenue was levied upon the South while it was disbursed at the North.

South Carolina, with the other Southern States, believed the revenue act of 1828 to be unconstitutional, because its principal object was not revenue but the encouragement of manufactures. She therefore betook herself to what she considered a constitutional right as the last resort in the working of the Federal Government. The State was led in this contest by Mr. Calhoun. No man of the time saw so clearly as he the fearful sectional strife that was threatened between the Northern and the Southern States. At present, it was one rather of money than of sentiment. But he foresaw that, besides the tariff, the fearful question of negro slavery must become fundamental in Federal politics. I knew Mr. Calhoun from my boyhood. He was a sincere Unionist. He dreaded the dissolution of the Federal Union only less than the loss of the local sovereignty of the States. He had studied the history and the constitution of the ancient Roman republic with far more interest and care than he had done that of England. He was, in fact, more of a Roman than an Englishman. His reading in political history had been extensive. His speculative and his logical faculty were both very powerful in the economy of his mind. If he had had the conservative training of continued practice at the bar, these faculties would have been moderated, and he would

have become a sounder constitutional lawyer. As it
was, he had become enamored of the Government of
the Roman republic with its checks and balances. He
saw two legislative assemblies, the *comitia centuriata* and
the *comitia tributa*, as antagonistic, legislating side by
side, for one hundred and fifty years, on the same subjects, and, because of their mutual respect and comity,
never coming into collision. He saw two consuls,
both chief executive officers, who must concur in all
acts. He saw ten tribunes, with constitutional power to
stop by veto the acts of the Senate, which was the
great central institution of this polity, giving to it its
enduring force. This Government — of such diversified checks, that David Hume, in his profound political essays, says it would only be considered a political
chimera, if it were not known to have existed, — Mr.
Calhoun saw had been the most active, most powerful,
and the most efficient ever established, extending, as
it did, its dominion by conquest over the whole
known world. With Roman studies and Roman pre-
dilections, he looked at our Federal Constitution from a
Roman rather than from an English point of view. As
the Federal Constitution had been established by every
State giving its assent, separately, in order to bind it,
and the Constitution authorizes three-fourths of the
States to change or amend it, he inferred by construction that the Constitution had conferred on three-
fourths of the States the authority to settle constitu-

tional questions of a political character raised between States and the Federal Government, just as it has conferred, on the Supreme Court of the United States, authority to decide all legal constitutional questions raised by parties to proceedings at law. From this general doctrine, he inferred the right of a State in a constituent convention to nullify, within her territory, any statute passed by the Congress of the United States which the State considered unconstitutional. And that when such an issue was presented by a State or States, it was the duty of the Federal Government to refer the question of the nullified law to the arbitrament of the States, and if three-fourths did not declare it constitutional, it would thereby become null and void; but if they declared it constitutional, then the State must submit, or might secede from the Union. Such was the doctrine of nullification which South Carolina put forth in justification of her refusal to permit the revenue acts to be enforced within her borders. General Jackson and his Cabinet, including his legal adviser, Mr. Taney, repudiated the doctrine of nullification as utterly subversive of all Federal authority; and, as we have seen, he brought the matter, in his annual message, to the attention of Congress, as likely to lead to difficulty between the Federal Government and the State of South Carolina.

According to the supposed right to do so, South

Carolina, on the 24th of November, 1832, passed, "An ordinance to nullify certain Acts of Congress of the United States purporting to be laws laying duties and imposts on the importation of foreign commodities." A copy of the ordinance was immediately sent to Mr. Vandeventer, who brought it to Mr. Blair, the Government printer, for publication in the *Globe*. Mr. Blair sent the ordinance to General Jackson by Mr. Vandeventer. Not long afterwards, Mr. Blair called to see General Jackson, and found him engaged in writing a proclamation. The General read to Mr. Blair what he had written. The proclamation, as written by General Jackson, was handed by the General to Mr. Livingston, the Secretary of State, to be elaborated and put into an appropriate form. When the instrument, as prepared by Mr. Livingston, was presented to General Jackson, he disapproved of the principles and doctrines of centralization contained in it. But as the conclusion suited him, he determined to issue it at once, without waiting to correct the erroneous doctrines contained in it; as promptitude was a cardinal principle of action with him. He authorized Mr. Blair to set forth his views in an editorial in the *Globe*, which was written by Mr. Blair under his dictation, and submitted to General Jackson before it was published. Mr. Taney has left a memorandum among his papers in these words: " I was at Annapolis attending Court, when General Jackson's proclamation at the time of the South Carolina nullification was prepared, and never saw it until it was in print, and certainly should have objected to some of the principles stated in it, if I had been in Washington. R. B. Taney. July, 1861."

The proclamation warned the people of South Carolina of the fatal consequences of nullification, and, with parental solicitude, begged them to desist from their purpose of open hostility to the authority of the Federal Government. But so infuriated were the people of the State, that, relying on support from other Southern States, they put themselves in an attitude of military defiance. The whole country was smitten with fearful anticipations at the thought of a fratricidal war. All knew that a man of imperious will held the sword of the country. They knew, too, that a personal dislike of Mr. Calhoun, the leader of this incipient rebellion against the laws of the Federal Government, influenced General Jackson's feelings as the executive head of the Government. The worst forebodings filled the country. That States, which had marched shoulder to shoulder in the war that achieved independence from foreign rule, should now slaughter each other in civil war, so roused the magnanimous patriotism of Mr. Clay, that, casting behind him all party feelings, he threw himself between the Government of the United States and South Carolina, and, like a true statesman, compromised the difficulty and rescued his country from disgrace. He introduced a revenue bill, which virtually gave up the policy of a protective tariff, that was accepted by the Congress of the United States, and achieved for himself an honor, as a statesman, that is a glory in our history. No blood was shed; and South Carolina, because of wise statesmanship, again embraced her sister States, and moved on with them in the march of nations. General Jackson felt great relief in being spared the dreadful necessity of enforcing the laws by the sword and by criminal prosecutions.

Mr. Taney was now unusually engaged in questions submitted to him by the President. Hurrying, one very cold morning, to his office, at an early hour, he saw a little negro girl striving in vain to bring water into a tin bucket hanging on the spout of a pump. When he came up to the pump, and saw the little girl shivering in the cold wind, he took the pump-handle and filled the bucket, and then placing it upon her head, said, "Tell whoever sent you to the pump, that it is too cold a morning to send out such a little girl." A negro woman, who came up just as Mr. Taney finished his act of kindness, communicated the fact to me, which had already been told me by a lady who heard of it when it occurred.

Mr. Taney, by his personal and official intercourse, had, by this time, so won upon the regard of General Jackson that he had become his most trusted and his

most confidential adviser. And as the great issue
which the administration had made with the Bank of
the United States and its adherents was now to be
tried, General Jackson relied especially upon the
faithfulness and the sagacious statesmanship of Mr.
Taney. He had learned that Mr. Taney, long before
he could have expected to be called into his Cabinet,
had often, to his friends, intimated the policy in regard to the bank that he was now about to make the
policy of his administration. He, with his intuitive
sagacity, had come to know that, with a moral courage
and a clearness of conviction in regard to duty never
surpassed by any statesman, Mr. Taney would, if duty
required it, sacrifice his aims in life for the good of his
country. Mr. Taney was, in fact, a man after Jackson's own heart.

In his first annual message after his second election,
General Jackson cordially congratulated Congress and
the people on the near approach of the extinction of
the national debt. The Government would thereby
cease to be a debtor to the people. And a high tariff,
raising revenue upon one section of the country and
expending it in another, would no longer be needed.
This policy was distasteful to the money power. The
deposits in the Bank of the United States would
thereby be diminished, its discounts lessened, and its
influence in the politics of the country circumscribed.
The bank was, therefore, averse to the extinguishment

of the national debt; and so was the money power of
the country, and also the politicians, who were debtors
or attorneys of the bank, or expected to be aided by
the bank influence in any way. The bank was considered by the whole country as solvent as the sun.
It was no more supposed that the deposits of the
Federal Government in the bank were in danger of
being lost in bankruptcy than that the light of the
sun would be lost in universal darkness. But not
so thought General Jackson and his Attorney-General, Mr. Taney. Mr. Taney thoroughly understood
finance and banking. Abhorring, as he did, all alliance between the Government and the money power
of the country, as fatal to liberty and a high civilization, he had for years watched the conduct of the
United States Bank, and believed that, while it was
corrupting the country, it was risking bankruptcy by
its adventurous dealings. He was calm while all were
excited by passion or suspicion or party feeling. In
the storm of party struggles, his judgment was as
sagacious and as unclouded as that of justice, with
even scales weighing the opposite considerations of a
dispute. His party could no more influence his judgment or his conduct than his political adversaries
could. General Jackson saw this, and trusted him.
For Jackson was, with all the fiery energy of his
nature, cautious in listening to trusted counsellors,
and, like Washington, enlightening and confirming
his judgment by their advice.

It was Mr. Taney as well as General Jackson who startled the country, when the annual message of the President intimated that the deposits of the Government were not safe in the Bank of the United States, in these terms. " Such measures as are within the reach of the Secretary of the Treasury have been taken to enable him to judge whether the public deposits in that institution may be regarded as entirely safe; but as his limited power may prove inadequate to this object, I recommend the subject to the attention of Congress, under the firm belief that it is worthy of their serious investigation. An inquiry into the transactions of the institution, embracing its branches as well as the principal bank, seems called for by the credit which is given throughout the country to many serious charges impeaching its character, and which, if true, may justly excite the apprehension that it is no longer a safe depository of the money of the people." The message recommended that the seven millions of stock held in the bank by the United States be sold; and also all other stock held by the United States in joint-stock companies: so as to sever the Government from all pursuits properly belonging to individuals.

A motion for a select committee to inquire into the condition of the bank was scornfully rejected by the House of Representatives, and the subject was referred to the Committee of Ways and Means. This com-

mittee, acting upon a report of the Treasury agent
founded upon statements furnished by the bank itself,
which were utterly false, reported, for the adoption of
the House, " That the Government deposits may, in
the opinion of the House, be safely continued in the
Bank of the United States." This resolution was
passed by a vote of 109 to 46. Of the members who
voted for it, fifty were borrowers from the institution,
and many were on the list of its retained attorneys.
The influence of money, like the miasm of the pesti-
lence, finds its way against all antidotes; and the history of man proves that he is as easily infected by the
one as the other.

Now was the great issue made by the bank, sustained
by the House of Representatives, with the Executive
Department of the Government, whether the bank,
that was insolvent, as it turned out to be, was to keep
the deposits of the Government for its own purposes,
or the Executive was to secure them from loss, for the
use of the people.

The bank had already, by prevarication and by
falsehood, evaded the payment of five millions of the
public debt which had been required to be paid out of
the public money on deposit. And it had, as even its
friends admitted, violated its charter by dealings to
which it had resorted in order to conceal its insolvency,
and its consequent inability to apply the deposits to
the payment of the five millions of public debt.

When a nation, at a crisis in its history, is left without a great man to conduct its affairs for the welfare of the people, it may be considered as given over by Providence to the power of evil. If ever a man was raised up for a crisis in the history of a country, that man was Andrew Jackson. His administration marks an epoch in the history of the United States. But the great actor in the contest with the money power, represented by the Bank of the United States was, as we shall see, Roger B. Taney.

General Jackson was at the Rip Raps, where, in the warm season, he usually retired from the cares and the intrusions of office. So deeply was Mr. Taney impressed with the importance of removing the Government deposits at once from the Bank of the United States, that he wrote to him the following letter:

[PRIVATE.] Washington, August 5, 1833.

My Dear Sir: — After reflecting on the conversation you held with me on the morning you left Washington, it seems to be proper that I should state to you, without reserve, my opinion on the present condition of affairs in relation to the bank.

In my official communications I have already expressed my conviction that the deposits ought to be withdrawn by order of the Executive, provided a safe and convenient arrangement can be made with the State banks for the collection and distribution of the revenue. And I have advised that the step should be taken before the meeting of Congress, because it is desirable that the members should be among their constituents when the measure is announced, and should bring with them, when they come here, the feelings and sentiments of the people. I rely, at all times, with confidence on the intelligence and virtue of the people of the United States; and believing it right to remove the deposits, I think they will sustain the decision.

The obstacles which have recently come in the way of such a proceeding have, without doubt, greatly strengthened the hands of the bank and increased the difficulties to be surmounted by the Executive. They have not, however, changed my opinion of the course to be taken. My mind has for some time been made up that the continued existence of that powerful and corrupting monopoly will be fatal to the liberties of the people, and that no man but yourself is strong enough to meet and destroy it; and that if your administration closes without having established and carried into operation some other plan for the collection and distribution of the revenue, the bank will be too strong to be resisted by any one who may succeed you. Entertaining these opinions, I am prepared to hazard much in order to save the people of this country from the shackles which a combined moneyed aristocracy is seeking to fasten upon them.

But although it is my duty frankly to state to you the opinion I hold on this subject, yet I do not desire to press the measure upon you. I am every day more and more sensible of the power and influence exercised by the bank; and I should feel deeply mortified, if, after so many splendid victories, civil and military, you should in the last term of your public life meet with defeat. You have already done more than any other man has done, or could do, to preserve the simplicity and purity of our institutions, and to guard the country from this dangerous and powerful instrument of corruption. And after a life of so many hazards in the public service, and after achieving so much for the cause of freedom, in the field and the Cabinet, I have doubted whether your friends or the country have a right to ask you to bear the brunt of such a conflict as the removal of the deposits under present circumstances is likely to produce.

With these feelings and opinions, I cannot wish you to adopt this measure, unless your own judgment is clear and decided that it is your duty to order the removal, and that the public interest requires it to be done. If you have any doubts on the subject, I would advise you not to proceed further until the meeting of Congress. For although my own opinion is firm in favor of the removal, as soon as the proper arrangements can be made, I have far more confidence in your decision than I have in my own. And if you determine against it, I shall most cheerfully acquiesce, and shall cordially support any other course of proceeding which you may think preferable.

But if you should finally make up your mind to adopt the measure, and should, as you intimated, find it necessary to call for my services, to aid in carrying it into execution, they will be promptly and willingly rendered; and I have thought it to be my duty, after what passed between us on the morning of your departure, to give you this assurance.

I should greatly regret the necessity for any change in your Cabinet. You will do me the justice to believe that I have no desire for the station you suggested. For, as I have already said to you, I do not think myself qualified for even its temporary occupation. But I shall not shrink from the responsibility, if, in your judgment, the public exigency should require me to undertake it.

I have now, my dear sir, laid before you all of my thoughts and feelings on this subject, and with cordial wishes for your health and happiness,

I am, with the highest respect and regard,

Your obedient servant,

R. B. TANEY.

General Jackson answered as follows:

RIP RAPS, August 11, 1833.

[PRIVATE.]

DEAR SIR: — Your letter of the 5th instant has been received, perused with much pleasure, and the contents *duly noted.*

I am still of opinion that the public deposits ought to be removed, provided a *more* safe depository, and as convenient for carrying on the fiscal operations of the Government, can be found in the State banks as is now found in the United States Bank.

The United States Bank attempts to overawe us. It threatens us with the Senate and with Congress, if we remove the deposits. As to the Senate, threats of their power cannot control my course or defeat my operations. I am regardless of its threats of rejecting my nominations. If Mr. Duane withdraws, you can, under an agency, carry on and superintend the Treasury Department until nearly the close of the next session of Congress; before which the battle must be fought and all things settled before your nomination would be sent in.

As to the threats about Congress, it may be observed, the bank, having been chartered contrary to the powers of Congress as defined by the Constitution, may find, when once the deposits are removed for *cause*, that Congress is not competent to order the deposits to be restored to this unconstitutional and corrupt depository, but must find another, and that can only be the State banks; *there is none other:* more of this when we meet.

I have no doubt of receiving, in a few days, in a report from the directors appointed by the Government, proof that about $40,000 have been paid by the United States Bank for printing essays, pamphlets, etc., etc., in favor of the bank, and in abuse of the Executive, and in subsidizing and corrupting journals. When this proof is furnished, of which I have no doubt, it will be considered by me *sufficient cause* for removing the deposits. If the bank can apply $8000 (being $\frac{1}{5}$ of $40,000) out of the public funds, without appropriation by law, it may one or two millions. Therefore, the deposits cannot be safe in such an institution. It might use the whole money of the Government, and stop its wheels.

I have been recently advised that a large amount of the six per cents., which have been paid off three or four years ago, remains uncollected, and the evidence of debt not surrendered to the Government; and, therefore, the Government is still bound for the debt to the holder of the scrip, whilst the bank has had, and still has, the use of the money. I have directed the Secretary to make a strict inquiry into this matter, and report the real facts of the case to me, that such steps may be taken to coerce the surrender of the stock, and to have the Government exonerated from its liability, as may be in our power to adopt. If it be that the original holders of the scrip are dead, it can only be justice to their representatives to publish to the world the fact that it appears from the books of the commissioner of loans that to A, B, and C there is money due, which will be paid to the individual who will present the evidence of debt and make satisfactory proof that he is legal heir or assignee. The bank has no claim to this money. If the proper owner is dead, without heirs or representatives or legal assignees, it belongs to the Government, not to the bank. I have suggested to the Secretary of the Treasury the propriety of calling in the loan-office books, and put an end to this agency of the bank, and having this duty performed in his own department; that when the debt is paid, the evidence may be surrendered, and put out of the power of the bank to make any more secret arrangements for postponing the payment of the public debt. To this it is intimated that the act of the 3d of March, 1817, which abolished the old commission of loans, and transferred it to the bank, will prevent the exercise of this power by the Government. This is not my idea of the law. I may be mistaken, as I have not referred to it lately, and have it not with me. You will find it in the sixth volume of the laws, page 192, and I ask your opinion on its proper construction and power of the Government in this particular. If the Government has no power to call for these books, and put an end to this bank agency, how can we know when the national debt is paid, or how much is and has been postponed by the bank, and remains unpaid by the bank, although it has been thought by the people, and reported by the tones of the Treasury, that the whole public debt has been paid except about seven millions, when seventeen may have been postponed by the bank, and the Government now liable for the same? Should I be mistaken, then I can only add that all legislation, from the charter establishing the bank, and in the charter, must have been to increase its powers, open avenues for its speculations and frauds, to the great neglect of the security of the Government and the interest of the people. Should we remove the deposits, I would not be surprised if the bank would rebel against our power, and even refuse to pay to the order of the Government the public money in its vaults, and lay claim to all the money that remains uncalled for on the books of the loan office. Every investigation gives us evidence of the assumed power of this *monster*. It must be thought by Mr. Biddle that it is above the law, and beyond any control of the Executive government. *He has boasted that it is.* We must test this matter, and meet it fearlessly and boldly; and no doubt remains on my mind but we will be sustained by the people.

I write in haste for the mail, and keep no copy. My health is improving, but I am much pestered with business, which is sent after me: this will hasten my return to the city, where the burden of so much writing will be lessened. I shall remain here eight or ten days more, perhaps a fortnight.

My little family all, *now*, enjoy health, and all join with me in a tender of kind salutations to you and your amiable family.

I am very respectfully your friend,

ANDREW JACKSON.

ROGER B. TANEY, ESQ.,

Attorney-General, U. S.

These letters furnish an instance of the private conferences between Mr. Taney and General Jackson on the question of the Bank of the United States. It is seen that Mr. Taney was so fully impressed that it was the duty of the President to remove the deposits of the Government from the Bank of the United States, that when the President had intimated that perhaps his agency would be required to effect the removal, he assured him he was ready to perform the duty at any sacrifice. And the letter of Mr. Taney strives to stimulate General Jackson to an act which his sense of duty to the people, as a constitutional adviser of the President, constrained him to think ought to be performed. Mr. Taney entered into this question with his whole heart. Of all men I have ever known, he had the deepest abhorrence of the influence of money. This appears even in his judicial opinions on usury laws, giving, as they do, a construction making the provisions as stringent

as possible.   But when an individual of wealth employed his money in promoting art, and in establishing
great charities during his lifetime, and in private gifts
to the needy, like the great American banker, Mr. W.
W. Corcoran, he had a peculiar admiration of him, as
he had of that gentleman.

General Jackson had now returned from the Rip
Raps.   The bank was the all-absorbing subject.   Mr.
William J. Duane, a lawyer of Philadelphia, and a
son of an old friend of General Jackson's, had been
appointed Secretary of the Treasury in June, 1833,
when Mr. McLane was transferred to the Secretaryship of State, made vacant by Mr. Livingston being
sent minister to France.   Mr. Duane was known to
General Jackson as an opponent of the bank, and
was supposed to concur in the contemplated measures
against that institution.   The very evening of the day
of his appointment, Mr. Duane had been informed
that General Jackson expected him to remove the public deposits from the bank.   This was the first of June.
On the twenty-sixth of the same month, General
Jackson wrote from Boston, to Mr. Duane, that it was
in his opinion desirable to appoint a discreet agent to
inquire into the practicability of making an arrangement with State banks, as fiscal agents of the Government, to receive and disburse the revenue.   Mr. Duane
opposed the scheme of removal of the deposits and
employing State banks.   He thought the matter ought

to be left to Congress.   In this state of the measure, Mr. Taney, at the request of General Jackson, prepared a paper on the subject, which was read to the Cabinet the 18th of September.   It concluded by appointing the 1st day of October for removing the deposits.   After it had been printed by Mr. Blair, the editor of the *Globe*, (the Government paper,) Wm. B. Lewis came to Mr. Blair and told him that Mr. McLane and General Cass would resign their places in the Cabinet, rather than be responsible for the removal of the deposits; and said that he thought the paper should be so drawn as to exempt them from all responsibility for the act.   Mr. Blair thereupon took the paper to General Jackson and told him what Mr. Lewis had said.   The General at once said he did not want any one to be responsible for his acts; and requested Mr. Blair to read the paper to him, so that he might see where he could insert a sentence assuming the sole responsibility.   It was accordingly read, and the assumption of the sole responsibility was inserted by the General.   Afterwards, Mr. Blair took the corrected copy to Mr. Taney to read it to him, that he might see whether it was correctly printed. When Mr. Blair read the inserted passage, Mr. Taney asked where it came from.   Mr. Blair informed him. Mr. Taney said it would be better that Mr. McLane and General Cass should leave the Cabinet than remain in it with feelings of hostility to so cardinal a measure; that it was better to encounter their hostility out of the Cabinet than in it.   The paper was read to the Cabinet the 18th of September, and was published in the *Globe* and other papers.   Mr. Duane now halted between two opinions.   He first promised General Jackson that, if he could not bring himself to remove the deposits, he would resign.   He at last told the General that he would do neither. Upon which General Jackson removed him the 23d of September; and the same day addressed Mr. Taney the following letter:

WASHINGTON, September 23, 1833.

SIR: — Having informed William J. Duane, Esq., this morning, that I have no further use for his services as Secretary of the Treasury of the United States, I hereby appoint you Secretary in his stead, and hope you will accept the same, and enter upon the duties thereof forthwith, so that no injury may accrue to the public service.

Please signify to me your acceptance or non-acceptance of this appointment.

I am, with great respect,
Your obedient servant,
ANDREW JACKSON.

R. B. TANEY, ESQ.,
Attorney-General, U. S.

I have not been able to find Mr. Taney's letter of acceptance.   He entered upon the duties of the Treasury Department on the 24th of September,

1833. On the twenty-sixth of the month, he gave the
order for the removal of the deposits, to take effect on
the 1st of October, in accordance with the day designated in the President's "Cabinet Paper." On the
day that the order was given for the removal, letters
were written to the banks which were at that time
selected as the depositories of the public money, noti-
fying them of their appointment. It was well understood by the public that there was strong opposition
in the Cabinet to the removal. And it was only
because Mr. Taney had urged the removal that he felt
himself in honor bound to take charge of the Treasury
Department when Mr. Duane unexpectedly refused to
carry out the policy of the President. He therefore
entered office with his mind made up to remove the
deposits. The order of removal merely directed that
thereafter the revenue should be deposited in the
selected State banks. The deposits already in the
Bank of the United States were only to be drawn out
when needed for the use of the Government. The
withdrawal would therefore be very gradual.

The bank at once put forth its whole strength,
which reached every point in the country, to bring
about as much distress as possible, by the time Congress met, with a view to compel a restoration of the
deposits. It had from the first formed its plan for
the contest with the Government. In order to gain
the favor of the country, so as to secure the renewal

of its charter, it had, as we have seen, extended its
loans and discounts to more than seventy millions.
Now, under the pretence that the loss of the deposits
compelled it, the bank called in its loans and discounts
to such an extent, and constrained the State banks to
do likewise, as to make the whole nation groan under
the pressure.   For months there were the most fearful
scenes of dismay and ruin, when the paper currency
was thus suddenly and violently contracted.   There
was hardly any gold in the country to take its place;
and though there was more silver, it was too heavy to
be used for currency in a commercial country, and
only served as change in small transactions.   Commerce became embarrassed.   Property became unsal-
able.   The price of produce and of labor was reduced
to the lowest point.   Thousands and tens of thousands
of laborers were thrown out of employment; and
many wealthy people were reduced to poverty.   The
friends of the bank were involved in common ruin
with its enemies.   All this distress, the bank strove to
make the sufferers believe, was caused by the removal
of the deposits.

Congress met on the second day of December, 1833.
This session was called the Panic Session.   Litanies
of woe came up to Congress from all parts of the
country.

In his annual message to Congress, General Jackson
said: "Since the last adjournment of Congress, the

Secretary of the Treasury has directed the money of the United States to be deposited in certain State banks designated by him, and he will immediately lay before you his reasons for this direction. I concur with him entirely in the view he has taken of the subject; and some months before the removal, I urged upon the department the propriety of taking that step. The near approach of the day on which the charter will expire, as well as the conduct of the bank, appeared to me to call for this measure upon the high considerations of public interest and public duty. The extent of its misconduct, however, although known to be great, was not at that time fully developed by proof. It was not until late in the month of August, that I received from the Government directors an official report, establishing beyond question that this great and powerful institution had been actively engaged in attempting to influence the elections of the public officers by means of its money; and that, in violation of the express provisions of its charter, it had, by a formal resolution, placed its funds at the disposition of its president, to be employed in sustaining the political power of the bank.

"It being thus established, by unquestionable proof, that the Bank of the United States was converted into a permanent electioneering engine, it appeared to me that the path of duty which the Executive department of the Government ought to pursue was not doubtful.   As, by the terms of the bank charter, no officer but the Secretary of the Treasury could remove the deposits, it seemed to me that this authority ought to be at once exerted to deprive that great corporation of the support and countenance of the Government in such a use of its funds, and such an exertion of its power.

"At this time the efforts of the bank to control public opinion, through the distresses of some and the fears of others, are equally apparent, and, if possible, more objectionable.   By a curtailment of its accommodations, more rapid than any emergency requires, and even while it retains specie to an unprecedented amount in its vaults, it is attempting to produce great embarrassment in one portion of the community, while through presses known to have been sustained by its money, it attempts, by unfounded alarms, to create a panic in all.

"These are the means by which it seems to expect that it can force a restoration of the deposits, and, as a necessary consequence, extort from Congress a renewal of its charter."

No great measure of state was ever more thoroughly vindicated and justified than the removal of the public deposits was by the letter of December 4, 1833, addressed by Mr. Taney, as Secretary of the Treasury, to the Speaker of the House of Representatives.   As the Treasury Department is intrusted with the administration of the finances, it is the duty of the Secretary of the Treasury, in the absence of any legislative provision on the subject, to take care that the public money is deposited in safe keeping, in the hands of faithful agents, and in convenient places, ready to be applied according to the wants of the Government. The law incorporating the Bank of the United States had reserved to the Secretary of the Treasury this power to its fullest extent. The sixteenth section of the law is in these words: "And be it enacted that the deposits of the money of the United States in places in which the said bank, and branches thereof, may be established, shall be made in said bank, or branches thereof, unless the Secretary of the Treasury shall at any time otherwise order and direct; in which case the Secretary of the Treasury shall immediately lay before Congress, if in session, and if not, immediately after the commencement of the next session, the reasons of such order or direction."

The right of the Secretary of the Treasury being undoubted, the bank itself admitting it, the question of removal of the public money was one solely of expediency. Mr. Taney, in his letter, showed beyond question that every interest of both the people and the Government required the removal. The bank was created solely as a fiscal agent of the Government, to be used for the benefit of the people; and the means of private emolument given in its franchises were in-

tended as a reward for the services it was expected and
required by its charter to perform.   It was never supposed that its separate interests would voluntarily be
brought into collision with those of the public.   Its
separate interests were wholly subordinate to its duties
as a fiscal agent to the Government.   Yet, in order to
secure a renewal of its charter, which was to expire
the 3d of March, 1836, the bank, as early as 1831,
entered the political arena, to influence the measures
of the Government by controlling the election of the
President of the United States and of the representatives in the Legislature.   For this purpose the bank
had, in effect, placed the whole capital of the institution, including the shares owned by the United States,
and the public deposits, at the disposal of the president of the institution.   And while the whole country
was in an agony of distress produced by his measures
of pure selfishness, the president of the institution sat
in his office as calm as a summer's morning, as was
boasted by one of his friends.   And so wanton and
hazardous had been the conduct of the bank in using
its own money and that confided to its care, that the
deposits of the Government were no longer safe in its
custody.   And as the re-election of General Jackson
had virtually decided that the charter of the bank was
not to be renewed, it was imperatively demanded that
the State banks, which had been substituted for the
United States Bank, should be gradually possessed of

the public deposits, to enable them to supply the place of that institution, in honoring each other's notes and drafts, and thereby supply a general currency in their mutually guaranteed notes.

Mr. Taney's opposition to the renewal of the charter of the bank was avowedly placed by him upon the ground of its great power. "It is [said he] a fixed principle of our political institutions, to guard against the unnecessary accumulation of power over persons and property in any hands. And no hands are less worthy to be trusted than those of a moneyed corporation."

And the constitutional power of the President to remove Mr. Duane, when he thought he was derelict in duty, is no less clear than the expediency of removing the deposits. Mr. Calhoun, in a speech of singular denunciation of both General Jackson and Mr. Taney, delivered in the Senate, admitted this. "But while I thus [said Mr. Calhoun] severely condemn the conduct of the President in removing the former Secretary, and appointing the present, I must say that, in my opinion, it is a case of the abuse, and not of the usurpation, of power. I cannot doubt that the President has, under the Constitution, the right of removal from office; nor can I doubt that the power of removal, wherever it exists, does, from necessity, involve the power of general supervision; nor can I doubt that it might be constitutionally exercised in reference to the deposits.   Reverse the present case: suppose the late Secretary, instead of being against, had been in favor of the removal; and that the President, instead of being for, had been against it, deeming the removal not only inexpedient, but, under the circumstances, illegal, would any man doubt that under such circumstances he had a right to remove the Secretary, if it were the only means of preventing the removal of the deposits?   Nay; would it not be his indispensable duty to have removed him? and had he not, would not he have been universally and justly held responsible?"

But notwithstanding the wisdom of the policy of General Jackson and Mr. Taney in regard to the bank, as subsequent events proved, as we shall see, the Senate, under the lead of Mr. Clay, co-operating with other Senators as able and as full of partisan zeal as himself, passed resolutions condemning the act of General Jackson as unconstitutional, and that of Mr. Taney as inexpedient and unjustifiable.   But the House of Representatives, just elected by the people, justified both General Jackson and Mr. Taney, and declared against the renewal of the charter of the bank.   This action of the House of Representatives was the death-blow to the bank.   The purpose of General Jackson was thereby accomplished.   The State banks showed themselves adequate to the function of fiscal agents of the Government.   But the

distress brought upon the country by the Bank of the
United States, in its death struggle for the renewal of
its charter, frightened the administration of Mr. Van
Buren into the recommendation of a league of State
banks, different from the plan of Mr. Taney, which
brought discredit on his plan because it was supposed
to be the same by many, and was said to be the same
by others who knew better.

Mr. Taney had, according to the practice of the
Government, made a report on the state of the finances,
and the probable revenue for the next fiscal year,
which had been laid before Congress. Early in May,
1834, the Senate, by a resolution, called on Mr. Taney,
as Secretary of the Treasury, for a report on the finances, believing, from the memorials of distress that
were sent up to Congress, that the Government would
soon be without adequate revenue, and would have to
resort to loans. The panic created by the bank was
at its height. It was still hoped, by the bank and its
friends, that the report of the Secretary would show
the revenue to be in such ruin that, in order to relieve
himself from the indignation of the people, the President would be compelled to restore the deposits to the
bank, and that, as a consequence, the charter would
be renewed. By the middle of June, Mr. Taney sent
in his report. Instead of showing the financial decline which had been expected, it showed an increase
in every branch of the revenue, and proved that Mr.

Taney, in his report on the revenue for the coming year, had not over-estimated it. It vindicated his administration of the Treasury Department, while it presented facts which proved that in localities where the bank influence was greatest, there was the greatest distress and commercial embarrassment. The friends of the bank found that they had committed a great blunder, as a party measure, in calling for the report. Mr. Taney's great abilities as a financier and statesman had been entirely underrated; as he had been supposed to be only a profound lawyer. He had never before been in the councils of the Federal Government.

The bank question was one not only of political power, but also of currency. The nation had been so completely strewed over with bank notes, that they were almost as numerous, and nearly as worthless, as the leaves on the ground, when the forests have been touched by autumnal frosts. The people had been made to know that paper is not money, but only gold and silver is, as their forefathers had declared when they framed the Constitution of the United States. The unquenchable thirst of gain, seeking for loans which cannot be obtained when gold and silver are the currency, had built up so many banks issuing paper under the lead of the United States Bank, that gold and silver were almost banished from the dealings of the country. In this state of things, Mr. Benton introduced into the Senate a bill for equalizing the value of gold and silver, and legalizing the tender of foreign coins of both metals. Mr. Taney advocated this measure with great zeal, giving Mr. Benton the aid of his sagacity throughout the preparation of the measure, as I find from many letters from Mr. Benton asking for interviews with him, from time to time, both before and while the measure was pending. Mr. Taney was for keeping every department of the Government within the limits of the Constitution. He was, therefore, for preventing paper from taking the place of gold and silver not only as a matter of policy, but of constitutional law also. The bill of Mr. Benton was passed, and gold began to come forth from its hiding-places and flow in from all the channels of commerce, giving confidence to all the pursuits of industry.

The opposition to the policy of General Jackson on the bank question was urged by an array of great men hardly to be paralleled in any country. Clay, Webster, and Calhoun in the Senate, and McDuffie, Binney, Adams, and others in the House, who gave an intellectual dignity to our legislative annals, assailed the administration, and especially Mr. Taney, with peculiar force and fierceness of denunciation. If the spirit of ruin had been administering the Government, more terrible evils could not have been foretold as sure to come upon the country. And there is always some truth in predictions of woes at such a crisis in a nation's history. When a Government has instituted a policy even of ultimate ruin, interests spring up under that policy, upon which thousands of fortunes depend, that must suffer in the transition to even a policy which only can save the country from destruction. Of all powers on earth, the money power is the most mighty, the most unscrupulous, the most craving, the most unrelenting, and the most sure to have devotees. It has not only bought individuals, but Governments, and, in fact, the ruling majority of nations. And there is nothing so fatal to all that is great in man as the dominion of money. There is no more important civil achievement in the working of our Government than the overthrow of the Bank of the United States.

As the transactions of to-day can only be tested by time, we must look at the ultimate fate of the Bank of the United States to judge correctly of General Jackson's and Mr. Taney's policy. This fate will be seen in the following announcements in the Philadelphia papers of the day.

First announcement: "Resolved (by the stockholders), that it is expedient for the Bank of the United States to make a general assignment of the real and personal estate, goods and chattels, rights and credits, whatsoever and wheresoever, of the said corporation, to five persons, for the payment or securing of the debts of the same, agreeably to the provisions of the Acts of Assembly of this Commonwealth (Pennsylvania)."

Second announcement: "It is known that measures have been taken to rescue the property of this shattered institution from impending peril, and to recover as much as possible of those enormous bounties which it was conceded had been paid by its late managers to trading politicians and mercenary publishers for corrupt services rendered to it during its charter — seeking and electioneering campaigns."

Third announcement: "The amount of the suit instituted by the Bank of the United States against Mr. N. Biddle is $1,018,000, paid out during his administration, for which no vouchers can be found."

Fourth announcement: "The United States Bank is a perfect wreck, and is seemingly the prey of the officers and their friends, who are making away with its choicest assets by selling them to each other, and taking pay in the depreciated paper of the South."

Fifth announcement: "Besides its own stock of $35,000,000, which is sunk, the bank carries down with it a great many other institutions and companies, involving a loss of about $21,000,000 more — making a loss of $56,000,000, besides injuries to individuals."

Sixth announcement: "There is no price for the United States Bank stock. Some shares are sold, but as lottery-tickets would be. The mass of the stockholders stand and look on, as passengers on a ship that is going down, and from which there is no escape."

Seventh announcement: " By virtue of a *venditioni exponas*, directed to the Sheriff of the City and County of Philadelphia, will be exposed to public sale to the highest bidder, on Friday, the 4th day of November next, the marble house and grounds known as the Bank of the United States, etc."

Eighth announcement: " By virtue of a writ of *levari facias*, to me directed, will be exposed to public sale the estate known as ' Andalusia,' ninety-nine and a half acres, one of the most highly improved places in Philadelphia: the mansion-house, and out-houses and offices, all on the most splendid scale; the green-houses, hot-houses, and conservatories extensive and useful; taken as the property of Nicholas Biddle."

Ninth announcement: " To the honorable Court of General Sessions. The grand jury for the County of Philadelphia respectfully submit to the Court, on their oaths and affirmations, that certain officers connected with the United States Bank have been guilty of a gross violation of the law, colluding together to defraud those stockholders who had trusted their property to be preserved by them. And that there is good ground to warrant a prosecution of such persons for criminal offences, which the grand jury do now present to the Court, and ask that the Attorney-

General be directed to send up for the action of the grand jury bills of indictment against Nicholas Biddle, Samuel Jaudon, John Andrews, and others to the grand jury unknown, for a conspiracy to defraud the stockholders in the Bank of the United States of the sums of, etc."

Tenth announcement: "Bills of indictment have been found against Nicholas Biddle, Samuel Jaudon, and John Andrews, according to the presentment of the grand jury, and bench - warrants issued, which have been executed upon them."

Eleventh announcement: "On Tuesday, the 18th, the examination of Nicholas Biddle and others was continued and concluded; and the Recorder ordered that Nicholas Biddle, Thomas Dunlap, John Andrews, Samuel Jaudon, and Joseph Cowperthwaite each enter into a separate recognizance, with two or more sufficient sureties, in the sum of $10,000, for their appearance at the present session of the Court of General Sessions for the City and County of Philadelphia, to answer the crime of which they stand charged."

Twelfth announcement: "The criminal proceedings against these former officers of the Bank of the United States have been brought to a close. To get rid of the charges against them without trial of the facts against them before a jury, they had themselves surrendered by their bail, and sued out writs of *habeas corpus* for the release of their persons. The opinions of the judges, the proceedings having been concluded, were delivered yesterday. The opinions of Judges Barton and Conrad were for their discharge; that of Judge Doran was unfavorable. They were accordingly discharged. The indignation of the community is intense against this escape from the indictments without jury trials."

As the session of Congress was near its close, General Jackson, on the 23d of June, sent to the Senate the nomination of Mr. Taney as Secretary of the Treasury. He was the next day rejected; and it was the first time, in the history of our Government, that a Cabinet minister nominated by a President had been rejected by the Senate. Mr. Taney, the day after, resigned his office by the following letter:

WASHINGTON, June 25, 1834.

SIR: — The Senate having, yesterday, refused to confirm my nomination as Secretary of the Treasury, I beg leave to resign the commission with which you honored me during the last recess. It would expire by its own limitations at the end of the present session of Congress, which is now at hand. But after the appointment has been submitted to the Senate, and acted on by them, it is due to you and to myself that I should conform to their decision, and retire at once from the office.

I cannot, however, take my final leave of the official relations which have connected me with your administration without returning my cordial thanks for the

many and continued proofs of kindness and confidence
which I have received at your hands. I shall always
bear them in grateful recollection.

I am, sir, with the highest respect,

Your obedient servant,

R. B. TANEY.

General Jackson's answer was as follows:

WASHINGTON, June 25, 1834.

DEAR SIR: — Your resignation of the appointment
of Secretary of the Treasury, conferred upon you in
the recess of the Senate, and now relinquished in consequence of the refusal of that body to confirm your
nomination, has been received.

I cannot refrain from expressing, on this occasion,
my profound regret at the necessity for your retirement from that important office; nor can I suffer the
opportunity to pass without paying a just tribute to
the patriotism, firmness, and ability which you have
uniformly exhibited since your introduction into my
Cabinet. Knowing that such a situation was not
desired by you, and was in opposition to your course
of life, I could not but feel grateful to you, when, in
compliance with my invitation, you exchanged the
independence of professional pursuits for the labors
and responsibilities of the office of Attorney-General
of the United States. This sentiment was greatly and
deservedly increased during the last year, when, upon
becoming acquainted with the difficulties which sur-
rounded me and with my earnest desire to avail myself of your services in the Treasury Department, you
generously abandoned the studies and avocations to

which your life had been devoted, and encountered the responsibility of carrying into execution those great measures which the public interest and the will of the people alike demanded at our hands. For the prompt and disinterested aid thus afforded me, at the risk of personal sacrifices which were then probable and which have now been realized, I feel that I owe you a debt of gratitude and regard which I have not the power to discharge. But, my dear sir, you have all along found support in a consciousness of right; and you already have a sure promise of reward in the approbation and applause which an intelligent and honest people always render to distinguished merit. The plan of financial policy which you have initiated by your acts and developed in your official reports, and which has thus far received the full approbation of the representatives of the people, will ultimately, I trust, be carried into complete operation; and its beneficial effects on the currency of the country and the best interests of society will be, in all future time, more than an adequate compensation for the momentary injustice to which you have now been subjected. And as it is the martyrs in any cause whose memory is held most sacred, so the victims in the great struggle to redeem our Republic from the corrupting domination of a great moneyed power will be remembered and honored in proportion to their services and their sacrifices.

I am, very respectfully and sincerely,

Your friend and obedient servant,

ANDREW JACKSON.

Hon. R. B. TANEY.

Mr. Taney was now relieved from official station, and rejoiced to resume the practice of the law, in which he had always found the pleasant duties of life. He at once began practice in Baltimore, and business hastened to get his aid.

His return from official station was hailed in Baltimore, with every demonstration of approval of his administration of the Treasury Department. He entered the city in a barouche drawn by four gray horses, accompanied by the committee of reception, amidst a multitude of citizens. The barouche was escorted by a cavalcade of several hundred horsemen. The procession repaired to the Columbian Gardens, where Mr. Taney addressed the assembly from a rostrum prepared for the occasion. It was a civic triumph of greater worth than those of arms celebrated by Roman generals on the Capitoline Hill.

A few days afterwards, a public dinner was given to Mr. Taney. There were many distinguished invited guests. Among those who could not attend the festivity was Martin Van Buren. He sent the following letter of apology :

NEW YORK, July 21, 1834.

GENTLEMEN : — I regret that I cannot accept your kind invitation to the public dinner to be given, by the Republicans of Baltimore, to Mr. Taney on the occasion of his return to that city.

An unreserved intercourse with Mr. Taney at a

vitally interesting period in our public affairs, and whilst he was in the discharge of his official duties, of the most arduous and responsible character, has enabled me fully to appreciate his intellectual and moral worth and his unsurpassed devotion to the best interests of our country.

Nothing would give me greater pleasure than to participate in a compliment so richly merited and so honorably bestowed; the state of my engagements will not allow me to do so further than to ask the favor of you to offer the annexed sentiments to the company in my name.

I have the honor to be, gentlemen, with the greatest respect, your friend and obedient servant,

MARTIN VAN BUREN.

ROGER B. TANEY.—He has, in his last best brilliant official career, passed through the severest ordeal to which a public officer can be subjected, and he has come out of it with imperishable claims upon the favor and confidence of his countrymen.

Resolutions approving of Mr. Taney's course in the administration of General Jackson were passed at primary meetings all over the United States, and public dinners tendered to him. He could not refuse the public dinner tendered to him at Frederick, in Maryland. The dinner took place the 6th of August. On his arrival at Frederick, Mr. Taney was welcomed, in behalf of the people, by Francis Thomas, the representative of that district in Congress.   To which Mr. Taney said :

"Sir : I am gratified for the honors with which my fellow-citizens of Frederick City and County have this day received me. I lived so many years in the midst of them, and that residence is endeared to me by so many cherished recollections, that I never find myself approaching Frederick without feeling as if I were again bending my footsteps to my own home, again to dwell in the midst of a people whose long-continued kindness to me I can never forget, and shall warmly and gratefully bear in my memory to the latest hour of my life.

"I see around me many citizens who were well known to me during almost the whole period of my residence in Frederick. And the deep emotions with which the events of this day are so well calculated to inspire me, are greatly increased when I behold so many well-remembered faces greeting my arrival with looks of friendship and approbation.

" Under any circumstances, such proofs of the confidence of my fellow-citizens would be gratefully acknowledged.   But the recent incidents of my life give them peculiar value.   When I entered on the high and delicate office which I recently filled, the great body of the people of the United States were strangers even to my name.   I had never been a member of either House of Congress.   The office of Attorney-

General of the United States, from the nature of its duties, was not calculated to make my name familiar to the ears of the people, in the brief space for which I held it. And when I was unexpectedly called to the office of Secretary of the Treasury, in a season of severe trial, when the best and highest interests of this great nation of freemen were vitally connected with the measures of that department, I could not but feel that my humble name would give no weight to the measures I had determined to adopt; that out of Maryland I was unknown to the great body of the American people, and could not, therefore, if attacks should be made upon me, appeal for my vindication to their previous knowledge of me, and a long life passed in the honest endeavor to discharge, to the best of my power, my duties as a man and a citizen. Yet a crisis had come which did not allow me to hesitate as to the path of duty.

"It was obvious to my mind, from the facts before me, that a great moneyed corporation, possessing a fearful power for good or for evil, had entered into the field of political warfare, and was deliberately preparing its plans to obtain, by means of its money, an irresistible political influence in the affairs of the nation, so as to enable it to control the measures of the Government. It was evident, if this ambitious corporation should succeed in its designs, that the liberties of the country would soon be destroyed, that the power of self-government would be wrested from the people, and they would find themselves, at no distant day, under the dominion of the worst of all possible governments—a moneyed aristocracy.   In this posture of affairs, full of peril, and of the deepest interest to this great nation, I saw the gray-haired patriot now at the head of the Government, who has so often breasted every danger in defence of the liberties of his country, once more prepared to plant himself in the breach, to defend his countrymen, at every hazard to himself, from the impending danger.   I firmly believe, and still believe, that the safety of the country depended on his prompt and decisive action.   I had long, as one of his Cabinet, advised the proceeding which he finally made up his mind to adopt.   Under such circumstances it was impossible that I could, without dishonor, have hesitated about accepting the office he proffered me, or have shrunk from the responsibility of executing a measure which I had myself advised at a time when it was believed that the duty would be performed by another person.   It was impossible, in a crisis when the dearest interests of the country were at stake, that I would, without just disgrace, have refused to render my best services in its defence.   I should have been unworthy of the friendship of the high-spirited and patriotic citizens who are now around me, if I could have thought of myself, and my own poor interests, at such a moment.

"The measures which I adopted as Secretary of the Treasury are now before the public, and I am ready to abide the judgment which the American people shall pass upon them. They have, indeed, brought upon me, it seems, a deep and enduring spirit of hostility. I have been singled out from among the number who advised, and who approved of the measure I pursued, as a fit object to receive a peculiar mark of indignity. The most unsparing efforts have been made to impeach the integrity of my motives, and to destroy me in the estimation of the citizens of the United States; and although I am no longer in office, the same spirit is still abroad, and still pursues its object with unwearied perseverance. I do not mention these things to complain of them. I should have been blind to the examples of history, if I had not expected them. No man who has at any period of the world stood forth to maintain the liberties of the people against a moneyed aristocracy grasping at power has ever met with a different fate. Its unrelenting, unquenchable hate has never failed to pursue him to the last hour of his life, and when in his grave. Money can always buy instruments; and I was not weak enough to suppose that I should escape what all others in a like situation have been doomed to encounter.

"Having, as I have already said, had no connection, until recently, with the general Government, I was

altogether unknown to the great body of the citizens
of other States, and cannot therefore, in reply to
assaults made upon me, appeal to their previous knowledge of my principles and conduct. But in Maryland it is otherwise. Born in the State, my life has
been passed in the midst of its citizens until age is
now coming upon me. To them I can confidently
appeal, for they have known me from my childhood.
To the citizens who now surround me, I can still more
confidently, for among them I passed twenty-two
years of the prime of my life ; taking an active part
during all that time in their public concerns. It is
from the people of Maryland that the citizens of other
States must in a great measure learn my character and
my principles ; and of none more justly can the
inquiry be made than of the citizens of this county,
who have so long and so intimately known me. And,
gratifying as their approbation and support would at
all times have proved, I acknowledge that, at a moment like this, I feel it with more than ordinary sensibility. The honors with which they have been pleased
to receive me ; the numerous body of freemen who
are now gathered about me ; the public expression of
their undiminished confidence and esteem, which, at
their request, you have just made to me, is a proud
and cheering testimony to which I can point to repel
the calumnies which are continually heaped upon me.

"The time will come, sir, I doubt not, when every

man who loves the institutions of the country will be ready to admit the misconduct of the Bank of the United States, and the danger to be apprehended from any similar corporation. Many honest and estimable men are now opposed to us who are led away by mistaken notions of party obligations, or are too much under the influence of party prejudices to examine the subject fairly, and form an impartial judgment for themselves. The time will soon come when such men will look back with deep regret at the course they have pursued, and are still pursuing, and will do justice to those who have shown themselves ready to make personal sacrifices to maintain unimpaired, for this great people, the blessings of freedom.

" It is an additional gratification to find you, sir, selected as the organ to communicate to me the sentiments of this large assemblage of my fellow-citizens. As the representative of this district, I received from you, during my brief and eventful administration of the Treasury Department, the most firm and steady support. It was to the committee of the House of Representatives, of which you were the head, that the people of this country are indebted for the proof that the affairs of the bank have been so managed that it is compelled, in the face of the plain provisions of its charter, to hide its proceedings from the public eye. The official report of your committee shows that the bank, aware of the conclusions which must inevitably be drawn from its refusal to submit itself to a fair and full examination, made every effort to escape, without coming to a direct denial. But the talents, firmness, and perseverance of the committee baffled the design, and compelled it to decide directly and unequivocally whether it would lay open its proceedings to strict and impartial scrutiny, or would, in direct violation of its charter, and in contempt of the House of Representatives of the United States, refuse it. Driven from every attempt of evasion, the bank finally refused, and thus gave to the people the most convincing and conclusive evidence of the truth of the charges against it, and that it dared not meet the searching investigation of such a committee.

"The distinguished share which you took in the conflict, and the efficient services you performed, will always be remembered and honored by a people whom you have so signally served."

As soon as Mr. Taney closed his remarks, the shouts of the multitude rent the air with cheers of approbation. He then repaired, with the committee, to the court-house square, where, under the canopy of trees, on a luxuriant grass-plot, seventeen tables were prepared with a sumptuous feast, where many hundreds of citizens and guests from abroad dined. Here, after the toasts were over, Mr. Taney made an elaborate speech, reviewing with the most masterly exposition all the topics involved in the politics of that trying time.

Mr. Taney considered this compliment of the citizens of Frederick City and County, made in the presence of the old court-house, whose bar he so long adorned, one of the glories of his life. Friendship mingled in the compliment, giving to its political signification the higher tribute to his character as a man.

On the 4th of September, in a speech delivered by Mr. Taney at a public dinner given to him at Elkton, Maryland, besides making a general defence of himself, he took occasion to repel the personal assaults which had been made upon him. Mr. Webster had suffered himself, in a public address, to speak of Mr. Taney as the " pliant instrument " of the President. Mr. Taney reproved him in the following language : " It is well understood, that when my nomination was before the Senate for their decision, no charge was brought against me; not a word of accusation was uttered, and I was rejected by a silent vote. If there was supposed to be anything in my character and conduct which justified my rejection, then was the time to have brought it forward. The charge then could have been investigated. But this was not done. And I had therefore a right to expect that no Senator, who had given a silent vote for my rejection, would, after the close of the session, follow me, with the spirit of hostility, into private life. In one instance, and in but one, so far as my knowledge extends, has this expectation been disappointed. And I find that at a public dinner at Salem, some time ago, Mr. Webster, of the Senate, took occasion to speak of me as the 'pliant instrument of the President, ready to do his bidding.'" After correcting some of Mr. Webster's misstatements of facts, and showing how entirely gratuitous were his accusations, Mr. Taney, rising, in the conscious grandeur of his moral superiority, to the sublimity of heartfelt scorn, said, "Neither my habits nor my principles lead me to bandy terms of reproach with Mr. Webster or any one else. But it is well known that he has found the bank a profitable client; and I submit to the public, whether the facts I have stated do not furnish ground for believing that he has become its 'pliant instrument,' and is prepared on all occasions to do its bidding, whenever and wherever it may choose to require him. In the situation in which he has placed himself before the public, it would far better become him to vindicate himself from imputations to which he stands justly liable, than to assail others."

The men at Washington little knew the man they were dealing with. In the mysterious drama of human life, there has never yet trod the stage a more chivalric man than Roger B. Taney. The fiery temper of his soul had been chastened by that form of Christianity which is ministered by the Church that sits on the seven hills of Rome, the imperial mistress of the moral order of the modern world. In his Christian faith was his security from inflicting upon insolence the punishment which an angry temper would suggest.

Mr. Taney was an inordinate smoker of cigars. While he was Secretary of the Treasury, a friend of his, meeting with the peculiar cigars which Mr. Taney used, sent him two boxes of them. As he could not find out the donor, he retained them unopened. A few days after he ceased to be Secretary of the Treasury, he ascertained that a Mr. Thomson, of Baltimore, connected temporarily with the Custom-House at New York, was the donor. Such was his high sense of official integrity, and his scorn of the custom of receiving presents by public men, that, though he was then only a private citizen, he wrote to Mr. Thomson the following letter:

WASHINGTON, June 28, 1834.

DEAR SIR: — Some weeks ago I received two boxes of cigars, and, as I had no letter of advice on the subject, I was at a loss to know from what quarter they came. A short time afterwards, Mr. Smith, the Register of the Treasury, asked me if I had received them; and in answer to my inquiry to whom I was indebted for them, he told me they were sent by you; and that they were intended as a token of your good will to one who had been the neighbor of your family in Maryland, and with whom you had yourself formed a friendly acquaintance in your late visit to Washington. I sincerely thank you for this proof of your kindness, and you must not feel mortified at what I am about to say. I cannot accept the cigars from you as a present. But I will be glad to keep them, and pay you the market value of them. And I must ask the favor of you to say how much they are worth, that I may send you the money. I meant to say this to you before, as I heard that you had sent them. But a thousand official engagements continually pressing on me left but little time to attend to anything else. Now I am a private citizen and have more command of my time.

I repeat that you must not feel any mortification at my refusal to accept the cigars as a present. But it has been a fixed rule with me to accept of no present, however trifling, from any one the amount of whose compensation for a public service depended on the department over which I presided. You will, perhaps, smile at what you may think my fastidiousness about such a trifle as your cigars. But I have thought it the true rule for a public man, and that it ought to be inflexibly adhered to in every case, and without any exception in the smallest matters. And having constantly acted upon it, I cannot consent to depart from it in this case, and trust that you will not suspect me of doubting for a moment the kindness and integrity of the motive which influenced you to send them.

With many thanks, my dear sir, for this token of your friendly recollection, and expecting soon to hear from you,

I am, very truly, your friend and obedient servant,
R. B. TANEY.
SAMUEL THOMSON, ESQ.

Mr. Thomson answered.

New York, July 3, 1834.

Dear Sir: — Yours of the 28th ultimo has just been received; and while I regret that the rule laid down for the government of your conduct has prevented your acceptance of the small token of my regard which I forwarded, I must, at the same time, acknowledge that the rule itself as a *general* one has the homage of my respect. But really the application of it to the *particular* case in question does appear almost " fastidious." Public men certainly cannot be too careful in guarding their actions and their motives against all suspicion; and perhaps, while an application of mine was before your " department," I ought not to have done what I did; and yet it would be esteeming your integrity as a very supple affair indeed, to suppose that it would be influenced by a box of cigars. However, my motives you duly appreciate, and I as duly appreciate the delicacy of your feelings.

And now you will permit me to say that " rules " which apply to R. B. Taney as Secretary of the Treasury do not apply to R. B. Taney as a private citizen; and you will oblige me much by accepting, in this *character*, of the trifle now in your possession as a mark of my respect for your great private worth and invaluable public services; or, if your fine feelings and independent spirit will not allow this, then either return the cigars or enclose me $10. I do sincerely hope, however, that the first proposition will be satisfactory to you.

With great respect, believe me to be yours, etc.

Samuel Thomson.

Mr. Taney replied.

WASHINGTON, July 11, 1834.

DEAR SIR:— Although, in conformity with the rule which I have always prescribed to myself, I must send you, as I now do enclosed, ten dollars for the cigars I received from you, yet I hope you do not doubt that I feel as much obliged by your kind intentions as if I had accepted them as a present. And having long known and respected your family in Maryland, it has given me real pleasure to meet you; and I hope that our acquaintance, although but brief, will be remembered by both of us with mutual kindness. And with best wishes for your health and happiness,

I am, dear sir, very truly

Your friend and obedient servant,

R. B. TANEY.

$10 enclosed — postage paid.

Have the goodness to let me know that this letter comes safely to you.

To Mr. SAMUEL THOMSON, New York.

Mr. Taney had been a diligent student of history, and his character had been formed under the influence of its solemn teachings. He well remembered that, two centuries and a quarter before, Lord-Chancellor Bacon had been impeached by the Commons of England, condemned by the House of Lords, fined forty thousand pounds, and disabled from holding office, and sent to the Tower, because he had received presents. It was not pretended that the gifts had influenced his conduct in office; but the Commons wished to signalize their abhorrence of the practice of receiving gifts by public men; and they selected the greatest man of their country, and indeed of all countries, and made him an example, to future ages, of the infamy of receiving presents while in public office.

Gabriel Duvall, before whom Mr. Taney argued his first case in the Mayor's Court of Annapolis, as we have seen in his autobiography given in the first chapter of this Memoir, had been, after holding many important offices, appointed in the year 1811, by Mr. Madison, an Associate Justice of the Supreme Court of the United States. He was violently opposed to General Jackson and his policy. He was now advanced in age, and wished to resign his seat on the bench. But he feared that General Jackson would appoint a gentleman of great abilities as a lawyer, but of too much political ambition, as he thought, to be elevated to the Supreme Court. He expressed this opinion to a particular friend, Thomas William Carroll, the Clerk of the Supreme Court of the United States. Mr. Carroll, who was opposed in politics to Mr. Taney, knew that Judge Duvall, like himself, had the greatest admiration of his abilities and his character. He, in some way, found out that General Jackson would appoint Mr. Taney in case Judge Duvall resigned, and communicated this information to the Judge. Judge Duvall thereupon resigned his seat upon the bench in January, 1835. General Jackson immediately nominated Mr. Taney to supply the vacancy.

The great Chief-Justice Marshall was still presiding over the Supreme Court. He had a peculiar dislike to General Jackson and to his policy. But so high was his estimate of Mr. Taney, that he privately endeavored to secure the confirmation of his appointment. With that view, he wrote the following note to Benjamin Watkins Leigh, a Senator from Virginia. Mr. Leigh was opposed to General Jackson's administration.

MY DEAR SIR: — If you have not made up your mind on the nomination of Mr. Taney, I have received some information in his favor which I would wish to communicate.

Yours,   J. MARSHALL.

MR. LEIGH.

This letter from Chief-Justice Marshall was sent to Mr. Taney, in the following letter, by the son of the Senator to whom it was written.

SAN FRANCISCO, December 5, 1854.

To the Hon. ROGER B. TANEY, Chief Justice of the Supreme Court of the United States.

SIR: — I have the honor to send you a note from Chief-Justice Marshall to my father, which I feel assured will give you much pleasure. An evidence of the esteem of that illustrious man is a fit offering of respect to one who worthily fills the exalted station he so long occupied, to his own immortal honor and that of these United States. The enclosed paper [the note] was found by me among my father's papers soon after his death.

I am, sir, with the highest respect,
Your most obedient servant,
B. W. Leigh.

Mr. Taney answered.

Washington, January 15, 1855.

My Dear Sir: — I have received your letter enclosing Chief-Justice Marshall's note to your father, while my nomination as one of the Associate Justices of the Supreme Court was pending before the Senate. You rightly suppose that it is exceedingly gratifying to me; and I thank you for it. I shall preserve it.

Allow me to thank you also for the kind language of your own letter. Your father and myself were early friends. Politics separated us for a time. But it gives me now sincere pleasure to remember that, years before his death, the cloud which had arisen between us passed away, and our early relations of mutual friendship were cordially restored. And I am glad to have this opportunity of renewing with the son the friendship and regard I cherished for the father.

With best wishes to you,
I am, dear sir, your friend,
R. B. Taney.

B. W. Leigh, Esq.

At the last moment of the session, the nomination of Mr. Taney was brought up in the Senate, and was *indefinitely postponed,* which was equivalent to a rejection.

It is sad to a reflecting man to witness in an august body like the Senate, composed at that time of men who, by their eminent abilities, would give the highest dignity to any legislative assembly in the world, the unreasoning domination of party spirit, making it do an act of which every member was afterwards ashamed.

In January, 1836, Mr. Taney was invited to a public dinner in Cincinnati, to be given on the 4th day of March next, in celebration of the expiration of the charter of the Bank of the United States. Engagements constrained him to decline the invitation. He therefore sent the following toast: "The gold coins — long exiled from our country for the benefit of the few — they are now returning for the benefit of the many."

Mr. Taney was singularly devoted to the State of his nativity, and was profoundly interested in whatever concerned her honor. In all emergencies, therefore, he stepped forward, and endeavored, by his advice, to save his State from any dishonor.

In 1835, the Bank of Maryland, situated in Baltimore, which had been chartered in 1790, failed in the general disasters which befell the banks of the country. The losses fell upon so many dependent persons that great indignation seized a portion of the community. Mr. Reverdy Johnson, and other gentlemen of the highest standing, having implicit confidence in the integrity and capacity of the managers of the bank, had, from motives of generosity, suffered their names to appear as directors of the institution, though they never looked into the management of the institution, and derived no profit from it. The feeling of resentment pervaded more especially the breakers of the peace, who, assembling in a mob, destroyed the dwellings and other property of the mere nominal directors of the bank. These gentlemen were opponents of the administration of General Jackson; and the vengeance against them was intensified by political prejudice. Mr. Taney at once took a decided stand against the outrage and the resentment; and maintained that the sufferers from the mob were entitled to indemnity for their losses from the city of Baltimore, which was bound to protect every member of the community from violence by other members of the same community. By his advice, a petition was sent up to the Legislature asking for indemnity. Mr. Taney prepared himself to argue the question before the Legislature, but was prevented from doing so because he had in the mean time been nominated for Chief Justice of the Supreme Court of the United States; and though the nomination was still pending, his scrupulous sense of propriety forbid him to argue a cause.

His notes were placed in the hands of Mr. John V. L. MacMahon, who argued the case in Mr. Taney's stead: Mr. Taney, however, appearing as a citizen present to council the passage of the bill. The Legislature was intensely Jacksonian in politics; and notwithstanding Mr. MacMahon, who called up all the resources of his vast capacity, made, as Chancellor Johnson told me, the greatest speech he ever heard, would have refused the indemnity, had it not been for the determination of Mr. Taney to vindicate his State from dishonor by his advice to the Legislature. It was an act of moral heroism in Mr. Taney; for those opposed to the bill used the name of General Jackson as decidedly against it. To do away with the influence of General Jackson's supposed hostility to the measure, Mr. Key, Mr. Taney's brother-in-law, wrote the following letter:

WASHINGTON, March 14, 1836.

MY DEAR TANEY: — I got your letter this morning, and am surprised you have not received mine of Saturday.

I saw the President this morning. He expressed himself, as I wrote you he did before, in strong and decided terms, that the persons whose property had been destroyed ought to be fully indemnified by the community where the outrage had occurred, and denied positively that he had ever expressed any other opinion. He allows me to say this to you, and to say that you may make any use of it you please.

Your nomination was to have been called up to-day. It will most probably be done to-morrow.

Yours truly,

F. S. KEY.

The Legislature passed a bill which, in its operation, made the city of Baltimore pay the full amount of the losses sustained from the violence of the mob. Still, as I personally know, some of the members of the Legislature who voted for the bill were afterwards voted against, by members of their own party, when they became candidates for place, because of their vote.

There is another memorable instance in the history of Maryland where Mr. Taney rebuked the action of his party in an important political movement in the State.

The growth of Baltimore City and of the western counties had made them dissatisfied with certain features of the State Constitution. By the Constitution, the Senate, the Governor and Council, and a majority of the House of Delegates could be elected by a minority of the people. This disparity had existed since 1776, when the Constitution was ordained and established, but was now much increased. The mode of electing the Senate through electors was considered particularly objectionable.

As early as 1807, a bill was introduced into the House of Delegates to give each county a Senator,

and the counties, delegates in proportion to population. The bill failed. In the next year a similar bill
was introduced, but it was lost in the Senate.

After the War of 1812, the agitation of the subject
was renewed, and became an element in State politics
more or less obtrusive at different junctures. It at
last waxed so warm, that, on the 6th of June, 1836,
delegates chosen from Cecil, Harford, Baltimore,
Frederick, Montgomery, and Washington Counties,
and Baltimore City, met at Baltimore, and adopted
resolutions advising the people to elect delegates at the
ensuing election pledged to introduce into the Legislature a bill to take the sense of the people upon the
amendment of the Constitution; and providing for
calling a convention for that purpose, if a majority of
the popular vote should be for it. And they empowered their president to re-assemble the convention,
if the Legislature did not pass such a bill within forty
days, "to take such ulterior measures as might then
be deemed expedient, just, and proper, and best calculated, *without the aid of the Legislature*, to ensure the
accomplishment of the desired results."

The election of President of the United States was
near at hand, and was mingled in the question of
amending the State Constitution. The Senate of the
State was about to expire. An election of electors to
choose a State Senator took place, and resulted in 19
Van Buren electors and 21 Whig. According to the

Constitution of the State, the electors met at Annapolis on the proper day. Twenty-four electors were necessary to constitute a quorum in the college. The 21 Whig electors qualified to take their seats in the college. The 19 Van Buren electors refused to meet in the college, unless the Whig electors would agree beforehand that 8 Van Buren Senators should be elected and 7 Whig. They based their proposition on the ground that the 19 Van Buren electors represented counties which contained a majority of the people. This proposition entirely ignored the Constitution of the State, which was not founded upon the numerical majority, but upon the majority as the people were organized under the established Government. The Whig electors refused to yield. So determined was Governor Veasy, who was a Whig, to maintain the Government and the Constitution, that he issued a proclamation calling on the military authority to hold itself in readiness to aid the civil to maintain its power. The 19 Van Buren electors finally went into the college, and a Senate was elected according to the provisions of the Constitution. Afterwards the reform was effected lawfully which was attempted to be effected by revolution. Mr. Taney had just been made Chief Justice of the Supreme Court of the United States. He had discountenanced this movement of his party to get the control of the State. And I find letters from distinguished persons of his party, who favored the movement, expressing the hope that he would not oppose it, which he answered, expressing strong condemnation of it as ill-advised, rash, and unfortunate.

Neither friendship, nor politics, nor religion, so far as I have ascertained from access to all that remains to testify of the secrets of his life, ever induced him even to hesitate to follow the dictates of his judgment, enlightened by a conscience ever looking up for guidance to Him to whom he owed his first allegiance.

CHAPTER IV.

JUDICIAL LIFE.

A. D. 1836 — 1856.

WE now enter upon the narrative of that part of Mr. Taney's life in which we shall contemplate him in the full dimensions of his greatness.

Chief-Justice Marshall died in the summer of 1835. On the succeeding 28th of December, President Jackson nominated to the Senate Mr. Taney, to fill his place in the Supreme Court. Since his nomination as Associate Justice, the political complexion of the Senate had changed. Yet the nomination was opposed with great determination. Mr. Clay and Mr. Webster led the opposition. So violent were his feelings of hostility to Mr. Taney, engendered during the strife with the Bank of the United States, that Mr. Clay permitted his assaults to degenerate into scurrility. Little did he and Mr. Webster dream that the great Chief-Justice Marshall had endeavored to help Mr. Taney to sit by his side as an Associate Justice. On the 15th of March, 1836, the nomination was confirmed by a majority of fourteen votes.

Members of the Senate and distinguished persons everywhere congratulated Mr. Taney upon his appointment. But I shall pass by all their letters of congratulation, to give place to one from James Dixon, of the Frederick bar, who, as we have seen, studied law under Mr. Taney, and was appointed by him one of his deputies when he was made Attorney-General of Maryland.

FREDERICK, MARYLAND, March 17, 1836.

DEAR SIR: — I have just understood that your nomination as the Chief Justice has been ratified, and I cannot but take leave to offer you my sincerest congratulations. I know you will believe me, when I say frankly that I have no selfish motive in this communication, but write simply to utter a few thoughts which I am unwilling to stifle, though to you of small value. There never lived a mortal, except my mother, for whom I have felt so much unmixed regard and friendship; yea, I may add any other word the language affords, and yet fail to express my feelings — deep feelings — on that subject. There is no one alive to whom I feel so deep a debtor; though I have always known that you neither knew nor dreamed I was under any obligation. In a word, I never left your presence without feeling in love with virtue, and have often and often recorded the same in my diary; for I have kept one almost all my life. I am proud that you will be now the very head itself of a profession you have always loved and honored; but though fitly then, you will never receive, even in that exalted seat, a single particle more of my respect than you have

long had already.   You have had my best and purest,
and more I shall never attempt to offer.

Yours sincerely,   J. DIXON.
Hon. R. B. TANEY.

This letter I found among the papers of the Chief
Justice.   The writer is long since dead, and his diary
is destroyed.   I know full well that I act in harmony
with the sentiments of the Chief Justice, when I present this letter from his old pupil, in this memoir, in
preference to congratulations from those high in places
of ambition.   And, besides, it gives insight into Mr.
Taney's character.   It shows how he appeared to Mr.
Dixon, who knew him so entirely.

It has been said, and perhaps was true, that Mr
Taney was appointed Chief Justice of the Supreme
Court because of his aid to General Jackson on the
bank question, and especially for the act of removing
the public deposits.   And it is quite certain that
his great predecessor, Marshall, was appointed Chief
Justice because of his defense, when a representative
in Congress, of Mr. Adams's administration, in the case
of Jonathan Robbins, who claimed to be an American
citizen, but was delivered up to the British Government as a deserter, and was hanged at the yard-arm of
a British man-of-war.   The act was seized upon by
the opposite party and denounced by resolutions offered
in the House of Representatives; but the transcendent speech of Marshall on the floor of the House

shut their mouths. The office in each case was bestowed as a reward for political services. But the
eminent fitness of each man justified his appointment
on grounds of patriotism and good government. The
rewards were not offered beforehand, but after great
services rendered in the interests of the country. And
as the great Marshall fulfilled the high trust to the
uttermost, so, we shall see, did his successor. Their
successive administration of justice is the noblest chapter in the history of our Government.

In order to show the services which Mr. Taney
rendered to his country as Chief Justice, it is first
necessary to give some account of the Court over
whose deliberations he presided, and point out its functions in the working of the Federal Government.

The framers of the Constitution of the United
States were men familiar with the history of nations.
They had studied human society in its progress
through all recorded time, in relation to Governments
as they had sprung up in various forms suited to the
peculiarities of different peoples. When, therefore,
they were about to frame a general Government for
the purpose of uniting a number of small, independent
sovereign States into one body politic, their thought
was some device by which questions which lead to war
between States should be settled by judicial adjustment. For this purpose they gave to a Supreme
Court, and such inferior courts as Congress may from

time to time ordain and establish, judicial power over all cases in law and equity arising under the Constitution, the laws of the United States, and treaties made, or which shall be made under their authority; over all cases affecting ambassadors, other public ministers and consuls; over all cases of admiralty and maritime jurisdiction; over controversies to which the United States shall be a party; to controversies between two or more States; between a State and citizens of another State; between citizens of different States; between citizens of the same State claiming lands under grants of different States, citizens, or subjects.

In all cases affecting ambassadors, or other public ministers and consuls, and those in which a State shall be a party, the Supreme Court shall have original jurisdiction.   In all other cases before mentioned, the Supreme Court shall have appellate jurisdiction, both as to law and fact, with such exceptions and under such regulations as Congress shall make.

The trial of all crimes, except in cases of impeachment, shall be by jury; and such trials shall be held in the State where the said crime shall have been committed; but when not committed within any State, the trial shall be at such place or places as the Congress may, by law, have directed.   The judicial power of the United States shall not be construed to extend to any suit in law or equity commenced or prosecuted against one of the United States by citizens of another State, or by citizens or subjects of any foreign State.

All the legal ideas of the framers of the Constitution, and especially of the judicial department, were derived from the common law of England. The fundamental principle of the common law, as a scheme of administrative justice, is, that a decision once made by a Court of the last resort, like the Supreme Court, shall not only bind the parties to the suit, but, the principle decided, shall be a precedent which all subsequent judges must follow as fixed law.

The Supreme Court, with the jurisdiction given to it under the Constitution, is a co-ordinate department of the Government. It is the equal, under the Constitution, with the legislative and executive departments. It sits in the Capitol the supreme dispenser of Federal law. It has the high function because of the limitations which the Constitution has imposed upon the legislative department, to declare any of its enactments null and void which it may deem in conflict with the Constitution, when the question arises in a case litigated before it by parties to a suit. This is the highest function ever bestowed upon a Court. And it is the provision of the Constitution' which, above all others, signalizes it as having ordained and established a Government of limited powers. It clothes the Supreme Court with moral sublimity. It supposes that, without patronage, and without any other power than its own character for learning, virtue, patriotism, and a love of justice, it will declare, as it is its duty under the Constitution to do, an act passed by Congress and approved by the President, null and void, when not authorized by the Constitution. And above all, it supposes that the people will have such reverence for its decisions that they will go into effect by the simple forms of civil process as certainly as the silent laws of nature take effect.

It was over the deliberations of such a tribunal, the most august ever established among men, that Mr. Taney was called to preside. No man ever realized more entirely the grandeur of high judicial functions, and felt more profoundly its responsibilities. And never did a man bring to the discharge of duty a more sublime moral courage. As to. his qualifications as a lawyer for the office, they were the most complete. He had not only mastered every branch of legal learning in every form of judicial tribunal, from the highest to the lowest, but he was extraordinarily familiar with practice in every species of Court. No matter from what Court, whether on the law or the equity side, a record came up on writ of error or appeal, he could see at once its full import. And his long and diversified experience as a practising lawyer in courts of original jurisdiction, had made him as familiar with rules of practice as the most experienced clerk of a Court. He was marshalled to his place by a divine tactic, for the good of his country, if ever a public functionary was, just as his great predecessor had been.

Before I sketch the judicial career of Mr. Taney, it is important, in order to understand the influence of the Supreme Court in the working of the Federal Government, to give some account of the conduct of his predecessors in the high office of Chief Justice.

John Jay, the first Chief Justice, was a Federalist of the extremest political views of his party. He may be said to have had none but an entirely perverted view of the character of the Federal Government. In 1785, in a letter to a friend, he wrote: "It is my first wish to see the United States assume and merit the character of *one great nation,* whose territory is divided into different States merely for more convenient government and the more easy and prompt administration of justice; just as our several States are divided into counties and townships for the like purposes." And in a letter to General Washington, just before the convention which framed the Constitution met, he wrote: "What powers should be granted to the Government so constituted is a question which deserves much thought. *I think the more the better;* the States retaining only so much as may be necessary for domestic purposes, and all their principal officers, civil and military, being commissioned and removable by the national Government." When the Constitution was agreed upon and submitted to the States for ratification, he became its zealous advocate. He saw it through his theoretic view of what he

thought it ought to be. His theory made him mag-
nify its powers. He carried his political views, as all
judges do, upon the bench. He saw all constitutional
questions through their modifying influences.

At the February Term of the Court, 1793, held at
Philadelphia, the case of Chisholm *vs.* Georgia came
up for argument. The doctrine of the sovereignty of
the States of the Union was, for the first time, brought
before the Court, at the suit of a citizen of another State
against the State of Georgia. The question raised by
the suit for adjudication was whether a State was
amenable to the jurisdiction of the Supreme Court
at the suit of a citizen of another State. Chisholm,
a citizen of South Carolina, had brought the suit by
serving process on the Governor and the Attorney-
General of Georgia. Georgia, not recognizing the
jurisdiction of the Supreme Court, refused to appear.
Thereupon the Attorney-General of the United States
moved that, unless Georgia caused her appearance to
be entered by the next term, judgment should be rendered against her by default, and a writ of inquiry
issued. Georgia, still denying the jurisdiction of the
Court, presented, by Mr. Dallas and Mr. Ingersoll, of
the bar of Philadelphia, a written protest. In this
state of the case, involving a question which determines
the character of the polity embodied in the Constitution of the United States, the Court pronounced its
judgment. The Chief Justice, looking at the question

through his political theory, considered a State as merely an aggregate of individuals, resting as to suability on the same ground with a corporation; and that, therefore, there was nothing in the character of a State of the Union incompatible with its being sued in a court of law, by a citizen of another State, in an action of assumpsit for the breach of a contract. In this view a majority of the Court concurred, and a judgment was given accordingly at the February Term, 1794, and a writ of inquiry awarded.

A decision so obnoxious to the sense of the people, who had but the other day ratified the Constitution, produced such excitement in the public mind that the matter was taken up by several of the State Legislatures. And to settle the question forever, an amendment was added to the Constitution which declared that the jurisdiction of the Supreme Court should not extend to suits against a State by citizens of another State, or subjects of a foreign State. In obedience to this amendment, the Court, at the February Term, 1798, unanimously determined that no further jurisdiction could be exercised in any case, past or future, wherein a State should be sued by the citizens of another State. The sovereignty of the States was thus declared by the amending power of the Constitution, and then proclaimed by the Supreme Court of the United States. At this time all the departments of the Government were co-operating, under the in-

fluence of centralizing doctrines, to reduce the States
to the low level of counties.   This amendment of the
Constitution rebuked their usurping policy.

Nothing can show more conclusively than this decision, how prone the Federal Government is, in its
working, to the usurpation of powers not granted by
the Constitution.   For even Alexander Hamilton, in
the eighty-first number of The Federalist, when it was
objected to the ratification of the Constitution that
under its provisions a State might be sued by the
citizens of another State, scouted the notion as inconsistent with the admitted sovereignty of the States.
" It is inherent [said he] in the nature of sovereignty,
not to be amenable to the suit of an individual *without its consent*.   This is the general sense and the
general practice of mankind ; and the exemption, as
one of the attributes of sovereignty, is now enjoyed
by the government of every State in the Union.   Unless, therefore, there is a surrender of this immunity
in the plan of the convention, it will remain with the
States, and the danger intimated must be ideal.   The
circumstances which are necessary to produce an
alienation of State sovereignty, were discussed in considering the article of taxation, and need not be repeated here.   A recurrence to the principles there
established will satisfy us that there is no color to pretend that the State governments would, by the adoption of that plan, be divested of the privilege of pay-

ing their own debts in their own way, free from every constraint but that which flows from the obligations of good faith. The contracts between a nation and individuals are only binding on the conscience of the sovereign, and can have no pretension to a compulsive force. They confer no right of action independent of the sovereign will. To what purpose would it be to authorize suits against States for debts they owe? How could recoveries be enforced? It is evident that it could not be done without waging war against the contracting State; and to ascribe to the Federal Courts, by mere implication, and in destruction of a pre-existing right of the State government, a power which would involve such a consequence, would be altogether forced and unwarrantable."

Chief-Justice Jay presided for the last time, at the term of the Supreme Court, in February, 1794. Soon afterwards he was commissioned as Minister to England. He accepted the appointment without vacating his seat on the bench. When he returned to America, in 1795, he had been elected Governor of New York. Thereupon he resigned the office of Chief Justice of the Supreme Court of the United States.

At no period of his life was the sublime majesty of Washington's character, and his extraordinary administrative ability, more apparent than at this time, when the Government had only begun its working. He had not only to conduct affairs amidst the contentions

of the Federal and Republican parties, but also amidst
the strifes and intrigues of the factions of the Federal
party.   He knew that in his own Cabinet the success
of his administration was far from being the only aim
of its members.   Therefore it was that, with scarcely
any intimation to his Cabinet, he appointed John
Rutledge, of South Carolina, to the office of Chief
Justice, immediately upon the resignation of Jay.
Rutledge was one of the leading minds of that age of
great men.   His courage and administrative ability, as
Governor of South Carolina, contributed, in an eminent degree, to the success of the American arms in
expelling the British from the South.   His eloquence,
together with his genius for organization, as a member
of the convention which framed the Federal Constitution, was of signal service.   He had, perhaps, the
wisest view of what should be the function of the
judiciary in the Federal Government, of any member
of the convention.   His cardinal idea was that "the
judges ought never to give their opinion on a law till
it comes before them."   This view was adopted in
opposition to that of Mr. Madison and others who
proposed that the supreme national judiciary should
be associated with the executive in the revisionary
power.   Such was his recognized ability, that he was
made the chairman of the committee which reported
the first draft of the Federal Constitution.   He had
held high judicial stations in his own State; and had

been an Associate Justice of the Supreme Court of the United States. He was, too, of the Federal party. But because he had, in common with other Federalists of the South, opposed the ratification of the treaty which Chief-Justice Jay had negotiated with Great Britain, he was denounced by Washington's own Secretary of the Treasury, Wolcott, as a "driveller and a fool." Having been appointed during the recess of Congress, his nomination was rejected by his own party in the Senate. Marshall, in his Life of Washington, speaks of him as "a gentleman of great talents and decision." He presided one term in the Supreme Court.

The class of Federalists who had defeated the nomination of Rutledge were held together not only by the cohesive force of party aims, but by personal ambition for power, and would have taken the reins of government out of the hands of Washington, as they afterwards did out of the hands of Adams, had it not been for his great faculty for rule. Yet Washington, notwithstanding he was well aware that they had other aims than the success of his administration, and that they reproached him in secret, selected one of their class, because he was not blind to his fitness, and appointed him to succeed Chief-Justice Rutledge. This was Oliver Ellsworth, of Connecticut. He was Senator from his State, and had voted against the nomination of Rutledge.

Chief - Justice Ellsworth was among the most moderate of the class of Federalists to which he belonged, and brought to the bench the eminent qualifications of extensive judicial experience in the Courts of his State. His nomination was not dictated to Washington, but was the result of his administrative wisdom in selecting officers in every department of Government. His imperial eye penetrated character in all classes of men.

Ellsworth had been a member of the convention which framed the Constitution; and was a strenuous advocate for preserving the identity and sovereignty of the States. " What we wanted [said he] was domestic happiness. The national Government could not descend to the local objects on which this depended. It could only embrace objects of a general nature. He turned his eyes, therefore, for the preservation of their rights, to the State governments. From them alone he could derive the greatest happiness he expected in this life. His happiness depended on their existence as much as a new-born infant on its mother for nourishment." It was by his exertions as much as by those of any member, that the identity and sovereignty of the States were preserved in the Federal Government. He opposed with especial hostility every attempt to confer on the Federal Legislature the power to interfere with the elective franchise in the States, or to impose unnecessary restrictions on the qualifications of its own members. "The right of suffrage [said he] is a tender point, and strongly guarded by most of the State Constitutions. The people will not readily subscribe to the national Constitution, if it should subject them to be disfranchised. The States are the best judges of the circumstances and temper of their own people."

After the Constitution had been framed upon the compromises between the consolidationists and the advocates of State sovereignty, Ellsworth characterized the Government established by it as "partly national and partly Federal;" language afterwards employed by Mr. Madison, in the thirty-ninth number of The Federalist, in describing the Government. As a Senator, Ellsworth legislated upon the assumption of this twofold character of the Government, and ceased to be so entirely under the influence of the idea of State sovereignty as he was when he was one of the architects of the Constitution.

The Constitution had declared that the judicial power of the United States should be vested in one Supreme Court, and such inferior Courts as the Congress may from time to time ordain and establish; leaving it to legislation to organize the whole edifice. When, therefore, Congress met, so important was the matter deemed, that on the day after the opening of the Senate, and before the President's inaugural had been delivered, a committee of the Senate was appointed "to bring in a bill for organizing the judiciary of the United States." Ellsworth had the honor of being placed at the head of the committee. The bill was drafted by him; and time has proved it to be a masterpiece of legislation, touching as it does all the points of relation between the Federal and State Governments, and so organizing jurisdiction as, under the legislation of Congress, to afford adequate legal remedy in our complex political system.

Chief-Justice Ellsworth took his seat on the bench of the Supreme Court at the February Term, 1796. Most of the cases in the Court at that early period related to the jurisdiction of the Federal Courts. He presided for the last time at a general term of the Court in August, 1799. At this session the case of Turner *vs.* the Bank of North America was decided; and the principle settled that, because of the limited character of Federal jurisdiction, a cause in the Circuit Court must affirmatively, and upon the face of the pleadings, appear to be within the jurisdiction of the Court, otherwise the judgment will be reversed in the Supreme Court, as jurisdiction is never to be presumed. The objection to the record was that the pleadings did not show the parties to be citizens of different States, or one of them an alien; and it was decided to be a fatal jurisdictional defect.

Now it was that President Adams sent Chief-Justice Ellsworth to France, just as Washington had sent

Chief-Justice Jay to England; it being deemed compatible to hold both offices at the same time. After the treaty with France was negotiated, and before his return to America, Chief-Justice Ellsworth resigned his seat upon the bench. President Adams thereupon nominated to the Senate, John Marshall, of Virginia, who was then his Secretary of State, to fill the vacancy of Chief Justice. The nomination was unanimously confirmed; and on the 31st of January, 1801, he was commissioned, but continued to act as Secretary of State until the 4th of March, when President Adams's term of office expired.

Chief-Justice Marshall was a moderate Federalist, and as little of a partisan as any man could be who had held so many political posts. When a member of the Virginia convention which ratified the Constitution of the United States, he maintained that the sovereignty of the States was not merged in the plan of Government, so that a State could be sued in a Federal Court by a citizen of another State. In defending the judiciary clause against the objections of those who contended that it conferred jurisdiction on the Federal Court in such a case, he said: "I hope that no gentleman will think *that a State will be called at the bar of a Federal Court*. Is there no such case at present? Are there not many cases in which the Legislature of Virginia is a party, and yet the State is not sued? It is not rational to suppose *that the sovereign power shall be dragged before a Court.* The intent is to enable States to recover claims of individuals residing in other States. *I contend this construction is warranted by the words."* His strict views of constitutional limitations were so well known, that when he took his seat as a member of Congress, in December, 1799, that venomous Federalist, Oliver Wolcott, in a letter to Fisher Ames, said: "A number of distinguished men appear from the southward, who are not pledged by any act to support the system of the last Congress; these men will pay great respect to the opinions of General Marshall: he is doubtless a man of virtue and distinguished talents, but he will think much of the State of Virginia, and is too much disposed to govern the world *according to rules of logic;* he will read and expound the Constitution *as if it were a penal statute,* and will sometimes *be embarrassed with doubts, of which his friends will not perceive the importance."*

Chief-Justice Marshall took his seat on the bench of the Supreme Court at the February Term, 1801. So little had been done by his predecessors towards developing Federal jurisprudence, that he had to lay its very foundations. And it is fortunate for the success of our Federal system of local self-government by sovereign States, that the foundations should have been laid by one who so fully recognized the limitations of the Constitution as conferring only specific powers expressly granted.

At the term of the Court in February, 1803, the case of Marbury vs. Madison was argued and decided. It involved the question whether the Constitution of the United States is to be regarded as an absolute limit to the legislative power, or is, as in England, at the mercy of the Legislature.

In disposing of this question, which involved the determination of the nature of our Federal Government, the Chief Justice said: "The powers of the Legislature are defined and limited. To what purpose are powers limited, and to what purpose is that limitation committed to writing, if these limits may at any time be passed by those intended to be restrained? The distinction between a Government of limited and unlimited powers is abolished, if these limits do not confine the persons on whom they are imposed. It is a proposition too plain to be contested, that the Constitution controls any legislative act repugnant to it, or that the Legislature may alter the Constitution by an ordinary act. Between these alternatives there is no middle ground. The Constitution is either a superior, paramount law, unchangeable by ordinary means, or it is on a level with ordinary legislative acts, and, like other acts, is alterable when the Legislature shall please to alter it.

" If the former part of the alternative be true, then a legislative act contrary to the Constitution *is not law:* if the latter part be true, then written Constitutions are absurd attempts, on the part of the people, to limit a power in its own nature illimitable.

"Certainly all those who have framed written Constitutions contemplate them as forming the fundamental and permanent law of the nation; and, consequently, the theory of every such Government must be, that an act of the Legislature repugnant to the Constitution is void.

"This theory is essentially attached to a written Constitution, and is consequently to be considered by this Court as one of the fundamental principles of our society."

The Chief Justice then claims for the judicial department the authority to declare an act of Congress repugnant to the Constitution null and void; and decided that the Act of Congress conferring jurisdiction on the Supreme Court to issue a mandamus, it being an original process, is not authorized by the Constitution, and therefore is null and void. The mandamus was refused on that ground.

He completed his view of the limited powers of the Federal Government, in his opinion in the case of Bank of Hamilton vs. Dudley's Lessees, that the State Courts have exclusive power to construe the Constitution and legislative acts of their respective States. "The judicial department of every Government [he said] is the rightful expositor of its laws; and emphatically of its supreme law."

But where a State law is repugnant to the Federal Constitution, he maintained the supremacy of the Federal judiciary over the State tribunals in cases of constitutional construction brought up on writ of error.

Such were the settled rules of constitutional construction in the Supreme Court of the United States when Chief-Justice Taney came to preside over its deliberations.

He first took his seat on the bench, at a Circuit Court held in Baltimore, for the District of Maryland, in April, 1836. He had been so long familiar with the practice of Courts in which the grand and petty juries perform functions in the administration of justice, that he was at once, as a judge, prepared to correct what he had observed to be vicious practice. It had been customary, before a grand jury entered upon the discharge of its functions, for the judge, in open Court, to instruct them regarding their duties. He disapproved of this practice. Therefore, in place of the customary charge, he remarked: "He had a few words to say to them, not so much in compliance with the usage which had prevailed, of charging grand juries,—of which he disapproved, and would in future dispense with altogether,— but more for the purpose of giving his reasons for departing from it; and his present charge would necessarily be brief. He thought the Court should enter at once with promptness and industry upon the discharge of its duties, disconnected with all unnecessary forms. The age had passed by which called for particular instructions from the Court; the public mind had become enlightened, and the intelligence of juries was adequate to the discharge of their duties. The District Attorney was ready to counsel them in all matters of law. It was unnecessary that the Court should enter the wide field of jurisprudence, when the attention of the jury would be called to but few infractions of the criminal law of the land." He ever after dispensed with the custom of charging the grand jury. On this occasion, after his preliminary remarks, he advised the jury that it was their duty carefully to examine the testimony laid before them, and find no bill except upon their clear conviction of the guilt of the accused.

In the January Term, 1837, he took his seat for the first time on the bench of the Supreme Court.

The judicial administration of Chief-Justice Taney must be considered as a reaction against the later tendency of that of Chief-Justice Marshall, and a return to the earlier constitutional construction of that great Judge. In the case of McCulloch vs. The State of Maryland, Chief-Justice Marshall was made to swerve from his earlier strictness of construction by the moulding and transforming logical power, aided by the delusive light of the seductive fancy, of Pinkney. The great orator put his own thoughts into the mind of the Chief Justice without his knowing it, until he made him see in the auxiliary provision of the Constitution, " to make all laws which shall be necessary and proper for carrying into execution " the specific powers granted, powers as original as those they are to carry into execution. And the Chief Justice never afterwards freed himself from this persuasive coercion of that master of the forum.

My chief purpose in this Memoir is to show the influence of Mr. Taney on the working of the Federal Government, in the political system of the United States, both while he was a Cabinet officer and while he was Chief Justice of the Supreme Court. I shall therefore confine my review to his judicial opinions on constitutional questions. At the moment he took his seat on the bench of the Supreme Court, there were pending three cases of great interest, each of them involving the validity of a State law, and the discussion of the relative powers of the State and the Federal Governments. The cases had been discussed in the time of Chief-Justice Marshall, and it was understood that he was of opinion that the State law involved in each was repugnant to the Constitution of the United States. Those who were familiar with the current of judicial decisions while Marshall presided over the Supreme Court, were curious to see, from the decision of these cases, whether that current was to flow in the same channel of construction, under the influence of the new Chief Justice.

The first of these cases is the City of New York *vs.* Miln. The Legislature of the State of New York had passed a statute, requiring the master of every vessel arriving in the port of New York, under certain penalties, to report in writing, respecting his passengers, within twenty-four hours after his arrival. The question in the case was, whether the requirement of the statute did not interfere with the right of Congress, under the express grant of the Federal Constitution, to regulate commerce.

It had been decided in 1824, by the Supreme Court, in the case of Gibbons *vs.* Ogden, that a statute of the State of New York, granting to certain persons the exclusive privilege to navigate all the waters of the State with vessels moved by steam, was repugnant to the clause of the Constitution giving to Congress the power to regulate commerce among the several States, and was therefore void. And in 1827, it was decided by the Supreme Court, in the case of Brown *vs.* The State of Maryland, that an Act of the Legislature of Maryland which required every importer of goods, by wholesale, bale, or package, to take out a license, and pay for it, under certain penalties or forfeitures for neglect, was void; because it was virtually laying a duty on imports, which the States were by the Constitution prohibited from doing, and because it interfered with the power of Congress to regulate foreign commerce. In both cases, Chief-Justice Marshall delivered the opinion of the Court.

It was argued, by those opposed to the validity of the State law, that the case came within the decisions just mentioned. But the majority of the Court, including Chief-Justice Taney, decided that the Act of New York was not a regulation of *commerce*, like the statutes involved in those cases, but a regulation of *police*, and was therefore in the exercise of a power belonging to the State. *Persons*, it was argued, are not the subject of *commerce;* and not being imported goods, they do not fall within the reasoning founded upon the construction of the power given to Congress to regulate commerce, and a prohibition of the States from imposing a duty on imported goods. The opinion of the Court was pronounced by Justice Barbour.

The second case was Briscoe *vs.* The Bank of the Commonwealth of Kentucky. The Act of the Legislature of Kentucky established the bank "in the name and behalf of the Commonwealth of Kentucky." It was argued, against the validity of the Act, that it was repugnant to the provision in the Federal Constitution which restrains the States from emitting bills of credit. The case had been argued before Chief-Justice Marshall, and he and a majority of the Court were of opinion that the Act was unconstitutional and void. A re-argument was ordered; and the case was argued before Chief-Justice Taney. The Act was declared constitutional; as the States were only prohibited from emitting such paper as was denominated bills of credit before and at the time of the adoption of the Constitution, and there was no limitation in the Constitution on the power of a State to incorporate a bank, a power incident to sovereignty. The judgment of the Court, in which the Chief Justice concurred, was pronounced by Justice McLean.

The last of these cases was the Charles River Bridge *vs.* Warren Bridge. The Chief Justice now delivered his first judgment regarding the Constitution. The case had been argued before Chief-Justice Marshall, and was ordered to be re-argued. It was a question of law that involved a great principle of public policy, requiring for its solution the forecast of the statesman as well as the learning of the lawyer. It was a question just suited to the statesmanly judicial mind of the Chief Justice.

The question in this case involved the power of the several States relative to the corporations which they have chartered, as it is affected by the provision in the Federal Constitution prohibiting a State from passing any law impairing the obligation of contracts.

The Charles River Bridge held its franchises under Acts passed by both the Colonial and the State Legislatures of Massachusetts. It was claimed that the corporation had, in perpetuity, the exclusive right to erect and maintain a bridge over the Charles River, and receive tolls; and that the Act of the Legislature of Massachusetts which authorized the erection of the Warren Bridge — which was a free bridge, diverting all the travel — impaired the implied contract contained in the charter of the Charles River Bridge not to authorize another such structure.

The case came by appeal before the Supreme Court, on a bill in equity for an injunction to prevent the erection of the Warren Bridge, filed in the State Court.

The Chief Justice maintained that public grants are to be construed strictly : that nothing passes by implication. And as there was no express grant of an exclusive privilege to the Charles River Bridge, an implied contract to that effect cannot be inferred. And that therefore the Act authorizing the erection of the Warren Bridge does not come in conflict with the provision in the Federal Constitution prohibiting the several States from passing laws impairing the obligation of contracts. "We cannot [he said] deal thus with the rights reserved to the States, and by legal intendments and mere technical reasoning take away from them any portion of that power over their own internal police and improvement which is necessary to their well-being and prosperity."

And having disposed of the case by the well settled rules for construing public grants, the Chief Justice vindicates his decision on grounds of statesmanly policy. "If this Court [he said] should establish the principles now contended for, what is to become of the numerous railroads established on the same line of travel with turnpike companies, and which have rendered the franchises of turnpike corporations of no value? Let it once be understood that their charters carry with them these implied contracts, and give this unknown and undefined property in a line of travelling, and you will soon find the old turnpike corporations awaking from their sleep, and calling upon this Court to put down the improvements which have taken their places. The millions of property which have been invested in railroads and canals in lines of travel which had been before by turnpike corporations, will be put in jeopardy. We shall be thrown back to the improvements of the last century, and obliged to stand still until the claims of the old turnpike corporations shall be satisfied, and they shall consent to permit these States to avail themselves of the light of modern science, and to partake of the benefit of those improvements which are now adding to the wealth and prosperity, and the convenience and comfort, of every other part of the civilized world."

This decision, enforced with the most convincing reasoning, founded on sound legal doctrine and expressed in the most felicitous diction, was most auspicious for the country. It left the States free to push forward the great improvements by which the earth has been subdued to the dominion of man.

Justice Story delivered an elaborate dissenting opinion. The great force of this first opinion of the Chief Justice, and the principles maintained in the two previous opinions, circumscribing, as he thought, the powers of the Federal Government, filled him with despondency for the fate of Federal supremacy. Writing from home to Justice McLean, he said: "There will not, I fear, ever, in our day, be any case in which a law of a State, or of Congress, will be declared unconstitutional; for the old constitutional doctrines are fast fading away, and a change has come over the public mind from which I augur little good. Indeed, on my return home, I came to the conclusion to resign. But my friends have interposed against my intention, and I shall remain on the bench, at least for the present."

Mr. Justice Story was originally a Republican, and as such was appointed to the Supreme Court by President Madison. In 1803, writing to Mr. Nathaniel Williams, of the Baltimore bar, but a native of New England, he said: "I have long had a desire to sojourn in some Southern clime, more congenial with my nature than the petty prejudices and sullen coolness of New England." But raised to distinction, and his great merits as a jurist becoming fully recognized at home, he gradually grew into sympathy with New England and with New England opinions. In an autobiographical letter to his son and biographer,

written in 1831, he said: " Nay, a Virginia Republican of that day [administration of Jefferson and
Madison] was very different from a Massachusetts
Republican; and the anti-Federal doctrines of the
former State then had, and still have, very little support or influence in the latter State, notwithstanding
a concurrence in political action upon general subjects." And writing to Mr. Everett, he said: " I was
avowedly a believer in the doctrines of Washington,
and little infected with Virginia notions as to men or
measures."

These three cases, which so disturbed Mr. Justice
Story, and made Chancellor Kent, in a letter to him,
say, " I have lost my confidence and hopes in the constitutional guardianship and protection of the Supreme
Court," are reported in the eleventh volume of Peters's
Reports; and the extracts from Mr. Justice Story's
letters are taken from his life by his son.

At the next term of the Court, the State of Massachusetts was summoned by the State of Rhode Island
to answer a suit involving the question of the territorial
boundary line between them. Rhode Island claimed
political sovereignty and jurisdiction over about one
hundred square miles of territory, with about five
thousand inhabitants whose rights of property in the
land were not questioned. Massachusetts had always
exercised sovereignty and jurisdiction over the territory. Rhode Island alleged that a mistake had been

made in the location of the boundary line between the
two States, and prayed that this boundary line might
now be established by the judgment of the Supreme
Court, and the State might be restored to and confirmed in the sovereignty and jurisdiction of the disputed territory. The case was brought by bill in
equity. The counsel for the State of Massachusetts
moved to dismiss the bill for want of jurisdiction ;
first, because of the character of the respondent, a
sovereign State; second, because of the nature of the
suit, being to recover sovereignty and jurisdiction.

The opinion of the Court, which was delivered by
Mr. Justice Baldwin, sustained the jurisdiction. Chief-
Justice Taney dissented. "It has, I find, [said the
Chief Justice,] been the uniform practice in this
Court for the Justices who differed from the Court on
constitutional questions to express their dissent."

The Chief Justice then proceeded to state the grounds
of his dissent. He did not doubt the jurisdiction of
the Court, under the Constitution, to hear and determine a controversy between States as well as between
individuals, in relation to the boundaries between the
States, where the suit is to try a right of property in
the soil. But the jurisdiction does not extend to
political rights. Sovereignty and jurisdiction, which
Rhode Islands seeks to recover, are not matter of property, but are political rights. The Court therefore
cannot take cognizance of the suit. He was therefore

of opinion that the bill ought to be dismissed for want
of jurisdiction.   After various proceedings in the case,
running through ten years, the matter was argued on
its merits in the winter of 1846, and decided against
Rhode Island on the ground that no mistake in the
location of the boundary line was proved; and that
even if a mistake had been proved, it would be difficult to disturb a possession of two centuries by Massachusetts, with a claim of right which was admitted by
Rhode Island and other colonies in the most solemn
form.   The Chief Justice concurred in the judgment
dismissing the bill, solely on the ground of want of
jurisdiction, which was his position from the beginning.

At the same term, January, 1839, the Chief Justice delivered the opinion of the Court in the case of
the Bank of Augusta *vs.* Earle, and two other cases
depending on the same principle, called the corporation cases, in which the sovereignty of the several States
is presented in another aspect.   It was decided that the
comity which obtains between independent nations,
applies to the several States of the Union, and must
be recognized by the Federal Courts.   The question
involved in the cases was, whether the corporations of
one State created by statute, within its territorial
limits, are permitted by the comity of nations to make
contracts in the other States and sue in their Courts.
" They are [said the Chief Justice] sovereign States;

and the history of the past, and the events which are daily occurring, furnish the strongest evidence that they have adopted towards each other the laws of comity in their fullest extent." Upon this doctrine of comity, it was decided that the corporations of one State can sue in the Courts of the other States.

At the term of the Court in 1841 was decided the case of Prigg vs. Commonwealth of Pennsylvania. It is reported in 14 Peters. Prigg, a citizen of Maryland, had taken a fugitive slave by force from the State of Pennsylvania, and carried her to the State of Maryland to her owner. The State of Pennsylvania had passed an Act which provided that the taking and carrying away of a negro or mulatto by force and violence out of the State should be deemed felony, punishable by fine and imprisonment. The Act provided a mode for the rendition of fugitive slaves by the State authorities to their owners. It professed to be passed to give effect to the constitutional provision relative to fugitives from labor, and to prevent kidnapping. The fugitive slave had been brought, by virtue of this law, before the Pennsylvania magistrate; but the magistrate refused to take cognizance of the case. Prigg thereupon, of his own will, carried off the slave and her children into Maryland. He was acting as the agent of the owner. For this act, Prigg was indicted under the law of Pennsylvania. The State of Pennsylvania and the

State of Maryland, in the most friendly spirit, agreed that judgment might be entered against Prigg, and the case be taken to the Supreme Court of the United States, and the question involved be decided by that final arbiter of constitutional questions of a judicial character.

Mr. Justice Story delivered the opinion of the Court, declaring the Act of the Legislature of Pennsylvania unconstitutional. The ground upon which Mr. Justice Story based his judgment was, that the Constitution places the remedy for fugitives from labor *exclusively* in Congress. While concurring in the judgment, the Chief Justice dissented from the doctrine that the States could not pass laws to aid in giving effect to the provisions in the Constitution. The Chief Justice had a clearer view than his associates, of the international character of the Federal Union, and of the co-operative duty and function of the several States in giving effect to all the provisions of the constitutional compact. His cast of mind was essentially statesmanly in considering constitutional questions. He knew that political law was an essential element in constitutional questions that arise in the working of our complex system of government. The Chief Justice said, in his dissenting opinion, "The language used in the Constitution does not, in my judgment, justify the construction given to it by the Court. It contains no words prohibiting the several States from passing laws to enforce this right. They are in express terms forbidden to make any regulation that shall impair it. But there the prohibition stops. And according to the settled rules of construction for all written instruments, the prohibition being confined to laws injurious to the right, the power to pass laws to support and enforce it is necessarily implied. And the words of the article which directs that the fugitive 'shall be delivered up,' seem evidently designed to impose it as a duty upon the people of the several States to pass laws to carry into execution, in good faith, the compact into which they thus solemnly entered with each other. The Constitution of the United States, and every article and clause in it, is a part of the law of every State in the Union, and is a paramount law. The right of the master, therefore, to seize his fugitive slave, is the law of each State; and no State has the power to abrogate or alter it. And why may not a State protect a right of property acknowledged by its own paramount law? Besides, the laws of the different States, in all other cases, constantly protect the citizens of other States in their rights of property, when it is found within their respective territories; and no one doubts their power to do so. And in the absence of any express prohibition, I perceive no reason for establishing, by implication, a different rule in this instance, where, by the national compact, this right of property is recognized as an existing right in every State of the Union."

At the January Term, 1847, in the case of Cook *vs.* Moffat, the Chief Justice again maintained, as he had done in the corporation cases, that the comity of nations existed among the States. The question was the effect of a debtor's discharge, under the insolvent laws of one State, on a contract made in another State. It had been decided in Chief-Justice Marshall's time, that a discharge under the insolvent law of a State was not a discharge of a debt due to a citizen of another State. As the question was no longer open to controversy, the Chief Justice, while acquiescing in the judgment of the Court, following the previous decisions, expressed his disapprobation of the principle on which it was decided. He was of opinion that the true doctrine was, that the insolvent law of one State should receive in the tribunals of a sister State the respect and comity which the established usages of civilized nations extend to the bankrupt laws of each other.

The principles of the decisions of the Supreme Court, since Chief-Justice Taney presided over the Court, continued to dissatisfy Mr. Justice Story. In April, 1845, he wrote to Hon. Ezekiel Bacon: " I have been long convinced that the doctrines and opinions of the ' Old Court ' were daily losing ground, and especially those on great constitutional questions. New men and new opinions have succeeded. The doctrines of the Constitution, so vital to the country, which in former times received the support of the whole Court, no longer maintain their ascendency.   I am the last member now living of the old Court, and I cannot consent to remain where I can no longer hope to see those doctrines recognized and enforced.   For the future, I must be in a dead minority of the Court, with the painful alternative of either expressing an open dissent from the opinions of the Court, or, by silence, seeming to acquiesce in them."

With these views, Mr. Justice Story had determined to resign his seat on the bench, and for the future devote his life to his law professorship at Harvard University.   But he died on the 10th of September, 1845; and America lost one of her greatest judges, and the world, one of its greatest jurists.

At the opening of the Court at the next session, in the winter of 1846, in response to the Attorney-General, who had announced the death of Mr. Justice Story, and moved the usual testimonials of respect, Chief-Justice Taney said: "It is difficult for me to express how deeply the Court feels the death of Mr. Justice Story.   He had a seat on this bench for so many years, and was so eminently distinguished for his great learning and ability, that his name had become habitually associated with the Supreme Court, not only in the mind of those more immediately connected with the administration of justice, but in that of the public generally throughout the Union.   He had, indeed, all the qualities of a great judge; and we are

fully sensible that his labors and his name have contributed largely to inspire confidence in the opinions
of this Court, and to give weight and authority to its
decisions.

"It is not, however, in this country only, that the
name of Justice Story is respected and honored. His
works upon various branches of jurisprudence have
made him known to eminent men wherever judicial
knowledge is esteemed and cultivated; and wherever
he is known, his opinions are quoted with respect; and
he is justly regarded as one of the brightest ornaments
of the age in which he lived. But it is here, on this
bench, that his real worth was best understood, and it
is here that his loss is most severely and painfully
felt. For we have not only known him as a learned
and able associate in the labors of the Court, but he
was endeared to us as a man, by his kindness of heart,
his frankness, and his high and pure integrity. We
most truly and deeply deplore his death, and cordially unite with the bar in paying appropriate honors
to his memory.

"The proceedings of to-day will therefore be entered on the records of the Court, as a lasting testimony
of our respectful and affectionate remembrance of our
departed brother."

The relations between Mr. Justice Story and Chief-
Justice Taney were of the most intimate friendship.

No Justice on the Supreme Court Bench wrote as many letters to the Chief Justice as Mr. Justice Story. Some of them were wholly personal, others relating to cases on his circuit, but one and all breathe the most friendly spirit. And his friendship for the Chief Justice extended to his family. He never passed through Baltimore, that he did not pay his respects to Mrs. Taney either in person or by a note of apology for not calling. He fully appreciated the great abilities and learning of Chief-Justice Taney. In a letter to the Chief Justice, dated at Cambridge, April 19, 1839, Justice Story says: "Your opinion in the corporation cases has given very general satisfaction to the public; and I hope you will allow me to say that I think it does great honor to yourself as well as to the Court." And in another letter from the same place, dated March 25, 1843, he says: "Whether I shall go abroad this spring is very uncertain. If my health improves, so that I need not go, I shall assuredly remain at home, for at my age, and with my feelings, I have no desire to visit foreign countries ; and although I have every reason to believe that I should be most hospitably received in England, — the only country which I feel a sincere desire to see and understand, — yet I confess that my heart misgives, whenever I think of quitting my home to embark among strangers, in new scenes and interests, and new habits of life. I am sure that you will sympathize with me in this respect, and feel that, when age is upon one, it is most for our happiness to be at rest at our own fireside.

"I read the opinion of the Court in the Illinois case, respecting the stay laws of that State, with the highest satisfaction, and entirely concur in it. I think your opinion is drawn up with great ability, and in my judgment is entirely conclusive. I hope that the opinion was unanimous : but within a few days it has been suggested in Boston that Brother McLean differed from the Court. But the information has not reached me in such a way as to make me feel that it is entitled to credit. At all events, I should regret to find it true. There are times in which the Court is called upon to support every sound constitutional doctrine in support of the rights of property and of creditors.

"I was exceedingly grieved in hearing of the death of poor Key. His excellent talents, his high morals, his warm and active benevolence, and his most amiable and gentle temper, endeared him to all who knew him. To you and Mrs. Taney the loss is irreparable, and to the public, in the truest sense of the word, a deep calamity. 'Our dying friends come o'er us like a cloud.' Jones is almost the only one left at the bar who was there when I first knew the Court; and it is sad to know how many glorious lights have been extinguished."

The Mr. Key spoken of in this letter is the author
of "The Star-Spangled Banner," and the Mr. Jones
was Walter Jones, of whom I have spoken as Judge
Advocate in General Wilkinson's trial, a lawyer of
surpassing abilities, but now dead.

Justice Story, in a letter, dated May, 1840, to Mr.
Peters, the Reporter of the Supreme Court, said: "In
my judgment, the opinion of the Chief Justice in the
habeas corpus case is a masterly one, and does his sound
judgment and discrimination very great credit. I
think it will (as it ought) elevate his judicial reputation. I entirely concurred in that opinion with all my
heart; and was surprised that it was not unanimously
adopted." Mr. Peters, in an official letter to the
Chief Justice, quoted this opinion of Mr. Justice
Story. The Chief Justice, in his official answer, said:
"I am very glad to hear that Judge Story is getting
well, and not a little gratified at the judgment he pro-
nounces on my opinion in the *habeas corpus* case. It
is praise worth receiving." And when, five years
afterwards, Judge Story died, the Chief Justice, in a
letter to Mr. Peters, dated November, 1845, said:
"What a loss the Court has sustained in the death of
Judge Story! It is irreparable, utterly irreparable in
this generation; for there is nobody equal to him.
You who have seen me sitting there for so many years
between Story and Thompson, will readily understand
how deeply I feel the loss of the survivor of them,

especially so soon after the death of the other; and I feel it still more deeply, as the time approaches when I must again take my seat there under such altered circumstances."

The *habeas corpus* case mentioned in the letter of Judge Story to Mr. Peters, I have deferred mentioning until now, because the Chief Justice, in his opinion in that case, guarded the rights of the Federal Government, while in all the opinions I have mentioned, he guarded the rights of the States. He never became confused in defining the boundaries between the powers of the Federal Government and the reserved rights of the States. His marvellous power of analysis enabled him to discern the exact boundary in all the mutual relations of Federal and State sovereignty and jurisdiction. Our complex political system was a perfect logical harmony, undisturbed by any conflict of powers, in the comprehensive view of his judicial mind. He had thoroughly studied it in the light of its history, and of the inferences founded, on both the indestructible love of local self-government in the respective States and the felt need of a Federal Union.

In the case of Holmes *vs.* Jennison, reported in 14 Peters, the members of the Court were so divided that no opinion was delivered as the opinion of the Court. Justice Story, McLean, and Wayne concurred in the view of the Chief Justice. The question in the

case was, can a State, since the adoption of the Constitution of the United States, deliver up an individual
found within its territory to a foreign Government, to be
there tried for offences alleged to have been committed
against it? The relative powers of the Federal and
State Governments were directly involved in the inquiry.

Before the merits of the question could be determined, there was a preliminary point to be decided.
Holmes, the plaintiff, had, upon demand by the authorities of Canada, been arrested in the State of Vermont, on a warrant issued by Jennison, as Governor of
the State, directed to a sheriff, commanding him to arrest
Holmes for the crime of murder, and deliver him, on
the confines between the State and Canada, to such
person as was empowered by the Canadian authorities
to receive him. Holmes sued out a *habeas corpus* from
the Supreme Court of Vermont, and the Court decided
in favor of the Governor's authority. The case was
brought before the Supreme Court of the United
States by a writ of error.

The Chief Justice decided, after reasoning the point
thoroughly, that the Supreme Court had jurisdiction.
The case being therefore before the Court, the Chief
Justice proceeded to inquire whether the authority exercised by the Governor of Vermont was repugnant
to the Constitution of the United States. He first admitted that the respective States have the power to

remove from their territory any persons whose presence they may think dangerous to their peace, or in any way injurious to their interests : that being an ordinary police power which has never been surrendered to the Federal Government.   But in the case of Holmes, the State did not act in order to protect itself, but to assist another nation which had asked its aid. The act of the State is one of foreign intercourse. All foreign intercourse belongs, by express grant, to the Federal Government.   "The framers of the Constitution [said the Chief Justice] manifestly believed that any intercourse between a State and a foreign nation was dangerous to the Union; that it would open a door of which foreign powers would avail themselves to obtain influence in the separate States. Provisions were therefore introduced to cut off all negotiations between the State authorities and foreign nations.   If they could make no agreement, either in writing or by parol, formal or informal, there would be no occasion for intercourse between the State authorities and a foreign Government.   Hence, prohibitions were introduced, which were supposed to be sufficient to cut off all communication between them."

After showing that such a power in the States is so inconsistent with the power on the same subject conferred on the United States, that, without any express prohibition on the States, they would be excluded from its exercise, the Chief Justice said: " It was one of the main objects of the Constitution, to make us, so far as regarded our foreign relations, one people and one nation, and to cut off all communications between foreign Governments and the several State authorities. The power now claimed for the States is utterly incompatible with this evident intention, and would expose us to one of those dangers against which the framers of the Constitution have so anxiously endeavored to guard."

Notwithstanding the masterly argument of the Chief Justice for reversing the judgment of the Supreme Court of Vermont, the Court was so divided that a different judgment had to be entered.

From the important character of this case, and of those which I have already reviewed and others yet to be noticed, deciding questions of the relative powers of the Federal and State Governments, the majesty of the Supreme Court of the United States, as one of the co-ordinate departments of Federal Government, becomes conspicuous. No wonder that, under the inspirations of such a tribunal, Pinkney pronounced it "a more than Amphictyonic Council." The dignity of the Supreme Court, Chief-Justice Taney never, for a moment, forgot. When President Harrison died, the news was immediately communicated to the Chief Justice. And the next day, April 5th, 1841, Mr. Carroll, the Clerk of the Supreme Court, in a letter to the Chief Justice, said: "I now write, at the instance

of Mr. Webster, to say not only that it would be highly
gratifying that you would be present on Wednesday,
at the funeral, but also that the Cabinet would be
pleased to see and confer with you at this most interesting moment." To this letter the Chief Justice
made the following answer:

Baltimore, April 6, 1841.

My Dear Sir: — I have this moment received
your letter of yesterday. I do not suppose I could
with propriety come to Washington unless I am requested to do so by the Cabinet, or by the Vice-President when he arrives. It is certainly my sincere wish
as well as my duty, to pay every respect to the memory of the President, and to render every service in
my power, in the new and painful condition of public
affairs. But if you look at the published invitations
of the Cabinet, you will, I think, agree with me, that
the presiding officer of a co-ordinate branch of the
Government would hardly be authorized to consider
himself as invited; and could not, after that publication, make his appearance at the funeral without a
direct invitation from the Cabinet. Of course, I am
speaking of my official character, in which it is my
duty to look at what is due the Judiciary Department
of the Government from the Executive, and from those
who act in its behalf. Yet do not, for a moment, suppose that I think any disrespect was intended. There
was no particular reason why I should have been
invited; and therefore no disrespect in the omission.

So also as to the other matter referred to in your
communication, [whether another oath must be taken

by the Vice-President,] the same reasons apply. In the intercourse between the Executive Department of the Government and the Judicial, whenever their official characters are involved, the communication from the one to the other ought to be direct and from the proper organ. I should be most unwilling to subject myself to the suspicion of desiring to intrude into the affairs which belong to another branch of the Government; and if I say or do anything in the matter, it must be upon a request in such a form as would make it my duty to comply; and, in that case, I should perform the duty with pleasure.

You will please regard this letter, as well as the former one, as intended for yourself only; and not to be even mentioned to the Cabinet or the Vice-President. It is designed to enable you to say why I am not in Washington: provided inquiries are made from quarters where you think it proper to answer, in order to prevent mistakes as to my intentions or motives. I repeat, that I am quite sure that no unkindness to me has been designed, and that I shall not be suspected of acting under any such feeling.

And with great respect and regard,

I am, dear sir, very truly yours,

R. B. TANEY.

WM. THOS. CARROLL, ESQ.,
    Clerk of the Supreme Court,
        Washington.

By this defence of the dignity of the Judicial Department, Chief-Justice Taney has set an example of high official spirit, which I record for the lesson it teaches to all who may succeed him as the head of administrative justice in our country. But for the function which the Supreme Court has performed in the working of the Federal Government, our Union would long ago have perished.

At the January Term, 1847, there came before the Supreme Court the Massachusetts, Rhode Island, and New Hampshire License cases, reported in 5 Howard. The question in the cases arose under the power vested in Congress, by the Constitution, to regulate commerce. The question was precisely the same in the first two cases. It was whether a State can regulate or prohibit the retail of wines and spirits which Congress has authorized to be imported from foreign countries. It was unanimously decided that a State can, and that the statutes authorizing it were constitutional.

The Chief Justice in his opinion, marked by singular facility of discrimination, admitted that if the statutes had obstructed the importation, or prohibited the sale in the original cask *in the hands of the importer*, they would have been unconstitutional, because in conflict with the power of Congress to regulate foreign commerce. But the State laws involved in the cases were designed to act upon the article after it had passed the line of foreign commerce into the hands of the dealer, and had become a part of the general property of the State.

In the New Hampshire case, the liquor had been imported from Massachusetts into New Hampshire, and had been sold by the importer in the same cask in which it was imported. The New Hampshire statute prohibited such a sale. The question was whether, in the absence of a law of Congress regulating commerce between the States, all State laws on the subject are unconstitutional. This involves the question whether a mere grant of a power to the Federal Government amounts to a prohibition to the exercise of a similar power by the States. The Chief Justice, in his opinion in the case of Prigg *vs.* Pennsylvania, as we have seen, had pronounced that a mere grant of power to Congress was not exclusive, or prohibitory upon the States. Upon this doctrine he bases his opinion in this case. "The controlling and supreme power over commerce with foreign nations and the several States, is undoubtedly [he said] conferred upon Congress. Yet, in my judgment, the State may nevertheless, for the safety or convenience of trade or for the protection of the health of its citizens, make regulations of commerce for its own ports and harbors, and for its own territory; and such regulations are valid, unless they come in conflict with the laws of Congress. Such evidently, I think, was the construction which the Constitution universally received at the time of its adoption, as appears from the legislation of Congress and of the several States; and a careful examination of the decisions of this Court will show that, so far from sanctioning the opposite doctrine, they recognize and maintain the power of the States."

It was a fundamental rule of construction with the Chief Justice, that our political system is a co-operative one on the part of the States in aid of the Federal Government. This principle he applied again in the passenger cases, 7 Howard Reports. These cases came up from New York and from Massachusetts. They were decided at the session of the Court in 1849. They had, because of the difficulty the Court had in a concurrence of opinion, been argued at several terms. And after all, "there was no opinion of the Court as a Court," so great was the conflict of views among the Judges.

The question presented in the New York case was, whether a law of the State of New York laying a tax upon the masters of vessels arriving from a foreign port, of one dollar on every steerage passenger, and one dollar and fifty cents for every cabin passenger, and upon the masters of coasting vessels, of twenty-five cents for each passenger such vessel might contain, for " hospital moneys," was repugnant to the Constitution of the United States, and void. The Massachusetts case depended upon the same question.

It was supposed that the question had been settled by previous adjudications; but this not being the view of the Court, the Chief Justice delivered an elaborate

dissenting opinion, maintaining what he had considered as settled by previous cases.

The points in the cases were: 1st. Is the power to
regulate commerce *exclusively* vested in Congress?
2d. Is a tax upon persons or passengers in vessels a
regulation of commerce? The Chief Justice maintained, as he had done before, that the power to regulate commerce is not *exclusive* in Congress; and that
persons are not, like goods, subjects of *commerce*, and
a tax upon passengers is not a regulation of commerce.
These propositions he discussed with a subtlety and a
perspicuity never surpassed in any judicial opinion.
He showed that a State may make regulations regarding commerce, where they do not conflict with the
paramount legislation of Congress. And his micro-
scopic discrimination cleared up the confusion, that a
tax upon persons coming into harbors in vessels is a
regulation of commerce. But so many of his associates were unable to appreciate the convincing force
of his argument, that his masterly opinion is one of
dissent.

The confused notion prevalent in this country, in
relation to the right of the people to change their form
of Government, confounding, as it does, the right of
revolution with a constitutional right, misled a portion of the people of Rhode Island into an attitude of
treason towards their State Government. It is not ade-
quately discriminated, that any attempt to change a

Government except in the mode pointed out in the Constitution where a mode is provided, or where there is none, under the authority of a law authorizing it, is revolutionary. A Constitution was framed in Rhode Island without the forms of law; and a Government was set up under it, to the attempted exclusion of the existing Government. Then another Constitution was framed in the forms of law, to which the old Government gave sanction, and yielded up its authority. The matter was brought before the Supreme Court by a suit between two individuals for an assault and battery, involving the authority of the Government under which the act was justified. It came up from the State Court.

"The questions decided [said the Chief Justice] are not such as commonly arise in an action of trespass. The existence and authority of the Government under which the defendants acted were called in question." This involved the question which of the two opposing Governments was the legitimate one. This the Chief Justice said was purely a question of political power, to be decided by the political department of the Government, and not by the judicial; and that the political department of the State had determined it, and the State Courts had recognized and acted upon this determination. That whatever might be the propriety of that decision, the Federal tribunals must not step over the boundaries of their jurisdiction, and invade the proper domain of the political department. "Much of the argument [he said], on the part of the plaintiff, turned upon political rights and political questions, upon which the Court has been urged to express an opinion. We decline doing so. The high power has been conferred on this Court of passing judgment upon the acts of the State sovereignties, and upon the legislative and executive branches of the Federal Government, and of determining whether they are beyond the limits of power marked out for them respectively by the Constitution of the United States. This tribunal, therefore, should be the last to overstep the boundaries which limit its own jurisdiction. And while it should be always ready to meet any question confided to it by the Constitution, it is equally its duty not to pass beyond its appropriate sphere of action, and to take care not to involve itself in discussions which properly belong to other forums." This case was decided at the session of 1849, and is reported in 7 Howard.

I come now to the December Term, 1851. A question involving the extent of the maritime jurisdiction of the Federal Courts was presented in the case of *The Genesee Chief.* It was a case of collision and loss on Lake Ontario. The vessel had been libelled in the District Court for the Northern District of New York.

By the law of England, maritime jurisdiction extended only over tide-water. And the Supreme Court had decided, in 1825, that the maritime jurisdiction of the Federal Courts was, as in England, limited by the ebb and flow of the tide. Mr. Justice Story, who delivered the opinion of the Court, adopted the strict letter of the English decisions.

In 1845, Congress had passed an Act extending the admiralty jurisdiction over the lakes and the connecting navigable waters. The question now for judicial determination was whether this act was authorized by the Constitution. The Chief Justice delivered the opinion of the Court, maintaining the constitutionality of the Act of Congress. In the decision of the question, the politic insight of the statesman enlightened and enlarged the legal view of the judge. It is a remarkable instance of a thoroughly technical lawyer realizing that enlightened jurisprudence requires the judge to adapt our borrowed law to the conditions of our own country, where tide-water does not, as in England, cover the whole expanse over which navigation prosecutes its work in commerce. This decision alone is sufficient to place the Chief Justice among the greatest of judicial characters. It was the politic element in the judgments of Mansfield which signalized his administration of justice as among the wisest known to judicial history. None of his judgments have more of the circumspect forecast of the judicial legislator than this leading decision fixing the boundaries of maritime jurisdiction beyond tide-water. And the decision illustrates, in an especial manner, the liberal wisdom of the Chief Justice, extending as it does the area of Federal legislation, where it might have been supposed that a Judge so jealous of the rights of the States would have been restrained by political preconceptions. The decision is a signal example of impartial judicial wisdom. None but lawyers who are familiar with the transactions embraced in maritime law, can appreciate the disastrous effects of a judgment confining maritime jurisdiction in this country, with its vast inland waters, within the limits of the ebb and flow of the tide. The Chief Justice rose to the elevation of mind proper to one presiding over so august a tribunal. "It is evident [said the Chief Justice] that a definition that would at this day limit public rivers in this country to tide-water rivers is utterly inadmissible. We have thousands of miles of public navigable waters, including lakes and river, in which there is no tide. And certainly there can be no reason for admiralty power over a public tide-water which does not apply with equal force to any other public water used for commercial purposes and foreign trade. The lakes, and the waters connecting them, are undoubtedly public waters; and we think are within the great admiralty and maritime jurisdiction in the Constitution of the United States."

In regard to the former decision, the Chief Justice

said, as it was " founded in error, and the error, if not corrected, must produce serious public as well as private inconvenience and loss, it becomes our duty not to perpetuate it."

As this Memoir is not intended for the professional reader only, I must leave the notice of his opinions on constitutional questions, and pass by altogether his opinions in cases in the Supreme Court not involving constitutional questions, with the single remark that for apposite learning, wise legal discrimination, calm judicial spirit, and perspicuity and finish of language, they are unsurpassed by those of any Judge who has ever administered law in a Court founded on the common law of England.

But as the practice is so important a part of the administration of justice, I will say a few words in regard to what Chief-Justice Taney did for that of the Supreme Court. When he came to the bench, the practice was very uncertain. As all matters of practice are particularly under the direction of the Chief Justice, from time to time, as exigencies growing out of cases presented themselves, Chief-Justice Taney accommodated the English practice and process to the circumstances of the cases. As an example of his perfect knowledge of the remedies furnished by the law of England in all their changed adaptations from age to age, his dissenting opinion in the case of Kendall vs. The United States, 11 Peters, should be studied.

A *mandamus* had been sued out from the Circuit
Court of Washington County, in the District of Columbia, to compel Amos Kendall, Postmaster-General,
to pay certain money claimed to be due to a contractor
for carrying the mail.   When the case came before
the Supreme Court, the Chief Justice delivered a dissenting opinion, denying that the Court had authority
to issue a *mandamus* as a prerogative writ.   He
founded his opinion upon the history of the use of the
writ in Maryland up to the time of the cession of the
District of Columbia.   And his clear comprehension
of equity pleading and practice is evinced in his
opinion in the case of Rhode Island *vs.* Massachusetts,
before mentioned.   But in order to see how he gradually built up the practice of the Court, all his
opinions on mere points of practice must be read.   The
practice of the Court has at last been ably treated by
Mr. P. Phillips, in his Jurisdiction and Practice just
published.

When Chief-Justice Taney's opinion in the case of
Kendall *vs.* The United States was delivered, he was
pelted by the party newspapers as influenced by
political feeling to protect General Jackson's Postmaster-General.   Mr. Peters, the reporter, in a letter
to him said that at one time he thought he would
notice the comments of the newspapers.   To this the
Chief Justice responded:

Baltimore, March 27, 1838.

My Dear Sir : — I have received your kind letter, and return my acknowledgments for the honor you propose to me in the dedication of your Digest. I esteem it no small honor to have my name associated with a work destined, I have no doubt, to be extensively useful, and to be more generally acceptable to the profession in this country than any law-book that has issued from the American press. Yet I shall chiefly value it as the evidence of the friendship and kind feelings we have cherished for each other.

You were certainly right in declining to notice, in any way, the statements in the newspapers in relation to the opinions delivered by the Court and its different members in the case of the Postmaster-General. The daily press, from the nature of things, can never be "the field of fame" for Judges; and I am so sensible that it is the last place that we should voluntarily select for our discussions, that on more occasions than one, where I have seen my opinions at Circuit incorrectly stated, I have declined publishing the opinion really delivered, because I did not think it proper for a Judge of the Supreme Court to go into the newspapers to discuss legal questions.

Since I wrote to you, I have received Judge Baldwin's dissenting opinion in the case of the Postmaster-General. It was arranged between him and myself before he left Washington, that he should send me the opinion which he told me he had determined to write out; and it was then my intention merely to express my concurrence with him, and to say nothing more. But the publications afterwards led me to

change that intention, and to determine to write out
my opinion. It is already written; but I find it
longer than I like, and I retain it for the purpose of
condensing my argument. As soon as it is brought
within proper dimensions, I will send it to you with
Judge Baldwin's. You know my settled dislike to
long opinions, when justice to the case can be done by
a short one. Yet I fear I sin in unnecessary length
as often as any of my brethren.

With best wishes, I am, dear sir,
Your friend and obedient servant,
R. B. TANEY.

RICHARD PETERS, ESQ.,
         Philadelphia.

I must now speak of Chief-Justice Taney as a
Judge at Circuit. His opinions from April Term,
1836, to April Term, 1861, have been reported by his
son-in-law, the late James Mason Campbell, of the
Baltimore bar. They embrace cases at common law,
equity, and admiralty. If the reader will look at the
first two opinions in the volume, they will be evidence
of the ability of all the rest. The ability of a Judge
at Circuit cannot be fully seen in his opinions. The
matters which are not reported manifest much more
the capacity of the Judge. The supreme excellence
of the Chief Justice at Circuit will go down to other
generations as a tradition of the Baltimore bar. My
honored friend, the late J. V. L. McMahon, of the
Baltimore bar, in a letter to me, dated December 11,

1865, written while he was ill, thus speaks of the Chief Justice at Circuit:

"Thus situated, I cannot now undertake [says Mr. McMahon] to furnish you with such a statement of the case of Budd *vs.* Brooke's Lessee as you would desire to have or I would be willing to give.

"I will refer you, however, on the subject, to my old friend Thomas S. Alexander, Esq., my associate in that case, who must still have a vivid recollection of all the circumstances of that intricate and most perplexing case, which was on trial before C. J. Taney and J. Heath for nearly a month. He will remember that this case was prosecuted on what was called the old title, for about three weeks, during which we had prepared, with great care, and after much reflection and consultation, a great number of prayers embodying all our views upon the novel and perplexing questions involved in that title, but which were never presented to the Court, because the old title was ruled out for the want of proper location. He will also recollect that the plaintiffs then threw themselves upon their later title, under the escheat warrant which they sought in the first instance to repudiate, by setting up the old title. And that the case was decided in our favor, as to the escheat title, upon a single prayer of the plaintiffs. He will also recollect that after thus disposing of this new title, the Chief Justice remarked that as the old title might come up again in the case on amended locations, he deemed it due to the cause of justice to avoid, as far as possible, further delay and expense to the parties, by giving them his views as to the old title also, which had been fully and completely exhibited before the objection as to location had been taken.

"Then it was that he delivered the verbal opinion as to the old title, which gave us such a display of intellect and judicial ability as has seldom, if ever before, been displayed in any case under the same circumstances. The questions involved in that title, many of which were very novel, and even perplexing to ourselves after much reflection, had not only never been argued, but had not even been presented for the cause before stated. The facts as to the old title, extending over a period of nearly or quite a century, and through several generations, were such as required the closest attention to obtain even a mastery of these.

"It was expected by all parties that at the close of the case, all these complicated facts, and the difficult questions growing out of them, would have been fully presented to the Court by the prayers and arguments of the counsel on both sides. For it could not reasonably be expected that the Court, whilst its attention was engrossed by the reception of the evidence, and the decisions of the questions arising in the course of its reception, could have mastered the whole case, so as to have rendered prayers or arguments unnecessary. When, then, the old title was unexpectedly ruled out, without a prayer or argument on either side, I was entirely unprepared for the display of intellect by the Chief Justice in his opinion disposing of it. And accustomed as I had been to the manifestations of his forensic and judicial ability on many previous occasions, I confess that, in my judgment, this outstripped them all. His opinion not only showed a perfect acquaintance with all the complicated facts of the case, but it also referred to and covered all the numerous questions of law which were to have been presented by our carefully prepared prayers. It is to be remarked also, that when this occurred there were other circumstances calculated to distract the attention of the Chief Justice. The case, at its close, was hurried through to enable him to attend the Supreme Court, and the opinion was delivered after the session had commenced. What I have said will serve to refresh the recollection of my friend, Mr. Alexander; although I am sure he will need no such refresher. I think I cannot be mistaken when I say that his surprise and admiration were equal to my own. Should there be any favorable turn in my disease which will enable me to say more, you will hear from me; and let me add, I shall always be glad to hear from you."

This letter, written by a lawyer of the greatest power and resources of any I have ever heard in a court of justice, will furnish the reader some idea of Chief-Justice Taney as a *nisi prius* judge.

In Campbell's Reports will be found the case of Reed *vs.* Carusi, relating to copyright for a musical composition. What took place on the trial before Chief-Justice Taney, at Circuit Court in Baltimore, is given in a letter to Mr. Campbell, written, by one of the counsel in the case, for my use.

BALTIMORE, February 8, 1867.

J. MASON CAMPBELL, ESQ.

DEAR SIR : — I can only comply, in a very general way, with your request that I should furnish you with a narrative of the proceedings in the case of George P. Reed *vs.* Samuel Carusi, tried before C. J. Taney, at November Term, 1845, in the Circuit Court United States, in Baltimore.

The papers I have been able to find present a very meagre record of the case; and, after the lapse of more than twenty years, I cannot pretend to recall with accuracy the special circumstances of the trial. But I furnish you with such as I can recollect.

Reed was a music seller in Boston, and had published and copyrighted an air set to the words of a popular ballad of the day, composed by Miss Eliza Cook and called " The Old Arm-Chair." The authorship of the music was claimed by Mr. Henry Russell, a famous singer; and the piece was in great demand. Carusi was a music publisher in Baltimore, who, availing himself of the popularity of the song, had adapted to the words another somewhat similar air, which he claimed to be a different composition, and published

and sold it; and he was sued by Reed, in the Circuit
Court before Chief-Justice Taney, for an infringement
of his copyright. The case was entirely novel in its
features, and presented some very perplexing questions as to what constituted "originality" in musical
composition, and as to the right of Mr. Russell to be considered the "author" of the air which had been copyrighted. There was a great deal of learned musical
testimony and forensic discussion on these very important points, the particulars of which, and the Chief
Justice's ruling thereon, I do not remember.

But I recall very distinctly one circumstance in the
case which was so peculiar that it could not easily be
forgotten. There was a question of fact, whether the
air adapted by Carusi to the words was substantially
the same as that which had been used by Mr. Russell.
On this point, the musical experts, proverbially discordant among themselves, differed widely in their
testimony. Some insisted that the airs were identical;
others, that there was a marked and easily to be recognized difference between them. To reconcile this
conflict of opinion, it was proposed by Mr. Latrobe,
who was the plaintiff's counsel, that Mr. John Cole, an
old professional singer, should be sworn as a witness,
and required to sing the two songs to the jury, that
they might judge for themselves whether the two airs
were similar or not. I remember resisting most stren-
uously, on behalf of the defendant, the introduction
of this novel species of evidence; but the Chief Justice overruled the objection, stating that he would
make a rule for the case, which he considered a reasonable one, however novel and peculiar it might be;

and that as the jury were to determine whether the two airs were substantially the same, the best evidence with which they could be furnished, would be the singing of them by an expert witness. Mr. Cole accordingly proceeded in the gravest manner, under the direction of the Chief Justice, to intone the two songs successively in open court; and the appearance of the singer, the lamentable, monotonous cadence of both airs, the bathos of the words, which, as nearly as I recollect, ran somewhat in this way,

> "I love it! I love it! And who shall dare
> To chide me for loving that old arm-chair," etc.,

together with the singular and varied expressions of pleasure or disapprobation on the faces of the musical *dilettanti* present, produced by Mr. Cole's emphatic rendering of the songs, would, under any other circumstances, have created in the crowd of bystanders irresistible laughter and confusion. But the Chief Justice, with that power peculiarly his own, of restraining almost by a glance the slightest breach of decorum in his Court, overawed and repressed every demonstration of disrespect by the placid and dignified attention which he bestowed throughout upon Mr. Cole's musical efforts. I doubt if the same scene could have been enacted in any other Court without inducing some, at least, of the listeners to forget and violate the customary rules of judicial decorum.

The case was argued to the jury, who made up their minds that there was only a difference in the songs between "Tweedledum and Tweedledee," and there was accordingly a verdict for the plaintiff.

I am, very truly yours,   WM. F. FRICK.

There was always in the Court the most perfect order. As a presiding officer, dignity and authority sat upon his brow. His own singular courtesy not only diffused itself through the bar and all the officers of the Court, but it was contagious among the crowd. No officer was permitted to look at a newspaper, but was required to be intent upon the proceedings of the Court. Every one was made to feel that he was where solemn duties were to be performed.

At the beginning of a term, when the list of jurors was called, he attended to every name. And if a juror from Frederick County, where he so long lived, was called, and the name was familiar in his recollection, he always asked the Marshal to tell the juror to come to him after the adjournment. He generally found them the sons or more distant relatives of his old professional acquaintances and friends; and made the kindest inquiries into their family matters. Often have jurors from Frederick County told me, when they returned home, of these friendly talks of the Chief Justice. He was a true citizen, interested in all the affairs of his State. And the reverence and the almost filial affection with which he was regarded, showed that he was the first in the hearts of the people.

I must pause for a moment and open the door, and let the world look in upon the domestic life of the Chief Justice.

Guizot, the minister of Louis Philippe, King of France, in the third volume of the Memoirs of his administration, while descanting on his own success in climbing to power and fame, steps aside from matters of State to tell to men who walk in the paths of ambition a great truth in human life. " Even in the midst of great undertakings, [says he,] domestic affections form the basis of life; and the most brilliant career has only superficial and incomplete enjoyments, if a stranger to the happy ties of family and friendship." He found at home that peace which fame and power cannot give.

Chief-Justice Taney had the great blessing of a wife who was to him "the gust of joy and the balm of woe." On the forty-sixth anniversary of their marriage, he wrote her the following letter:

WASHINGTON, January 7, 1852.

I cannot, my dearest wife, suffer the 7th of January to pass without renewing to you the pledges of love which I made to you on the 7th of January forty-six years ago. And although I am sensible that in that long period I have done many things that I ought not to have done, and have left undone many things that I ought to have done, yet in constant affection to you I have never wavered — never being insensible how much I owe to you — and now pledge to you again a love as true and sincere as that I offered on the 7th of January, 1806, and shall ever be

Your affectionate husband,   R. B. TANEY.

Mrs. ANNE TANEY.

Such was the reputation which the Chief Justice had now acquired for all the qualities of a great Judge, that all his old political enemies had become his greatest admirers. Mr. Clay had long ago, in the presence of Mr. Reverdy Johnson, of the Maryland bar, made a personal apology for the style of his remarks upon his nomination to the Senate, and paid the highest possible tribute to his great judicial abilities. And ever after, Mr. Clay, as his many letters to the Chief Justice show, seemed to strive for the generous forgiveness of the Chief Justice, by his courteous and kind bearing towards him. And the many instances in which Mr. Webster sought the counsel of the Chief Justice on matters of state, show his estimate of his great capacity and wisdom. And so high did he stand in the estimation of the whole country, that his judgment was counted as a sure measure of truth in all matters pertaining to justice and right. Mr. Senator William H. Seward, appreciating the weight of the Chief Justice's character, addressed to him the following letter :

WASHINGTON, January 31, 1851.

SIR : — I am prepossessed with a belief that your convictions must be in favor of the justice of the claims of the American merchants for indemnities for French spoliations; and I am sure that these convictions, if known, would have great influence upon the public mind in favor of the law relating to that sub-

ject which has passed the Senate. I am desirous of
the honor of inscribing my speech, recently delivered
on that subject, to you, as well for the consideration
I have already presented, as because it would be an
expression of the high regard which, in common with
the whole American people, I entertain for you as the
head of the Judiciary Department. But I dare not
take so great a liberty, without first obtaining your
consent. I beg leave therefore to submit a copy of my
argument, and to request your permission to use your
name in the manner I have indicated.

I am, dear sir, with high respect and esteem,
Your humble servant,
WILLIAM H. SEWARD.
The Hon. R. B. TANEY, Chief Justice, etc.

To this letter, the Chief Justice responded as
follows:

WASHINGTON, January 31, 1851.

SIR: — I thank you for the copy of your speech on
the claims of American merchants for indemnities for
French spoliations which you have been good enough
to send me, with a request for permission to inscribe it
to me.

Ever since I have been on the bench, I have felt
very unwilling to have my name in any way connected
with a measure pending before the Legislative or Executive Departments of the Government; and have
studiously abstained from doing anything that might
be construed into interference on my part. I have
adopted this course from the belief that it would enable me to discharge my judicial duties more usefully

to the public.   And acting upon that opinion, I must
beg leave respectfully to decline the honor you have
proposed to do me.

With great respect, I am, sir,

Your obedient servant,

R. B. Taney.

Hon. William H. Seward.

As this book is designed not only to be a memoir
of Chief-Justice Taney, but also to show the working
of the Federal Government, I will now give the correspondence between General Taylor, when he was
about to take the oath of office as President of the
United States, and Chief-Justice Taney.   Though the
President may have his official oath administered to
him by any functionary competent to administer an
oath, the Chief Justice of the Supreme Court of the
United States has always sworn in every President of
the United States.   This seems befitting the dignity
and the solemnity of the occasion.   The ancient kings
of England, while the memories of the separate States
of which the kingdom was composed had not yet died
away, in order to secure themselves from sectional
feelings in the suspicions of the people, before they
took their official oath, turned to the East, and to the
West, and to the North, and to the South, and then
swore to govern according to law.   The Chief Justice
of the Supreme Court of the United States, from his

high judicial position, can administer no sectional oath. He represents the Constitution and the laws over the East and the West, the North and the South. And without sectional difference he administers the oath to the President.

WASHINGTON, D. C., March 3, 1849.

SIR : — Expecting to take, on the 5th instant, the oath of office as President of the United States, I have the honor to request, if it be agreeable to you, that you will attend for the purpose of administering the oath at the time and place indicated by the committee of the Senate.

In soliciting the favor of your attendance, I not only comply with a long-established custom, but also give expression to the high respect which I entertain for the Supreme Bench and its august presiding officer.

I have the honor to be,
    With the highest esteem,
        Your most obedient servant,
            Z. TAYLOR.
His Honor ROGER B. TANEY,
    Chief Justice of the United States.

To this invitation, Chief-Justice Taney responded:

SIR : — It will give me much pleasure to administer to you the oath of office as President of the United States, on the 5th inst. And the duty will be the more agreeable because the high trust to which you are called has been spontaneously bestowed by the American people upon a citizen already so eminently distinguished for the able and faithful discharge of great public duties.

I have the honor to be, sir,
With the highest respect,
Your obedient servant,
R. B. TANEY.

General Z. TAYLOR,
President-Elect of the United States.

As law reform has become an engrossing subject, it is important to know the opinion of Chief-Justice Taney on changes in common law pleading. I will therefore give a letter of his on the subject, which also shows, incidentally, his opinion on the importance of trial by jury.

In 1852, a constituent convention met in the State of Maryland to change the Constitution of the State. Among other matters, an order was offered to incorporate into the Constitution a provision prohibiting the use of special pleading in the Courts of the State. As I well knew the confusion and increased expense any substitute for special pleading would bring into the administration of law in the State, I addressed an elaborate argument to the convention against such a provision, and suggested that provision be made to simplify common law pleading instead of abolishing it. This suggestion was adopted; and the first Legislature which met under the new Constitution appointed Mr. William Price, Mr. Frederick Stone, and myself, commissioners to simplify the pleadings and practice in all the courts of record in the State. It devolved upon me to simplify the preliminary procedure and the pleading. I made an elaborate report on the whole subject to the Legislature; and sent a copy of the report to Chief-Justice Taney. He wrote me the following letter:

BALTIMORE, June 12, 1854.

DEAR SIR: — I have received your letter, and certainly take much interest in the law reforms proposed in Maryland; and, as you desire it, would be glad to examine the report on pleading, if it was in my power, and give you my opinion of it. But at my time of life, the labors of a long session of the Supreme Court are sensibly felt when the Court is over, and I require repose and relaxation from business to regain my strength. Now, if I undertook to examine the report on pleading in all its bearings, and to give you my opinion of it, it would occupy nearly the whole summer, in order to make up an opinion upon which I would myself be disposed to rely. The task of reforming — in other words, of radically changing — the system of pleading, which is interwoven with the common law itself, is one of extreme difficulty and delicacy. I am by no means satisfied that the experiments made in other States and in England have been successful. For I observe there are quite as many cases upon pleading now — if not more — than before the change was made. For more disputes arise as to the meaning of words in new combinations and new modes of averment; while in common law pleading as it now

stands, the ordinary counts in a declaration and
ordinary pleas have a certain definite form which
conveys a certain definite meaning, about which
lawyers can never doubt or dispute. I am sensible,
indeed, that there are many more forms and technicalities in common law proceedings which the Courts
ought to have reformed long ago. The power has
been given to them by the Legislature to give judgment
according to the right of the matter, without regard to
matters of form; and yet they have *obstinately* (I
must say) continued to treat as a matter of substance
what evidently was nothing but form, merely because
it was called substance in some of the old law books.
I fear they will continue to do so, without some
specific direction from the Legislature. But when that
direction is given, it will require the greatest care and
consideration to preserve all that is really essential to
the common law and trial by jury, and dispense with
everything else. For certainly the proceedings ought
to be so moulded that the party having right on his
side, should not be defeated by technicality or nicety
in pleading. But to do this by legislation, and yet
preserve in full vigor and usefulness the great principles of the common law and trial by jury (without
which, in my judgment, no free government can long
exist), will require much reflection and care in matters
of detail, and great perspicuity in language. And I
should be most unwilling to express any opinion upon
such a proposed system of reform without ample time
to examine it and think about it. It would require
more labor and thought than I am willing to bestow
on any subject this summer. And you must pardon

me, therefore, for declining to express any opinion
on the reform in pleading proposed by the commissioners.

With great respect and regard,
I am, dear sir, truly yours,
R. B. TANEY.

SAMUEL TYLER, ESQ.,
Frederick, Frederick County, Md.

After the Legislature had passed into a statute all
the recommendations proposed in my report,—the
statute having been prepared by me,—at the suggestion
of that great lawyer, my friend, Mr. Horace Binney,
of Philadelphia, I prepared a treatise to uphold the
simplified pleading, and sent a copy of it to Chief-
Justice Taney. He made his acknowledgments for
it in the following letter:

BALTIMORE, November 9, 1857.

MY DEAR SIR: — Upon my arrival here to hold
the Circuit Court for the District of Maryland, Mr.
Campbell handed me your note, together with your
treatise on Maryland's Simplified Preliminary Procedure and Pleading.

Although my infirm health and many engagements
put it out of my power to examine carefully the
whole volume; yet I have looked enough into it to
see the judicious arrangement of the topics of which
you treat, and the condensed yet clear commentary
which you make upon them. Your book, under the
new system of pleading, must be exceedingly useful to
the student, and very convenient to the profession generally.

Accept my thanks for your book, and also for the kind language of your note which accompanied it.
With best wishes, I am, dear sir,
Your friend and servant,
R. B. TANEY.
SAMUEL TYLER, ESQ.,
Frederick.

Chief-Justice Marshall had belonged to a quoit club near Richmond. He was one of its most active members; as he had from boyhood been peculiarly fond of quoits. Many other distinguished persons belonged to the club; so that membership was considered a high honor. Upon his first official visit to Richmond to hold the Circuit Court, Chief-Justice Taney was elected a member, as the following letter shows:

RICHMOND, May 12, 1843.

DEAR SIR: — I have the honor to acknowledge the receipt of your letter, enclosing the resolution of the Quoit Club at Buchanan's Spring, by which I am elected an honorary member.

It is with much pleasure that I find myself so kindly received on my first visit to Richmond by this ancient club, distinguished, as it is, by the honored names associated with it. And you have made my election still more gratifying by the manner in which you have been pleased to connect my name with one so justly venerated and cherished as that of Chief-Justice Marshall.

I shall most gladly avail myself of the privileges

conferred upon me by the club whenever it is in my power.

I am, with high respect,

Your obedient servant,

R. B. TANEY.

JOHN G. BLAIR, ESQ.

A great affliction now falls upon the Chief Justice, which makes him peculiarly a man of sorrows. He had repaired, as was his custom, to Old Point Comfort, with his family, in the summer of 1855. The yellow fever suddenly made its appearance; and on the 29th of September carried off Mrs. Taney, and the next day, the 30th, took away the youngest child, Miss Alice, who was "made up of loveliness alone."

The following letter tells how profoundly his brother on the Bench of the Supreme Court, Mr. Justice Curtis, felt for the Chief Justice in his sore trial.

BOSTON, October 22, 1855.

DEAR SIR : — It has not been by reason of my constant labors on the Circuit, still less because I have been forgetful of you, that I have not written to you since I heard of the affliction which you have suffered. I assure you, my dear sir, that I have very often considered whether it might not seem to you almost intrusive, if I were to express to you, as early and as strongly as I wished, the sympathy which I felt. Perhaps I formed a mistaken opinion, remembering my own feelings when my children and my wife died.

For I was young, and little schooled in the submissiveness and acquiescence in the will of God which you have derived from a long and wise life.   Allow me now to say — alas, that it should be all I can say! — that you have my deepest sympathy.   How little any human feeling can aid us in such trials, I know.   But I think I also know that you have that strength which is " in quietness and confidence."   Quietness of a mind which can look back over a long life usefully spent, and confidence in the goodness and mercy of God.

I am not willing you should take the trouble to write to me; but if Mr. Campbell would do so, and say how you are, I should take it as a favor.   I strongly hope I shall meet you at Washington, at the beginning of the term, as well as you were during the last winter.

With great respect and regard,

I am your obedient servant,

B. R. CURTIS.

Mr. Chief-Justice TANEY,
Baltimore.

The Chief Justice responded to this kind letter as follows:

BALTIMORE, November 3, 1855.

DEAR SIR : — I cannot turn your letter over to Mr. Campbell as you suggest, but must answer it myself, to thank you for the kind terms in which it is written, and to assure you that I am grateful for it.

It would be useless for me to tell you what I have passed through.   But it has pleased God to support me in the trial, and to enable me to resign myself in

humble submission to his will. And I am again endeavoring to fulfil the duties which may yet remain
to me in this world.

The Circuit Court for this District begins on Monday next, and I propose to take my seat on the bench,
and busy myself, if I can, in the business of the term.
I hope also to meet you at the Supreme Court at the
beginning of the session, and have made my arrangements with that view.

But I shall enter upon those duties with the painful
consciousness that they will be imperfectly discharged.
The chastisement with which it has pleased God to
visit me has told sensibly upon a body already worn by
age, as well as upon the mind; and I shall meet you
with broken health and with a broken spirit.

May you and Mrs. Curtis be long spared to one
another, and with best wishes for the health and happiness of you both,

I am, dear sir, very truly your friend,

R. B. TANEY.

Hon. B. R. CURTIS,
Boston.

It was not from the great alone that the Chief
Justice received words of sympathy. It was befitting
that the humble should feel the private sorrow of this
great and good magistrate. I have, in the second
chapter of this Memoir, spoken of the happy plantation home where Mrs. Taney was born, and lived at
her marriage. The negroes, who there had so often
looked with pleasure and pride at the beauty and

grace and gentleness and fulness of feeling of their young mistress, and received so many kindnesses from her gracious hands, could never forget her. So that now, when she had been taken from earth, one of these servants, who had for many years been living in Pennsylvania, far away from the scenes of early life, wrote the Chief Justice the following letter:

QUAKERTOWN, November 26, 1855.
BUCKS COUNTY, PA.

DEAR SIR:—Being informed lately of the irreparable loss you have sustained in the death of your affectionate wife, one who I had every reason to respect and regard for the many kindnesses and attentions shown me while a servant in her father's family, I thought perhaps a few lines from one, though in inferior station, who remembers her virtues and amiable disposition, in the way of consolation to you, sir, suffering under the privation of so valuable a companion, might not be considered arrogant or improper, for I can truly say I was very sorry when I was informed of her death, and hope you may so bear your affliction as that it may be sanctified to your eternal comfort and a reunion in a better world with her.

I am getting to be an old man, failing some in bodily strength, but my mind I believe pretty sound, and my memory a little failing of things recently past, but of things that happened in early life I have clear recollections, and hence the remembrance of the respected Mrs. Taney. Excuse me for thus approaching you, but I have written as I felt best, and therefore hope it will be accepted in all good feeling by you.

I shall forward this by Dr. Samuel Bradshaw, a member of Congress from our place, for whom I have a high regard, having labored for him often.

With sentiments of profound respect, I remain your humble friend, who was one of the servants of General J. Ross Key.

JARAD.

The Chief Justice's answer to this letter I have not been able to recover; though I wrote to Dr. Samuel C. Bradshaw, who, as a member of Congress, franked the letter, and was living when I wrote, and I suppose is now. Jarad, I suppose, is dead.

CHAPTER V.

NOTWITHSTANDING the exalted place which, as we have seen, Chief-Justice Taney had attained in the esteem of the great men of all political parties, we shall now see him assailed, for political ends, until he becomes an object of especial hate to a powerful political combination. As the head of the Federal judiciary, he stood between that political combination and the Constitution, which was a barrier in the way to their purposes.

It is a sad chapter in the history of the United States upon which we now enter. Chief-Justice Taney was a grand actor in its successive melancholy scenes. By the part he took, he consummated the glory of his high career.

Before the Federal Government was formed, and even before the war of independence, there were two diverse forms of civilization in this country — that of Virginia and the other Southern States, and that of Massachusetts and the other New England States. Besides that, the first settlers of the two regions were very different in character and opinions — the Cavaliers having settled the Southern States, and the

331

Puritans the New England States — the soils and the climates of the two regions were so different as to necessitate such different pursuits in life as to enhance the original diversity of character of the two distinct peoples. But, nevertheless, the peoples of the two regions had much in common. Besides their common language and laws, their political rights were the same. England was their common mother country, with the same governmental relation to them. Therefore, when their common liberties were invaded by the mother country, they joined with alacrity in a common defence, and in the struggle a more fraternal feeling grew up between the two peoples. But when the war with the mother country was over, and a common government was formed by all the colonies now become States, the antagonism of the Southern and the New England States began at once to manifest itself in the politics of the country and the working of the Government. Each people aspired to rule the country through Federal power, permitting the other to only a participation in the trusts of office. Sectional influence was therefore, at the very origin of the Federal Government, an element, and a powerful one, in the politics of the country and the working of the Government. At first, as we have seen, New England held the sceptre, after Washington laid it down. And when the alien and sedition laws were passed and attempted to be enforced, Virginia and

Kentucky, representing the Southern States, proclaimed the right of the States to interpose their
sovereignty to prevent the enactment and execution
of unconstitutional laws.   The New England States
at once repudiated any such right.   But when the
Southern States attained the control of the Federal
Government under Jefferson's administration, and
Louisiana was purchased in 1803, to be formed into
new Southern States, thereby increasing their political
power, the doctrine of State sovereignty was proclaimed in New England, to preserve the balance of
Federal power between the two sections of the country.
Massachusetts asserted that, as the purchase was a violation of the constitutional compact between the
States, she was no longer bound by it.   Her Legislature passed the following resolution : " *Resolved,* That
the annexation of Louisiana to the Union transcends
the constitutional power of the Government of the
United States.   It formed a new confederacy, to which
the States united by the former compact are not
bound to adhere."   And when, in 1811, a bill was
before Congress for the admission of Louisiana into
the Union as a State, Josiah Quincy, an able and
leading representative from Massachusetts, in discussing the bill, said, " If this bill passes, it is my deliberate opinion that it is virtually a dissolution of the
Union ; that it will free the States from their moral
obligation ; and as it will be the right of all, so it will

be the duty of some definitely to prepare for separation, amicably if they can, violently if they must." And when the war measures, in 1815, pressed heavily upon Massachusetts and other New England States, they met in convention, at Hartford, Connecticut, to consider how they might obtain relief. The convention, in considering the rights of the several States, declared, "That Acts of Congress, in violation of the Constitution, are absolutely void, is an indisputable position. It does not, however, consist with the respect from a confederate State towards the general Government, to fly to open resistance upon every infraction of the Constitution. The mode and the energy of the opposition should always conform to the nature of the violation, the intention of the authors, the extent of the evil inflicted, the determination manifested to persist in it, and the danger of delay. But in case of deliberate, dangerous, and palpable infractions of the Constitution, affecting the sovereignty of the State and liberties of the people, it is not only the right, but the duty, of each State to interpose its authority for their protection, in the manner best calculated to secure that end. When emergencies occur which are either beyond the reach of judicial tribunals or too pressing to admit of the delay incident to their forms, States, which have no common umpire, must be their own judges, and execute their own decisions."

Having thus asserted the right of each State to redress its own wrongs inflicted by the working of the Federal Government, and that the State is to judge for itself when it is wronged, the convention proceeds to suggest amendments to the Constitution which would prevent the New England States from being oppressed, in future, by the working of the Federal Government in the hands of a majority from some other section of the country. The first amendment proposed was to lessen the relative power of the Southern States, by taking from them any representation in Congress based upon their slaves. The second amendment proposed was to prevent the admission of any new State into the Union without the concurrence of two-thirds of both houses of Congress. " The admission of new States into the Union [said the convention] formed at pleasure in the Western region, has destroyed the balance of power which existed among the original States, and deeply affects their interests. . . . . None of the old States can find an interest in creating prematurely an overwhelming Western influence, which may hereafter discern (as it has heretofore) benefits to be derived to them by wars and commercial restrictions."

It was now the year 1819, and so dominant had been the influence of the Southern States in the working of the Federal Government, that all the Presidents, as we have seen, except one, had been elected from a slave State. And the exceptional one was defeated for the second term. The New England States, therefore, determined to persist in their policy begun in 1803, and declared in the Hartford Convention in 1815, of resisting the admission of any new State into the Union which would be adverse to their relative power in the working of the Federal Government. When, therefore, Missouri, which was a slave territory identified with the Southern States because of slavery, asked for admission, as a State, into the Union, the New England States opposed it, unless she would, by her Constitution, abrogate slavery forever. William Pinkney, the great lawyer, was then a Senator from Maryland in the Congress of the United States, and stood forth as the champion of the equality and sovereignty of a State when admitted into the Union. Rufus King, a Senator from New York and a man of great ability and high honor, was the leader of the party which wished to introduce States into the Union manacled by Federal authority. Such was the marvellous power of Pinkney's vindication of the right of States to be admitted, if admitted at all, into the Union on no other conditions than those imposed by the Constitution of the United States, that the enemies of State sovereignty quailed under his mighty blows. And Rufus King, while yet subdued by Pinkney's Titanic strength, remarked to John Nelson, whom I have mentioned as my preceptor in the law, then just elected a representative in Congress, that the speech of Pinkney had enlarged his admiration of the capacity of the human mind.*

The argument of Pinkney so far prevailed, that political managers on both sides settled the question, for the time, by the Missouri compromise—an Act of Congress which provided that slavery should not be carried into any territory north of a certain geographical line. Upon this settlement, Missouri was admitted as a slave State into the Union in 1820.

This was the first direct attack, made by the representatives of New England civilization, upon the provisions of the Constitution which guarantee equal rights to the slave States. Because slave labor was not profitable in the New England States, slaves had gradually passed from those States, by sale, to the Southern States. The question of the balance of power in the politics of the country was, therefore, becoming a sectional question between slave-holding and non-slaveholding States. That the question was, at this time, rather a question of political power than of hostility to slavery, is shown by the fact that while the New England States were opposing the admission of Missouri into the Union, some of their prominent citizens were engaged in the African slave-trade, and Judge Story was, throughout his circuit, charging the grand juries, by elaborate arguments, to bring the nefarious traffickers to punishment. The African slave-

trade had been made a crime by Act of Congress.
But before the Act, and from the first settlement of
the country, the colonies, and afterwards the States,
both of New England and of the South, had acted
upon the principle that a negro has no rights which
a white man is bound to respect. All the wealth of
New England, and all her institutions, have their
roots in the nefarious traffic of men and women torn
from their African homes, and subjected to the sufferings and cruelties of a prison-ship, to be sold into
perpetual slavery to a different people.

" The *Boston Gazette* and *Country Journal*," on
Monday, July 22d, 1776, then published at Water-
town, contains the Declaration of Independence and
the proceedings of many towns in Massachusetts in
regard to it; and it also contains the following adver-
tisement:

"TO BE SOLD.

" A stout, strong, healthy negro man, about twenty-
five years of age; has had the small-pox; can turn his
hand to almost anything. He likes farming business
the best: he is well clothed. The pay may be on
interest, giving security. Inquire of the printer."

When the Federal Constitution was established, in
1789, it recognized in a special manner the institution
of slavery, founding upon it even the relative sectional
representation in Congress, and by an express provision gave the authority and guaranteed the right to

slave owners to seize their fugitive slaves in any State in the Union, and take them home, as they would their ox or their horse. And the Federal Government was established on slave territory, and the purchase and sale of negroes were carried on under the eaves of the Capitol, in the presence of Congress and the other departments of the Government, as it had been on the ceded territory when it was a part of the States of Maryland and Virginia. Slavery was one of the fundamental institutions in our system of federative local self-government.

In 1828, while John Quincy Adams was President of the United States, the Federal party having been rendered odious in New England by the Hartford Convention, Harrison Gray Otis, and others to whom the stigma attached of having plotted the secession of the New England States in time of war, inquired, by letter, of Mr. Adams, whether he ever charged New England Federalists with a purpose to set up a separate confederacy. Mr. Adams frankly admitted that he had made such a charge to Mr. Jefferson and to others. He asserted that such a plot began in 1803, and culminated in the Hartford Convention. In a communication in the *National Intelligencer*, of October 21, 1828, Mr. Adams said, "That their object was, and had been for several years, a dissolution of the Union and the establishment of a separate confederation, he knew from unequivocal evidence, although

not provable in a court of law; and that, in the case
of a civil war, the aid of Great Britain to effect that
purpose would be as surely resorted to as it would be
indispensably necessary to the design."

In his letters to Mr. Otis and others, he denied the
right of a State to secede from the Union, by reasoning, in which I fully concur. "My principles," he
said, "do not admit the right even of the people, still
less of the Legislature, of any one State to secede at
pleasure from the Union. No provision is made for
the exercise of this right, either by the Federal or
any of the State Constitutions. The act of exercising
it presupposes a departure from the principle of the
compact, and a resort to force.

"If, in the exercise of their respective functions, the
legislative, executive, and judicial authorities of the
Union on one side, and one or more States on the
other, are brought into direct collision with each other,
the relations between the parties are no longer those
of constitutional right, but of independent force.
Each party construes the common compact for itself.
The constructions are irreconcilable together. There
is no umpire between them, and the appeal is to the
sword — the ultimate arbiter of right between independent States, but not between members of one body
politic."

After the expiration of his presidential term, Mr.
Adams was, notwithstanding his charge against lead-

ing New England Federalists, elected from Massachusetts a representative in the Congress of the United States. He was essentially a New England man, with all the idiosyncrasies of the descendants of the Puritans. All his travel, observation, study, and varied experience had but nurtured his original type of character. He became in Congress the representative man of New England civilization. He was the first ex-president who had taken a seat in Congress. This alone rendered his position peculiar.

Up to this time the agitation in regard to slavery was political, having reference exclusively to the territories; its aim being to prevent the Southern States from growing in political strength, and perpetuating their rule in the Federal Government. But a party was now forming, with political aims, who regarded slavery as *a sin*. And as the Constitution guaranteed the right to slaves, they soon declared the Constitution to be "a covenant with death and an agreement with hell," and proclaimed that there is a "higher law" which makes it a duty to disregard the Constitution. The party soon acquired the name of abolitionists. Being radical in regard to slavery, it soon became radical in regard to everything opposed to their aim. Radicalism belongs rather to the instincts of man than to his reason. What it calls *nature*, is the basis of its doctrines. It strives to extirpate all distinctions of every kind, political and social. It aims at equality

and unity in politics; and at the apotheosis of the
will of the numerical majority, without regard to the
political rights of a community as organized under
established government. It is philanthropic rather
than patriotic. It moves to its ends through paths of
destruction; and always terminates by an inevitable
recoil of society to save itself from anarchy in a military despotism.

Abolition now knocked at the doors of Congress
for admission. It selected Mr. Adams to present its
wishes to the Federal Legislature. On the 12th day
of December, 1831, it being the second week of the
first session of the Twenty-Second Congress, he presented fifteen petitions, all numerously signed, from
sundry citizens of Pennsylvania, praying for the
abolition of slavery and the slave-trade in the District of Columbia. At this time abolition was considered so odious a fanaticism, that Mr. Adams did
not venture to advocate the abolition of slavery in the
District of Columbia. He thought Congress might
legislate on the slave-trade in the District. Year after
year Mr. Adams continued to present the petitions of
the abolitionists from New England and other States.
The Southern States were, at this time, oppressed by
the high tariff; and were threatening nullification.
Every possible means were used to excite the free
States against the slave States, and also to incite the
slaves against their masters. The spirit of the agita-

tion is exemplified in the extracts which I have given
from Mr. Gruber's sermon.   Yet Mr. Adams stood
forth in the House of Representatives, under the pretext of guarding the right of petition, the fomentor of
discord between the two great sections of the country.
All discreet men abhorred the purposes of the abolitionists.   In order, if possible, to stop the nefarious
agitation, the House of Representatives, in May, 1836,
by a large majority, passed the following resolution:

"*Resolved*, That all petitions, memorials, resolutions, propositions or papers, relating in any way, or
to any extent whatever, to the subject of slavery, shall,
without being either printed or referred, be laid upon
the table, and that no further action whatever shall be
had thereon."

The resolution only gave Mr. Adams the position
of one seemingly defending the right of petition,
and it roused his perverse nature to a more determined purpose.   The petitions now came to him in
such numbers that he sometimes presented two hundred a day.   He was, with all his might, fomenting
sectional strife.   He turned his back upon the Missouri compromise; and when, on the 13th of June,
1836, the bill for the admission of Arkansas as a State
was before the House of Representatives, he offered
this amendment, saying he wished it to be inserted in
italics: "And nothing in this Act shall be construed
as an assent by Congress to the article in the Consti-

tution of the said State, in relation to slavery or the
emancipation of slaves, etc." He, with the other
abolitionists, voted against the admission of the State.
Arkansas was within the territory where slavery was
allowed by the Missouri compromise. Mr. Adams
was bent upon agitating the question of slavery, with
the hope that it would tear up the institution by the
roots. He was now the great leader of New England
radicalism. He felt happy in his power of mischief.
Strife had always been his delight. And a peculiar
zest was given to the present contest, as it was with those
who had dismissed both his father and himself from
power — the people of the Southern States. In this
work of discord, on the 25th of February, 1839, he
proposed, in the House of Representatives, the following
amendments to the Constitution of the United States:

" *Resolved, by the Senate and House of Representatives in Congress assembled,* two-thirds of both Houses
concurring therein, That the following amendments to
the Constitution of the United States be proposed to
the several States of the Union, which, when ratified
by three-fourths of the Legislatures of the said States,
shall become and be a part of the Constitution of the
United States : —

" 1. From and after the 4th day of July, 1842, there
shall be throughout the United States no hereditary
slavery ; but on and after that day every child born
within the United States, their territories or jurisdiction, shall be born free.

"2. With the exception of the territory of Florida, there shall henceforth never be admitted into this Union any State the Constitution of which shall tolerate within the same the existence of slavery.

"3. From and after the 4th of July, 1845, there shall be neither slavery nor slave-trade at the seat of Government of the United States."

The course of Mr. Adams greatly encouraged the abolitionists in their work of mischief. The Legislatures of Massachusetts and Vermont approved his course, and pledged him their support. Large bodies of people in the Eastern, Northern, and Middle States gave him their pledges of co-operation in his work of aggression. Mr. Adams was now the hero of an agitation pregnant with civil war.

In order to justify a course so perilous to the peace of the country, Mr. Adams conceived a new theory of the Constitution of the United States. He had been invited, by the New York Historical Society, to deliver a discourse on the fiftieth anniversary of the inauguration of George Washington as President of the United States. This he did on the 30th of April, 1839, two months after he had proposed his amendments to the Constitution of the United States abolishing slavery. In his discourse he asserted that, by the Declaration of Independence, the inhabitants of the Colonies became *one people*, and that the rights proclaimed were "the natural rights of mankind." That

the Articles of Confederation, in which it was declared
"each State retains its sovereignty," were a usurpation, by the Legislatures of the several States and
their delegates in Congress, upon the rights of the
people of the United States constituting one blended
community. And that afterwards the Articles of
Confederation were abolished, and the people reclaimed
their rights, and in their own name, " we the people,"
ordained and established the Constitution of the
United States upon the principles of the Declaration
of Independence proclaiming " the natural rights of
mankind." If it were true that the Constitution of
the United States was founded upon "the natural
rights of mankind," and not upon the separate rights
of the respective peoples of the different States, then
his proposed amendments were no breach of the implied faith to the South, but only a measure carrying
out the principles of the Constitution. But when, as
is seen in the first part of this chapter, the Declaration of Independence was at once published in the
same newspaper, in Massachusetts, with advertisements
for the sale of negro slaves, and that the slave-trade
from Africa was tolerated until 1808, increasing the
number of slaves in the States, and the right to catch
fugitive slaves everywhere was guaranteed by the
Constitution, and the Federal Government was established in slave territory, it becomes manifest that Mr.
Adams's theory of the Federal Constitution is an

absurdity.   It was invented, by perverse ingenuity, to
serve a fanatical purpose; and it has since been invoked to justify acts of machination in the course in
which Mr. Adams was the forerunner.

The House of Representatives, finding that their
resolution in regard to the petitions of the abolitionists had not answered its purpose of quieting the agitation, rescinded it in 1845, and consented to receive
the petitions and treat them considerately.   But this
was only considered by the abolitionists as a triumph
in the progress of their cause.

I knew Mr. Adams personally, when he was a very
old man, and I a very young one; and I remember
his conversations with singular pleasure.   But, conscious of no motives but the love of truth and justice,
and a wish to present to the world the political lessons
which our history teaches, I am writing of Mr. Adams
as a great actor in a movement which, as we shall see,
has shattered to pieces the Constitution of 1789, and
has exhibited the dreadful spectacle of a land drenched
in fraternal blood, which the grand orator of New
England, in his sublime protest, in the Senate of the
United States, against the right of nullification, prayed
to God his eyes might never behold.

Only a few weeks before Mr. Adams broached the
theory that, by the Declaration of Independence, the
colonies were merged into one homogeneous community, founded upon "the natural rights of mankind,"

and that it was continued under the Constitution, Mr. Webster argued the case of Earle *vs.* The Bank of Augusta before Chief-Justice Taney, in which it was, as we have seen, decided that the States are sovereign, in accordance with the doctrine of the Supreme Court, pronounced by Chief-Justice Marshall in the case of Gibbons *vs.* Ogden, and in McCulloch *vs.* Maryland; two cases in which he, nevertheless, leaned unusually towards the enlargement of Federal power. In the first of these cases, Chief-Justice Marshall said, "As preliminary to the very able discussion of the Constitution which we have heard from the bar, and as having some influence on its construction, reference has been made to the political situation of these States anterior to its formation. It has been said that they were sovereign, were completely independent, and were connected with each other only by a league. This is true." In the other case, the Chief Justice declared that the States retained their sovereignty under the Constitution.

Mr. Webster, in discussing the question of sovereignty in relation to our complex political system, said, "The term 'sovereignty' does not occur in the Constitution at all. The Constitution treats States as States, and the United States as the United States; and by a careful enumeration declares all the powers that are granted to the United States, and all the rest are reserved to the States. If we pursue, to the extreme point, the powers granted and the powers reserved, the powers of the general and the State Governments will be found, it is to be feared, impinging and in conflict.   Our hope is, that the prudence and patriotism of the States and the wisdom of this Government will prevent that catastrophe. . . . The States of this Union, as States, are subject to all the voluntary and customary laws of nations."

In the same year Mr. Webster considered the question of sovereignty, in a letter to the Barings of London, who inquired of him whether the States had power to contract loans at home and abroad.   " Every State [said Mr. Webster] is an independent, sovereign, political community, except in so far as certain powers, which it might otherwise have exercised, have been conferred on a general Government, established under a written Constitution, and exerting its authority over the people of all the States.   The general Government is a limited Government.   Its powers are specific and enumerated.   All powers not conferred upon it still remain with the States and the people.   The State Legislatures, on the other hand, possess usual and extraordinary powers of government subject to any limitations which may be imposed by their own Constitutions, and with the exception, as I have said, of the operation on those powers of the Constitution of the United States.

" The security for State loans is the plighted faith

of the State as a political community. It rests on the
same basis as other contracts with established Governments — the same basis, for example, as loans made in
the United States under the authority of Congress;
that is to say, the good faith of the Government
making the loan, and its ability to fulfil its engagements."

The considerations which I have presented show
the enormity of the heresy presented by Mr. Adams
in his Jubilee oration, as it is called.

Chief-Justice Taney was invited by the New York
Historical Society to be present on the occasion of Mr.
Adams's oration. He answered the invitation by the
following letter :

BALTIMORE, April 18, 1839.

GENTLEMEN : — I regret very much that it will not
be in my power to be present at the celebration of the
fiftieth anniversary of the inauguration of George
Washington as the President of the United States,
by the Historical Society of New York. The event
about to be commemorated has been followed with so
many public blessings, and is connected with so many
grateful and cheering recollections, that I should have
rejoiced in the opportunity of uniting in its celebration.   But the Circuit Court for the District of
Maryland will be in session at the time, and my
official duties therefore compel me to remain in Baltimore.

Accept my thanks for the invitation with which you

have favored me, and I am with great respect, your
obedient servant,

R. B. Taney.

To J. Blunt and others,
Committee.

When General Jackson's second term expired,
there was no one to continue the restoration in the
working of the Federal Government begun by that
great ruler. Martin Van Buren succeeded him as
President. He was cold and crafty, always watching
for an opportunity, but had nothing heroic in his
nature, which is so essential to the character of a ruler
of the people. He had, by machination, broken up
the first Cabinet of General Jackson, and by playing
upon his hatred of Mr. Calhoun, whom the General
thought had been treacherous to him, he succeeded in
gaining his favor for himself as his successor. Van
Buren was called a "Northern man with Southern
principles." He was certainly an extreme State-
rights man, as his "Inquiry into the origin and
course of political parties in the United States"
abundantly shows. The Southern State-rights party,
led by Mr. Calhoun, felt for him the contemptuous
hatred borrowed from their great leader. When Van
Buren became a candidate for re-election, all the
political factions and cliques and rings, led by log-
rolling politicians, combined with the disintegrated
national Republican party into an opposition, — for

such a combination cannot be called a party, — and called themselves *Whigs*, to indicate that their aim was to overthrow the one-man power, which, as they pretended, General Jackson had endeavored to establish. The great leaders, Clay and Webster, were repudiated by this motley group led by political tricksters; and recognizing *availability* as the only qualification for candidates for the Presidency and Vice-Presidency, they nominated William Henry Harrison and John Tyler, a Federalist and a Nullifier, to secure all the votes of such a heterogeneous multitude as were concealed under the appellation, *Whig*. Pandering to the lowest feelings of human nature, this combination succeeded in electing their candidates by the instrumentalities of log-cabins, coon-skins, and hard cider. From that moment, the great party which Alexander Hamilton organized fell to the lowest level in politics.

"Its principles [to use an expression of John Randolph of Roanoke,] were seven — five loaves and two fishes." When a nation comes to think that it no longer stands in need of great men to lead it, but relies upon the wisdom of the intuitions of the multitude, it soon brings upon itself woes, which, perhaps, may be esteemed curses for repudiating the great men whom God has endowed with superior wisdom for the benefit of the country in which they are born. The Federalist died, and the Nullifier became President,

and administered the Government upon his special
views of the Constitution. The Democratic party,
fighting the opposition upon the level of *availability*,
now nominated James K. Polk for President; and the
other party nominated Henry Clay as their candidate.
Polk was elected by a large majority, which elicited
from Mr. Clay the remark that he was always nominated when his defeat was certain, and never when
his election was probable. The truth is, both parties
had ceased to appreciate great men. Amidst the
extraordinary development of the material resources
of the country, the nation had come to consider physical power and territorial extent the chief glory of a
great people. Therefore it was that combinations of
corporations and public companies, and speculators,
and money changers, became a great power in the
politics of the country. Their schemes of personal
aggrandizement could not receive the same favor from
great statesmen, aspiring to a proud name in history
as wise rulers, as they would from men of narrow
understandings, neither knowing what constitutes historical honor nor caring for it. As early as 1833, it
had been attempted to make the election of President
of the United States turn upon the question of Masonry
or anti-Masonry; and so respectable a man as the
eminent lawyer William Wirt consented and became
the candidate for the Presidency upon so preposterous
an issue. John Quincy Adams had written the ques-

tion into a factitious importance. Mr. Wirt received
the entire vote of Vermont. I mention anti-Masonry,
to show what silly elements had entered into the
politics of the country, along with the demoralizing
influences of a universal greed for gain attempting to
work the Government for its aggrandizement.

By an unrighteous war with Mexico we had, by
conquest, added an immense territory to our wide
domain. General Taylor, who was one of the military
actors in the conquest, was now, in 1849, made President, more by a prurient political sentiment than anything else, for he had not a qualification for the high
place. Wise men, lovers of republican institutions,
were grieved to see that the elective franchise can, in
an enlightened country, elevate to the highest places
of responsibility just as incompetent persons as hereditary right has ever done. General Taylor died in
a few months, and Mr. Fillmore, the Vice-President,
succeeded to his place. He was a man of high character and respectable abilities.

A momentous crisis had come in the progress of the
nation. The addition of more territory to the country
had fomented anew the hostility against slavery. The
possible admission of more slave States, formed out of
this territory, into the Union, made anti-slavery feel
that, after all the progress of the country, the sceptre
of Federal rule might be wielded by the *slave power*,
as it was contemptuously designated. The " Life of

John Quincy Adams," written by William H. Seward, was now published, to couple his own name and that of Mr. Adams with the abolition movement, which, he foresaw, was likely in the course of events to become the soul of the Free-soil party, now growing mighty in strength and in daring. He knew full well that all movements in politics are apt to reach their logical consequences; and that Free-soil might culminate, either by peaceful means or by violence, in abolition. He knew that he himself was but watching his opportunity to take advantage of the culmination, however it might be.

It is a fact, which this nation, so mighty for good or for evil, ought ever to remember with gratitude to God, that their great statesmen, Clay and Webster, were spared to effect the settlement or compromise of 1850, and leave one more example of statesmanship in the legislation of the Federal Government, and thereby postpone civil war, so that the eyes of such patriots should not behold its bloody scenes.

The compromise of 1850 declared that Congress would not interfere on the question of slavery in the territories acquired since the Missouri compromise, but would leave the question to the inhabitants of the respective territories. It prohibited the public sale of slaves in the District of Columbia. And it enacted a law for the recovery of fugitive slaves, which was supposed to be less obnoxious to the free States than the law of 1793. This settlement only inflamed the abolitionists to a more fanatical zeal, in which they were encouraged by politicians who pretended to be only Free-soilers. The settlement of the slavery agitation in the territories would make politics too rational and too tranquil for their coarse ambition, which breathed the spirit of "rule or ruin." The Legislatures of many of the free States passed laws not only hindering and obstructing the execution of the fugitive slave laws, but subjected the owners of slaves, in the exercise of their right of recovery, to punishment in the penitentiary. Mr. Webster, in his celebrated speech of the 7th of March, 1850, on Mr. Clay's compromise measures, had maintained, as Chief-Justice Taney had in the case of Prigg *vs.* Pennsylvania, that it was the duty of the several States, under the Constitution, to aid the Federal Government in executing the provision in the Constitution relative to fugitives from labor. Mr. Webster knew that, as long as the free States disregarded this important provision of the Constitution, and obstructed the execution of it, they were estopped from charging breaches of the Constitution against the slave States. In a speech at Capon Springs, in Virginia, on the 28th of June, 1851, in alluding to this subject, he said, "How absurd it is to suppose that, when different parties enter into a compact for certain purposes, either can disregard any provision, and expect, nevertheless, the other to observe the rest!

I intend, for one, to regard and maintain and carry out, to the fullest extent, the Constitution of the United States, which I have sworn to support in all its parts and all its provisions. It is written in the Constitution : 'No person held to service or labor in one State, under the laws thereof, escaping into another, shall, in consequence of any law or regulation therein, be discharged from such service or labor, but shall be delivered up on claim of the party to whom such service or labor may be due.'

"That is as much a part of the Constitution as any other, and as equally binding and obligatory as any other on all men, public or private. And who denies this? None but the abolitionists of the North. And pray, what is it they will not deny? They have but one idea; and it would seem that these fanatics at the North and the secessionists at the South are putting their heads together to devise means to defeat the good designs of honest and patriotic men. They act to the same end and the same object; and the Constitution has to take the fire from both sides.

"I have not hesitated to say, and I repeat, that if the Northern States refuse, wilfully and deliberately, to carry into effect that part of the Constitution which respects the restoration of fugitive slaves, and Congress provide no remedy, the South would no longer be bound to observe the compact. A bargain cannot be broken on one side, and still bind the other. I say to you, gentlemen in Virginia, as I said on the shores of Lake Erie and in the city of Boston, as I may again in that city or elsewhere in the North, that you of the South have as much right to receive your fugitive slaves as the North has to any of its rights and privileges of navigation and commerce."

Mr. Calhoun died in 1850, and Mr. Webster and Mr. Clay died in 1852. Lesser stars now began to shed disastrous light, from the political firmament, upon the national destiny. The line of statesmen had ended; and politicians had succeeded to the government of the people. Political managers began to disturb the work of pacification commenced, by Mr. Clay, in the Missouri compromise; continued in the Revenue bill to arrest, by peaceful means, threatened nullification; and consummated in the compromise of 1850 — constituting a civic crown of glory for that celebrated statesman.

In 1852, the Democratic party nominated and elected Franklin Pierce; pledging, in their political platform, to maintain the compromise of 1850 relative to slavery. But Mr. Senator Douglas, from Illinois, aspiring to succeed either Mr. Pierce or his successor as a Democratic President, assuming that he was only carrying out the policy of the compromise of 1850, introduced the Kansas-Nebraska bill into the Senate in 1854, and it became a law by which territory that had, by the Missouri compromise, been assigned to occupation only as free territory, was brought within the non-intervention principle of the compromise of 1850, so that slave-owners might occupy it with their slaves; and the Missouri compromise was repealed. Now ensued a contest for the occupation and control of that territory by emigrants from the slave and the free States, which ended in murder and plunder, and other outrages which would disgrace even a barbarous people. The opposing sections of the country became infuriated with the spirit of the murdering factions of Kansas. Abolition, and its aiders and abetters, gloated over a contest which they hoped was the fore-runner of a crusade for the extirpation of slavery in the States, and the humiliation of the slave-owners.

In the midst of these premonitions of a coming catastrophe, James Buchanan was, in 1856, elected President of the United States by the Democratic party. His was not the hand to hold the sceptre in such times. Looking at the fearful scenes around him, and forecasting still more fearful consequences, knowing, as he did, that the accumulated wrath of a struggle that began in 1820 was pent up in the contest, catching at a straw, he announced in his Inaugural that a case relative to the constitutional question about the occupation of the territories was pending in the Supreme Court of the United States, the decision of which might appease the storm; as he, as the President, should abide by it. It was the celebrated Dred Scott case.

The day after the inauguration, the decision was announced. Instead of the quiet which President Buchanan's blind hope anticipated, the decision excited more rancorous hate than any other judgment of a Court since man first submitted disputes to the arbitrament of law. The abolitionists considered it a decision enforcing "A covenant with death and an agreement with hell," as they called the Constitution of the United States. And the Free-soilers, from that moment, caught the fanatical spirit of the abolitionists.

The great question involved in the case was, *whether it be competent for the Congress of the United States, directly or indirectly, to exclude slavery from the territories of the Union?* The Supreme Court decided that it is not. This was the opinion of six Judges out of the eight who composed the Court. Justice McLean and Justice Curtis dissented.

The opinion of the Court was delivered by Chief-Justice Taney, though the other five Judges, who concurred in the opinion, delivered separate opinions.

The opinion of Chief-Justice Taney, and a supplement which he afterwards prepared, because of the clamor against him, to justify his opinion before the publicists of the world and before the judgment of future ages, are published among the appendices to this volume. The two combined constitute the most comprehensive and best-reasoned politico-judicial opinion ever pronounced by any tribunal. No such question could arise before any other judicature in the world. It sprung out of our peculiar polity and form of government.

The opinion is based upon the doctrine that when the American colonies were settled, property in African negroes was recognized by the public law of Europe; and that trade in negroes as merchandise was regulated by public treaties and by municipal legislation. That European States vied with each other in getting control of the trade, because of its enormous profits. England, whose royal family was especially reaping its profits, obtained by the treaty of Utrecht, in the year 1713, as it had done years before, the almost entire control of the trade of supplying the American colonies with slaves. That the people of England, dissatisfied with the monopoly by a few royal favorites of such a profitable trade, forced Parliament to open it to all subjects. That the crown lawyers of England, and the Judges of the Courts of Westminster, in giving opinions to the British Government on the navigation act, put negroes on the same footing, as property, with rum, and included them in the words *goods and merchandise.* That States of Europe, in this phase of public law and national practice, introduced slavery into their American colonies, and established property in negroes, as recognized by public law, just as slavery on the continent of Europe had

always been recognized by the law of nations. That
when the Constitution of the United States was formed,
negroes were just as much property as any other goods
and merchandise; and that the right to their slaves
as property, in accordance with the common law of
the Colonies, was guaranteed, by its provisions, to their
owners when they escaped to other States than those
in which they were held to labor; and that the States
to which they had fled were bound to deliver them to
their owners on demand. That, such being the law
of property recognized by the Constitution, and incorporated into its provisions, a master had as much
right to take his slaves, as any other property, into
the common territories of the United States, held by
the Government in trust for all citizens, no matter in
what State they resided; and that, as the Missouri
compromise was in violation of this right, it was null
and void. And that negroes, being considered by the
Constitution as only property, could not, when freed
by their masters, thereby become citizens of the
United States.

In order that this decision, which has been reversed
by one of the most terrible and bloody wars ever enacted by infuriated man, may be tested by the objections of the dissenting Judges, I will consider the
opinion of Justice Curtis; it being esteemed as embracing the whole dissenting argument.

Justice Curtis, when he comes to the main question,—

and I shall consider none other,— looks at it through the pinhole of a provincial creed, which excluded all the light of history by which alone the question could be properly understood. One sentence embraces the pith of his dissenting doctrine. "Slavery," says Justice Curtis, " being contrary to natural right, is created only by municipal law." From his doctrine, that slavery is *created* only by municipal law, he argues that a citizen of the United States cannot take his slaves into a territory, and own them there, because the Constitution of the United States " has neither made nor provided for any municipal regulations which are essential to the existence of slavery."

The doctrine that slavery was created by municipal law, is one of the most extraordinary aberrations from a great fundamental principle of public law to be found in the history of judicial administration ; and that one of such well - ordered faculties as Justice Curtis should have enunciated such a doctrine in a case of so much import, can only be accounted for by the bias of the political aspect of the question. Mr. Curtis should have remembered that Plato based the lawfulness of slavery upon the ground of captivity in war ; and that, following this theoretical view of the matter, the Roman jurists, more than fifteen centuries ago, based it upon the same ground, and established it as a principle of Roman jurisprudence that slavery originated in the *jus gentium,* the law of nations. And the institution of slavery, in all the nations of Europe, was recognized, by publicists, as reposing upon a right originating in, and protected by, the law of nations. If a slave ran away, the owner had a right, under the law of nations, which was the law of every State, to capture him in any country to which he may have escaped, and carry him home, like any other property. This right is shown by the following extract from a letter written by Vatinius, Governor of Illyricum, to Cicero : " Being informed that the slave you employed as your reader, had run away from you into the country of the Vardaei, I have caused diligent search to be made after him, although I did not receive your commands for that purpose. I doubt not of recovering him, unless he should take refuge in Dalmatia; and even in that case, I do not entirely despair." Where any right is recognized by the law of nations, it would be a breach of comity for any State to deny a remedy to one seeking the enjoyment of that right, whether to a slave or to the enforcement of a contract recognized by the law of nations. The Roman law, as every jurist knows, puts slavery, and almost all contracts, upon the same legal basis, of having been introduced by the law of nations. No State can abrogate the legal right to a slave escaping from another State; but it may refuse a remedy, just as it may refuse a remedy upon a contract, because every State is sovereign over the remedies in its forums.

That African slavery, like the slavery under the Roman dominion, originated in the law of nations, or in the common practice of European States of dealing in negroes as ordinary merchandise, with no rights to be respected, being, as it was thought, an inferior order of beings, is a fact of history so indubitable, that only egregious ignorance or a blinding fanaticism can deny it. As an inferior order of beings, having no human rights, negroes were brought as property, called slavery, into all the colonial settlements of America. They were property on the shores of Africa, were received as property into the slave-ships, were held as property on the ocean, and were sold as property to the white inhabitants of the American colonies. It is difficult for a publicist to treat with respectful forbearance the doctrine that such a right of property was "created only by municipal law." And even down to and after the Declaration of Independence, negroes were so little thought of as human beings, that they were not considered as embraced in the words of that instrument, but were, as we have seen, advertised for sale in the same paper published in Massachusetts in which that instrument was first declared to the people of that Commonwealth in July, 1776.

But the reason which Justice Curtis gives for his extraordinary doctrine, that slavery was *created only* by municipal law, is even more extraordinary than the doctrine. "Being contrary to natural right" is the reason upon which he rests the doctrine. Certainly, Roman slavery was contrary to natural right; and surely he will not say that was created by municipal law, in the face of all Roman jurists to the contrary. Can it be that Justice Curtis was led into this extraordinary doctrine by reading mistranslations of Justinian's Institutes, where the words *servitus contra naturam* are rendered *slavery is contrary to natural right*, and, confusedly remembering that the law of nations is sometimes called, by jurists, the law of nature, jumped to the conclusion that slavery, being contrary to natural right, cannot be created by the law of nations, which is the law of nature, therefore it must be created by municipal law?

The law of nature, in the writings of jurists, is a very ambiguous thought. It sometimes means opposite things. Cicero, in the first book and third chapter of the Tusculan Questions, makes the consent of all nations in regard to any thing the law of nature. *Omni in re consensio omnium gentium lex naturæ putanda est.* Gaius, who wrote about two centuries after Cicero, makes no allusion, in treating of slavery in his Commentaries on the Roman law, to the *jus naturale,* law of nature. But Ulpian introduced the *jus naturale,* by way of theoretical completeness, into Roman law; and it was afterwards incorporated into Justinian's Institutes, which were published in the year 533 of the Christian era. In order to understand

what is meant by the *jus naturale, law of nature,* in
Roman jurisprudence, we must refer to a passage in
the first book and second title of Justinian's Institutes.
"The law of nature is that law which nature teaches
to all animals. For this law does not belong exclusively to the human race, but belongs to all animals,
whether of the earth, the air, or the water. Hence
proceeds the union of male and female, which we term
matrimony; hence the procreation and education of
children. We see, indeed, that all other animals besides man are considered as having a knowledge of
this law." It is seen that this law of nature is not a
moral law at all. Nothing ethical is involved in its
meaning. It merely describes relations in the order
of nature, which suggest the notion of law, like physical law binding things in certain relations. When,
therefore, in the first book and second title of Justinian's Institutes, it is said that slavery is contrary to
the law of nature, it means such a law as that just
mentioned. And when it is said to be contrary to
nature, the same thing is meant. Slavery does not
come by nature; it is not a natural relation like that
of children. It comes by the law of nations.

Dr. Harris, more than a hundred years ago, translated *contra naturam, contrary to natural right;* and
Dr. Cooper and others have adopted his blunder.
When the commissioners of Justinian came to sys-
tematize the Roman law, they introduced, as Ulpian

had done, ideas drawn from the philosophy of the
Stoics. This philosophy classed some things as *according to nature*, and other things as *contrary to
nature*. The commissioners carried this theory into
the Roman law. The notion of *natural right* had not
yet entered into human thought. It did not enter the
mind of man till ages had elapsed after the publication of the Institutes of Justinian. It is a purely
modern notion. In considering moral questions and,
much more, political questions, Pagan civilization
looked at them solely from the point of *duty*, never
from the point of *right*. All Pagan ethical philosophy culminated in the *De Officiis* of Cicero; and in
that treatise virtues and duties only are discussed. To
ascribe to the Roman Jurists the doctrine that slavery
is contrary to *natural right*, or *right of any kind*, is to
ignore the spirit of the Imperial Jurists, and of the
civilization of the epoch. The Romans did not possess the abstract idea of rights. Though Justinian
had, by an edict in the year 529, closed the schools
of Athens, and thereby Paganism was extinguished,
still Christianity, out of which the abstract idea of
rights has emerged, had but little influence on jurisprudence at that time.

Having postulated that slavery is created only by
municipal law, Justice Curtis argues that slave property cannot exist in the territories, because the Constitution of the United States "has neither made nor

provided for any municipal regulations which are essential to the existence of slavery." Now, Justice Curtis seems to have forgotten that it was the opinion even of Mr. Jefferson that the United States had no authority to acquire any territory when Louisiana was purchased by him. Then, surely, the Constitution could not have provided for any municipal regulations essential to the existence of slavery in territories never to be, in contemplation of the Constitution, procured. Mr. Webster, late in life, expressed the opinion that the Constitution never contemplated the acquisition of any more territory. And this was the opinion of all public men who can be considered publicists.

Down to the formation of the Articles of Confederation, so entirely did the comity between the Colonies enable masters to recover runaway slaves, that no provision on the subject was incorporated into the articles. But when the Constitution was framed, as slavery was no longer valuable in the Northern States, those States where it was valuable, deemed it important to incorporate into the Constitution a provision containing the principle of the comity in regard to fugitive slaves, which had always existed between the Colonies when all were interested in that species of property; and it was accordingly done.

All must rejoice when men once slaves have so far improved as to become freemen, occupying a sphere of

higher duties and higher rights. But to speak of the
institution of slavery as political sciolists do, as an
unmitigated evil, crime, and sin, only betrays an ignorant presumption. It is coeval with human society;
and it is the one great educational institution by
which, for thousands of years, the lowest classes of
people in all nations have, in the progress of society,
been raised up from barbarism to a degree of intelligence and self-control, when their restraints can be
removed. The greatest thinker of antiquity, Aristotle,
and who looked, perhaps, more profoundly into all
forms of human polity and institutions than any
thinker even since his time, based slavery upon the
law of nature, as co-ordinate with the other social
relations, and originating in the necessities and good
of society. He saw so profoundly into the great
order of nature, that he acquired the philosophical
title of "The Interpreter of Nature," — "'Αριστοτέλης
τῆς φυσέως γραμματεὺς ἦν." And when Christianity
was sent into the world, slavery was a distinguishing
feature of the social arrangements of both the Jewish
and the Gentile world. Christianity did not single it
out for reprobation, but recognized it as a lawful institution, and gave precepts for regulating the relation
of master and slave, as it did for the other social
relations.

We must look at the institution of slavery as publicists, and not as casuists. It is a question of law, and

not a case of conscience. Chief-Justice Marshall, in the year 1825, in the case of the slave-ship *Antelope*, in the Supreme Court, 10 Wheaton Reports, in pronouncing that the slave-trade was authorized by the law of nations, said, "Slavery, then, has its origin in force; but as the world has agreed that it is a legitimate result of force, the state of things which is thus produced by general consent cannot be pronounced unlawful." Many of the fundamental rules of the law of nations have no moral foundation. By the law of nations, the States of Europe claimed that, by the mere fact of the discovery of America, as it was inhabited by heathen barbarians, they acquired the absolute title and dominion in the soil, and that the aboriginal inhabitants had a mere right of occupation and use. And in the case of Johnson *vs.* McIntosh, in 8 Wheaton Reports, in the year 1823, Chief-Justice Marshall, delivering the opinion of the Supreme Court, decided that, because of the law of nations, the Indians have only the right of possession to their lands, and cannot sell them except to the United States. And force is recognized by the law of nations as the final arbiter in political disputes. And even the most flagrant usurpations are recognized by public law as having established legitimate governments. Radicalism looks at all questions of public law as cases of conscience; and is, therefore, ever on a crusade against the perennial institutions of society. And it should ever be remembered that, — at the time when conscience played the most important part in the politics of Europe, — by the laws of Oleron, which were recognized every-where, infidels were put upon the same footing with pirates, as perpetual enemies, and subject to the extreme rights of war.

Each age fixes the standard of right and wrong, of legality and illegality, for itself; and all its rights of every kind, and the corresponding duties and obligations express and implied, descend to the next age, binding it just as they bound the previous age, who fixed the standard by which the obligations were contracted or incurred. In order to do justice, therefore, all rights, or claims of rights, which originate at each epoch, must be determined by the opinions of that epoch, and not by the opinions of subsequent times. This is the doctrine of political and legal justice. "Private opinions," said Lord Stowell, in deciding the lawfulness of the slave-trade, "cannot be carried into public judgments on the quality of actions." When the enlightened opinion of this century first condemned the slave-trade, and, afterwards, the institution of slavery, all nations and all communities who had co-operated in establishing slavery, and had shared in the profits of the trade, should have shared in the losses of its abolition. This would be political justice.

I rejoice that slavery no longer exists in our country ; and as it is now a historical question, it is a part of my duty to pass upon it such reflections as may enable all men to think wisely in regard to the real question which was involved in the judgment pronounced by Chief-Justice Taney in the Dred Scott case.

The opinion of Chief Justice Taney, in the Dred Scott case, had hardly been read in open Court, before the panders of the Free-soil party circulated, by all means of communication, over every place where a voter lived, that the Chief Justice had proclaimed, as his personal opinion and not as a matter of public law, that negroes have no rights which a white man is bound to respect. A sentiment so atrocious, notwithstanding the elevated position the Chief Justice had attained, as we have seen, in public estimation, was readily believed, and is still believed by perhaps a majority of the people of the United States, had been really expressed by the Chief Justice. In the wild, willing imaginations of the party in whose path to power the Dred Scott decision was a stumbling-block, the Chief Justice appeared as a monster robed in the habiliments of justice, in collusion with the Democratic party, and delivering unrighteous judgments in their interests. In the midst of this frantic state of party feeling, the territory of Kansas, in the winter of 1858, petitioned Congress to be admitted into the Union with a Constitution allowing slavery. Whether the Constitution expressed the wishes of the people of the

territory or not, I have never been able to satisfy myself; but whether it did, or did not, was not of the
slightest weight in the contest then waging in Congress.   It had become the fixed purpose of the Free-
soil party, that no slave State should ever be admitted
into the Union.   The question of slavery had been
discussed for forty years, and had now passed beyond
the frontier of reason.   There was one man, prominent
in the politics of the country, who had been for many
years striving to fix it as a system of policy, that the
country should be governed by sectional animosities.
He hoped to wield the animosities of the strong section against the weak, with his own hand, from the
Presidential chair.   That man was William H. Seward.
He was now a Senator from the great State of New
York.   By no means forgetting that he had sought the
moral influence of the name of Chief-Justice Taney,
as we have seen, to influence the public mind on a
measure in which, perhaps, he was interested in other
ways than as a Senator, but regardless of the fact, he
now denounces him for another purpose of his own.
It was on the 3d day of March, 1858, in his speech on
the bill for the admission of Kansas into the Union,
that William H. Seward, as Senator of the United
States, uttered the following grave accusations against
Chief-Justice Taney in his judicial character.   " At
this juncture, the new Federal administration came in,
under a President [Buchanan] who had obtained suc-

cess by the intervention at the polls of a third party—an ephemeral organization built upon a foreign and frivolous issue, which had just strength enough and life enough to give to a pro-slavery party the aid required to produce that untoward result. The new President, under a show of moderation, masked a more effectual intervention than that of his predecessor, in favor of slave labor and a slave State. Before coming into office, he approached, or was approached, by the Supreme Court of the United States. On their docket was, through some chance or design, an action which an obscure negro man, in Missouri, had brought for his freedom against his reputed master. The Court had arrived at the conclusion, on solemn argument, that, inasmuch as this unfortunate negro had, through some ignorance or chicane in special pleading, admitted what could not have been proved, that he had descended from some African who had been held in bondage, therefore he was not, in view of the Constitution, a citizen of the United States, and therefore could not implead the reputed master in the Federal Courts; and on this ground the Supreme Court was prepared to dismiss the action for want of jurisdiction over the suitor's person. This decision, certainly as repugnant to the Declaration of Independence and the spirit of the Constitution as to the instincts of humanity, nevertheless would be one which would exhaust all the power of the tribunal, and exclude consideration of all other questions that had been raised upon the record. The counsel who had appeared for the negro had volunteered from motives of charity, and ignorant, of course, of the disposition which was to be made of the cause, had argued that his client had been freed from slavery by operation of the Missouri prohibition of 1820. The opposing counsel, paid by the defending slave-holder, had insisted, in reply, that that famous statute was unconstitutional. The mock debate had been heard in the chamber of the Court, in the basement of the Capitol, in the presence of the curious visitors at the seat of Government, whom the dulness of a judicial investigation could not disgust. The Court did not hesitate to please the incoming President, by seizing the extraneous and idle forensic discussion, and converting it into an occasion for pronouncing an opinion that the Missouri prohibition was void; and that, by force of the Constitution, slavery existed, with all the elements of property in man over man, in all the territories of the United States, paramount to any popular sovereignty within the territories, and even to the authority of Congress itself.

"In this ill-omened act the Supreme Court forgot its own dignity, which had always before been maintained with just judicial jealousy. They forgot that the province of a Court is simply '*jus dicere*,' and not at all '*jus dare*.' They forgot, also, that one ' foul sentence does more harm than many foul examples ;

for the last do but corrupt the stream, while the former corrupteth the fountain.' And they and the President alike forgot that judicial usurpation is more odious and intolerable than any other among the manifold practices of tyranny.

"The day of inauguration came, the first one, among all the celebrations of that great national pageant, that was to be desecrated by a coalition between the Executive and Judicial departments to undermine the national legislature and the liberties of the people. The President, attended by the usual lengthened procession, arrived, and took his seat on the portico. The Supreme Court attended him there, in robes which yet exacted public reverence. The people, unaware of the import of the whisperings carried on between the President and the Chief Justice, and imbued with veneration for both, filled the avenues and gardens far away as the eye could reach. The President addressed them in words as bland as those which the worst of all the Roman emperors pronounced when he assumed the purple. He announced (vaguely, indeed, but with self-satisfaction,) the forthcoming extra-judicial exposition of the Constitution, and pledged his submission to it as authoritative and final. The Chief Justice and his Associates remained silent. The Senate, too, were there — constitutional witnesses of the transfer of administration. They, too, were silent, although the promised usurpation was to subvert the authority over more than half of the empire which Congress had assumed contemporaneously with the birth of the nation, and had exercised, without interruption, for nearly seventy years. It cost the President, under the circumstances, little exercise of magnanimity now to promise to the people of Kansas — on whose neck he had, with the aid of the Supreme Court, hung the millstone of slavery — a fair trial in their attempt to cast it off and hurl it to the earth when they should come to organize a State government. Alas! that even this cheap promise, uttered under such great solemnities, was only made to be broken.

"The pageant ended. On the 5th of March, the Judges, without even exchanging their silken robes for courtiers' gowns, paid their salutations to the President in the Executive palace. Doubtless the President received them as graciously as Charles the First did the Judges who had, at his instance, subverted the statutes of English liberty. On the 6th of March, the Supreme Court dismissed the negro suitor, Dred Scott, to return to his bondage; and having thus disposed of that private action for an alleged private wrong, on the ground of want of jurisdiction in the case, they proceeded with mock solemnity to pronounce the opinion that, if they had had such jurisdiction, still the unfortunate negro would have had to remain in bondage unrelieved, because the Missouri prohibition violates rights of general property involved in slavery, paramount to the authority of Congress. A few days later, copies of this opinion were multiplied by the Senate's press, and scattered in the name of the Senate broadcast over the land; and their publication has not yet been disowned by the Senate. Simultaneously, Dred Scott, who had played the hand of *dummy* in this interesting political game, unwillingly, yet to the complete satisfaction of his adversary, was voluntarily emancipated; and thus received from his master, as a reward, the freedom which the Court had denied him as a right.

"The new President of the United States having organized this formidable judicial battery at the Capitol, was now ready to begin his active demonstrations of intervention in the territory."

This bungling sketch of an historical scene, by unskilful literary ambition, is an unmitigated calumny from beginning to end, invented by a bad man to serve in his machinations for the Presidency.

William H. Seward, in his place as Senator of the United States, thus charged in an elaborate and carefully prepared speech, which has since been published in one of the volumes of his printed writings, a corrupt coalition between the chief executive magistrate of the Union and the Judges of the Supreme Court of the United States. He charges — and his charge is put into a form to enter into history — that the Judges of our highest Court, and the parties to the Dred Scott case, got up a mock trial, to serve a purpose in a political game, by previous agreement with the President-elect of the United States.   Chief-Justice Taney is represented as whispering the terms of the nefarious bargain into the ear of the President at the very moment when he was administering to him the oath of office, by which the majesty of Heaven was invoked to witness the purity of his intentions in the administration of the government of his country.

By way of answer to this base accusation, it is only necessary to state, for the information of future ages, that years before Mr. Buchanan was even a candidate for the Presidency, and years before even the meeting of the Congress of 1854, which passed the Kansas-Nebraska Act, Dred Scott had sought his freedom by a suit in the State Courts of Missouri.   It reached the Supreme Court of Missouri, and was decided adversely to Dred Scott, as early as 1852.   In November, 1853, because of failure in the State Courts, the case was carried into the Federal Court in the city of St. Louis.   The Kansas bill, which Mr. Seward made the occasion of his charges, as though the case was got up to aid in its passage, was not, at that time, even in the imagination of any one.   The case was decided in the lower Federal Court, and was taken by writ of error to the Supreme Court of the United States while Mr. Buchanan was in England as American Minister.   The case came upon the docket of the Supreme Court by the agency of the parties, like any other case; and after argument and re-argument it was, in the regular order of the docket, decided.

Mr. Seward could not have believed one word of his charges. He knew the truth; but it was of no use to him, and I believe hardly ever is to a man of crooked ways.

In order to make his charge of judicial corruption the more pointed, Mr. Seward alleged that the Court said they had no jurisdiction over the case, but nevertheless decided it. So far from this being true, every Judge held that the Court had jurisdiction over the merits of the case; though they were divided in regard to jurisdiction over the plea in abatement. This allegation of Mr. Seward was made in order that the decision might be considered an *obiter dictum*, and therefore not binding as a precedent.

As Chief-Justice Taney has been singled out for the vituperation of a political party, and of fanatics all over the world, I publish the following letters from Mr. Justice Campbell and Mr. Justice Nelson, the only surviving Judges, except Mr. Curtis, who sat in the Dred Scott case. From delicacy, I did not ask a letter from Mr. Curtis. The letters will show the course of Chief-Justice Taney in the consultation-room, and vindicate him from all purpose to give the case a political bearing on the issue with which Mr. Seward endeavored to connect it.

New Orleans, Nov. 24, 1870.

My Dear Sir: — Your letter of the 18th inst., requesting me to communicate "the facts or history of
the decision in the case of Dred Scott," that you may
vindicate the late Chief-Justice Taney from the imputation of complicity with Mr. Buchanan, has been received. I am aware of no objection to the statement
of any fact concerning the judgment, but I hesitate to
believe that testimony is required to relieve the name
of the Chief Justice from a charge so improbable,
and so obviously calumnious and spiteful. The case of
Dred Scott was argued for the first time in the spring
of 1856.

There were several discussions at the conferences of
the Judges upon the case. There was much division
among them, and especially upon the first question
presented. This was whether a plea in abatement that
decided that Dred Scott was a citizen of Missouri, or
capable of maintaining a suit in the Courts of the
United States, because he was a negro of African
descent, and his ancestors were African negroes imported and held as slaves, was for consideration. The
minority of the Court, at that time, were of opinion
that this plea was not open for examination, nor
the judgment on it for review, because a demurrer
had been filed to it, and sustained. The defendant had
then pleaded to the merits, and had succeeded in the
action. The writ of error had been taken by Dred
Scott, whose demurrer to the plea in abatement had
been sustained, and the judgment upon it submitted to
and complied with on the part of the defendant by
answering over.

This minority was composed of Justices McLean, Catron, Grier, and Campbell. The majority were Chief-Justice Taney, Justices Wayne, Nelson, Daniel, and Curtis. Justice Nelson hesitated, and proposed a re-argument of that and other questions to be had at the next term, and this was assented to, none objecting.

At the next term, these questions were again argued. Upon the re-argument, Justice Nelson's opinion concurred with that of the minority above mentioned, and they, by this addition, became the majority. Each of these Judges has recorded in his opinion that there was nothing in the plea in abatement before the Court for review. I understand that four of them have decided that the plaintiff, Dred Scott, was a slave upon the facts established on the trial, and that he was not capable of maintaining a suit in the Courts of the United States for that cause.

The other question of political, sectional, and party interest arose upon the fact that Dred Scott, while in the service of his master, went with him to a place in the present State of Minnesota, north of the Missouri line, and remained there two years in attendance on him, when he returned to Missouri. This was about fifteen years before the suit. He claimed that he became free under the operation of the Act of Congress of the 6th of March, 1820, prohibiting slavery in the territory north of 36° 30′ north latitude. The majority of the Court determined that the Act of Congress did not operate upon Dred Scott under the particular circumstances of his case, and also that it was inoperative in any case to liberate a slave. The instruction of the majority, in reference to the preparation of this

opinion, was to limit the opinion to the particular circumstances of Dred Scott; and Mr. Justice Nelson
prepared his opinion, on file, under this instruction, to
be read as the opinion of the Court. Subsequently,
and before it was read, upon a motion of Mr. Justice
Wayne, who stated that the case had created public
interest and expectation, that it had been twice argued,
that an impression existed that the questions argued
would be considered in the opinion of the Court, he
proposed that the Chief Justice should write an opinion
on all of the questions as the opinion of the Court.
This was assented to; some reserving to themselves to
qualify their assent as the opinion might require.
Others of the Court proposed to have no question, save
one, discussed. It was under these circumstances that
the Chief Justice undertook that opinion. The motion
of Mr. Justice Wayne was made without any notice to
me, and I do not know that he gave notice to any one
of the members of the Court. The apprehension had
been expressed by others of the Court, that the
Court would not fulfil public expectation or discharge
its duties by maintaining silence upon these questions;
and my impression is, that several opinions had
already been begun among the members of the Court,
in which a full discussion of the case was made, before
Justice Wayne made this proposal.

I have not the slightest information of any connection between Mr. Buchanan or any other person, with
the discussions in the Court or the conference, or with
the preparation of any opinion of either of the Judges,
save the Judges themselves.

Very respectfully, yours,   J. A. CAMPBELL.
SAMUEL TYLER, ESQ.

I left this letter from Judge Campbell with Mr. Justice Nelson, and requested him to give me his views in regard to its contents. In answer, he wrote me the following letter:

WASHINGTON, May 13, 1871.

DEAR SIR: — I have read with care the letter of Judge Campbell, dated 24 Nov., 1870, addressed to you on the subject of the opinion in the "Dred Scott case," and concur with him as it respects the facts or history of the decision in that case so far as they came within my knowledge. I was not present when the majority decided to change the ground of the decision, and assigned the preparation of the opinion to the Chief Justice, and, when advised of the change, I simply gave notice that I should read the opinion I had prepared as my own, and which is the one on file. The accuracy and fulness with which Judge Campbell has stated the facts render it unnecessary to go over them.

Yours, truly,   S. NELSON.
SAMUEL TYLER, ESQ.

Soon after Mr. Seward uttered the abuse of the Supreme Court, and of Chief-Justice Taney in particular, which I am noticing, a public meeting was held in Baltimore, which Mr. Reverdy Johnson was invited to address. As his engagements at Washington were such that he could not be present at the meeting, he wrote a letter of excuse, dated March 6th, 1858, from which I make the following extract. "It was but the other day, that a Senator [Mr. Seward] from a North-

ern State — a State, more interested, perhaps, if that be
possible, than any other in the undisturbed continuance of the Union, and whose past and present position
should have taught him better, — in a speech carefully
elaborated, and in print before spoken, desecrated the
Senate - chamber by virtually threatening the South
with early practical subjugation ; hurling the bitterest
anathemas at their system of labor, denouncing it as at
war with the Declaration of Independence, repugnant
to the instincts of humanity, and an outrage upon the
laws of God.   Never was there a more direct incentive
to servile insurrection.   Could the slaves of the South
hear such teachings, and be as mad and reckless as the
speaker, many a homestead would swim in blood, and
many a cry would find its way to the throne of
Heaven, invoking retributive justice upon the author
of its agony.   Even a co-ordinate branch of the
Government, because only of its having differed with
him on a question of constitutional law judicially before it, in a due course of legal proceeding, was, and
evidently from mere party ends, subjected to as calumnious an attack as ever dishonored human lips.   These
are strong terms to apply to a Senator of the United
States ; but the relation which I held to what is known
as the Dred Scott case, and which furnished the pretext for the libel, and the knowledge which this gives
me, justifies me in their use.   There is not, I know, a
word of truth in his direct charges, nor the slightest

foundation for the uncharitable and unmanly insinuations in which he indulged. The case itself was originally commenced by Scott, under the advice of counsel,— no advocate of slavery,— in one of the State Courts of Missouri. This was done in perfect good faith, and with no view to political effect there or elsewhere; and the defence was carried on in the same spirit. The judgment of that Court was in favor of Scott; but, on writ of error, sued out by the master, it was reversed, and the case remanded for final judgment. Scott's counsel then abandoned that case, and instituted another for the like purpose in the Circuit Court of the United States for that district. By that Court his legality to sue, if free, was maintained; but on the merits, the judgment was against him, when he and his counsel — *not the master or the master's counsel* — brought the controversy to the Supreme Court of the United States.

"This was all done before the Kansas and Nebraska Act was passed or anticipated. On the first hearing in that Court, the argument for Scott was made by Mr. Blair, and for the master by Mr. Geyer (one of the Senators from Missouri), and myself. A re-argument was ordered, and that was conducted by Mr. Blair and Mr. G. W. Curtis (the brother of Mr. Justice Curtis) for Scott, and with signal ability; and the master was again represented by Mr. Geyer and myself. The Senator's insinuation that the case was made by the

master for the purpose of obtaining a decision by the
Supreme Court is so far from being true, that the
suspicion at the time was that the political friends of
the Senator — the abolitionists — had had it instituted
and brought here with that exclusive end. But this
was equally unfounded, as was stated by Mr. Blair in
open Court, and a few days afterwards in a communication to the *National Intelligencer*.

"The allegation, also, that the counsel of the defendant slave-holder were paid by him, is in keeping with
the recklessness of this portion of the entire speech.
It is absolutely untrue. The questions that the case
involved were mentioned to me by a Southern gentleman; and always entertaining the opinion afterwards
announced by the Supreme Court, and seeing, as I
thought, how deeply the country was interested in
their decision, I volunteered to argue the case for the
defendant, and never received, or would have received,
the ordinary compensation. My colleague was, I am
certain, actuated by the same motives, and was re-
warded only by a sense of duty performed. The
charge that the majority of the Judges, in ruling the
Missouri restriction unconstitutional, acted extra-judi-
cially, I leave every lawyer to decide, after he shall
have read the opinion of the venerable Chief Justice.
If that does not convince him of the utter ground-
lessness of the complaint, all reason or authority would
be lost upon him. In this respect, however, there is

one view which the public generally cannot fail, I think, readily to comprehend, that what may have passed at the consultations of the Court no one perhaps but the Judges will ever know.   But this would seem to be obvious, that if it was the duty of the dissenting Judges, Messrs. McLean and Curtis, to pass upon a question of such importance, and to argue it with unwonted zeal and rare ability, and with a practical appeal to Northern prepossession and sympathy calculated to impress upon the public mind of that section a conviction of the right of Congress to prohibit slave labor in the territories then or thereafter to belong to the Union, — a power so pregnant with danger to our continuance as one people, — it was equally proper that the Judges who entertained a different opinion should have expressed it, and maintained it with all the ability and research within their power.

"Mr. Justice McLean's opinion occupies thirty-five pages of the Report, in 19th Howard, and Mr. Justice Curtis's opinion one hundred and three.   The greater part of each is devoted to this very question, and as to the right to consider and decide it.   The last-named Judge concludes his with an apology for its length by saying the 'questions are so numerous, and the grave importance of some of them require me to exhibit the grounds of my opinion.   I have treated no question which, in the view I have taken, it was not absolutely necessary for me to pass upon to ascertain whether the

judgment of the Circuit Court should stand or be
reversed. I have avoided no question on which the
validity of that judgment depends. To have done
either more or less, would have been inconsistent with
my sense of duty.'

"Were these two opinions to be spread, as they were,
with unexampled haste, broadcast over the land, and
the rest of the Court, who differed so widely and so
decidedly, to remain silent? Were they, by that very
silence, to leave the public to infer, as they might then
have fairly done, that they did not, or were unable, to
maintain different doctrine? Assuming, therefore, —
what is, I think, palpably unsound, — that the decision
of the Court on this question was in any sense extra-
judicial, I hold it to be perfectly clear that the course
adopted by the dissenting Judges rendered it the duty
of the Court to correct, to the whole extent of their
power, what they believed to be the serious constitutional errors which that course, if left unobstructed,
was likely to fasten upon the public judgment. But,
not content with assailing the motives of the South by
totally misrepresenting them, and the alleged extra-
judicial character of the Court's decision, the independence and integrity of the Judges were shamelessly
impeached. No gentleman can be guilty of the injustice even of supposing that it can be necessary to
vindicate them against such a charge, coming from
such a quarter, and dictated by unhallowed party

motives so obviously apparent. With lives honestly spent in the service of their country in almost every department in which she could be served, without stain or blemish, and with constantly increasing honor; with a judicial career, by its admitted ability, learning, and independence, challenging the respect and admiration of the good and the wise; with every incentive to continue to the last the pure administrators of the jurisdiction with which the Constitution clothes them, and especially the watchful guardians of all the rights, personal and political, secured by that sacred instrument, which may, by proper judicial proceeding, be submitted to them, — with all these persuasions to duty, the charge that they have been at last false to it, and, forgetful of honest fame, have pandered to party or Executive influence, is a slander so gross and revolting, that, instead of finding a lodgment in, it cannot but ultimately, if not at once, disgust the public mind."

In such abhorrence did Chief-Justice Taney hold the conduct of Mr. Seward, in so wantonly assailing the Supreme Court, that he told me, if Mr. Seward had been nominated and elected President instead of Mr. Lincoln, he should, if requested, as was customary, have refused to administer to him the official oath, and thereby proclaim to the nation that he would not administer that oath to such a man.

I now leave Mr. Seward, as the accuser of Chief-

Justice Taney, to the calm judgment of his fellow-men.

Antislavery, which had long ago denounced the Constitution of the United States as " a covenant with death and an agreement with hell," had now become openly rebellious against Federal authority in such an important and defiant manner, that it had assumed a judicial form because of positive violation of law, and the case was brought to the Supreme Court of the United States. And one year after Mr. Seward, in the Senate of the United States, had poured out his abuse upon Chief-Justice Taney, that patriotic magistrate delivered one of his most important, and to himself one of the most satisfactory (as he told me), opinions against this incipient treason. The case arose under the fugitive slave law. It was the State of Wisconsin, both by its Courts and Legislature, that openly defied the judicial authority of the Supreme Court of the United States.

There were two cases; both, however, constituting one transaction, which originated under the fugitive slave law passed in 1850, as one of the great measures of pacification of Mr. Clay, of which I have already spoken.

Sherman M. Booth had, in the State of Wisconsin, aided and abetted the escape of a fugitive slave from the United States Deputy Marshal who had him in custody, under a warrant issued by the District Judge

of the United States for that district, under the Act
of Congress of 1850. On the 4th of January, 1855,
Booth was indicted, in the District Court, by the
grand jury, for the offence. He was tried by a jury,
found guilty, and was sentenced to imprisonment for
one month, and to pay a fine of a thousand dollars,
and remain in custody until the sentence was complied with. Upon application to the Supreme Court
of the State of Wisconsin, the prisoner was released
upon *habeas corpus* by that Court. Then upon a
petition of the Attorney-General of the United States
to the Chief Justice of the Supreme Court of the
United States, based upon a certified copy of the proceedings, a writ of error was allowed and issued, to
bring the judgment of the Supreme Court of Wisconsin before the Supreme Court of the United States, to
correct the error of the judgment. The Supreme Court
of Wisconsin thereupon directed its Clerk to make
no return to the writ of error, and to enter no order
upon the journals or record of the Court concerning
the same. And accordingly the Clerk contumaciously
refused to make return to the mandate of the Supreme
Court of the United States. It was, in fact, the con-
tumacy of the Supreme Court of Wisconsin: first,
taking a prisoner from the custody of the law of the
United States, defying the grand jury who indicted
him, the jury who found him guilty, and the District Court that passed sentence upon him; and then

refusing to permit the Supreme Court of the United States to review their conduct for withdrawing a case from a Federal Court.

Upon this open nullification of the process of the Supreme Court of the United States by the State Court, the Supreme Court of the United States, under a rule laid, ordered the certified copy of the record of the Supreme Court of Wisconsin, which the Attorney-General had before procured, to be entered on its docket, to have the same effect and legal operation as if returned by the Clerk with the writ of error. Thus the judicial nullification of Federal authority was baffled by the regular order of practice being adapted to the exigency; and the case stood on the docket for review.

Chief-Justice Taney, in the opening of his opinion, in speaking of the extraordinary claim of a State to set aside and annul a judgment of a Federal Court, and discharge a prisoner who had been tried and found guilty of an offence against the laws of the United States, and sentenced to imprisonment, said, "These propositions are new in the jurisprudence of the United States, as well as of the States; and the supremacy of the State Courts over the Courts of the United States, in cases arising under the Constitution and laws of the United States, is now for the first time asserted and acted upon in the Supreme Court of a State."

The Chief Justice then proceeded in an argument

which may well be termed a bulwark of the Constitution of the United States. It defines, with boundaries of light, the respective spheres of Federal and State sovereignty. "Although," says he, "the State of Wisconsin is sovereign within its territorial limits to a certain extent, yet that sovereignty is limited and restricted by the Constitution of the United States. And the powers of the general Government and of the State, although both exist and are exercised within the same territorial limits, are yet separate and distinct sovereignties, acting separately and independently of each other within their respective spheres. And the sphere of action appropriated to the United States is as far beyond the reach of the judicial process issued by a State Judge or a State Court, as if the line of division was traced by landmarks and monuments visible to the eye. And the State of Wisconsin had no more power to authorize these proceedings of its Judges and Courts than it would have had if the prisoner had been confined in Michigan, or in any other State of the Union, for an offence against the laws of the State in which he was imprisoned."

The Chief Justice then proceeds to define the scope of the judicial power granted to the Supreme Court of the United States, and enumerates the general constitutional questions that belong to its jurisdiction. "And as the final appellate power in all such questions," says the Chief Justice, "is given to this Court,

controversies, as to the respective powers of the United
States and the States, instead of being determined by
military and physical force, are heard, investigated, and
finally settled, with the calmness and deliberation of
judicial inquiry.   And no one can fail to see, that, if
such an arbiter had not been provided in our complicated system of government, internal tranquillity
could not have been preserved ; and if such controversies were left to the arbitrament of physical force,
our Government, State and National, would cease to be
governments of laws, and revolutions by force of arms
would take the place of Courts of justice and judicial
decisions."

After showing that, in organizing the Supreme
Court of the United States, its function was considered
so high and indispensable in the working of so complex a system of government that the great statesmen
of the time made the Court a part of the Constitution
itself, the Chief Justice said : "So long, therefore, as
this Constitution shall endure, this tribunal must exist
with it, deciding in the peaceful forms of judicial proceeding the angry and irritating controversies between
sovereignties, which in other countries have been
determined by the arbitrament of force."

After saying that, in the judgment of the Court,
the Act of Congress of 1850, commonly called the
fugitive slave law, is, in all its provisions, constitutional, and that all the proceedings in the cases were

regular and conformable to law, the Chief Justice
said: "The judgment of the Supreme Court of Wisconsin must therefore be reversed in each of the cases
now before the Court."

This judgment was pronounced on the seventh of
March, 1859. The State of Wisconsin had been
watching for the judgment with a fanatical anxiety;
and, on the nineteenth of the same month, the Legislature of the State passed the following joint resolutions :

WHEREAS: The Supreme Court of the United States
has assumed appellate jurisdiction in the matter of
the petition of Sherman M. Booth for a writ of *habeas
corpus* presented and prosecuted to a final judgment
in the Supreme Court of this State, and has, without
process, or any of the forms recognized by law, assumed
the power to reverse that judgment in a matter involving the personal liberty of the citizen, asserted by
and adjusted to him by the regular course of judicial
proceedings upon the great writ of liberty secured to
the people of each State by the Constitution of the
United States :

And whereas: Such assumption of power and authority by the Supreme Court of the United States, to
become the final arbiter of the liberty of the citizen,
and to override and nullify the judgments of the State
Courts declaration thereof, is in direct conflict with
that provision of the Constitution of the United States
which secures to the people the benefits of the writ of
habeas corpus :

Therefore, *Resolved* (*the Senate concurring*), That we regard the action of the Supreme Court of the United States, in assuming jurisdiction in the case before mentioned, as an act of arbitrary power unauthorized by the Constitution, and virtually superseding the benefit of the writ of *habeas corpus*, and prostrating the rights and liberties of the people at the foot of unlimited power.

Resolved, That this assumption of jurisdiction by the Federal judiciary in the said case, and without process, is an act of undelegated power, and, therefore, without authority, void, and of no force.

Resolved, That the Government formed by the Constitution of the United States was not made the exclusive or final judge of the extent of the powers delegated to itself; but that, as in all other cases of compact among parties having no common judge, each has an equal right to judge for itself, as well of infractions as of the mode and measure of redress.

Resolved, That the principle and construction contended for by the party which now rules in the councils of the nation, that the general Government is the exclusive judge of the extent of the powers delegated to it, stop nothing short of despotism; since the *discretion* of those who administer the Government, and not the *Constitution,* would be the measure of their powers; that the several States which formed that instrument, being sovereign and independent, have the unquestionable right to judge of its infractions; and that a *positive defiance* of those sovereignties of all unauthorized acts done under color of that instrument is the rightful remedy.

Approved March 19, 1859.

This conduct of the State of Wisconsin, in first, by her Supreme Court releasing a criminal imprisoned by a Court of the United States, and then ordering its Clerk to disregard a writ of error from the Supreme Court of the United States; and, secondly, by her Legislature declaring a decision of the Supreme Court of the United States "void and of no force," "and that a *positive defiance*" of all acts of the Federal Government which it may deem unauthorized "is the rightful remedy," is without parallel for audacity in the history of our Government up to that time. From the time (about forty years ago) that the emissaries of the abolition societies of Great Britain began to inculcate their doctrines in New England, the anti-slavery sentiment had increased in intensity, until it had become an epidemic fanaticism of both countries. In England, it had infected, more or less, all classes of minds. Max Müller, the Oriental scholar, and Professor at Oxford, could not lecture in London on "the Science of Language," without venting his fanatical spleen against negro slavery in America. And even Earl Russell, in Parliament, seemed to have found relief from a moral oppression at other people's transgressions by pronouncing slavery a sin. In fact, for thirty years, there had been an active co-operation between the radicals of both England and America to overthrow the institution of slavery in the United States. This co-operation of radicals in different countries is now, through the International Society, threatening to destroy the proper order of society all over Europe and America.

South Carolina, before she threatened nullification, and even while doing so, was willing and anxious that a question involving the constitutionality of a revenue laid primarily for protection, like that by the Act of 1828, should be put into judicial form, and submitted to the Supreme Court of the United States. South Carolina had faith in that tribunal, though presided over at the time by Chief-Justice Marshall, who differed so entirely in political views from that State. But such men as William H. Seward now taught the people that the Judges of the Supreme Court were utterly corrupt; and that the Chief Justice was a monster, who could, and did, administer the official oath to the President of the United States while whispering in his ear a corrupt political bargain with him.

CHAPTER VI.

JUDICIAL LIFE.

A. D. 1860 — 1864.

A NEW era now begins in the political history of the United States. The conservative, statesmanly civilization of the Southern States, which had, by its Federal rule, conducted the country through a period of so much honor among nations and so much happiness at home, becomes entirely excluded from all influence in the working of the Federal Government. The civilization of New England, with its radical spirit, is inaugurated, to direct and control the policy of the Government and the destiny of the people.

We must now recount how this great change was brought about, and show what part Chief-Justice Taney acted in the drama of this transition from one civilization to another as the controlling power in the Government of the country.

When that great statesman, Thomas Jefferson, heard, in his retirement at Monticello, that the Missouri compromise was passed, dividing political parties by a geographical line, making them sectional instead of national, he said it was like the sound of a fire-bell in the night, and made him fear that the revolu-

tionary struggle for self-government had been in vain.
But up to this period, the Southern political doctrines
and policy of Federal administration had received
such wise and powerful aid in the Northern States,
that no political party had yet been organized upon
a geographical line. But now so complete was the
alienation of the free States from the slave States,
that even Christian churches had been broken asunder
on the question of slavery, and were divided by a
geographical line. A Christian on one side of the
line was not a Christian on the other. The United
States were, in fact, only held together by a written
Constitution, which was denounced, by a constantly
increasing political party on one side of a geographical
line, as "a covenant with death and an agreement
with hell." And the provision incorporated into the
Constitution for the special protection of the peculiar
institution, on which the present prosperity and safety
of the Southern States depended, was openly and per-
sistently violated and nullified, upon a principle whose
obligation was assumed to be above the Constitution.
A party breathing this sectional spirit, assuming the
name Republican, nominated, in May, 1860, Abraham
Lincoln, of Illinois, as their candidate for President
of the United States, and Hannibal Hamlin, of Maine,
as their candidate for Vice-President. This nomination of both candidates, contrary to unbroken usage,
from one side of the geographical line between the

slave States and the free States, proclaimed, with the
fearful sound of a fire-bell at night, the policy of the
party now aiming at the control of the Federal Government.

Three other candidates for President and Vice-
President were also nominated by three other parties;
but each presented candidates chosen from both sides
of the geographical line between the slave and free
States. They were national parties, deprecating sectional strife, and stood upon the national ground that
their candidates must represent both the North and
the South, pledged to a policy of equal protection to
every section of the country.

It was felt by all who could forecast coming events,
that the question was now presented in the political
issue, whether the Constitution and Union were to be
one and inseparable in the future, as they had been in
the past, or the Union preserved and the Constitution
disregarded. For those conversant with the history
of popular movements inspired by one idea, foresaw
that the Republican party, if successful in the election
of their candidates, would be hurried on, even in spite
of itself, by the mere momentum of a developing idea,
from step to step — the opinions and conscience of the
party changing as it moved — to the entire extirpation
of the institution of slavery. Mr. Lincoln but uttered
this truth, when, at Springfield, Illinois, in 1858, he
said, in his speech to the Convention which nominated

him for the Senate of the United States: "In my opinion, it [slavery agitation] will not cease until a crisis shall have been reached and passed. A house divided against itself cannot stand. I believe this Government cannot endure permanently half slave and half free. I do not expect the Union to be dissolved — I do not expect the house to fall; but I do expect it will cease to be divided. It will become all one thing or the other. Either the opponents of slavery will arrest the farther spread of it, and *place it where the public mind shall rest in the belief that it is in the course of ultimate extinction,* or its advocates will push it forward till it shall become alike lawful in all the States — old as well as new, North as well as South." It was a thing impossible, that the South could see the triumph of such a party at the coming election, without feeling that the polity of the United States was to be moulded, sooner or later, so as to discriminate between local self-government in the different sections of the country.

With calm judgment and serene dignity, Chief-Justice Taney foresaw, in the signs of the times, the coming storm. He felt now, more than ever, the importance of the Judicial Department of the Government, and the high function of the Chief Justice of the Supreme Court. To keep clear of the defiling influences of politics had always been the fixed purpose of his judicial life. No tempter could beguile him from the path of his duty as a Judge.

Each party was now using, in the canvass for the Presidency, every available influence to promote the election of their candidate. A communication appeared in a newspaper, stating that Chief - Justice Taney was favorable to the election of Mr. Douglas, to influence, as it was said, the Roman Catholic vote in his favor. George W. Hughes, an intimate friend of the Chief Justice, and a Democratic representative in Congress from Maryland, called the attention of the Chief Justice to the statement, with a request that he be permitted to contradict it, as he knew that the Chief Justice did not prefer Mr. Douglas. The Chief Justice wrote the following letter in answer:

WASHINGTON, August 22, 1860.

MY DEAR SIR: — I received your kind letter yesterday, with Mr. M——'s to you inclosed, and should have answered immediately, had not the calls of friends prevented me from writing until after the mail was closed. And I must now answer briefly, as I am not strong enough to remain long at my desk without fatigue.

In regard to Mr. M——'s suggestion, I answer that I cannot take any notice of such an anonymous publication myself, nor authorize any one else to take the slightest notice of it; and for the following reasons:

Whatever I might say or authorize to be said in this matter would be regarded as said not merely by an individual, but by the Chief Justice of the Supreme Court; and I must neither say, nor authorize to be said, anything that it would not become the Chief Justice to say.

Now, it would be most unseemly in that officer to take any notice in any way of anonymous publications in newspapers, upon exciting political questions, in which his name is improperly used.

In the second place, every one whose opinion is worth anything knows that, since I have been on the Bench, I have carefully abstained from taking any part in political movements or elections; and that I have done this from a sense of duty, and under the firm conviction that any other course would destroy the usefulness of the Supreme Court, and create the belief that it was a mere party body, and acting for the interests of a party. And no one will place the least confidence in the anonymous statement Mr. M—— speaks of; and it will be forgotten in a week, unless public attention is called to it, and a factitious importance attached to it by a formal or authorized contradiction.

And if such a contradiction was made, by authority from me, to such a publication, it would naturally be regarded as a mere pretext on my part, and as an excuse for entering into the political campaign. The publication has, it seems, not been thought worthy of notice, even by the newspapers; for I have never seen it noticed in any one, although I am accustomed to look over papers on every side of this mixed-up and confused election.

And in addition to the insuperable objection as Chief Justice of the Supreme Court of the United States, any sort of contradiction authorized by me would get up dis-

cussions about me among all the small-fry politicians ;
and I should be constantly annoyed by seeing my name
mixed up in the slavery discussions, and speeches,
and publications, by that class of politicians who are
always appealing to some unworthy passion or supposed prejudice, instead of discussing the great principles of government which are in issue in the election.

I never speak upon political issues of the day in
public, nor in mixed companies ; nor do I enter into
any argument, or ever express an opinion to friends
who I know differ from me, or who I think may be so
inconsiderate as to repeat what I say, in a way to involve my name in public discussions as one who is
taking part in the canvass, and supporting or opposing
a particular candidate. To my intimate and confidential friends, *as you know,* I speak freely and without
reserve. And I do this because I know them well
enough to be quite sure that they understand the
nature of these conversations and guard them as you
have done.

Pardon me for saying that I was sorry to see the
remarks in Mr. M——'s letter pointing to the class
upon whom he expects my opinion to operate; and I
fear he has, unconsciously to himself, imbibed some
of those deep-rooted prejudices which gave rise to the
" Know-Nothing" clubs. I say this without any feeling of unkindness to him. But his remark implies
that the Irish Roman Catholics vote from religious
bigotry, and blindly follow leaders because they happen to be Roman Catholics. I presume he has had
but little association with that class, and forms his
opinion of them from sectarian books, and not from

his own observation. For if he would look at the Catholics of Baltimore and the Irish Catholics, he would see that they are as much divided as other churches, and vote as independently of leaders. And if they for a moment supposed that an appeal was made to their supposed bigotry in an election, they would resent it, and it would recoil upon the party who sought to use it. I know them better than Mr. M——; and if he attempts to exercise that sort of influence, he will find himself detected by those whom, I have no doubt, he thinks too ignorant and bigoted to be influenced by reason.

I have made this letter much larger than I had intended. But its length will show you how sincerely I respect your opinion, and how anxious I am to prove to you that I am right.

When we are able, few things would give me more pleasure than to pass some days at Tulip Hill, not only on account of its present occupants, but the memories of the past that the place would bring so freshly back to me. Best regards to Mrs. Hughes.

Ever, dear Sir, truly and
Respectfully your friend,
R. B. TANEY.
Hon. G. W. HUGHES, Tulip Hill.

The above letter, like all the other private letters of the Chief Justice published in this Memoir, was procured by letters of general inquiry addressed by me to persons with whom I knew the Chief Justice to be on terms of intimacy. It shows with what studious care he held himself aloof from party politics. No one knows better than I do his undeviating conduct on this important matter of duty in a Judge as he thought it to be. It was, like his religion, ever present to his mind.

Chief-Justice Taney wrote the "Farewell Address" of General Jackson on his retirement from the Presidency of the United States. The views of the Chief Justice in regard to sectional discord may be seen in the following extract from that address: "We behold systematic efforts publicly made to sow the seeds of discord between the different parts of the United States, and to place party divisions directly upon geographical distinctions: to excite the South against the North, and the North against the South, and to force into controversy the most delicate and exciting topics—topics upon which it is impossible that a large portion of the Union can ever speak without strong emotion. Appeals, too, are constantly made to sectional interests, in order to influence the election of the Chief Magistrate, as if it were desired that he should favor a particular quarter of the country, instead of fulfilling the duties of his station with impartial justice to all; and the possible dissolution of the Union has at length become an ordinary and familiar subject of discussion. Has the warning voice of Washington been forgotten? or have designs already been formed to sever the Union? Let it not be supposed that I impute to all of those who have taken an active part in these unwise and unprofitable discussions a want of patriotism or of public virtue. The honorable feelings of State pride and local attachments find a place in the bosoms of the most enlightened and pure. But while such men are conscious of their own integrity and honesty of purpose, they ought never to forget that the citizens of other States are their political brethren; and that, however mistaken they may be in their views, the great body of them are equally honest and upright with themselves. Mutual suspicions and reproaches may in time create mutual hostility; and artful and designing men will always be found who are ready to foment these fatal divisions, and to inflame the natural jealousies of different sections of the country! The history of the world is full of such examples, and especially the history of republics."

The chief question involved in the presidential election of 1860 was, whether the decision of the Supreme Court in the Dred Scott case was to stand or not as the true construction of the Constitution of the United States. It was a fearful thing, to submit to a popular vote a question of constitutional construction which had been decided, after the most mature deliberation, by a judicial tribunal which had been made a co-ordinate department of the Government by the Constitution, and jurisdiction over all constitutional questions expressly given to it, that the Government might stand forth, in the most declared manner, as one of constitutional limitation. The party whose great purpose was to disregard that decision elected Abraham Lincoln to carry out their policy. And on the day that he took his official oath that he would, to the best of his ability, preserve, protect, and defend the Constitution of the United States, he, in his Inaugural Address, foreshadowed that the policy of his administration would disregard the decision of the Dred Scott case. "I do not forget," said President Lincoln, "the position assumed by some, that constitutional questions are to be decided by the Supreme Court; nor do I deny that such decision must be binding, in any case, upon the parties to a suit, while they are also entitled to very high respect and consideration in all parallel cases by all other departments of the Government. And while it is obviously possible that such decision may be erroneous in any given case, still the evil effect following it, being limited to that particular case, with the chance that it may be overruled, and never become a precedent for other cases, can better be borne than could the evils of a different practice. *At the same time, the candid citizen must confess that if the policy of the Government, upon vital questions affecting the whole people, is to be irrevocably fixed by decisions of the Supreme Court, the instant they are made in ordinary litigation between parties in personal actions the people will have ceased to be their*

*own rulers, having to that extent practically resigned
their Government into the hands of that eminent tribunal.*" The lines which I have put in italics proclaim the most pernicious political heresy ever uttered
in the politics of our country. It saps the foundations
of the Constitution, and substitutes the fluctuating and
alternating will of a party majority of the people in its
stead. This was, however, the cardinal doctrine of the
party which elected President Lincoln, and he but
spoke their creed.

We have already seen how that party in Wisconsin, in the case of Ableman and Booth, had set the
authority of the Supreme Court at defiance, in order
to carry out its policy in regard to slavery. And at
the very time that President Lincoln was delivering
his Inaugural, a case was pending in the Supreme
Court, arising out of the determination of his party
to carry out its anti-slavery policy in defiance of the
Constitution. Willis Lago, a free man of color, was,
in October, 1859, indicted by the grand jury of a
Court of the State of Kentucky, under a law of that
State, for the crime of assisting a slave to escape.
Lago fled to the State of Ohio. A copy of the indict-
ment, properly authenticated according to the Act of
Congress of 1793, was presented to the Governor of
Ohio, by the authorized agent of the Governor of
Kentucky, and the arrest and delivery of the fugitive
from justice demanded. The Governor of Ohio re-

ferred the matter to the Attorney-General of the State
for his opinion. The Attorney-General gave an opinion in conformity with his politics. Though the law
of Kentucky made the act of assisting a slave to
escape a crime, the politics of the Attorney-General
forbade him to consider the act otherwise than meri-
torious. He therefore advised the Governor of Ohio
that "The offence charged against Lago does not rank
among those upon which the constitutional provision
was intended to operate; and you have therefore no
authority to comply with the requisition made upon
you by the Governor of Kentucky." The Governor,
of course, refused to cause the arrest and delivery of
the fugitive from justice. Upon this refusal, the State
of Kentucky moved the Supreme Court of the United
for a *mandamus* against the Governor of Ohio to compel him to perform his duty in the premises. On the
13th of March, 1861, a few days after President Lincoln's inauguration, Chief-Justice Taney delivered the
opinion of the Court in the case.

After deciding that the Court had jurisdiction of the
case, the Chief Justice said : "This brings us to the
examination of the clause of the Constitution which
has given rise to this controversy. It is in the following words :

"'A person charged in any State with treason,
felony, or other crime, who shall flee from justice, and
be found in another State, shall, on demand of the

Executive authority of the State from which he fled, be delivered up, to be removed to the State having jurisdiction of the crime.'

"Looking to the language of the clause, it is difficult to comprehend how any doubt could have arisen as to its meaning and construction. The words 'treason, felony, or other crime,' in their plain and obvious import, as well as in their legal and technical sense, embrace every act forbidden and made punishable by a law of the State. The word crime of itself includes every offence, from the highest to the lowest in the grade of offences, and includes what are called 'misdemeanors' as well as treason and felony."

The Chief Justice, then, in order to show that the framers of the Constitution intended to make the clause as comprehensive as possible, it being intended to enable each State to maintain its local policy, says: "They [the words 'treason and felony'] were introduced for the purpose of guarding against any restriction of the word 'crime,' and to prevent this provision from being construed by the rules and usages of independent nations in compacts for delivering up fugitives from justice. According to these usages, even where they admitted the obligation to deliver the fugitive, persons who fled on account of political offences were almost always excepted, and the nation upon which the demand is made also uniformly claims and exercises a discretion in weighing the evidence of the crime and the character of the offence. . . . And as treason was also a 'felony,' it was necessary to insert those words, to show, in language that could not be mistaken, that political offenders were included in it. For this was not a compact of peace and comity between separate nations who had no claim on each other for mutual support, but a compact binding them to give aid and assistance to each other in executing their laws, and to support each other in preserving order and law within its confines, whenever such aid was needed and required ; for it is manifest that the statesmen who framed the Constitution, were fully sensible that, from the complex character of the Government, it must fail, unless the States mutually supported each other and the general Government ; and that nothing would be more likely to disturb its peace, and end in discord, than permitting an offender against the laws of a State, by passing over a mathematical line which divides it from another, to defy its process, and stand ready, under the protection of the State, to repeat the offence as soon as another opportunity offered."

The Chief Justice then argues that the right given to " demand " implies that it is an absolute right, and that the obligation or duty to deliver is correlative. " The performance of this duty, however," says the Chief Justice, " is left to the fidelity of the State Executive to the compact entered into with the other States when it adopted the Constitution of the United States, and became a member of the Union. . . .

"But if the Governor of Ohio refuses to discharge this duty, there is no power delegated to the general Government, either through the Judicial Department or any other department, to use coercive means to compel him.

"And upon this ground the motion for the *mandamus* must be overruled."

This case consummated the determination of the anti-slavery party to set the provisions of the Constitution bearing upon the subject of the institution of slavery at defiance. These provisions could no longer be enforced. And a réference to the statutes of the free States will show that the party was not moved by any regard for the welfare of the negro race, but by hostility to the Southern States. At the very time the Governor of Ohio was disregarding his constitutional duty in refusing to deliver up a fugitive from justice, merely because he was a negro and his crime was connected with the institution of slavery, there was a statute of the State, passed in 1859, prohibiting any free negro or mulatto from voting in the State, and inflicting a fine of five hundred dollars and imprisonment for six months on any Judge "who shall receive the vote of any person where such person has a distinct and visible admixture of African blood." And in Indiana there was a statute, in 1862, punishing any white person who should marry another with one-eighth, or more, of negro blood by a fine of five thousand dollars and an imprisonment for ten years. And in President Lincoln's own State, Illinois, there was a statute, when he was inaugurated, to prevent the immigration of free negroes into the State, which enacted that if any negro or mulatto, bond or free, came into the State and remained more than ten days, with the intention of residing in the State, he should be " deemed guilty of a high misdemeanor," and be liable to a fine, and to be advertised and sold at public auction, to pay the fine by the proceeds of the sale.

In the case just mentioned, the Supreme Court decided that the constitutional compact had been deliberately broken by a State, and that there was no redress by law. In all the other cases regarding slavery which came before the Supreme Court, it was decided that the Constitution had not only guaranteed a right, but had also furnished a remedy. The opinions of the Chief Justice in all these cases are to be found among the appendices to this volume. And the same calm, serene spirit of justice pervades them — though delivered amidst the throes of civil war, the causes of which the cases involved — as pervades his opinions on ordinary matters of litigation. Neither the thoughts nor the style of any one of his opinions are ever tinctured in the slightest degree by the circumstances of the case. Never, perhaps, was so calm a judgment given to a judicial magistrate.

Many of the slave States had now passed ordinances

of secession, by which they claimed that they had dissolved their connection with the other States and had set up a confederate Government, organized into executive, legislative, and judicial departments, upon the plan of the Government of the United States. Virginia, reluctant to leave a Union which she had done so much to form, and in which she had acted so glorious a part, appealed to her sister States still within the Union to meet her in a Congress, where the discord might be harmonized. The Congress met in Washington City, February 4, 1861, and adjourned February the 27th, without accomplishing anything. Virginia then bade the free States farewell, across the widening gulf of civil discord, and joined her fortunes, for better or worse, with her sister States of the South.

No candid man, capable of considering the lessons of history, can doubt, when he looks over the events in the working of our Government which I have recited, that any other group of States in our Union would, under like peril to any great interest of theirs from the course of political events, have endeavored to secede from the Union, or would have resisted by arms. No power or right is constitutional but what can be exercised in a mode pointed out in the Constitution for its exercise. Secession is, therefore, not constitutional, but revolutionary; and is only justifiable, like war, upon failure of justice without hope of relief under the Government. But, constituted as man is, *peaceable* secession would have been impossible, even if the right to secede at pleasure had been expressly guaranteed by the Constitution of the United States to each State. The common interests of all the States had become too interdependent and identified, since the establishment of the Federal Government, to admit of severance without disasters worse than the bloodiest war in defence of the Union. But, nevertheless, no publicist, judging by the practices of nations, can doubt that, in the forum of political ethics, the slave States were justified in their course. And every publicist knows that it is not the party which fires the first shot that is responsible for the war, but the party which makes war necessary. "Neither is the opinion of some of the schoolmen to be received," says Lord Bacon, "*that a war cannot justly be made but upon a precedent injury or provocation. For there is no question but a just fear of an imminent danger, though there be no blow given, is a lawful cause of war.*"

Mr. Lincoln had the misfortune to be inaugurated President of a divided country, without any hope of amicable adjustment. He had grave and difficult official responsibilities laid upon him, besides those which ordinarily belong to the office of President. He was President of a Government of only expressly granted powers under a written Constitution. To exercise any other powers would be usurpation. No motive of patriotism could rescue the acts from a

breach of the Constitution. The very whisperings of
one's heart, placed in such circumstances, are likely to
be deceitful. For it may well be doubted, whether
the worst of usurpers and tyrants do not believe that
they are moved only by a regard to the welfare of their
country. Even the Earl of Strafford, on his trial for
treason, defended his usurpations, on the ground that
they were done for the welfare of the people. "*Salus
populi*," said he, "*suprema lex;* nay, in cases of extremity, even above acts of Parliament."

President Lincoln and his Cabinet were from the
first in great alarm, and at once began to lean for support on the military arm of Lieutenant-General Scott.
Suspecting, very naturally, that Maryland sympathized
with her sister slave States, every citizen of the State
was imagined to be engaged in plots against the Federal Government. Hence it was that, on the 25th of
May, 1861, John Merryman, a citizen of Baltimore
County, in the State of Maryland, was arrested by a
military force, acting under orders of a Major-General
of the United States Army commanding in the State
of Pennsylvania, and was committed to the custody of
the General commanding Fort McHenry, within the
district of Maryland. On the 26th of May, 1861, a
writ of *habeas corpus* was issued, upon the petition of
Merryman, by Chief-Justice Taney, sitting at chambers, directed to the commandant of the Fort, commanding him to produce the body of the petitioner

before the Chief Justice, in Baltimore City, on the 27th of May, 1861. On that day, the writ was returned "served," and the officer to whom it was directed declined to produce the petitioner, giving as his excuse the following reasons:

1. That the petitioner was arrested by the orders of the Major-General commanding in Pennsylvania, upon the charge of treason in being publicly associated with and holding a commission as lieutenant in a company having in their possession arms belonging to the United States, and avowing his purpose of armed hostility against the Government.

2. That he (the officer holding the prisoner in custody) was duly authorized by the President of the United States, in such cases, to suspend the writ of *habeas corpus* for the public safety.

The Chief Justice immediately passed the following order:

"*Ordered,* That an attachment forthwith issue against General George Cadwalader for a contempt, in refusing to produce the body of John Merryman, according to the command of the writ of *habeas corpus* returnable and returned before me to-day, and that said attachment be returned before me at twelve o'clock to-morrow, at the room of the Circuit Court. Monday, May 27, 1861. R. B. TANEY."

The attachment was issued as ordered.

At twelve o'clock on the 28th of May, 1861, the

Chief Justice again took his seat on the Bench, and called for the Marshal's return to the writ of attachment. It was as follows:

" I hereby certify to the Honorable Roger B. Taney, Chief Justice of the Supreme Court of the United States, that, by virtue of the within writ of attachment to me directed on the 27th day of May, 1861, I proceeded, on this 28th day of May, 1861, to Fort McHenry, for the purpose of serving the said writ. I sent in my name at the outer gate; the messenger returned with the reply, 'that there was no answer to my card,' and therefore could not serve the writ, as I was commanded. I was not permitted to enter the gate. So answers   WASHINGTON BONIFANT,
U. S. Marshal for the District of Maryland."

After the Marshal's return was read, the Chief Justice said that the Marshal had the power to summon the *posse comitatus* to aid him in seizing and bringing before the Court the party named in the attachment, who would, when so brought in, be liable to punishment by fine and imprisonment; but where, as in this case, the power refusing obedience was so notoriously superior to any the Marshal could command, he held that officer excused from doing anything more than he had done.

After expressing his views of the law of the case in general but very decided terms, he said that he should cause his written opinion, when filed, and all the proceedings, to be laid before the President, in order that he might perform his constitutional duty, to enforce the laws by securing obedience to the process of the United States.

In a day or two afterwards, the Chief Justice put his opinion in writing, and filed it in the office of the Clerk of the Circuit Court.

After stating the facts of the case, the Chief Justice, in the written opinion, says: "As the case comes before me, therefore, I understand that the President not only claims the right to suspend the writ of *habeas corpus* at his discretion, but to delegate that discretionary power to a military officer, and to leave it to him to determine whether he will or will not obey judicial process that may be served upon him. No official notice has been given to the courts of justice, or to the public, by proclamation or otherwise, that the President claimed this power, and had exercised it in the manner stated in the return. And I certainly listened to it with some surprise, for I had supposed it to be one of those points of constitutional law upon which there was no difference of opinion, and that it was admitted on all hands that the privilege of the writ could not be suspended except by act of Congress."

The Chief Justice then inquires into the law of *habeas corpus* in England, in order to show what must be the law in our country, which inherited, and endeavored to improve the guarantees of personal

liberty derived from the mother country. He finally
shows what are the views of great American jurists
upon the subject. Mr. Justice Story is referred to as
maintaining, in his Commentaries on the Constitution
of the United States, that the right to suspend the
privilege of *habeas corpus* is vested in Congress. Mr.
Justice Story does not raise any question about the
right; as no jurist, unless maddened by some passion
or self-deluding sophistry, could ever doubt that the
right belonged to Congress. " Hitherto," says Story,
" no suspension of the writ has ever been authorized
by Congress since the establishment of the Constitution. It would seem, as the power is given to Congress
to suspend the writ of *habeas corpus* in cases of rebellion or invasion, that the right to judge whether the
exigency had arisen must exclusively belong to that
body." And Chief-Justice Marshall, in the case of
Ex parte Bollman, 4 Cranch R., says, " If at any time
the public safety should require the suspension of the
powers vested by this Act [Judiciary Act of 1789] in
the Courts of the United States, it is for the Legislature to say so. That question depends on political
considerations on which the Legislature is to decide;
until the legislative will be expressed, this Court can
only see its duty, and must obey the laws." " I can
add nothing," said Chief-Justice Taney, " to these clear
and emphatic words of my great predecessor."

" But the documents before me," continues Chief-

Justice Taney, "show that the military authority in this case has gone far beyond the mere suspension of the privilege of the writ of *habeas corpus*. It has, by force of arms, thrust aside the judicial authorities and officers to whom the Constitution has confided the power and duty of interpreting and administering the laws, and substituted a military government in its place, to be administered and executed by military officers."

After showing that other guarantees besides the *habeas corpus* had been disregarded, the Chief Justice says : " These great and fundamental laws, which Congress itself could not suspend, have been disregarded and suspended, like the *habeas corpus*, by a military order, supported by force of arms. Such is the case now before me; and I can only say that, if the authority which the Constitution has confided to the Judiciary Department and judicial officers may thus, upon any pretext or under any circumstances, be usurped by the military power at its descretion, the people of the United States are no longer living under a Government of laws ; but every citizen holds life, liberty, and property at the will and pleasure of the army officer in whose military district he may happen to be found.

" In such a case, my duty was too plain to be mistaken. I have exercised all the power which the Constitution and laws confer on me ; but that power has been resisted by a force too strong for me to overcome. It is possible that the officer who has incurred this grave responsibility may have misunderstood his instructions, and exceeded the authority intended to be given him. I shall, therefore, order all the proceedings in this case, with my opinion, to be filed and recorded in the Circuit Court of the United States for the district of Maryland, and direct the Clerk to transmit a copy, under seal, to the President of the United States. It will then remain for that high officer, in fulfilment of his constitutional obligation to 'take care that the laws be faithfully executed,' to determine what measures he will take to cause the civil process of the United States to be respected and enforced."

The Clerk did accordingly transmit the proceedings and the opinion in the case to the President, as ordered by Chief-Justice Taney. But the President paid no respect to the opinion of that great magistrate, nor to his constitutional obligation to "take care that the laws be faithfully executed."

There is not, in the history of nations, a more flagrant usurpation, than this act by which President Lincoln suspended all the guarantees of personal liberty, and put the military power above the civil. From that moment, the Government of the United States was converted into an instrument by which the whole power of one section of the country was wielded by a sectional party against another section. And there is nothing more sublime in the acts of great magistrates that give dignity to Governments, than this attempt of Chief-Justice Taney to uphold the supremacy of the Constitution and the civil authority in the midst of arms. His Court was open; and he sat upon the Bench to administer the law. The cannon of Fort McHenry, where Merryman was imprisoned, pointed upon the city of Baltimore. But the Chief Justice, with the weight of eighty-four years upon him, as he left the house of his son-in-law, Mr. Campbell, remarked that it was likely he should be imprisoned in Fort McHenry before night; but that he was going to Court to do his duty. It is considered the chief glory in our history, that Washington delivered up his sword to the civil authority after he had performed his duty as a soldier. The scene, as it occurred at Annapolis, depicted on canvas, adorns the rotunda of the Capitol of the United States. And the day will come, when some painter, inspired with the sublime conception of this great magistrate struggling for the cause of constitutional government, will sketch this scene for the instruction of future ages.

The opinion of Chief-Justice Taney, which is among the appendices to this volume, pronounced against the claim of President Lincoln, that the Executive of the United States is an Imperial Cæsar, with authority to suspend all civil authority and govern the country by the army. Disguise the matter as partisans may, this is the great political issue made in the Merryman case.

Emergencies will occur in the progress of a nation,
when the exercise of much greater power is necessary
for public order and safety than is needed for the
ordinary course of affairs. In every constitutional
Government, provision must therefore be made for such
emergencies. Because, says Hume, in his Essays, " It
is a maxim in politics, which we readily admit as undisputed and universal, that a power, however great,
when granted by law to an eminent magistrate, is not
so dangerous to liberty as authority, however incon-
siderable, which he acquires from violence and usurpation. For, besides, that the law always limits every
power which it bestows, the receiving it as a concession establishes the authority whence it is derived,
and preserves the harmony of the Constitution." The
remedy furnished by the Constitution of England for
emergencies of state, is the suspension, by Parliament,
of the writ of *habeas corpus*, enabling the Government,
for the time, to retain in prison persons who may be
dangerous to the State. Such prisoners, however, are
amenable only to the civil authority, and entitled to
all the guarantees of a fair trial according to " the
frame and ordinary course of the common law."
They can, too, sue the highest officers of the Government, if they have been imprisoned illegally.

In France, and other countries on the continent of
Europe, where the Roman civil law, with the maxim,
" Whatever pleases the Prince has the force of law,"

has nurtured the spirit of the nation, the Government has the authority to imprison at pleasure, and to declare the state of siege and martial law. And the officers of the Government are shielded by perfect impunity for all their acts.

Our ancestors brought with them to this country the laws and institutions of England; and the framers of the Constitution of the United States have provided for emergencies of state, by authorizing Congress to suspend the writ of *habeas corpus*, subject to the same conditions as in England. In England, at all times and under all circumstances, the military is subject to the laws and civil authority. There is in England, neither in war nor peace, any such thing as martial law, like that employed by the other Governments of Europe. " Where martial law," said Lord Loughborough, 2 H. Blackstone's Reports, " is established and prevails in any country, it is of a totally different nature from that which is inaccurately called martial law merely because the decision is by a court-martial; but which bears no affinity to that which was formerly attempted to be exercised in this kingdom, which was contrary to the Constitution, and which has been for a century totally exploded.... Therefore, it is totally inaccurate to state martial law as having any place whatever within the realm of Great Britain." Without the Mutiny Act, and the power granted by Parliament to the king to make articles of war, even soldiers would be amenable only to trial by "the frame and ordinary course of the common law."

We have arrived at a point in the career of national progress, when it behooves us to pause and to reflect upon the nature of the peculiar polity under which we have accomplished such great things as a people; in order that, in refitting our institutions for the new era which is opening before us, we may build according to the ancient models, which have hitherto weathered national disasters. Nationality is not determined more by peculiarity of race, than it is by the character of the institutions under which a people is developed. Let us beware, lest we exchange a Government with the writ of *habeas corpus* and trial by jury for a Government with the right to declare the state of siege and martial law!

A few days after Chief-Justice Taney made his decision in the Merryman case, he wrote the following private letter to an intimate friend:

WASHINGTON, June 8, 1861.

MY DEAR SIR: — I returned from Baltimore yesterday, having remained there to try a case in admiralty in the Circuit Court after I had disposed of Merryman's case; and this morning I received your kind letter. I thank you for the kind terms in which you have spoken of my opinion in the *habeas corpus* case. I certainly desire no conflict with the Executive Department of the Government; and would be glad, as

you will readily suppose, to pass the brief remnant of
life that may yet be vouchsafed to me in peace with all
men, and in the quiet discharge of every-day judicial
duties.   Yet, I trust I shall always be found ready to
meet any responsibility or any consequence that my
official duty may require me to encounter.   Ellen is
still an invalid — improves slowly; and is seldom
strong enough even to drive out.

I looked at the envelope of your letter carefully.   I
think it had not been opened.   And indeed if it had
been read, there certainly was no opinion in it, nor
anything said, that you could have any reason for
wishing to conceal.

The girls all send, with me, affectionate remembrances to Mrs. Hughes, and best wishes to yourself.

And I am, dear Sir, very truly,

Your friend and servant,

R. B. Taney.

Hon. George W. Hughes,

Tulip Hill, Anne Arundel Co., Md.

After the President of the United States had authorized petty military officers to suspend the writ of *habeas
corpus*, and the judicial authority of the Chief Justice
of the Supreme Court of the United States was treated
with contempt, the will of Congress and of the President
was paramount over the Constitution.   But subsequent
usurpations were committed under the forms of law.
Congress, in its career of unconstitutional legislation,
passed an Act taxing the salaries of the Judges of the
Courts of the United States; and the Secretary of the

Treasury deducted the tax from the salaries.   Because
of so monstrous an act, done in contempt of the express words of the Constitution, Chief-Justice Taney
addressed the following letter to the Secretary of the
Treasury:

WASHINGTON, February 16, 1863.

SIR: — I find that the Act of Congress of the last
session, imposing a tax of three per cent. on the salaries of all officers in the employment of the United
States, has been construed, in your department, to embrace judicial officers, and the amount of the tax has
been deducted from the salaries of the Judges.

The first section of the third article of the Constitution
provides that " The judicial power of the United States
shall be vested in one Supreme Court, and such inferior Courts as Congress may from time to time ordain
and establish.   The Judges of both the Supreme and
inferior Courts shall hold their offices during good
behavior, and shall at stated times receive for their
services a compensation, which shall not be diminished
during their continuance in office."   The Act in question, as you interpret it, diminishes the compensation
of every Judge three per cent.; and if it can be diminished to that extent by the name of a tax, it may, in
the same way, be reduced from time to time at the
pleasure of the Legislature.

The Judiciary is one of the three great departments
of the Government created and established by the
Constitution.   Its duties and powers are specifically
set forth, and are of a character that requires it to be
perfectly independent of the other departments.   And

in order to place it beyond the reach, and above even the suspicion, of any such influence, the power to reduce their compensation is expressly withheld from Congress and excepted from their powers of legislation.

Language could not be more plain than that used in the Constitution. It is, moreover, one of its most important and essential provisions. For the articles which limit the powers of the Legislative and Executive branches of the Government, and those which provide safeguards for the protection of the citizen in his person and property, would be of little value without a Judiciary to uphold and maintain them which was free from every influence, direct or indirect, that might by possibility, in times of political excitement, warp their judgments.

Upon these grounds, I regard an Act of Congress, retaining in the Treasury a portion of the compensation of the Judges, as unconstitutional and void; and I should not have troubled you with this letter, if there was any mode by which the question could be decided in a judicial proceeding. But all the Judges of the Courts of the United States have an interest in the question, and could not therefore with propriety undertake to hear and decide it.

I am, however, not willing to leave it to be inferred, from my silence, that I admit the right of the Legislature to diminish, in this or any other mode, the compensation of the Judges when once fixed by law; and my silence would naturally, perhaps necessarily, be looked upon as acquiescence, on my part, in the power claimed and exercised under this Act of Congress, and would be regarded as a precedent establishing the principle that the Legislature may at its pleasure regulate the salaries of the Judges of the Courts of the United States, and may reduce their compensation whenever Congress may think proper.

Having been honored with the highest judicial station under the Constitution, I feel it to be more especially my duty to uphold and maintain the constitutional rights of that department of the Government; and not by any act or word of mine have it to be supposed that I acquiesce in a measure that displaces it from the independent position assigned to it by the statesmen who framed the Constitution. And in order to guard against any such inference, I present to you this respectful, but firm and decided, remonstrance against the authority you have exercised under this Act of Congress. And request you to place this protest upon the public files of your office, as the evidence that I have done everything in my power to preserve and maintain the Judicial Department in the position and rank in the Government which the Constitution has assigned to it.

I am, Sir, very respectfully yours,

R. B. TANEY.

Hon. S. P. CHASE,
        Secretary of the Treasury.

The Secretary of the Treasury took no notice of the letter from Chief-Justice Taney. Thereupon the Chief Justice procured the following order to be passed by the Supreme Court of the United States:

"*Supreme Court of the United States, December*

Term, 1862. — *Order of Court:* Ordered, upon the request of the Chief Justice, that the following letter from him to the Secretary of the Treasury be entered on the records of the Court.   10th March, 1863."

The letter was, by this order, preserved, to testify to future ages that, in war no less than in peace, Chief-Justice Taney strove to protect the Constitution from violation.   Within a few days, (now April, 1872,) the present Secretary of the Treasury has adopted the views contained in the letter of Chief-Justice Taney, and declines to deduct, under the Act of Congress, any part of the salaries of the Judges.   And as wiser counsels regain ascendency in the Government of the United States, Chief - Justice Taney will recover, in public estimation, his commanding influence, which has been displaced by the infuriated rancor of a sectional political party.   He, as we have seen, was equally as much traduced by another political party before he was elevated to the Bench, and when the rage of the times passed away, those who traduced him felt themselves honored in doing his exalted worth reverence. And he, in his sublime magnanimity, forgot the past, and gave to every returning repentant the full measure of his friendly regard.   No man ever relied with more confidence upon the ultimate triumph of truth. This gave him his marvellous self-reliance.

In order to show the high moral views which Chief-Justice Taney took of the duty of Government officials in time of war, I transcribe from the *Baltimore Daily Gazette*, of June 4, 1863, the following case : —

" In the Circuit Court of the United States, yesterday morning, Chief-Justice Taney delivered his opinion in an appeal taken from the District Court of the United States, which has been under consideration for some days past, and is of great importance in various points of view.   The case was :

" *The claimants of a large lot of merchandise and goods* vs. *The United States.*

" A seizure made by Provost-Marshal McPhail, in October, 1862, heretofore reported, in which he was required to proceed to adjudication, by order of the District Court, on the application of the claimants' Proctor, A. Sterrett Ridgely, Esq.

" It appears from the evidence, which was fully reviewed by the Chief Justice, that, early in September, 1862, Marshal McPhail received from the War Department a communication stating a Colonel Stone had lately come from the Southern Confederacy, with authority and money to buy $25,000 of drugs; that he was the nephew of a dealer in artificial flowers, living in Baltimore, of the name of Rose ; and that Stone must be arrested.   Immediately thereupon the Provost-Marshal laid a trap to catch the party, giving *carte blanche* to his detectives.   One of these, Voltaire Randal, called on Mr. Rose at his store on Lexington

Street, and representing himself as a Captain Thomas, of Cone River, Virginia, inquired after Stone, stating that the Captain who had brought him from Virginia had recommended him (Thomas) to Stone as a person with whom he could safely return. Rose knowing no one of that name, so told Randal, *alias* Captain Thomas, and the latter left. He returned again at night, and, after further conversation, Rose, supposing he might refer to a young man formerly in his employ, named Stern, who had also lately come from Virginia, mentioned his name to Randal, adding that he was then in Philadelphia. The latter then asked Rose to write, and tell Stern what he said. This Mr. Rose refused to do, as he knew nothing of the matter, and it was none of his business.

"After a few days, Randal again called on Rose, with a letter addressed to Stern, which he requested should be sent to him. This was done by Rose. Randal, still under the assumed name of Thomas, insinuated himself into Rose's house and into an acquaintance with his children and family, visiting them frequently, and waiting until Rose came from his business, on the plea of inquiring if any answer to his letter had come from Stern. He made presents to the children, who became very fond of him; and otherwise sought to work himself into the family's confidence. On one of these visits (they were always made at night), he exhibited to Rose a handkerchief full of soft hats, telling him they cost but four dollars here, and would bring twenty dollars in Virginia. On another occasion, he showed him a pair of cavalry boots and a coat, which he declared he could get one hundred dollars for, asking Rose if he did not think that a pretty good business. He represented himself as in the confidence of the officers of the United States and Southern Confederacy — showed a pass and certificate of loyalty over what purported to be the signature of Marshal McPhail. His conversations were subsequently reported by Rose to Stern, who was still in Philadelphia, and who had received the letter from Randal, *alias* Captain Thomas, inviting him to return to Virginia with him. Some months or so afterwards, Stern, having purchased his goods, came to Baltimore, and having informed some of his young companions of Randal's conversations and assumed character, they had an interview with the latter. At this interview, Randal exhibited to them what he stated to be a clearance from the custom-house; told them he had a wagoner up to such jobs, who would collect and transport their goods to North Point, where his vessel lay; and concerted all the arrangements for so doing.

" The further to inspire their confidence, he showed them letters to and from distinguished persons in the South, and succeeded thoroughly in imposing upon them; and they appointed the next night for their departure. The goods were collected by Randal and the wagoner employed by him, and sent towards North Point, he (Randal) and the young men following down two hours later in another wagon. In the meantime, Marshal McPhail (who, privy to what was going on, and who in his testimony, filed in the case, states that he set traps to catch the parties, having sent to North Point the schooner *Caroline*, manned and in charge of other of his employees, who were to represent themselves as the schooner and crew of the fictitious Captain Thomas, and were to receive and take aboard the goods on their arrival,) had procured a tug-boat, with a view of intercepting and capturing the parties.

"In going aboard of the *Caroline*, the fictitious Captain Thomas, *alias* detective Randal, called on the parties for freight and passage-money; they paid him half. But he returned, and stated that he and the crew were sailing the schooner on shares, and that the latter demanded the whole amount, some two hundred and five dollars. This sum he succeeded in getting from the claimants in advance. After some delays and difficulties, evidently created by Randal, *alias* Captain Thomas, for the purpose of giving time to Marshal McPhail to get down in the tug-boat, they got underway, a few minutes after which they were boarded. The deception was still carried on by the Provost-Marshal and the supposed Captain and crew of the *Caroline*, the former pretending to treat the latter as prisoners and offenders. The schooner was taken in tow; they stopped at Fort McHenry, where the Marshal told Randal he would hand him over to the custody of General Morris, which was seemingly done, as Randal was then landed. The claimants were brought to Baltimore, and lodged in jail.

" Among other circumstances of deception sought to be practised by detective Randal on one of the claimants, was a package of letters addressed to parties in the South, which he was induced by Randal to place in his carpet-bag. These, it seems, were *bona fide* letters, which had previously got into the possession of Marshal McPhail, and which were used by Randal the better to enable him to impose upon the parties.

" There was also, in the case, the statement of Mr. Hoffman, the Collector of the Port, to the effect that some time in September or October, 1862, he was called on by Marshal McPhail, with the request that he would grant him blank permits, under the seal of the custom-house, to enable him (McPhail) to entrap persons engaged in contraband trade. This Mr. Hoffman did not think proper, and refused to do.

" The Chief Justice, in delivering his opinion, reviewed the facts in substance as above, stating that he had examined them with no less care than surprise, and could recall no similar case in the jurisprudence of either this country or England. He commented with severity on the visits of Randal to Rose's house, and the deceptions practised in the case; on the iniquity, as he felt called to term it, of this and other parts of his conduct; on his forged permits and clearances, and the evil design and consequences of placing letters, or allowing them to be placed, in the carpetbag of the claimants.

"The parties he considered as having been seduced and betrayed into the purchase of the goods by the Provost-Marshal's officers, and could see no possible benefit to accrue to the Government from such a seizure that would in any way compare with the great evil that would arise from a court of justice countenancing such conduct by a condemnation of the goods. It would encourage officers to betray the weak and imprudent into all sorts of violation of law, and would be demoralizing in the extreme to the officers themselves; and he was at a loss to see how any court of justice could condemn property under the circumstances of this seizure, unless the means employed be also countenanced.

"Besides the questions of public morality and public policy, there were other grounds on which the goods should be restored. He had no doubt that the parties had come originally from the South, and perhaps intended to return on the first favorable opportunity. There was, however, nothing connecting them with the Colonel Stone alluded to in the communication from the War Department but the fact that Stern was known to Rose, who was named in that communication. The goods of the claimants in this case were not of a hostile character, tending to aid or arm those in rebellion against the Government. They were simple articles of trade and merchandise, such as hats, ribbons, silks, and jewelry, and articles of that description. There was no evidence of the claimants ever having been before engaged in the contraband trade. The libel charged that the goods were proceeding from Baltimore to Virginia when seized.

"In deciding the case, you must seek for the substantial fact. Were they then, at the time of the seizure, proceeding from Baltimore to Virginia? The claimants may have desired to carry them there, and may have thought they were going there; but the Court is not to regard the outside coloring which imposed upon the claimants. The substantial fact is, that they were going to Marshal McPhail's office from the time they left their respective depositories in Baltimore till they arrived there. They were clearly not going to Virginia. The law, too, is express that not only the goods, but the vessel conveying them, must be forfeited. Now the vessel belonged to the Government officers. Was *she* going to Virginia, and is she liable to be condemned? Clearly not. She and the goods were, although unknown to the claimants, in the custody and control of the Government officers all the time, and cannot be condemned under the libel in this case, even though the Court should overlook the immorality of the proceedings, and look only at the case in its legal aspect.

" Part of the goods were bought in Philadelphia by Stern, and could not, of course, come under the provisions of the libel, which only refers to those in Baltimore.

" A decree was signed, reversing the decision of the District Court, and ordering the money or appraised value of the goods, which had been deposited (instead of stipulating in the case), to be restored or paid over to the claimants.   The Court, at the same time, stated that there was no *probable cause* for the seizure, which renders the informer (Marshal McPhail) responsible for the damages and costs sustained by the claimants."

This report of the case was submitted to Chief-Justice Taney by the reporter, and received his approval, before it was published.

The vile practices disclosed in this case that were authorized by the Government during the war, and the disregard of the Constitution and the law, have chiefly contributed to demoralize the public sense, and bring about in our country the stupendous official corruption of the present time.   And now, in the calm of peace, with a returning sense of truth and justice, it becomes us, as patriots, to pause, and reflect with instructive terror on the fate of nations like ancient Rome, which, because of public corruption and private profligacy, perished with such exemplary and appalling ruin. That Chief-Justice Taney, both as a statesman and a Judge, did all in his power to save his country from such a fate, must be manifest to all who may read this Memoir.

The Chief Justice of the Supreme Court of the United States is made, by an Act of Congress, *ex officio*, one of the Regents of the Smithsonian Institution. Chief-Justice Taney was the first to occupy that post. In order that it may be known how he performed the duties of the office, I give the following letter from the Secretary of the Institution, the eminent scientist, Dr. Joseph Henry:

SMITHSONIAN INSTITUTION,
WASHINGTON, D. C., January 4, 1872.

MY DEAR SIR: — Your letter, asking me to inform you as to the "manner in which Chief-Justice Taney performed his duties in his official relations with the Smithsonian Institution," has been received; and I take pleasure in complying with your request.

Chief-Justice Taney took a lively interest in the Smithsonian Institution, and was thoroughly imbued with an idea of its importance and the responsibility involved in its management. He frequently referred to the peculiarity of the bequest on which the Institution is founded, and to the fact that it was intrusted, by a foreigner, to the United States for the good of mankind, and that therefore the Government was responsible to the civilized world for the proper interpretation of the will as well as for the faithful administration of the trust; that the failure of the Institution would not alone involve the loss of money and reputation, but would prevent the founding of similar establishments through the influence of an unfavorable example. He acquiesced in the analysis of the will as given in the first report of the Secretary, and approved of the plan of increasing and diffusing knowledge by facilitating scientific research and by publishing original works of a scientific character.

Shortly after the commencement of the operations of the Institution, he was elected Chancellor, or, in other words, Chairman of the Board of Regents, which office he held until his death. He was regular in his attendance at the meetings of the Board, and evinced to the last a remarkable accuracy of memory in reference to all the acts and the numerous incidents connected with the history of the Institution. As a presiding officer, his manner was admirably adapted to produce harmonious action amidst diversity of opinion. When at one period, in the history of the Institution, conflicting views were urged and personal animosities engendered, even then the discussions of the Board were conducted with that dignity of manner and calmness of deliberation which characterized, under his direction, the proceedings of the Supreme Court of the United States.

In the interim of the annual sessions of the Board of Regents, the Secretary habitually consulted him with regard to the operations of the Institution, the disposition of the funds, and the course to be pursued in doubtful or perplexing cases. His advice was always judicious, founded as it was on a clear perception of what would be proper in view of the peculiarity of the bequest, and the character of the Government by which the bequest was to be administered.

In addition to the answer which I have given to the question which you have propounded to me, I beg leave to say that, from an unreserved intimacy with Judge Taney of nearly twenty years, I am led to a very high appreciation of his moral and intellectual character, and to entertain sentiments in regard to him which will ever induce me to cherish his memory as that of a great and good man.

Yours very respectfully,
JOSEPH HENRY.

To SAMUEL TYLER, ESQ.

By this letter it is seen that Chief-Justice Taney manifested, as Chancellor of the Smithsonian Institution, the same faithfulness to duty, and the same remarkable administrative ability, which characterized him in every station which he occupied throughout his long, eventful, and trying life.

CHAPTER VII.

PRIVATE LIFE.

I FEEL that in this chapter I am undertaking a task almost too delicate for the pen of the historian, while members of the family of Chief-Justice Taney (and they ladies) are still living. The incidents of his domestic circle, which would illustrate with most beauty the private life of the Chief Justice, cannot be unveiled to public view. But in the great trial of life the Chief Justice was destined to walk over the hottest ploughshares ever put under the feet of a public man by his countrymen; and it is my duty to show, by his virtues, that he passed through the ordeal unhurt. I must therefore say more of his private life than has thus far been revealed in this Memoir.

The private intercourse of Chief-Justice Taney with the officers and other officials of the Supreme Court deserves the first notice. It was such that they all had, and still have, and always will have, his praise upon their tongues. His very name warms their hearts and brightens their countenances. The memory of no father was ever cherished by his children with more affectionate reverence, than that of Chief-

Justice Taney is this day by every officer of the Supreme Court who was there when he presided over its deliberations. And such was the charm of his manner that every newly - appointed officer was, at his very first interview with the Chief Justice, brought to regard him with affectionate reverence. Soon after the death of the Chief Justice, Mr. Lamon, who had been appointed Marshal of the Supreme Court by President Lincoln, remarked to me : "Chief-Justice Taney was the greatest and best man I ever saw. I never went into his presence on business that his gracious courtesy and kind consideration did not make me feel that I was a better man for being in his presence." I said, "Your experience is that of every officer about the Court. Mr. Meehan, the Librarian, has often, when I have been in the library, come from the presence of the Chief Justice, and said, 'What a glorious old gentleman the Chief Justice is! He always treats me in such a way as to increase my respect for myself.'"

That a man of such an iron will, such determined purpose, such undaunted courage, and all the heroic elements of character, should have such a delicate sentiment of kindness manifested in his courtesy, has always been a subject of observation by those who knew the Chief Justice best. Its source was his charity of heart and his high breeding.

It was, for some years, the custom of the Judges of

the Court of Appeals of Maryland to write to Chief-Justice Taney a letter of compliment on his birth-day. I have been able to procure but one of his answers, which is the following letter:

WASHINGTON, March 19, 1860.

GENTLEMEN : — I return my cordial thanks for your very kind letter on my birthday. If I have done anything to merit in any degree the approbation you are pleased to express, I owe it to my training in the Maryland Courts and at the Maryland Bar; and no mark of approval could be more grateful to me, or more highly valued, than the one you have sent me from the highest judicial tribunal of the State.

At the same time I am sensible of the personal kindness which prompted your letter, and am grateful for it.

With the highest respect and esteem,

I am, gentlemen, your obedient servant,

R. B. TANEY.

Hon. JOHN C. LEGRAND, *Chief Justice.*
Hon. J. B. ECCLESTON,
Hon. WILLIAM F. TUCK, } *Judges of the Court of Appeals.*
Hon. JAMES L. BARTOL,

Chief-Justice Taney was of a singularly domestic nature. All through life he loved to talk of his early home in Calvert County, Maryland. The friends of his youth were remembered with great warmth of affection. But he lived so long that all had died and left him, except Mr. Justice Morsell, for many years one of the Judges of the Circuit Court in the District

of Columbia. Judge Morsell was older than himself.
They were born in the same neighborhood, and were
playmates, hunting wild game in the woods, and fish-
ing and bathing in the streams and rivers of their
native county ; and were linked together by their
youthful joys in an enduring friendship. They had
now walked down the hill of life together, to rest forever at its base; and the country they both had seen
moving in such a grand career was now torn by civil
war. As a last parting token of his friendship, Chief-
Justice Taney sent his friend a photograph of himself.
The note accompanying it, I could not procure. The
following is Judge Morsell's acknowledgment.

GEORGE TOWN, May 5, 1863.

MY DEAR SIR : — I have been favored with the
receipt of your card, — a most welcome token, indeed,
of a highly-prized, early, and long-continued friendship, formed in better days of law and order, and
without change continued. Let it never be severed!
With much esteem and respect, yours,

JAMES S. MORSELL.

The Hon. Chief-Justice TANEY,
Washington.

It surely is pleasant and exalting, to contemplate
such friendship as this between two such aged men.
I record it with unspeakable pleasure, to testify of the
noble nature of Judge Morsell, whom I knew well,
and to show how Chief-Justice Taney lived in the
hearts of those who knew him best.

In the first chapter of this Memoir, Chief-Justice Taney speaks of Joshua Williams, one of his class-mates at Dickinson College. When the Rev. Dr. Sprague was preparing his " Annals of the American Pulpit," he inquired, by letter, of Chief-Justice Taney about Mr. Williams. I find in the fourth volume of the Annals the following letter in answer:

WASHINGTON CITY, May 20, 1850.

DEAR SIR : — You ask for my recollections of my class-mate Joshua Williams. More than fifty years have passed since we graduated together at Dickinson College; but my recollection of him seems as fresh as the day after we parted, for he was not a man to be forgotten by his companions.

It is not in my power to give you any particular incidents in his life worth repeating. Indeed, in the calm and quiet life of a student faithfully performing his college duties, and preparing himself for future use-fulness, there is scarcely ever any striking event worth recording in his biography. Such, according to my recollection, was Mr. Williams. He was, I believe, a few years older than myself. His standing as a scholar was equal to the highest in the class. He was studi-ous, yet cheerful, social, and a general favorite. His life was pure and unsullied, and it is a pleasure to recall him to memory such as he then was. We all thought him eloquent; and, although he and I never met after we left college, I have often inquired after him and heard of him, and have been gratified to find that his future did not disappoint the anticipations of those who were his companions and fellow-students. I have ever cherished for him a high and cordial regard.

With great respect and esteem,

I am, dear sir, your obedient servant,

R. B. TANEY.

WILLIAM B. SPRAGUE, D. D.

This Mr. Williams became a distinguished minister in the Presbyterian Church, was pastor at Big Spring, Pennsylvania, and died in 1838.

After Chief-Justice Taney removed to Baltimore City, he formed an enduring friendship with Mr. David M. Perine, a gentleman of the highest character, and the most scrupulous attention to duty in one of the most important public offices in the city. The Chief Justice took pleasure in visits to his beautiful country-seat near Baltimore, to stroll under the shady trees on the banks of artificial lakes so natural as to seem to have been formed in the beginning of things.

The following letters, which I have procured from Mr. Perine, will show what manner of man the Chief Justice was in his friendships, and what tenderness of feeling he had for his suffering fellow-men :

WASHINGTON, March 16, 1862.

MY DEAR FRIEND : — To-morrow, if I live to see it, I shall, as you know, be eighty-five years old; and I cannot suffer it to close without expressing my gratitude to the Giver of all good, that I have been so long spared to those I love, and that age has not found me without true and tried friends to comfort and solace it. And among the foremost in that number, I need not say how sensible I am of your constant and unwearied friendship for now nearly forty years, and never forget the proofs you have given of it in the darkest and most sorrowful scenes of my long life.

I wish I could have seen my eighty-sixth year begin with brighter hopes. The one I have just passed has been a sad one. And there is, I doubt not, a million of persons — men, women, and children — in this now distracted country, who, at my last birthday, were full of bright hopes, and cheerful homes, who are now mourning over ruined fortunes, or weeping for husbands or sons or brothers who have fallen in battle or died of the diseases of a camp life.

How sad it is to look upon this picture, and see how suddenly it has come upon the country! Will the year in which I am about to enter be better? I fear not. . . . .

God's will be done; and we must meet it with the faith of Christians and the firmness and courage of manhood.

May you and yours pass through it safely and happily is the sincere prayer of me and mine, who all join me in affectionate remembrances.

Ever your friend,   R. B. TANEY.

D. M. PERINE, ESQ., Baltimore.

As the darkness grew thicker over our country torn by civil war, the letters of the Chief Justice to his friend had less and less of hope .for better things, as the following one shows :

Washington, August 6, 1863.

My Dear Friend : — I have been sick, very sick, since I last wrote to you, and have recovered slowly. But I am again in my office, and feel as well as usual, but not so strong, and am obliged to confine myself to my house.

During this hot season I have often thought of the pleasant days I have passed at your home, enjoying the fresh country air and walking over your grounds. But my walking days are over ; and I feel that I am sick enough for a hospital, and that hospital must be my own house.

Yet I hope to linger along to the next term of the Supreme Court. Very different, however, that Court will now be from the Court as I have heretofore known it. Nor do I see any ground for hope that it will ever again be restored to the authority and rank which the Constitution intended to confer upon it. The supremacy of the military power over the civil seems to be established ; and the public mind has acquiesced in it and sanctioned it. We can pray for better times, and submit with resignation to the chastisements which it may please God to inflict upon us.

With best regards to the ladies of your family,

I am ever your friend,

R. B. Taney.

D. M. Perine, Esq., Baltimore.

I next give the last letter which Chief-Justice Taney wrote to Mr. Perine :

WASHINGTON, March 18, 1864.

MY DEAR FRIEND : — I can hardly tell you with what pleasure I looked upon your well-known handwriting, when your birthday letter was handed to me yesterday. It brought back to memory many kindnesses and scenes of unbroken intimacy and friendship for forty years. At the age of eighty-seven, I cannot hope to see many more birthdays in this world, and can hardly hope to live long enough to see more peaceful and happier times. You I trust, who are so much younger than I am, will be spared to see and enjoy them. And that it may please God to lengthen your days in the enjoyment of every blessing, is the sincere and earnest prayer of

Your friend ever,   R. B. TANEY.

D. M. PERINE, ESQ., Baltimore.

On the day that the above letter was written, the *National Intelligencer*, published at Washington, contained the following notice of the eighty - seventh birthday of the Chief Justice:

" The venerable Chief-Justice Taney yesterday finished the eighty-seventh year of his age. Detained at his home more by recent indisposition (from which we are glad to learn he is steadily recovering) than by the infirmities of his age, he was yesterday waited upon, in a body, by his brethren the Associate Justices of the Supreme Court of the United States, who took this occasion to pay their respects officially to their Chief, and at the same time tender him personally

their congratulations on the returning anniversary of
his birthday.

"That this token of reverence and regard might be
the more marked, Mr. Justice Wayne, the presiding
Judge of the Court in the absence of the Chief Justice,
requested, as we learn, a member of the Bar, while
yesterday arguing a cause before that high tribunal,
to suspend his remarks at an earlier hour than that at
which the Court usually adjourns, that its members
might pay a complimentary visit to the Chief on the
return of his birthday.

"Immediately after the interview had by the Judges
of the Court, its officers, accompanied by several members of the Bar, and a few other friends, waited in
like manner on the Chief Justice at his house, where,
we need not add, all who called were received with
that urbanity and affability which characterize the
distinguished and venerable jurist in his intercourse
with society."

The son of his old friend Mr. Perine had sent the
Chief Justice, as a birthday present, a carved walnut
cigar-box of fine workmanship.   The pleasure with
which the Chief Justice received the token of respect
is manifested in the following letter to the donor:

WASHINGTON, March 18, 1864.

MY DEAR SIR: — I thank you for your very kind
letter and the beautiful and acceptable present, both
of which were received yesterday.   I took much

pleasure in showing your birthday present to the
Judges of the Supreme Court and other friends, who
did me the honor of paying me a birthday visit, and
hearing its beauty and taste admired by them all.
And I value it the more, because it is from the son
of the truest, and now one of the oldest, of my surviving friends, and tells me that the friendship which
the father and myself have so long cherished for each
other will not be forgotten by the son.

With great regard, very truly, your friend,

R. B. TANEY.

Mr. E. GLENN PERINE, Baltimore.

This letter manifests in a remarkable manner the
lively interest which the Chief Justice still took in the
ordinary acts of social life. His conduct, in showing
his present, is just what he would have done when he
was a young man. At this very time, I sat up with
him at night during his sickness, and, after he was
convalescent, he would, while lying in bed, smoke a
cigar, and talk to me to such a late hour that one of
his daughters would come into the room to break up
the conversation. The topics of conversation were
such as showed as great familiarity with every-day
life as any gentleman at any age would possess. My
brother, Dr. Grafton Tyler, had been for years the
family physician of the Chief Justice, and he remarked
again and again to me that the Chief Justice was like
a disembodied spirit; for that his mind did not, in
any degree, participate in the infirmities of the body.

Knowing that my friend Mr. S. Teackle Wallis, an eminent lawyer of the Baltimore Bar, was on intimate social relations with the Chief Justice, at my personal request he handed to me letters which he had received from the Chief Justice. I select the following, because of their allusion to public affairs, as appropriate to this Memoir.

WASHINGTON, March 20, 1863.

MY DEAR SIR: — I thank you for your birthday letter which I received to-day. After so many years passed in the public service, and often called on to act in seasons of popular excitement and passion, your approval of my conduct so cordially expressed is most grateful to me; for I know it is sincere, and comes from one who has had the best opportunities of knowing me, and who has himself given a bright example of public and private virtue amid severe trials.

At my advanced age, I can hardly hope to see the end of the evil times on which we have fallen. But I trust you will live to see the civil power restored in Maryland to its supremacy over the military, and the homes and firesides of its citizens once more safe under the protection and guardianship of law. Such is the constant and earnest prayer of

Your true and sincere friend,

R. B. TANEY.

S. T. WALLIS, ESQ., Counsellor-at-law, Baltimore.

On his eighty-seventh birthday, which has already been particularly noticed, Mr. Wallis wrote the Chief

Justice a letter of compliments. The Chief Justice returned the following answer:

WASHINGTON, March 20, 1864.

MY DEAR SIR: — I received your very kind birth-day letter to-day. When a man has arrived at the age of eighty-seven years, he will always find that he has outlived nearly all of the companions and friends of his early life; and it is then that he sensibly feels the assurances of regard from men whom he has known from their boyhood and who belong to another generation. He perhaps hopes that their approbation of his life and official conduct is evidence of the judgment which impartial and enlightened posterity will pass upon it. I have not only outlived the friends and companions of my early life, but I fear I have outlived the Government of which they were so justly proud, and which has conferred so many blessings upon us. The times are dark with evil omens, and seem to grow darker every day. At my time of life, I cannot expect to live long enough to see these evil days pass away; yet I will indulge the hope that you, who are so much younger, may live to see order and law once more return, and live long to enjoy their blessings.

With sincere respect and regard,
I am your friend and servant,
R. B. TANEY.

S. T. WALLIS, ESQ., Baltimore.

The following letter, which, because of its topics, comes in appropriately here, was written by the Chief

Justice to his friend, the eminent law-writer, Mr. Conway Robinson. Being intimate myself with Mr. Robinson, I learned from him the contents of the letter, and at my request he allows me to publish it.

WASHINGTON, April 10, 1863.

MY DEAR SIR : — I send you, according to your request, a reference to two State papers which were inadvertently omitted in my opinion in the *habeas corpus* case of John Merryman. I can hardly account now for the omission. But I had named a day on which I would file the opinion in the Clerk's office of the Circuit Court, and other official duties intervening, I found myself pressed for time. And after it was filed and a copy sent to the President, it was too late to correct it. These papers bear directly and strongly upon the point ; and to show how forcibly they apply, I give the reference in the words in which they should have appeared in the argument, inserted immediately before the last paragraph in the pamphlet edition as follows :

" The Constitution of the United States was framed upon the principles set forth and maintained in the Declaration of Independence; and in that memorable instrument one of the reasons assigned to justify the people of the several colonies in withdrawing their allegiance from the British monarch, and forming a new and separate government, is that ' He (the king) has affected to render the military independent and superior to the civil power.' "

And upon another occasion, scarcely less memorable, when Washington resigned his commission as

commander-in-chief of the American army, and surrendered to Congress the great military powers which
had been confided to him, Thomas Mifflin, then President of Congress, in accepting the resignation in behalf of the body over which he presided, said :

"Called upon by your country to defend her invaded rights, you accepted the sacred charge before it
had formed alliances, and while it was without funds
or a government to support you. You have conducted
the great military contest with wisdom and fortitude,
invariably regarding the rights of the civil power
through all disasters and changes."

Such was Washington through all the disasters and
changes of a seven years' war, while combating invasion from abroad and disaffection at home ; and such
the men who declared and achieved independence and
formed the Constitution of the United States. They
mark with emphasis his invariable respect for the civil
power ; and show that they regarded it as one of his
strongest claims to the confidence and gratitude of his
countrymen.

So much for the argument. But I may say to *you,*
how finely and nobly Washington's conduct contrasts
with the military men of the present day, from the
Lieutenant-General down.

Very respectfully and truly yours,

R. B. Taney.

Conway Robinson, Esq.

Washington's opinion of the relation which the
military power bears to the civil, and his determination that it should always act only as subordinate to

the civil, is evinced by his conduct during "The
Whiskey Boys' Insurrection" in 1794.   The in-
surgents resisted, by force of arms, the authority of
both the United States and the State of Pennsylvania.
So tender was the Government towards the insurgents,
that it endeavored for three years, by offers of con-
ciliation, to allay their discontent.   At length the
President proceeded to effect by force that which per-
suasion had failed to accomplish.   And even then,
Washington, in a letter of October 20, 1794, dated
"United States (Bedford)," addressed to "Henry Lee
Esq., commander-in-chief of the military army on its
march against the insurgents," says: "There is but
one point on which I think it proper to add a special
recommendation; it is this, that every officer and soldier will constantly bear in mind that he comes to
support the laws, and it would be peculiarly unbe-
coming in him to be in any way the infractor of them.
That the essential principles of free government confine the province of the military, when called forth on
such occasions, to these two objects: First, to combat
and subdue all who may be found in arms in opposition to the national will and authority; second, to aid
and support the civil magistrate in bringing offenders
to justice.   The dispensation of this justice belongs to
the civil magistrate; and let it ever be our pride and
our glory to leave this trust there unviolated."   Of
all the insurgents, only two were prosecuted for

treason, and they were pardoned; so that, by civil clemency, the rebellion was put down without the shedding of blood. I recount this striking instance in the conduct of Washington, to confirm the view of the relation of the military to the civil power taken by the Chief Justice. Washington had the highest moral tone, and the justest appreciation of authority and of individual right in proper adjustment, of any great ruler who has yet appeared in the history of nations.

Chief-Justice Taney had all his life, whenever occasion offered, been the composer of strife. It so happened that Mr. Peters, the Reporter of the Supreme Court of the United States, and Mr. Carroll, the Clerk, had got into unpleasant relations, after having been friends. They were both excellent officers, and both especially liked by the Chief Justice. Mr. Carroll was of the family of Charles Carroll of Carrollton, whose counsel the Chief Justice had been for many years, while he was at the bar, and together they had supported General Jackson's administration. So that, besides restoring peace between friends for whom he had so much kindly feeling, it may be supposed the Chief Justice would wish to restore amicable relations between two officers of his Court. Mr. Peters was at his home in Philadelphia. In May, 1848, the Chief Justice thus writes to him:

"What can I do to put things right between you

and the Clerk? When we meet again next winter, I will find time to have a full explanation with both of you, and see what can be done. I am persuaded that there are more misunderstandings than there need be between you, and that both of you sometimes act under the influence of excitement. Remember, I do not complain of this, or find fault with it; for I know it is unavoidable in the state of feeling in relation to one another which exists between you. But I will see, when we meet again, if there is not a place yet left for the peacemaker — for a peacemaker who sincerely respects and esteems both of you; and who would do much to re-establish friendly relations between you.

"But in the meantime I must take care that you are not interrupted in the performance of your duties. I am not sure that I understand exactly what records or opinions are still deficient. Do me the favor to say what you wish to be sent to you, that I may immediately attend to it."

The Chief Justice was a man of such a high sense of honor, having been bred in the old school of gentlemen, that he did not undertake to reconcile difficulties between gentlemen like Mr. Peters and Mr. Carroll, except upon the basis of honorable explanation. Therefore, when he undertook the office of peacemaker, he expected to have some trouble. It has been remarked by one who has read this letter, that it "does a higher honor to the memory of the

Chief Justice than the ablest opinion he ever gave. The latter may show that he was an able man; the former proves that he was a good one."

The relatives of Mrs. Taney were devotedly fond of the Chief Justice, and were a great deal at his house. Mrs. Alice Key Pendleton, wife of the Hon. George H. Pendleton, and daughter of the author of "The Star-Spangled Banner," requested the Chief Justice to give her his photograph with his autograph, and a sentiment. He sent the likeness with the following letter, written in his eighty-eighth year.

WASHINGTON, June 24, 1864.

MY DEAR ALICE: — I promised to send you a sentiment with my autograph; but, thinking the matter over since, I have sometimes felt disposed to ask you to release me from it; for I have been much puzzled to determine whether the sentiment should be religious, or moral, or political, or judicial. Nevertheless, as the promise has been made, I will fulfil it. And as I have the honor to belong to the Judicial Department of the Government, I have selected one which, although applicable to any situation in life, seems especially fit to be borne in mind by every Judge who, in the present times, is called on to administer and maintain the law.

I have not attached the sentiment to the autograph on the picture; for if I placed it there, I should appear to be making a speech to every person who looked at it, and, what would be still worse, always

saying over the same thing. I have therefore attached it to this note.

I know you could once read Latin, although it is
not a very common accomplishment in ladies of the
present day. I presume you have not forgotten it;
and I therefore make no apology for giving you the
sentiment in the language of Horace in his third
Ode, third Book.

Affectionately,   R. B. TANEY.

> " *Justum et tenacem propositi virum*
> *Non civium ardor prava jubentium,*
> *Non vultus instantis tyranni,*
> *Mente quatit solida.*"

The photograph had the following autograph :

" For Mrs. Alice Key Pendleton, as a token of the
respect and regard of her uncle.

R. B. TANEY.

" June 22, 1864."

And in order to show how dear the Chief Justice
was to those who knew him in private, I venture to
extract from Mrs. Pendleton's letter to me, without
her knowledge, the following passages :

" I am very glad you are writing uncle's biography.
I long to have the beauty of his life and character
more fully known and appreciated. And amid the
indignation that I feel daily at the wrong done him
at the present, I comfort myself with the hope for
history to right him. To your hands is intrusted

this work, and your name has been too long associated in my memory as a household friend, for me to feel otherwise than that the work will be well done.

.   .   .   .   .   .

"I have also copied the 'sentiment' from uncle, appended to his letter. It has a noble signification as emanating from him. So truly is it the precept and example of his life."

As I am now portraying the private life of one of the most abused men who ever served his country in high stations, I will show how he impressed all classes of persons who were admitted to his intimacy. Among these was General Robert E. Lee. I inquired of him whether he had any letters from Chief-Justice Taney, and received in answer the following letter:

Lexington, Va., November 14, 1865.

My Dear Sir: — I have just received your note of the 5th instant, and wish it was in my power to add to your stock of materials for the life of Chief-Justice Taney. I have no letters from him; and though my memory is full of the pleasure and improvement I always enjoyed in his company, and in my intercourse with his charming and intellectual family, I have no special reminiscences that would be useful to you.

I am much pleased to hear that your materials are so ample and satisfactory; and I hope, when his history is known, that it will exalt him in the estimation of all honorable men to the high position he holds in mine.

Very respectfully, your obedient servant,

R. E. LEE.

Mr. SAMUEL TYLER.

November 6, 1864, the Rev. Dr. Clover, of the Protestant Episcopal Church, preached a sermon in Springfield, Ill., the home of President Lincoln, from the Scriptural text : " Some say he is a good man, others say nay." The sermon was devoted entirely to the life and character of Chief-Justice Taney. I make the following extracts from a newspaper report of it:

" In the relations of social intercourse, it has happily fallen to my lot to know Mr. Taney in that sphere of life which most fairly and truly develops real character — in which a man, thrown off his guard, acts not for public applause, but acts out himself; and in so doing, shows what in him is good and great and noble, or what is mean, debasing, and selfish. In his private and domestic relations, Chief-Justice Taney was most exemplary, and has left a bright example, in this respect, for public men to follow. . . . .

" That he was great as a lawyer cannot be doubted; but in nothing did his attractiveness of character more appear than in his happy and affable manner, coupled with the most graceful and dignified bearing, which rendered his society, even to the humblest, most congenial and delightful.

"Few men in his profession were closer students than Mr. Taney, even after he had attained the period allotted to human life. In his library, pondering over some important principle of law, or investigating authorities to enable him to reach a safe and well-grounded conclusion in his decisions, with rare exceptions was he to be found during the day; but when evening came, at the simple announcement that some friend was in the parlor, it mattered not whether young or old, distinguished or obscure, the tall form of the old gentleman would enter, and the marked and peculiar features of his face light up and beam with a pleasant smile of welcome which no words can express."

It is impossible to have an adequate appreciation of one in his domestic life, unless we have also a view of his domestic circle. Therefore, I give this further extract from the sermon of Dr. Clover:

"Mrs. Taney was a woman of a noble and cultivated mind, of deep religious convictions, and of a truly catholic spirit. Courted by the influential, the affluent, and the fashionable, she cast aside the pleasures and attractions of the world, that she might the more fully and freely devote her life to the Saviour. From many an abode of virtuous poverty in the city of Baltimore, the prayer of gratitude has gone up in her behalf to heaven. One of the most unselfish women I have ever known, her life was a beautiful

exemplification, not only of active benevolence, but
of that spirit of true charity so admirably depicted
by the Apostle Paul." Such was the wife who knew
all the heart-secrets of the Chief Justice, and, by her
inspiring love, gave tone and vigor to his great soul,
and shed around his family circle the divine charm of
womanly charity and grace. The Chief Justice and
Mrs. Taney seemed to be made for each other. The
two together made their home all but perfect in parental love and filial piety. He was a devout Catholic,
she a devout Protestant; but so sure was each that
the other was a Christian, that no doubt ever hindered
their mutual belief that they would meet in heaven.

Mr. Campbell, the son-in-law of the Chief Justice,
in a letter to me, dated November 4, 1864, writes:
"Great men have often simple tastes, and the Chief
Justice was no exception. He was passionately fond
of flowers, and always thought well of one who liked
them." In his love of flowers, he shared in a common
love with Mrs. Taney. In his letters to her from
Washington, he often alluded to the flowers in the
public grounds, as is exemplified in the following
one:

WASHINGTON, April 1, 1850.

I write you a brief note, my dear wife, to tell you
that I have safely arrived, — with a journey less unpleasant and fatiguing than I usually experience in the
cars; for the day was fine and the cars not crowded,
and Howard and I sat together. We have adjourned

without transacting any business, as you will see by the newspapers, out of respect to the memory of Mr. Calhoun. His funeral takes place to-morrow, and we shall of course be expected to attend, and therefore do no business. On Wednesday morning we intend to go seriously to work. Judges Daniel and Grier have not arrived yet; but we expect them this evening. Judge McLean has come; but Mrs. McLean is not with him. I hear nothing from Judge McKinley, and do not know whether he will be here or not.

Having just left you all, my room is lonely and sad to-day, and I feel much more disposed to lie down and think of you all at home than do anything else. This bright weather will, I hope, continue, and enable you to exercise and be more in the open air. How glad I should be to walk with you.

I find the hyacinths in bloom in the Capitol grounds, and walked about them alone after the Court adjourned, to enjoy the marks of the opening spring. In a week they will be beautiful. Much love to all.

Most affectionately,

R. B. TANEY.

Because of my intimacy from my early years in the family of the Chief Justice, one of his daughters placed in my hands, as the biographer of her father, his letters to her mother running through a period of nearly fifty years. The contents were not known to herself. But so anxious was she that I should realize the beauty, as she termed it, of her father's and mother's married life, that she wished me to look into this sacred record of their daily thoughts and feelings in regard to their mutual doings. As only a few of such letters can be published, their chief use to me is to write with the greater confidence of the singular purity and felicity of the private life which these letters reveal. As Mrs. Taney was a woman of high intelligence as well as of cultivation, the Chief Justice, in his letters, often remarks upon public matters in an interesting way. And sometimes he mentions the mere courtesies which as Chief Justice he was required to fulfil. In a letter of 24th February, 1845, he writes: "The Court in a body, with the Marshal, Clerk, and Reporter, waited upon President Polk on last Wednesday morning in due form. We were, as you may suppose, (that is, the President elect and myself,) glad to meet here again under such circumstances, and talked about old times as much as we could in the five minutes we were together. I have not yet been able to wait on Mrs. Polk; but must do so before I leave Washington.

" In the evening we went to President Tyler's. There must have been, I think, a thousand people there, — well-dressed, well-behaved people; for none others were there. You know the President and I are good friends, and he and Mrs. President received me with great kindness; and I met there more old friends, and spent a more pleasant evening, than I expected; except only that I was greatly oppressed, as I always am on such occasions, by the crowded state of the rooms. I need not give you their names now, for it is not worth the trouble; and will tell you all about it when I come to Baltimore. President Tyler's Cabinet were all there; but I suppose you have heard that they are all to go out as soon as Mr. Polk comes in. But we do not yet know who will come in; and I am too busy in Court to make many inquiries."

Chief-Justice Taney's affections were by no means circumscribed within the circle of his own home. But wherever the blood of his kindred ran, there his affections extended. He was particularly attached, among his more remote kindred, to his cousin Ethelbert Taney, who lived an humble farmer near Hancock, Md. He had so true a nature, that his attachments grew stronger as age taught him that change is written on all the things of earth. The following letter reveals the great sorrow of his life to his kinsman Ethelbert Taney:

BALTIMORE, October 22, 1855.

MY DEAR ETHELBERT:— It gave me much pleasure to receive your letter; for when we are in affliction, we are most sensible of the kindness and sympathy of our friends. I have indeed passed through most painful scenes, and have not yet gained sufficient composure to attend to business. But it has pleased God mercifully to support me through this visitation, and to recall my bewildered thoughts, and enable me to feel this chastisement comes from Him, and that it is my duty to submit to it with calmness and resignation. And I do not doubt that, severe as the trial is to those who survive, it is, in the mysterious ways of Providence, introduced in justice and mercy to the living and the dead.

You too have lost a friend in my excellent wife. For neither she nor I ever lost our interest in you, and took pleasure in hearing from time to time of your good conduct and success in life.

My age and feeble health put it out of my power to accept your kind invitation to visit you. I should be glad to spend some time with you and your family; but my health has suffered from this shock, and, at my time of life, I can hardly hope it will be much better. My great duty is to prepare myself for that change which must soon come; and I trust that I shall mercifully be enabled to do so.

May you and those around you be long spared, and be a blessing to one another; and may we all meet hereafter in a happy eternity, is the prayer of

Your affectionate kinsman,

R. B. TANEY.

Mr. ETHELBERT TANEY,
    Near Hancock, Maryland.

In this letter is shown the great sorrow of the Chief Justice at the death of his wife. It was this great affliction which prevented the Chief Justice from ever resuming his autobiography. He had begun it the year before at Old Point Comfort, where the sad event occurred; and was writing it there when the blow fell upon him. He could not continue a work which would keep constantly in his mind so great an affliction.

The following extract is from another letter, written by the Chief Justice, to Mr. Ethelbert Taney. It shows his abiding and well-considered faith in his church. Such a declaration of his religious faith would only be made in the seclusion of private friendship. Never did he obtrude his religious doctrines upon any one. He often talked to me, in incidental conversations, on the general subject of religion; but the mantle of his charity was as broad as the sinning world.

" You are the only one left of the name from whom I ever receive a letter; and it is always with pleasure that I read a letter from you. I am truly glad to learn that you have recovered your health, and, as age is advancing upon you, that you have so many comforts and blessings about you, which I trust will continue to cheer you to the close of your life. When I count my years, I know that the close of mine cannot be distant, and that my duty is to be ready to meet it when it comes. Most thankful I am, that the reading, reflection, studies, and experience of a long life have strengthened and confirmed my faith in the Catholic Church, which has never ceased to teach her children how they should live and how they should die."

As religion was so prominent in the life of Chief-Justice Taney, it becomes me to give it due prominence in his biography. Therefore it is that I publish the following letter from Father McElroy, whom I have had the honor to know from my boyhood as one of the most useful and pious of men. He took charge of the little church in Frederick City (which I mentioned in the second chapter) the 29th September, 1822, when an intimacy and true friendship commenced between him and Chief-Justice Taney. He is still living in the maturity of his faculties at the age of ninety years. The first part of the letter relates to the Chief Justice while he lived in Frederick City :

FREDERICK, March 2, 1871.

MY DEAR SIR : — In answer to yours of the 28th ultimo, I have to state, at your request, the few particulars of which I am cognizant concerning Judge Taney's *practical religion*.

An essential precept (as we think) of the Catholic Church is confession for the remission of sins — very humiliating to the pride of human nature; but the well-known humility of Mr. Taney made the practice of confession easy to him. Often have I seen him stand at the outer door leading to the confessional, in a crowd of penitents, majority *colored*, waiting his *turn* for admission. I proposed to introduce him by another door to my confessional, but he would not accept of any deviation from the established custom.

A few days after the death of his wife, I called on

him in Baltimore. He was much crushed and broken in spirits after such a severe bereavement, as might be expected. He received me, however, with his usual kindness and courtesy. During my visit, a gentleman, with his carriage, sent to let Mr. Taney know that he came expressly to give him a little airing in a drive to the country for an hour or two. He [Mr. Taney] sent for answer that he must decline his kind offer; and then, turning to me, he said: "The truth is, Father, that I have resolved that my first visit should be to the Cathedral, to invoke strength and grace from God, to be resigned to his holy will, by approaching the altar and receiving holy communion,"—preceded, of course, by confession.

I must confess, this edified me very much. In Washington, he continued to practise all the duties prescribed by the Catholic Church.

I am pleased to find you engaged earnestly at the life of this great and good man, and hope to see it soon circulated extensively, as no doubt it will be.

With great respect, I am

Your obedient servant,

JOHN McELROY.

Mr. SAMUEL TYLER.

A little before this time, Mr. Justice Daniel, of the Supreme Court, (while all the Judges were boarding at the same house in Washington,) just before the hour for going up to the Court, opened the door of the room of the Chief Justice, and found him on his knees at prayer. He withdrew instantly, much mor-

tified that he had forgotten to rap before he entered
the room. He made an apology as soon as possible
for the intrusion, which the Chief Justice accepted,
with the remark that it was his custom, before he
began the duties of the day, to seek divine guidance
through prayer. Mr. Justice Daniel, though a particular friend of the Chief Justice, had never before
learned this religious practice. My information is
from Justice Daniel himself, and from a member of
the Chief Justice's family, and other intimates of the
household.

Chief-Justice Taney's religion was the moving
principle of his life. It filled him with every Christian grace. Faith, hope, and charity led him in the
high career which we have been reviewing. The
humblest received his kindness, while the great were
charmed with his courtesy. The servants of his
family could hardly understand his kindness, when
they contrasted it with the treatment of their servants
by others. In early life he manumitted all the slaves
he inherited from his father. The old ones he supported by monthly allowances of money till they died.
The allowances were always in small silver pieces —
none exceeding fifty cents — as more convenient, and
not so liable to be taken improperly by those with
whom they might deal. Each servant had a separate
wallet for their allowance, which was brought monthly
to the member of the Chief Justice's family who attended to the matter.

In 1860, the distinguished law-writer, Mr. Conway Robinson, asked Chief-Justice Taney for his photograph in his judicial gown, to be presented to two of the Judges of the Queen's Bench in England, whose acquaintance Mr. Robinson had made when in England. The Chief Justice, accordingly, had a large-size likeness of himself taken for the Judges. And, at the same time, he had two from the same negative put into gilt frames for his old negro servant-woman and his negro man-servant. At the bottom of one likeness was written : "To Martha Hill, as a mark of my esteem. R. B. Taney. February 14, 1860, Washington." At the bottom of the other : "To Madison Franklin, as a mark of my esteem. R. B. Taney. February 14, 1860, Washington."

But the Chief Justice did so many of these little charities, which he little thought would ever be brought to the notice of men, that I must recount no more. I recount what I have, more to put to shame those who have traduced the Chief Justice, than for any good it may do as an example to men walking in the paths of ambition and power.

Chief-Justice Taney had gone on the Bench of the Supreme Court when he was in full practice at the Bar, and was thereby cut off from all possibility of adding to his very small fortune. That fortune, small as it was, had been invested exclusively in Virginia

State stocks.   The following correspondence in regard
to that investment explains itself.

BALTIMORE, November 28, 1866.

DEAR SIR: — In compliance with your request, I
herewith send you a copy of Mr. Taney's letter to me
of the 18th July, 1861 ; and, in relation to the subject-
matter referred to in that letter, it may be proper for
me to state, that, after Mr. Taney moved from Baltimore to Washington, he appointed me his attorney
in fact to receive the interest due on his Virginia State
loan ; and from that time I was in the habit for years
of collecting it through the Union Bank of Maryland ;
and in the latter part of June, 1861, I sent the order
for its payment, according to my usual custom, through
that bank, not knowing at the time that any law had
been passed upon the subject ; and it was only when
my order was returned that I knew of the existence
of such a law.   I immediately communicated the facts
to Mr. Taney, and declined to renew the order ; and
his letter to me of the 18th July, 1861, was his answer
to that communication.

It is hardly necessary for me to add, that no part
of the interest due from the 1st January, 1861, was
ever received by Mr. Taney.

I am, very respectfully yours, &c.,

D. M. PERINE.

SAMUEL TYLER, ESQ., Frederick, Md.

The answer of Chief-Justice Taney, spoken of by
Mr. Perine, was the following letter to him :

WASHINGTON, July 18, 1861.

MY DEAR SIR: — I have received your letter informing me that the Union Bank of Maryland had received a letter from the bank in Richmond requesting the return of your order for the interest due me on my Virginia State stock, and the bank in Richmond would try and get it paid.

You did right in declining to renew the order until you communicated with me. I cannot receive the money. It is true, it is due to me from the State; but, under the law recently passed, the payment of dividends to stockholders in the non-seceding States is forbidden; and if mine is paid, it is a matter of favor and not of right, under the existing law of the State. If I were a private individual, I would accept it; but in my official position, and in the present posture of public affairs, I cannot consent to an exception in my favor when other stockholders in Maryland are refused payment.

I am sensible that this proposition has arisen from the personal kindness of friends in Richmond, who know that public life has not enriched me; and I am very sure that it never entered their minds that any one would suspect them of unworthy motives in offering it or me in receiving it. But yet I think the offer was made inadvertently, and under the impulses of kind feelings which prevented them from looking at the interpretation which baser minds might put upon the offer. Malignity would not fail to impute unworthy motives to them and to me; and in the present frenzied state of the public mind, men, who do not know my Virginia friends or me, would be ready to believe it. I mean to stand, in relation to this debt, upon the same ground with the other Maryland creditors, and cannot consent to any exception in my favor.

Your friend ever,

R. B. TANEY.

D. M. PERINE, ESQ., Baltimore.

Another striking instance of the scrupulous regard which Chief-Justice Taney had for his official reputation came under my own observation. His body-servant Madison, whom I have mentioned, was drafted during the late war as a soldier. He had waited on the Chief Justice so long that he had become indispensable to one of such extreme old age as the Chief Justice. My brother, the physician of the Chief Justice and of his family, had long known that Madison had organic disease of the heart, which wholly disqualified him for the duties of a soldier. This the Chief Justice knew himself. But when my brother proposed to make an affidavit to that effect, and write to the proper officer, and have Madison excused, the Chief Justice said he would rather buy a substitute, and did pay one hundred dollars for a substitute, while the Government of the United States was, in violation of the Constitution, withholding three per cent. of his salary.

Silence is the best criticism, when the facts of his

life are revealed, upon the conduct of the revilers of Chief-Justice Taney. Because, if I were to attempt to portray in words the strange injustice with which a large portion of his own countrymen have abused and persecuted him, while he was achieving such glory for the history of their common country, no matter how severe my censures might be, there would still be something wanting in the force of reprobation. I leave them, when they may have read this Memoir, to their own reflections, trusting that they may suffer nothing more than the pain of the repentance which enables those who have done injustice to respect themselves.

It will recur to the reader with what affection Chief-Justice Taney writes of his mother in the first chapter of this Memoir. She was a woman of the most eminent virtues. It will be remembered, too, that, in the second chapter of this Memoir, it is stated that, when the Chief Justice left Frederick to reside in Baltimore, he requested a friend, much younger than himself, to see that at his death he should be buried beside his mother in the graveyard by the little church where he worshipped. The following letter shows that, after forty years with all their trials had rolled on, his heart still clung to his mother with its early affection, and that his purpose to be buried by her side was unchanged:

WASHINGTON, May 6, 1864.

MY DEAR SIR: — I learned accidentally, some months ago, that some kind and pious hand had removed from the tomb of my beloved mother the moss and rubbish which fifty years had accumulated upon it, and restored it to the condition in which it was when placed there by her weeping children. Residing in a distant place, I could not myself guard it from desecration, nor even the ordinary injuries of time; and you may readily imagine how grateful I felt to the unknown friend who had, unasked and without my knowledge, performed that duty for me. I have often inquired and tried to discover to whom I was indebted for an act so touching and pious, but without success, until a few days ago, when my excellent friend and former pastor, the Rev. Father McElroy, called to see me, and from him I learned for the first time that I owed it to you, to whom I had hitherto been an entire stranger. But you are not now, nor can you hereafter be, a stranger. I am most grateful for your kindness, and when the brief space of life in this world which may yet be vouchsafed to me shall have passed, and I am laid by the side of my mother, I hope you will be near, and will feel assured that among my last thoughts will be the memory of your kindness.

With great respect and regard,
Your grateful friend,
R. B. TANEY.

Mr. H. McALEER, Frederick City, Md.

How little did the Chief Justice dream, when, in

the seclusion of his study, he penned this exquisite
letter, it would be handed down to future ages as one
of the chief witnesses to his great character, testifying
that no man with such a heart could be an unjust
Judge.

Chief-Justice Taney was a constant reader to the
end of his life of the current literature of the day.
He has often talked to me, with great satisfaction, of
Macaulay's "History of England," and Campbell's
"Lives of the Chief Justices and Lord Chancellors
of England." I found him, soon after it appeared,
reading Lord Campbell's disquisition on Shakespeare.
He laughed, and said : "Lord Campbell has failed to
convince himself that Shakespeare was an attorney's
clerk, but he has convinced me." Shakespeare was a
favorite author of his, and therefore he readily entered
into the topics of Lord Campbell's argument. Though
not what might be called a novel reader, he nevertheless read novels to the last. The "British Quarterlies"
and "Blackwood" he read with singular interest.
Newspapers, on all sides of politics, he had read to
him daily. Whenever friends came in to see him, he,
to the very last, inquired about everything that was
going on. In fact, he looked every day with unabated
interest over the great spectacle of the world, and
scanned all the doings of man with profound insight
and far-seeing forecast. He was emphatically an actor
in the drama of life. But the curtain falls. On the

12th of October, 1864, in the eighty-eighth year of
his age, he died. He was buried by the side of
his mother.

I append to this Memoir the proceedings of the Bar
of the Supreme Court of the United States on the
occasion of the death of Chief-Justice Taney. And
though similar proceedings were had by the Bars all
over the United States, I select from all the speeches
made that of Mr. B. R. Curtis, made at Boston, as
worthy both of himself and of Chief-Justice Taney,
and proper to be preserved as a part of this Memoir.

Upon the occasion of the death of Chief-Justice
Taney, in vacation, the members of the Bar of the
Supreme Court of the United States, and other officers
of the Court, having assembled in the court-room in
the Capitol, at noon, on Tuesday, the sixth day of
December, A. D. 1864, being the second day of the
Term, the following proceedings took place:

The meeting was called to order by James M.
Carlisle, Esq., of Washington; and on his motion
Jonathan Meredith, Esq., of Maryland, was called to
the chair, and D. W. Middleton, Clerk of the Court,
was appointed Secretary.

Upon being conducted to the chair, Mr. Meredith
spoke as follows:

" *Gentlemen of the Bar:* Before I take the seat
to which you have been pleased to invite me, I desire
to express not my own acknowledgment only, but that
of the Maryland Bar, for the honor reflected on both.

"Translated from that Bar, bearing the palm of professional renown, to preside over the deliberations of the most august tribunal of our country, the death of our late venerable Chief Justice — the last star in the glorious galaxy of the olden race of Maryland lawyers — could not fail to be sensibly felt and deeply deplored, not alone by his time-worn associates, but by those youthful aspirants for whom he marshalled the way and smoothed the ascent to that 'vantage ground' on which he had stood so long, so firmly, and so proudly. As their representative, I am here to mingle their sorrow with the sorrow of the whole American Bar, for the loss of a deeply-read and profoundly-learned lawyer, of an eloquent advocate, of a dignified, enlightened, and upright judge, and of a Christian gentleman, whose purity of life was high above all reproach. Let us, then, banded as brothers, now unite in paying a last sad tribute to the memory of a great and good man."

On motion, the Chair appointed the following members of the Bar a committee to report and recommend such resolutions and other proceedings as may be appropriate:

Ohio: Hon. Thomas Ewing, Mr. Henry Stanberry. *Maryland:* Hon. Reverdy Johnson, Mr. Wm. Schley. *Pennsylvania:* Hon. J. S. Black, Hon. Wm. B. Reed. *New York:* Hon. Charles O'Conor, Hon. J. V. L. Pruyn. *New Jersey:* Hon. J. C. Ten Eyck, Mr. C. Parker. *Illinois:* Hon. O. H. Browning, Mr. S. W. Fuller. *Wisconsin:* Hon. J. R. Doolittle, Hon. J. S. Brown. *Missouri:* Hon. J. S. Green, Mr. T. T. Gantt. *California:* Hon. Cornelius Cole, Mr.

John B. Williams. *District of Columbia:* Mr. P. R. Fendall, Mr. J. M. Carlisle. *Massachusetts:* Hon. Caleb Cushing, Mr. Sidney Bartlett. *Kansas:* Hon. Samuel A. Stinson.

The Committee, by Mr. Ewing, their chairman, reported the following preamble and resolutions, which were, on his request, read by Mr. Carlisle, the mover in committee.

In presenting the report, Mr. Ewing said:

"*Mr. Chairman:* I am instructed by the Committee to say that they have had the subject under consideration, and have agreed upon a report to be now presented. We all unite in the feelings expressed by yourself, Mr. Chairman, with respect to the deceased. I, for one, knew him from his first accession to the Bench. I have been present at every Term when he has presided in this Court since that time, from the first to the last; and I can bear ample testimony to his courtesy, to his kindness, to his consideration of the members of the Bar, to his judicial capacity, and his integrity as a Judge. Of a judge, it is true, little can be said, unless he be a judge in troubled times. The history of our Judiciary and the history of our Bar is written and spoken in few, brief words. All that we can say of the ablest and the best is what we are prepared to say of our deceased Chief Justice. I submit the report, and ask Mr. Carlisle to read it."

Mr. Carlisle read the report as follows:

"Roger Brooke Taney, of Maryland, fifth Chief Justice of the Supreme Court of the United States, having departed this life on the evening of Wednesday, the twelfth day of October last, at his residence in the city of Washington, in vacation of the Court, the members of the Bar and other officers of the Court desire, at the earliest moment and in advance of the business of the Term, to place upon record their profound sense of this national calamity, and a testimonial, individually and collectively, of their affectionate veneration for his memory.

"A man of spotless and benevolent life, he must, alike in the humblest as in the highest sphere, everywhere and always, have commanded the sympathy, respect, and homage of all good men who knew him or felt his influence. To see him and to speak with him was enough to give assurance of this. To know him intimately was to make this assurance doubly sure.

"But his was not the destiny of private life, where virtue, benevolence, and religion pursue the noiseless tenor of their way. And yet, upon the broad and lofty theatre to which he was called, and where, for more than a quarter of a century, he sat in judgment, between sovereign States as between private litigants, 'without fear and without reproach,' there was ever apparent this deep undercurrent, which marked him as the model of a good man and a Christian gentleman.

"Unambitious of political distinction or political office, he nevertheless served his native State as member of the House of Delegates, as Senator, and as Attorney-General of Maryland, when the interests of the State and people summoned him from his chosen quiet and thoughtful path of the jurist. He first extended his sphere of professional usefulness to the national councils when he had become the acknowledged head of the Maryland Bar, which, among the names of those who had preceded him, boasted of Martin, Dulaney, Pinkney, Wirt, and Harper.

"It was a notable tribute to his distinction as a lawyer and his worth as a private gentleman, that he was called by President Jackson to the office of Attorney-General at a time of great party strife, when a new order of things was about to be inaugurated, and when he was known to belong to the constitutional school, of which Chief-Justice Marshall was the living type, as his name remains the enduring monument.

"The brief period during which Mr. Taney held the office of Secretary of the Treasury, from which he was called to preside in this Court, was marked by the same firm, steady, and conscientious discharge of duty which characterized him in every situation of life, public or private. His convictions were ever the result of patient deliberation upon the whole matter before him; truth and right being his constant end and aim.

"Profoundly learned in the law, and naturally gifted with a clear, direct, and logical mind, he nevertheless listened for instruction from the humblest advocate who appeared before him in any cause. With all the qualities of a great Judge, and with the natural consciousness of his superiority to ordinary men, he was ever attentive and respectful to those whose duty brought them before him to attempt to influence his determination as a Judge; and none who knew him could doubt that his conclusions were always the result of conscientious and enlightened study and reflection.

"The Bar of this Court, as a body, heartily unite in this tribute to the memory of this great and good

magistrate.   His enduring record is perpetuated in
the official reports of this Court. His judgments, like
those of his illustrious predecessors, will be studied by
successive generations of barristers, and emulated by
successive generations of Judges, as long as American
jurisprudence shall exist.   Wherefore :

"*Resolved*, That the members of the Bar and officers
of the Court, deeply impressed by the great and good
qualities and acquirements, and the illustrious life of
the late Chief-Justice Roger Brooke Taney, deplore
the decree, inevitable at his advanced age, which has
removed him from his place of usefulness, dignity, and
honor here.

"*Resolved*, That they will wear the usual badge of
mourning during the Term.

"*Resolved*, That the Chairman of this Committee
move the Court, at its meeting to-morrow, to direct
these proceedings to be entered on the Minutes, and
that a copy be transmitted to the family of the deceased Chief Justice, with the respectful assurance of
the sincere sympathy of the Bar."

After the reading of the resolutions, Mr. Stanberry, of Ohio, said :

"*Mr. Chairman :* There are but few, I think not
more than three or four, of our brethren of the Bar
now present who were here when Chief-Justice Taney
took his seat on this Bench. I perfectly recollect the
time and the circumstances. There was a feeling of
disappointment, an impression that a more acceptable
appointment might have been made ; for at that time
Webster, Binney, Wood, and Sergeant were at the
Bar, and there was at least one Judge on the Bench

eminently fit for the place. The new Chief Justice took his seat under these unfavorable circumstances. It was not long, sir, before these doubts and apprehensions were all dissipated, and very soon it came to be generally acknowledged that the Chief Justice was fully equal to the duties and responsibilities of his high position.

"For more than a quarter of a century, year after year, I have argued cases in this Court whilst Chief-Justice Taney presided. That long experience gives me warrant and confidence in saying that he never failed to sustain the dignity and requirements of the office. Nay, Mr. Chairman, not to the last. Although before the close he had long passed the age when the most vigorous show signs of mental decay, his intellect seemed as clear as ever.

"But at this time, missing his kind and courteous presence in that accustomed seat, it is the man rather than the Judge whose loss afflicts me. It is that quiet dignity, that perfect composure, and, above all, that amiability and goodness of heart for which that venerable magistrate was so distinguished. He will be fortunate, who, succeeding to that vacant chair, shall occupy it so long and so well."

Mr. Stanberry was followed by Mr. Reverdy Johnson, of Maryland, who spoke as follows:

"*Mr. Chairman:* As a member of the Maryland Bar, with which the late Chief Justice was so long associated, it will not, I am sure, be esteemed obtrusive if I ask permission to add my personal regrets to the general sorrow which the Bar of the Union feels at his loss. In the beginning of my professional career,

I soon learned the great excellence, professional and
social, of the deceased. My first acquaintance with
him dates back as far as 1815. In that year I was
admitted to practice in the Court of Appeals of my
State. Its Bar was then adorned by Winder, Dorsey,
Harper, Pinkney, and Martin, all of them men of
profound legal learning, some of them of dazzling and
extraordinary eloquence. Without meaning in the
slightest degree to detract from the reputation of their
brethren in other States, — for in all at that time there
were, as there have been since, men of distinguished
ability, — I think I am safe in saying that they were at
least the equals of the most eminent of the profession.
In this galaxy of talent, Mr. Taney shone with a
splendor that challenged admiration, and made him,
in the opinion of all, their equal. Whilst enjoying
the confidence of his elder brethren and admitted to
be every way their peer, he was especially dear to his
juniors. It was my good fortune to have his confidence and his friendship almost from the first, and
greatly did I profit by it. Often his associate, and
often his opponent, I had constant opportunities of
judging of his legal learning, of his ability in its use,
and the fair and elevated ground upon which he ever
acted. In neither relation is it possible to exaggerate
his excellence. In those respects, he was a model that
his elder contemporaries were proud of, and his juniors
admired and kept before them as an example.

"In social life he was as attractive as he was instructive and eminent in professional life. No one knows
this better, Mr. Chairman, than you and I do. During
the many years of his practice at the Baltimore Bar,

and after his elevation to the Bench, whilst he continued a resident of our city, we, in common with all of our brethren, (for he was kind to all,) had constant opportunities of witnessing his demeanor, causing us to esteem him as much as a man, as we admired him as a lawyer and a Judge.

"Of his eminence in the latter character, in this presence, it is idle to speak. All of those who are around me to pay fitting respect to his memory have been themselves, during the sessions of the Supreme Court, the daily observers of it. In everything he said from the Bench, and in his uniform conduct as its chief, all saw how peculiarly fitted he was for his high office. Whilst his mind evidently was as capable of mastering, and uniformly mastered, the great, the momentous judicial questions which were often before him, it was as capable of solving, and did solve, the minutest which the rules of practice involved, and upon the correctness of which so much of a Judge's usefulness depends.

"At a recent meeting of our own Bar, Mr. Chairman, you will remember that I deemed it due to his character to vindicate it from an imputation utterly unjust, because utterly false. It is not amiss to repeat it here. In the opinion that he delivered in the Dred Scott case, speaking of the African race in this country, he said 'they had no rights which the white man was bound to respect.' Relying on this extract alone, though knowing that it is but the part of a sentence, by a certain class he has been denounced in bitter and malignant terms as entertaining the inhuman sentiment that the words taken by themselves convey; and this, too, although it is perfectly manifest, from what he said immediately before and after, that he mentioned the fact not to justify, but to deplore it. He gave it as an historical fact; and the archives, legislative and judicial, of all the Colonies, at and for some years after our Declaration of Independence, prove beyond all doubt that in that age the race was so esteemed. So far from entertaining himself any such opinion, long before that case was decided, he had manumitted the slaves that he owned, that they might have rights which all men would be bound to respect, and never declined to give his professional aid to such of the race as applied to the Courts to secure the rights of freedom. The charge is but one of the many calumnies with which the prejudices or passions of political partisans, in time of high excitement, cause them, in total disregard of truth, to fill the public ear. In this instance, I suppose, for a time, and with a certain portion of our people, it answered its purpose. But, if not already, it will be hereafter forgotten; and fair and intelligent men of the future, as do those of the present day, should they ever refer to it, will only marvel that an accusation so wholly groundles could at any time have been listened to by honest men, even for a moment, with anything but disgust and indignation.

" Mr. Chairman, I ask the patience of yourself and the meeting a few moments longer, to defend our late chief from a charge of a different character. This, perhaps, may be thought superfluous when it is known that, with many of the good and great men who made it, and once believed it, his pure administration of his late office soon satisfied them that they had done him

injustice. What I refer to is his order as Secretary of
the Treasury, in September, 1833, for the withdrawal
of the deposits from the late Bank of the United
States. Mr. Duane, his immediate predecessor in that
department, on the 23d of that month, was removed
by President Jackson because he would not give the
order, and it was alleged that Mr. Taney was appointed
to be the mere instrument, in that particular, of the
President's will. In this, as in the other instance,
though the parties making the charge were men of
high character and conscientiously believed in its
truth, the charge itself was equally without foundation in fact. I say this with confidence.

" I was, as I have stated, for some years immediately
preceding Mr. Taney's appointment to the Bench, on
the most intimate terms with him, and, as I have every
reason to believe, possessed his confidence. He often
conversed with me on all the political topics of the
day, and, amongst others, frequently of the character,
tendency, and actual condition of the bank. At this
time he had no reason to believe that he would be a
member of Jackson's Administration, nor had he, I am
sure, any wish upon the subject. The only office he
could have thought of, if he thought of any, as he did
not, was that of Attorney-General, then filled by the
late Mr. Berrien with the approval of the country, and
its duties discharged with consummate ability. He
had, of course, no reason to anticipate a vacancy. In
this condition he over and over again expressed to me
his conviction that the bank, as he thought it was being
administered, was dangerous to the true interests of
the country, because, as he said, it was being used for

party political purposes; and that,'under such management, its ruin was but a question of time. He,
therefore, considered it to be the duty and the interest
of the Government (the charter clearly giving the
power) to remove the public money from its custody,
and said that if the authority was with him he would
lose no time in exercising it. In this opinion I am
sure he continued to the period of his becoming Attorney-General.   When, therefore, Mr. Duane was
removed, and he was appointed, the order he gave
was his alone, and was but the carrying out of a
measure which he had long deemed — whether correctly or not is immaterial — to be important to the
public good.

"As to his acting in the matter merely at the bidding of General Jackson and against his own convictions of duty, and to attain a selfish end, no one who
knew him as well as you and I did, Mr. Chairman,
could believe; for if his kindness of nature was remarkable, his firmness was, if possible, even more so.
There was no man living to whom he would have
yielded a matured opinion of his own on a question of
moral or political duty; and he was not more able to
form one, than ever resolute in adhering to it when
formed, against every possible extraneous influence.
If influence, therefore, was exerted at all in relation to
the measure, it was the influence of Taney on Jackson,
and not of Jackson on Taney.   And let me further
add that, when in February, 1840, the bank finally
suspended payment, and was soon found to be insolvent, barely able to pay its debts, the stockholders
losing all, he reminded me how the fact established

the correctness of his predictions years before. That he had the legal right to pass the order, the bank never questioned, nor could it be questioned. He was said to have been but an instrument; when, on the contrary, his was the mind that determined upon and adopted the measure.

"What I have said, sir, has seemed to me to be due to the memory of the great Judge in whose honor we have assembled. It seemed to be a duty which I owed not only to a long friendship, but to a conviction which I shared with every enlightened jurist in the land, that jurisprudence itself had in him an able and enlightened disciple, whose labors in its behalf have greatly contributed to promote the highest interests of the country, and to keep, with the aid of his upright and learned associates, the character of our greatest tribunal as pure and high as it was left by Marshall. And the calm judgment of posterity, uncorrupted or unaffected by partisan passion, will ratify the conclusion of the Bar of the Union that a purer and abler Judge never lived than Roger B. Taney."

Upon the conclusion of Mr. Johnson's remarks, Mr. Charles O'Conor, of New York, rose and said:

"*Mr. Chairman:* The local Bar and Judiciary throughout the country have been already heard. Each in its proper place has expressed, in as strong terms as could be employed, a deep sense of the public loss sustained in the death of Chief-Justice Taney. His transcendent merits have been portrayed with a force measured only by the utmost capacity of human speech. The eulogies pronounced, as well elsewhere as here at this time, would seem, as we read or listen, to have exhausted all power of expressing the emotion of grief, for his departure from among us, and that of admiration for his high personal qualities. Yet I believe that no one who knew the illustrious deceased can fail to feel that language has not yet issued from human lips in any degree adequate to the melancholy dignity of the occasion. Nor is this because the wise, the learned, and the good of our land, who unite with us as mourners, have not used the most appropriate words that acquirement and genius could supply, but because human language is a feeble instrument, and wholly insufficient to express some ideas. They rise above its sphere; they are beyond its reach.

"Although our venerable and venerated friend had reached a period of life at which, in most instances, human usefulness is no longer displayed, it is not singular that his death should be deplored as a deprivation. From his clear, vigorous, and perfectly unimpaired intellect, there shone out, even to the latest moment, a force that seemed proof against decay. Well might we be excused for failing to realize his liability to the common lot, and for feeling towards him as towards one who was to bless the earth with his presence through all time.

"In approaching the subject before us, two great ideas present themselves: first, the majesty and power of this great tribunal, the Supreme Court of the United States; next, the chief column among the illustrious magistracy by which this grand moral structure is upheld. The history of the Court, and the character displayed by its Chief Justices, are most impressive and commanding. Whilst we may feel within us what seems a due perception of them, conscious incapacity compels us to shrink from any effort to portray in fitting colors the dignity of the one or the merits of the other. I will not attempt it. I will not recur to past history. I will speak only as a living witness, and of my own times. These bring into view the last two of our Chief Justices. Their acts have made their names immortal. They have left to us, and transmitted to posterity for their admiration and guidance, a series of judgments, not merely marked by profound learning and ability, but placing this august tribunal foremost amongst human authorities. The jurisconsult, of whatever clime or future age, cannot find a safer precedent than in these. They embody and enforce the cardinal virtues, Wisdom, Justice, Temperance, and Fortitude.

"Who shall hesitate to recognize the moral greatness of the Supreme Court under the presidency of John Marshall, and his most fit and worthy successor, Roger B. Taney? It secured justice to the humblest individual who appealed to it for the protection or enforcement of his rights; but, when occasion required, it also summoned to its Bar the greatest States in our united galaxy, and with mild dignity, but resistless power, executed justice upon them. It curbed their every attempt to transcend the just limits of their authority. Need I relate instances? The populous and powerful State which I have the honor here, this day, in part to represent — imperial New York — was called hither to answer wherefore she had ventured to deal lightly with the obligation of a contract. She obeyed the summons and abided judgment. Her great river was connected with the ocean as an arm thereof;

it was of right, and according to our fundamental law, justly open to navigation by all the people of our republic; yet New York had assumed to exercise exclusive authority over it. She was again called hither to justify, if she could, this high assumption. Again she came. She came full of pride and confidence. It was the pride of a mistaken conviction; the confidence of rectitude in her motives and supposed ability to vindicate her action. Her first minds, her loftiest intellects, appeared as her champions. Her statesmen, her lawyers, her social leaders, her whole people, sustained her with earnest zeal and perfect belief in her right to exercise this power. Some might say she went away rebuked; but not so. She was not less steadfast in her dutiful obedience than firm in the pride of her conscious rectitude. She heard the judgment of this Court, and standing corrected, not rebuked, she retired from its presence more majestic in her obedient submission than if she had gone forth triumphant. She was corrected, but not humiliated. Virginia, too, was in like manner corrected; and instances might be multiplied; but let these suffice. Such has the Supreme Court of the United States hitherto been; such no amount of mere physical power could have made it. Its real eminence, its moral grandeur, is due to the pure and enlightened intelligence which has directed its judgments.

" I will not attempt the hopeless task of intensifying by mere words the strong emotions of affectionate and reverential regret for our great loss universally felt. Those who knew Chief-Justice Taney, who witnessed in his administration of justice the gracious dignity of his bearing and the stern impartiality of his judgment, find in their own vivid recollections a voice with which mine cannot compete. Those who have not enjoyed that high privilege will gather from the perusal of his recorded decisions far better conceptions of his worth and intellectual greatness than any mere eulogium could inspire.

"I will only add my fervent prayer and express my anxious hope that He who determines the fate of nations, who has fostered this mighty Republic unto unsurpassed greatness — He, at whose footstool she now sits, though bereaved of her chief judicial magistrate, still radiant in the fulness of her power and majesty, may so direct the counsels of those who rule her destinies, that the future historian of our times may not be impelled to write, as he drops a tear upon the grave of Taney, *Ultimus Romanorum.*"

At the conclusion of these remarks, the resolutions were unanimously adopted, and the meeting adjourned *sine die.*

Supreme Court of the United States, December 7, 1864.
  Present: The Hon. Jas. M. Wayne, Hon. Samuel Nelson, Hon. Robert C. Grier, Hon. Nathan Clifford, Hon. Noah H. Swayne, Hon. Samuel F. Miller, *Associate Justices.*

At the opening of the Court, Mr. Ewing rose, and, with appropriate remarks, presented to the Court the proceedings of the Bar, and moved that they be entered on the Minutes of the Term.

After the reading of the resolutions, Mr. Justice

Wayne, the senior Associate Justice, presiding, replied as follows:

" *Gentlemen of the Bar:* The Court receive with sensibility your resolutions commemorative of the life, the virtues, and the judicial eminence of our deceased friend and brother ; and we cherish his memory with affectionate recollections and with respectful veneration.

" You have discriminated accurately and with feeling, the remarkable points of his life and character. Your tribute will be soothing to the hearts of his family, and it, with other notices of his death in the circuits, will be a memorial of his character, which lawyers and judges may emulate with advantage.

" His life was honorable and useful. In early manhood it gave assurances that in both respects he would become distinguished. It disclosed the qualities and acquirements which were the foundation of his distinction. They were the anticipations of it.

" In a few years after his admission to the Bar he was recognized to be a sound lawyer, by the distinguished advocates of that day in the Courts of Maryland, whose reputations were known in every part of the United States. His general demeanor, studious habits, and pure life, gave him the good-will and confidence of the people of the town and county in which he lived, and, without having been voluntarily a candidate, they elected him, at different times, their representative in places of trust and political interest, in which the whole State was concerned. In his discharge of them he was marked to be one who could be relied upon in those public exigencies which require firm character and statesmanlike ability to manage and control successfully. In such public employments, and in the practice of his profession, it was admitted by his associates, and the able men who watched his course with interest and with expectation, that he had made himself familiar with the history of the law, in all its relations, for the organization of government for the preservation of human rights, and also with those principles which had, from the instincts of men as to right and wrong, or which had been arbitrarily made in ancient and later times, to rule the rights of property and the general conduct of persons in society in connection with their obligations to authority. He had read and reflected upon all that had been written concerning society and the control of it; also as to its actual condition, as made known by sacred and profane history, and the history of modern times. That course of reading and reflection familiarized him with the consideration of human rights, and strengthened his ability and disposition to maintain them. But he was no enthusiast. He thought that men had not been solely the victims of power, but of circumstances, in all times, and in our day, before modern civilization had received the full impress of the principles and divine tendencies of Christianity, and when rulers and legislators forgot those obligations by permitting the violation of them for the advancement of State policy and trade. He thought that God had designed for men rights, whatever might be the condition of their humanity, which could not be taken from them by fraud, by violence, or by avarice, with impunity from God's chastisement. Under such convictions he gave freedom to the slaves he had inherited, aided them in their employments, and took care of them when they were in want. He often said that they had been grateful, and they had never caused him a moment's regret for what he had done.

"By temperament he was ardent. Its impulses, however, could only be seen in his eyes and heard in fervent language, when it was excited by an occasion; but he was never impetuous or vehement. He was courteous at all times, to every one, without affectation. He was cautious and circumspect without being indecisive; and the firm resolves of his purposes and principles were habitually expressed in words showing the sincerity of his convictions, without offence to any who thought differently. He was generous, and the only measure of his liberalities was his inability to give more. He was the willing advocate, professionally, of any one oppressed under color of the law, or who was too poor to litigate a legal right, or to seek in Court the redress of a wrong. In doing so he encountered responsibilities by opposing preconceived public opinion, and corrected this by reconciling popular misapprehension to himself and his client. The control of himself and his temper was no doubt the result in part of a practised philosophy, but it had its foundation in a higher source. In the full maturity of his life and mind he made a profession of his Christian belief, and, with the usual constancy of his nature, he died in the faith of his ancestors, in the communion of the Roman Catholic Church.

"He lived in Frederick City for twenty-three years, and then left it to reside in Baltimore. The prospect there of a larger practice and greater professional

eminence induced him to do so. Several of the distinguished lawyers of the Baltimore Bar had died
within a few years, leaving it without a leader. He
took that position, and maintained it with increased
reputation, when he was called to Washington, having
received the appointment of Attorney-General of the
United States. He was at that time the Attorney-
General of Maryland. He had been called to that
office by the Governor and Council, though they differed in politics, at a time of strong excitement. He
was an avowed supporter on the side in opposition to
that which they took. It was a magnanimous disregard of their differences, for which the Governor and
his Council were honored and are still remembered.
It led to his appointment as Attorney-General of the
United States, by which his State reputation became
national. When the latter office became vacant,
though the claims of other distinguished lawyers
and politicians were discussed, yet his fitness for the
discharge of the duties of the office, and for the
support of the principles of the Administration of
which he was to become a member, were admitted by
all. He was a worthy successor of those able men
who had held the office for twenty years. It would be
out of place at this time to particularize the cases of
his official success and ability. His arguments were
listened to with the marked attention of the Court,
and, whether successful or otherwise in the case, his
brief comprehended all the points of it, and all the
law applicable to them.

" Of the political course of Chief-Justice Taney
when he was the Attorney-General and the Secretary

of the Treasury, we need only say that the heated party contests of that day have passed away, with the admission of all who were engaged in them that his course was sincere, and sustained with ability; and that his virtues as a statesman and Judge were worthy of all the honors bestowed upon him, and that they have been illustrated by services to his country which will place him in its history among our ablest and best men.

"As his predecessor, our great Judge Marshall, had been, he was made Chief Justice, having but recently held high political office. Both were leaders in support of the policy of the Administrations of which they had been Cabinet officers. Each had to meet opposition of talent and eloquence — Marshall, from those who had the impress of services in our long revolutionary struggle with England for national independence, and for their conspicuous agency in the formation of the Constitution of the United States; his successor, the opposition of the men of talent and virtue who had, as legislators and in arms, carried the nation through a successful war with the same Power in support of its commercial interests and its rights of navigation. Neither of them passed through their political trials without being assailed by party resentments, but both received generous recantations from those who uttered them, in the spirit of kindness, confidence, and admiration of the purity of their lives and the able discharge of their official duties.

"It is a happy occurrence that two such men should have been Chief Justices in succession, and that the life of each of them should have been prolonged to their respective ages. They presided in this Court for sixty-three years, and by their decisions, aided by their associates and by the learning of the District Judges of the United States, we have a body of law, constitutional and otherwise, and in every department of the profession, unsurpassed in the records of Courts, for the security which it gives to political, personal, and municipal rights. It is truly a system upon which we can rely as our sure foundation for securing the rights and independence of the States of this Union, and our national liberty. Gentlemen of the Bar, it is a part of our mission to maintain it, and if it shall be done by us with discretion, exempted from the withering corruptions of party spirit, our great country will again become what it was before it became distracted by rebellion and scourged by civil war.

"The Court direct that your resolutions shall be placed on the Minutes, and that they shall have such other direction as you may desire."

And thereupon the Court adjourned.

At a meeting of the members of the Bar of the First Circuit, held at Boston on Saturday, the 15th day of October, A. D. 1864, to take measures for giving expression to the feelings of the Bar on occasion of the death of Chief-Justice Taney, the meeting having been called to order by Richard H. Dana, Jr., Attorney of the United States, Sidney Bartlett was appointed Chairman, and Elias Merwin, Secretary.

On motion of Mr. Dana, a Committee, consisting of Benjamin R. Curtis, Caleb Cushing, Richard H. Dana, Jr., and Sidney Bartlett, was appointed to prepare and report resolutions for the consideration of the Bar.

At an adjourned meeting, held Monday the 17th day of October, A. D. 1864, the following resolutions, reported by Benjamin R. Curtis in behalf of the Committee, were unanimously adopted, namely :

"*Resolved*, That the members of this Bar render the tribute of their admiration and reverence for the pre-eminent abilities, profound learning, incorruptible integrity, and signal private virtues, exhibited in the long and illustrious judicial career of the late lamented Chief-Justice Taney.

"*Resolved*, That the Attorney of the United States be requested to communicate these proceedings to the Court, and ask to have them entered on the records of the Court.

"SIDNEY BARTLETT, Chairman.
"ELIAS MERWIN, Secretary."

Mr. B. R. Curtis then addressed the Court :

"*May it please the Court :* I have been requested to second the resolutions which Mr. Attorney has presented. I suppose the reason for this request is, that for six years I was in such official connection with the late Chief Justice as enabled me to know him better than the other members of this Bar. My intimate association with him began in the autumn of 1851. He was then seventy-three years old, — a period of life when, the Scripture admonishes us and the experience of mankind proves, it is best for most men to seek that repose which belongs to old age. But it was not best for him.

"I observe that it has been recently said, by one

who had known him upwards of forty years, that
during all those years there had never been a time
when his death might not reasonably have been anticipated within the next six months. Such was the
impression produced on me when I first knew him.
His tall, thin form, not much bent with the weight of
years, but exhibiting in his carriage and motions great
muscular weakness, the apparent feebleness of his vital
powers, the constant and rigid care necessary to guard
what little health he had, strongly impressed casual
observers with the belief that the remainder of his
days must be short. But a more intimate acquaintance
soon produced the conviction that his was no ordinary
case, because he was no ordinary man. An accurate
knowledge of his own physical condition and its necessities; an unyielding will, which, while it conformed
everything to those necessities, braced and vivified the
springs of life; a temper which long discipline had
made calm and cheerful; and the consciousness that
he occupied and continued usefully to fill a great and
difficult office, whose duties were congenial to him,
gave assurance, which the event has justified, that
his life would be prolonged much beyond the allotted
years of man.

"In respect to his mental powers, there was not
then, nor at any time while I knew him intimately,
any infirmity or failure whatever. I believe the
memory is that faculty which first feels the stiffness
of old age. His memory was and continued to be as
alert and true as that of any man I ever knew. In
consultation with his brethren he could, and habitually
did, state the facts of a voluminous and complicated

case, with every important detail of names and dates, with extraordinary accuracy, and I may add with extraordinary clearness and skill. And his recollection of principles of law and of the decisions of the Court over which he presided was as ready as his memory of facts.

"He had none of the querulousness which too often accompanies old age. There can be no doubt that his was a vehement and passionate nature; but he had subdued it. I have seen him sorely tried, when the duly observable effects of the trial were silence and a flushed cheek. So long as he lived, he preserved that quietness of temper and that consideration for the feelings and wishes of others which were as far as possible removed from weak and selfish querulousness. And I believe it may truly be said, that though the increasing burden of years had somewhat diminished his bodily strength, yet down to the close of the last term of the Supreme Court, his presence was felt to be as important as at any period of his life.

"I have been long enough at the Bar to remember Mr. Taney's appointment; and I believe it was then a general impression, in this part of the country, that he was neither a learned nor a profound lawyer. This was certainly a mistake. His mind was thoroughly imbued with the rules of the common law and of equity law; and, whatever may have been true at the time of his appointment, when I first knew him, he was master of all that peculiar jurisprudence which it is the special province of the Courts of the United States to administer and apply. His skill in applying it was of the highest order. His power of subtle analysis exceeded that of any man I ever knew,—a power not without its dangers to a judge as well as to a lawyer; but in his case, it was balanced and checked by excellent common sense and by great experience in practical business, both public and private. His physical infirmities disqualified him from making those learned researches, with the results of which other great judges have illustrated and strengthened their written judgments; but it can be truly said of him that he rarely felt the need of them. The same cause prevented him from writing so large a proportion of the opinions of the Court as his eminent predecessor; and it has seemed to me probable, that for this reason his real importance in the Court may not have been fully appreciated, even by the Bar of his own time. For it is certainly true, and I am happy to be able to bear direct testimony to it, that the surpassing ability of the Chief Justice, and all his great qualities of character and mind, were more fully and constantly exhibited in the consultation-room, while presiding over and assisting the deliberations of his brethren, than the public knew, or can ever justly appreciate. There, his dignity, his love of order, his gentleness, his caution, his accuracy, his discrimination, were of incalculable importance. The real intrinsic character of the tribunal was greatly influenced by them; and always for the better.

"How he presided over the public sessions of the Court some who hear me know. The blandness of his manner, the promptness, precision, and firmness which made every word he said weighty, and made very few words necessary, and the unflagging attention which he fixed on every one who addressed the Court, will be remembered by all.

"But all may not know that he had some other attainments and qualities important to the prompt, orderly, and safe dispatch of business. In the time of his predecessor, the practice of the Court is understood to have been somewhat loosely administered. The amount of business in the Court was then comparatively so small, that this occasioned no real detriment, probably no considerable inconvenience. But when the docket became crowded with causes and heavy arrears were accumulated, it would have been quite otherwise. The Chief Justice made himself entirely familiar with the rules of practice of the Court and with the circumstances out of which they had arisen. He had a natural aptitude to understand and, so far as was needed, to reform the system. It was almost a necessity of his character to have it practically complete. It *was* a necessity of his character to administer it with unyielding firmness. I have not looked back to the reports to verify the fact, but I have no doubt it may be found there, that even when so infirm that he could not write other opinions, he uniformly wrote the opinions of the Court upon new points of its practice. He had no more than a just estimate of their importance. The business of the Supreme Court came thither from nearly the whole of a continent. It arose out of many systems of laws, differing from each other in important particulars. It was conducted by counsel who travelled long distances to attend the Court. It included the most diverse cases, tried in the lower Courts in many different

modes of procedure — some according to the course of
the common law; some under the pleadings and practice of the courts of chancery in England; some
under forms borrowed from the French law; many
under special laws of the United States framed for the
execution of treaties; and many more so anomalous
that it would not be easy to reduce them to any classi-
fication. And the tribunal itself, though it was absolutely supreme, within the limits of its powers, was
bounded and circumscribed in its jurisdiction by the
Constitution and by Acts of Congress, which it was
necessary constantly to regard. Let it be remembered,
also, for just now we may be in some danger of forgetting it, that questions of jurisdiction were questions
of power as between the United States and the several
States. The practice of the Court therefore involved
not merely the orderly and convenient conduct of this
vastly diversified business, drawn from a territory so
vast, but questions of constitutional law, running deep
into the framework of our complicated political system.
Upon this entire subject the Chief Justice was vigilant,
steady, and thoroughly informed. Doubtless it would
be the tendency of most second-rate minds, and of not
a few first-rate minds, to press such a jurisdiction out
to its extremest limits, and occasionally beyond them;
while for timid men, or for those who might come
to that Bench with formed prejudices, the opposite
danger would be imminent. Perhaps I may be permitted to say that, though on the only important occasions on which I had the misfortune to differ with the
Chief Justice on such points, I thought he and they
who agreed with him carried the powers of the Court

too far, yet, speaking for myself, I am quite sure he fell into neither of these extremes. The great powers intrusted to the Court by the Constitution and laws of his country he steadily and firmly upheld and administered; and, so far as I know, he showed no disposition to exceed them.

" I have already adverted to the fact that his physical infirmities rendered it difficult for him to write a large proportion of the opinions of the Court. But my own impression is that this was not the only reason why he was thus abstinent. He was as absolutely free from the slightest trace of vanity and self-conceit as any man I ever knew. He was aware that many of his associates were ambitious of doing this conspicuous part of their joint labor. The preservation of the harmony of the members of the Court, and of their good-will to himself, was always in his mind. And I have not the least doubt that these considerations often influenced him to request others to prepare opinions, which he could and otherwise would have written. As it was, he has recorded many which are important, some which are very important. This does not seem to me to be the occasion to specify, still less to criticize them. They are all characterized by that purity of style and clearness of thought which marked whatever he wrote or spoke; and some of them must always be known and recurred to as masterly discussions of their subjects.

" It is one of the favors which the providence of God has bestowed on our once happy country, that for the period of sixty-three years this great office has been filled by only two persons, each of whom has retained, to extreme old age, his great and useful qualities and powers. The stability, uniformity, and completeness of our national jurisprudence are in no small degree attributable to this act. The last of them has now gone. God grant that there may be found a successor true to the Constitution, able to expound and willing to apply it to the portentous questions which the passions of men have made."

End of the Memoir.

APPENDIX.

Supreme Court of the United States, December Term, 1856.
19 Howard R., 393.

Dred Scott, Plaintiff in Error, *vs.* John F. A. Sanford.

Mr. Chief-Justice Taney delivered the opinion of the Court:

This case has been twice argued. After the argument at the last Term, differences of opinion were found to exist among the members of the Court; and, as the questions in controversy are of the highest importance, and the Court was at that time much pressed by the ordinary business of the term, it was deemed advisable to continue the case, and direct a re-argument on some of the points, in order that we might have an opportunity of giving to the whole subject a more deliberate consideration. It has accordingly been again argued by counsel, and considered by the Court; and I now proceed to deliver its opinion.

There are two leading questions presented by the record:

1. Had the Circuit Court of the United States jurisdiction to hear and determine the case between these parties? And,

2. If it had jurisdiction, is the judgment it has given erroneous or not?

The plaintiff in error, who was also the plaintiff in the Court below, was, with his wife and children, held as slaves by the defendant in the State of Missouri; and he brought this action in the Circuit Court of the United States for that district, to assert the title of himself and his family to freedom.

The declaration is in the form usually adopted in that State to try questions of this description, and contains the averment necessary to give the Court jurisdiction; that he and the defendant are citizens of different States — that is, that he is a citizen of Missouri, and the defendant a citizen of New York.

The defendant pleaded in abatement to the jurisdiction of the

517

Court, that the plaintiff was not a citizen of the State of Missouri, as alleged in his declaration, being a negro of African descent, whose ancestors were of pure African blood, and who were brought into this country and sold as slaves.

To this plea the plaintiff demurred, and the defendant joined in demurrer. The Court overruled the plea, and gave judgment that the defendant should answer over. And he therefore put in sundry pleas in bar, upon which issues were joined; and at the trial the verdict and judgment were in his favor. Whereupon the plaintiff brought this writ of error.

Before we speak of the pleas in bar, it will be proper to dispose of the questions which have arisen on the plea in abatement.

That plea denies the right of the plaintiff to sue in a court of the United States, for the reasons therein stated.

If the question raised by it is legally before us, and the Court should be of opinion that the facts stated in it disqualify the plaintiff from becoming a citizen, in the sense in which that word is used in the Constitution of the United States, then the judgment of the Circuit Court is erroneous, and must be reversed.

It is suggested, however, that this plea is not before us; and that, as the judgment in the court below on this plea was in favor of the plaintiff, he does not seek to reverse it, or bring it before the Court for revision by his writ of error; and also that the defendant waved this defence by pleading over, and thereby admitted the jurisdiction of the Court.

But, in making this objection, we think the peculiar and limited jurisdiction of courts of the United States has not been adverted to. This peculiar and limited jurisdiction has made it necessary, in these courts, to adopt different rules and principles of pleading, so far as jurisdiction is concerned, from those which regulate courts of common law in England, and in the different States of the Union which have adopted the common law rules.

In these last-mentioned courts, where their character and rank are analogous to that of a Circuit Court of the United States,— in other words, where they are what the law terms courts of general jurisdiction,— they are presumed to have jurisdiction, unless the contrary appears. No averment in the pleadings of the plaintiff is necessary in order to give jurisdiction. If the defendant objects to it, he must plead it specially; and unless the fact on which he relies is found to be true by a jury, or admitted to be true by the plaintiff, the jurisdiction cannot be disputed in an appellate court.

Now, it is not necessary to inquire whether in courts of that description a party who pleads over in bar, when a plea to the jurisdiction has been ruled against him, does or does not waive his plea; nor whether upon a judgment in his favor on the pleas in bar, and a writ of error brought by the plaintiff, the question upon the plea in abatement would be open for revision in the appellate court. Cases that may have been decided in such courts, or rules that may have been laid down by common-law pleaders, can have no influence in the decision in this Court. Because, under the Constitution and laws of the United States, the rules which govern the pleadings in its courts, in questions of jurisdiction, stand on different principles, and are regulated by different laws.

This difference arises, as we have said, from the peculiar character of the Government of the United States. For, although it is sovereign and supreme in its appropriate sphere of action, yet it does not possess all the powers which usually belong to the sovereignty of a nation. Certain specified powers, enumerated in the Constitution, have been conferred upon it; and neither the legislative, executive, or judicial department of the Government can lawfully exercise any authority beyond the limits marked out by the Constitution. And in regulating the judicial department, the cases in which the courts of the United States shall have jurisdiction are particularly and specifically enumerated and defined; and they are not authorized to take cognizance of any case which does not come within the description therein specified. Hence, when a plaintiff sues in a court of the United States, it is necessary that he should show, in his pleading, that the suit he brings is within the jurisdiction of the court, and that he is entitled to sue there. And if he omits to do this, and should, by any oversight of the Circuit Court, obtain a judgment in his favor, the judgment would be reversed in the appellate court for want of jurisdiction in the court below. The jurisdiction would not be presumed, as in the case of a common-law English or State court, unless the contrary appeared. But the record, when it comes before the appellate court, must show, affirmatively, that the inferior court had authority, under the Constitution, to hear and determine the case. And if the plaintiff claims a right to sue in a Circuit Court of the United States, under that provision of the Constitution which gives jurisdiction in controversies between citizens of different States, he must distinctly aver in his pleading that they are citizens of different States; and he cannot maintain his suit without showing that fact in the pleadings.

This point was decided in the case of Bingham *vs.* Cabot, (in 3 Dall., 382,) and ever since adhered to by the Court. And in Jackson *vs.* Ashton, (8 Pet., 148,) it was held that the objection to which it was open could not be waived by the opposite party, because consent of parties could not give jurisdiction.

It is needless to accumulate cases on this subject. Those already referred to, and the cases of Capron *vs.* Van Noorden, (in 2 Cr., 126,) and Montalet *vs.* Murray, (4 Cr., 46,) are sufficient to show the rule of which we have spoken. The case of Capron *vs.* Van Noorden strikingly illustrates the difference between a common-law court and a court of the United States.

If, however, the fact of citizenship is averred in the declaration, and the defendant does not deny it, and put it in issue by plea in abatement, he cannot offer evidence at the trial to disprove it, and consequently cannot avail himself of the objection in the appellate court, unless the defect should be apparent in some other part of the record. For if there is no plea in abatement, and the want of jurisdiction does not appear in any other part of the transcript brought up by the writ of error, the undisputed averment of citizenship in the declaration must be taken in this Court to be true. In this case, the citizenship is averred; but it is denied by the defendant in the manner required by the rules of pleading, and the fact upon which the denial is based is admitted by the demurrer. And if the plea and demurrer, and judgment of the court below upon it, are before us upon this record, the question to be decided is, whether the facts stated in the plea are sufficient to show that the plaintiff is not entitled to sue as a citizen in a court of the United States.

We think they are before us. The plea in abatement and the judgment of the court upon it are a part of the judicial proceedings in the Circuit Court, and are there recorded as such; and a writ of error always brings up to the superior court the whole record of the proceedings in the court below. And in the case of the United States *vs.* Smith, (11 Wheat., 172,) this Court said, that the case being brought up by writ of error, the whole record was under the consideration of this Court. And this being the case in the present instance, the plea in abatement is necessarily under consideration; and it becomes, therefore, our duty to decide whether the facts stated in the plea are or are not sufficient to show that the plaintiff is not entitled to sue as a citizen in a court of the United States.

This is certainly a very serious question, and one that now for the first time has been brought for decision before this Court. But it is brought here by those who have a right to bring it, and it is our duty to meet it and decide it.

The question is simply this: Can a negro, whose ancestors were imported into this country, and sold as slaves, become a member of the political community formed and brought into existence by the Constitution of the United States, and as such become entitled to all the rights and privileges and immunities guaranteed by that instrument to the citizen? One of which rights is the privilege of suing in a court of the United States in the cases specified in the Constitution.

It will be observed that the plea applies to that class of persons only whose ancestors were negroes of the African race, and imported into this country, and sold and held as slaves. The only matter in issue before the Court, therefore, is whether the descendants of such slaves, when they shall be emancipated, or who are born of parents who had become free before their birth, are citizens of a State in the sense in which the word citizen is used in the Constitution of the United States. And this being the only matter in dispute on the pleadings, the Court must be understood as speaking in this opinion of that class only, that is, of those persons who are the descendants of Africans who were imported into this country and sold as slaves.

The situation of this population was altogether unlike that of the Indian race. The latter, it is true, formed no part of the colonial communities, and never amalgamated with them in social connections or in government. But although they were uncivilized, they were yet a free and independent people, associated together in nations or tribes, and governed by their own laws. Many of these political communities were situated in territories to which the white race claimed the ultimate right of dominion. But that claim was acknowledged to be subject to the right of the Indians to occupy it as long as they thought proper, and neither the English nor colonial Governments claimed or exercised any dominion over the tribe or nation by whom it was occupied, nor claimed the right to the possession of the territory, until the tribe or nation consented to cede it. These Indian Governments were regarded as foreign governments, as much so as if an ocean had separated the red man from the white; and their freedom has constantly been acknowledged, from the time of the first emigration to the English colonies to the present day, by the different governments which succeeded each other. Treaties have been negotiated with them, and their alliance sought for in war; and the people who compose these Indian political communities have always been treated as foreigners not living under our Government. It is true, that the course of events has brought the Indian tribes within the limits of the United States under subjection to the white race; and it has been found necessary, for their sake as well as our own, to regard them as in a state of pupilage, and to legislate to a certain extent over them and the territory they occupy. But they may, without doubt, like the subjects of any other foreign government, be naturalized by the authority of Congress, and become citizens of a State and of the United States; and if an individual should leave his nation or tribe, and take up his abode among the white population, he would be entitled to all the rights and privileges which would belong to an emigrant from any other foreign people.

We proceed to examine the case as presented by the pleadings.

The words, "people of the United States" and "citizens," are synonymous terms, and mean the same thing. They both describe the political body who, according to our republican institutions, form the sovereignty, and who hold the power and conduct the Government through their representatives. They are what we familiarly call the "sovereign people;" and every citizen is one of this people, and a constituent member of this sovereignty. The question before us is, whether the class of persons described in the plea in abatement compose a portion of this people, and are constituent members of this sovereignty? We think they are not; and that they are not included, and were not intended to be included, under the word "citizens" in the Constitution, and therefore can claim none of the rights and privileges which that instrument provides for and secures to citizens of the United States. On the contrary, they were, at that time, considered as a subordinate and inferior class of beings, who had been subjugated by the dominant race; and, whether emancipated or not, yet remained subject to their authority, and had no rights or privileges but such as those who held the power and the Government might choose to grant them.

It is not the province of the Court to decide upon the justice or injustice, policy or impolicy, of these laws. The decision of that question belonged to the political or law-making power; to those who formed the sovereignty and framed the Constitution. The duty of the Court is to interpret the instrument they have framed, with the best lights we can obtain on the subject, and to administer it as we find it, according to its true intent and meaning when it was adopted.

In discussing this question, we must not confound the rights of citizenship which a State may confer within its own limits and the rights of citizenship as a member of the Union. It does not by any means follow, because he has all the rights and privileges of a citizen of a State, that he must be a citizen of the United States. He may have all of the rights and privileges of the citizen of a State, and yet not be entitled to the rights and privileges of a citizen in any other State. For, previous to the adoption of the Constitution of the United States, every State had the undoubted right to confer on whomsoever it pleased the character of citizen, and to endow him with all its rights. But this character of course was confined to the boundaries of the State, and gave him no rights or privileges in other States beyond those secured to him by the laws of nations and the comity of States. Nor have the several States surrendered the power of conferring these rights and privileges by adopting the Constitution of the United States. Each State may still confer them upon an alien, or any one it thinks proper, or upon any class or description of persons; yet he would not be a citizen, in the sense in which that word is used in the Constitution of the United States, nor entitled to such in one of its courts, nor to the privileges and immunities of a citizen in the other States. The rights which he would acquire would be restricted to the State which gave them. The Constitution has conferred on Congress the right to establish a uniform rule of naturalization, and this right is evidently exclusive, and has always been held by this Court to be so. Consequently, no State, since the adoption of the Constitution of the United States, can, by naturalizing an alien, invest him with the rights and privileges secured to a citizen of a State under the Federal Government; although, so far as the State alone was concerned, he would undoubtedly be entitled to the rights of a citizen, and clothed with all the rights and immunities which the Constitution and laws of the State attached to that character.

It is very clear, therefore, that no State can, by any act or law of its own, passed since the adoption of the Constitution, introduce a new member into the political community created by the Constitution of the United States. It cannot make him a member of this community by making him a member of its own. And for the same reason it cannot introduce any person, or description of persons, who were not intended to be embraced in this new political family, which the Constitution brought into existence, but were intended to be excluded from it.

The question then arises, whether the provisions of the Constitution, in relation to the personal rights and privileges to which the citizenship of a State should be entitled, embraced the negro-African race, at that time in this country, or who might afterwards be imported, who had then or should afterwards be made free in any State; and to put it in the power of a single State to make him a citizen of the United States, and endue him with the full rights of citizenship in every other State without their consent? Does the Constitution of the United States act upon him whenever he shall be made free under the laws of a State, and raised there to the rank of a citizen, and immediately clothe him with all the privileges of a citizen in every other State, and in its own courts?

The Court think the affirmative of these propositions cannot be maintained. And if it cannot, the plaintiff in error could not be a citizen of the State of Missouri, within the meaning of the Constitution of the United States, and consequently was not entitled to sue in its courts.

It is true, every person, and every class and description of persons, who were at the time of the adoption of the Constitution recognized as citizens in the several States, became also citizens of this new political body, but none other; it was formed by them, and for them and their posterity, but no one else. And the personal rights and privileges guaranteed to citizens of this new sovereignty were intended to embrace those only who were then members of the several State communities, or who should afterwards, by birthright or otherwise, become members, according to the provisions of the Constitution and the principles on which it was founded. It was the union of those who were at that time members of distinct and separate political communities into one political family, whose power, for certain specified purposes, was to extend over the whole territory of the United States. And it gave to each citizen rights and privileges outside of his State which he did not before possess, and placed him in every other State upon a perfect equality with its own citizens as to rights of person and rights of property; it made him a citizen of the United States.

It becomes necessary, therefore, to determine who were citizens of the several States when the Constitution was adopted. And in order to do this, we must recur to the governments and institutions of the thirteen Colonies when they separated from Great Britain, and formed new sovereignties, and took their places in the family of independent nations. We must inquire who, at that time, were recognized as the people or citizens of a State, whose rights and liberties had been outraged by the English Government; and who declared their independence, and assumed the powers of Government to defend their rights by force of arms.

In the opinion of the Court, the legislation and histories of the times, and the language used in the Declaration of Independence, show that neither the class of persons who had been imported as slaves, nor their descendants, whether they had become free or not, were then acknowledged as a part of the people, nor intended to be included in the general words used in that memorable instrument.

It is difficult at this day to realize the state of public opinion, in relation to that unfortunate race, which prevailed in the civilized and enlightened portions of the world at the time of the Declaration of Independence, and when the Constitution was framed and adopted. But the public history of every European nation displays it in a manner too plain to be mistaken.

They had for more than a century before been regarded as beings of an inferior order, and altogether unfit to associate with the white race, either in social or political relations; and so far inferior, that they had no rights which the white man was bound to respect; and that the negro might justly and lawfully be reduced to slavery for his benefit. He was bought and sold, and treated as an ordinary article of merchandise and traffic, whenever a profit could be made by it. This opinion was at that time fixed and universal in the civilized portion of the white race. It was regarded as an axiom in morals as well as in politics, which no one thought of disputing, or supposed to be open to dispute; and men in every grade and position in society daily and habitually acted upon it in their private pursuits, as well as in matters of public concern, without doubting for a moment the correctness of this opinion.

And in no nation was this opinion more firmly fixed, or more uniformly acted upon, than by the English Government and English people. They not only seized them on the coast of Africa, and sold them or held them in slavery for their own use; but they took them as ordinary articles of merchandise to every country where they could make a profit on them, and were far more extensively engaged in this commerce than any other nation in the world.

The opinion thus entertained and acted upon in England was naturally impressed upon the colonies they founded on this side of the Atlantic. And, accordingly, a negro of the African race was regarded by them as an article of property, and held and bought and sold as such in every one of the thirteen Colonies which united in the Declaration of Independence, and afterwards formed the Constitution of the United States. The slaves were more or less numerous in the different colonies, as slave labor was found more or less profitable. But no one seems to have doubted the correctness of the prevailing opinion of the time.

The legislation of the different colonies furnishes positive and indisputable proof of this fact.

It would be tedious, in this opinion, to enumerate the various laws passed upon this subject. It will be sufficient, as a sample of the legislation which then generally prevailed throughout the British colonies, to give the laws of two of them,— one being still a large slave-holding State, and the other the first State in which slavery ceased to exist.

The province of Maryland, in 1717, (ch. 13, s. 5,) passed a law declaring " that if any free negro or mulatto intermarry with any white woman, or if any white man shall intermarry with any negro or mulatto woman, such negro or mulatto shall become a slave during life, excepting mulattoes born of white women, who, for such intermarriage, shall only become servants for seven years, to be disposed of as the Justices of the County Court, where such marriage so happens, shall think fit; to be applied by them towards the support of a public school within said county. And any white man or white woman who shall intermarry as aforesaid, with any negro or mulatto, such white man or white woman shall become servants during the term of seven years, and shall be disposed of by the justices as aforesaid, and be applied to the uses aforesaid."

The other colonial law to which we refer was passed by Massachusetts in 1705 (ch. 6). It is entitled " An Act for the better preventing of a spurious and mixed issue," etc.; and it provides that "if any negro or mulatto shall presume to smite or strike any person of the English or other Christian nation, such negro or mulatto shall be severely whipped, at the discretion of the justices before whom the offender shall be convicted."

And " that none of her Majesty's English or Scottish subjects, nor of any other Christian nation, within this province, shall contract matrimony with any negro or mulatto; nor shall any person duly authorized to solemnize marriage presume to join any such in marriage, on pain of forfeiting the sum of fifty pounds; one moiety thereof to her Majesty, for and towards the support of the Government within this province, and the other moiety to him or them that shall inform and sue for the same, in any of her Majesty's Courts of Record within the province, by bill, plaint, or information."

We give both of these laws in the words used by the respective legislative bodies, because the language in which they are framed, as well as the provisions contained in them, show, too plainly to be misunderstood, the degraded condition of this unhappy race. They were still in force when the Revolution began, and are a faithful index to the state of feeling towards the class of persons of whom they speak, and of the position they occupied throughout the thirteen Colonies, in the eyes and thoughts of the men who framed the Declaration of Independence and established the State constitutions and governments. They show that a perpetual and impassable barrier was intended to be erected between the white race and the one they had reduced to slavery, and governed as subjects with absolute and despotic power; and which they then looked upon as so far below them in the scale of created beings, that intermarriages between white persons and negroes or mulattoes were regarded as unnatural and immoral, and punished as crimes, not only in the parties, but in the person who joined them in marriage. And no distinction in this respect was made between the free negro or mulatto and the slave, but this stigma, of the deepest degradation, was fixed upon the whole race.

We refer to these historical facts for the purpose of showing the fixed opinions concerning that race, upon which the statesmen of that day spoke and acted. It is necessary to do this, in order to determine whether the general terms used in the Constitution of the United States, as to the rights of man and the rights of the people, were intended to include them, or to give to them or their posterity the benefit of any of its provisions.

The language of the Declaration of Independence is equally conclusive.

It begins by declaring that, "when in the course of human events it becomes necessary for one people to dissolve the political bands which have connected them with another, and to assume among the powers of the earth the separate and equal station to which the laws of nature and nature's God entitle them, a decent respect for the opinions of mankind requires that they should declare the causes which impel them to the separation."

It then proceeds to say: "We hold these truths to be self-evident: that all men are created equal; that they are endowed by their Creator with certain unalienable rights; that among them are life, liberty, and the pursuit of happiness; that to secure these rights governments are instituted, deriving their just powers from the consent of the governed."

The general words above quoted would seem to embrace the whole human family, and if they were used in a similar instrument at this day would be so understood. But it is too clear for dispute, that the enslaved African race were not intended to be included, and formed no part of the people who framed and adopted this declaration; for if the language, as understood in that day, would embrace them, the conduct of the distinguished men who framed the Declaration of Independence would have been utterly and flagrantly inconsistent with the principles they asserted; and instead of the sympathy of mankind, to which they so confidently appealed, they would have deserved and received universal rebuke and reprobation.

Yet the men who framed this declaration were great men, — high in literary acquirements, high in their sense of honor, and incapable of asserting principles inconsistent with those on which they were acting. They perfectly understood the meaning of the language they used, and how it would be understood by others; and they knew that it would not, in any part of the civilized world, be supposed to embrace the negro race, which, by common consent, had been excluded from civilized governments and the family of nations, and doomed to slavery. They spoke and acted according to the then established doctrines and principles, and in the ordinary language of the day, and no one misunderstood them. The unhappy black race were separated from the white by indelible marks and laws long before established, and were never thought of or spoken of except as property, and when the claims of the owner or the profit of the trader were supposed to need protection.

This state of public opinion had undergone no change when the Constitution was adopted, as is equally evident from its provisions and language.

The brief preamble sets forth by whom it was formed, for what purposes, and for whose benefit and protection. It declares that it is formed by the *people* of the United States, that is to say, by those who were members of the different political communities in the several States; and its great object is declared to be to secure the blessings of liberty to themselves and their posterity. It speaks in general terms of the *people* of the United States, and of *citizens* of the several States, when it is providing for the exercise of the powers granted or the privileges secured to the citizen. It does not define what description of persons are intended to be included under these terms, or who shall be regarded as a citizen and one of the people. It uses them as terms so well understood, that no further description or definition was necessary.

But there are two clauses in the Constitution which point directly and specifically to the negro race as a separate class of persons, and show clearly that they were not regarded as a portion of the people or citizens of the Government then formed.

One of these clauses reserves to each of the thirteen States the right to import slaves until the year 1808, if it thinks proper. And the importation which it thus sanctions was unquestionably of persons of the race of which we are speaking, as the traffic in slaves in the United States had always been confined to them. And by the other provision, the States pledge themselves to each other to maintain the right of property of the master, by delivering up to him any slave who may have escaped from his service, and be found within their respective territories. By the first above-mentioned clause, therefore, the right to purchase and hold this property is directly sanctioned and authorized for twenty years by the people who framed the Constitution. And by the second, they pledge themselves to maintain and uphold the right of the master in the manner specified, as long as the Government they then formed should endure. And these two provisions show, conclusively, that neither the description of persons therein referred to, nor their descendants, were embraced in any of the other provisions of the Constitution; for certainly these two clauses were not intended to confer on them or their posterity the blessings of liberty, or any of the personal rights so carefully provided for the citizen.

No one of that race had ever migrated to the United States voluntarily; all of them had been brought here as articles of merchandise. The number that had been emancipated at that time were but few in comparison with those held in slavery; and they were identified in the public mind with the race to which they belonged, and regarded as a part of the slave population rather than the free. It is obvious that they were not even in the minds of the framers of the Constitution when they were conferring special rights and privileges upon the citizens of a State in every other part of the Union.

Indeed, when we look to the condition of this race in the several States at the time, it is impossible to believe that these rights and privileges were intended to be extended to them.

It is very true, that in that portion of the Union where the labor of the negro race was found to be unsuited to the climate and unprofitable to the master, but few slaves were held at the time of the Declaration of Independence; and when the Constitution was adopted, it had entirely worn out in one of them, and measures had been taken for its gradual abolition in several others. But this change had not been produced by any change of opinion in relation to this race, but because it was discovered, from experience, that slave labor was unsuited to the climate and productions of these States; for some of the States, where it had ceased, or nearly ceased to exist, were actively engaged in the slave-trade, procuring cargoes on the coast of Africa, and transporting them for sale to those parts of the Union where their labor was found to be profitable, and suited to the climate and productions. And this traffic was openly carried on, and fortunes accumulated by it, without reproach from the people of the States where they resided. And it can hardly be supposed that, in the States where it was then countenanced in its worst form, that is, in the seizure and transportation, the people could have regarded those who were emancipated as entitled to equal rights with themselves.

And we may again refer, in support of this proposition, to the plain and unequivocal language of the laws of the several States; some passed after the Declaration of Independence and before the Constitution was adopted, and some since the Government went into operation.

We need not refer, on this point, particularly to the laws of the present slave-holding States. Their statute-books are full of provisions in relation to this class, in the same spirit with the Maryland law which we have before quoted. They have continued to treat them as an inferior class, and to subject them to strict police regulations, drawing a broad line of distinction between the citizen and the slave races, and legislating in relation to them upon the same principle which prevailed at the time of the Declaration of Independence. As relates to these States, it is too plain for argument, that they have never been regarded as a part of the people or citizens of the State, nor supposed to possess any political rights which the dominant race might not withhold or grant at their pleasure. And as long ago as 1822, the Court of Appeals of Kentucky decided that free negroes and mulattoes were not citizens within the meaning of the Constitution of the United States; and the correctness of this decision is recognized, and the same doctrine affirmed, in 1 Meigs's Tenn. Reports, 331.

And if we turn to the legislation of the States where slavery had worn out, or measures taken for its speedy abolition, we shall find the same opinions and principles equally fixed and equally acted upon.

Thus, Massachusetts, in 1786, passed a law similar to the colonial one of which we have spoken. The law of 1786, like the law of 1705, forbids the marriage of any white person with any negro, Indian, or mulatto, and inflicts a penalty of fifty pounds upon any one who shall join them in marriage; and declares all such marriages absolutely null and void, and degrades thus the unhappy issue of the marriage by fixing upon it the stain of bastardy. And this mark of degradation was renewed, and again impressed upon the race, in the careful and deliberate preparation of their revised code published in 1836. This code forbids any person from joining in marriage any white person with any Indian, negro, or mulatto, and subjects the party who shall offend in this respect to imprisonment, not exceeding six months, in the common jail, or to hard labor, and to a fine of not less than fifty nor more than two hundred dollars; and like the law of 1786, it declares the marriage to be absolutely null and void. It will be seen that the punishment is increased by the code upon the person who shall marry them, by adding imprisonment to a pecuniary penalty.

So, too, in Connecticut. We refer more particularly to the legislation of this State, because it was not only among the first to put an end to slavery within its own territory, but was the first to fix a mark of reprobation upon the African slave-trade. The law last mentioned was passed in October, 1788, about nine months after the State had ratified and adopted the present Constitution of the United States; and by that law it prohibited its own citizens, under severe penalties, from engaging in the trade, and declared all policies of insurance on the vessel or cargo made in the State to be null and void. But up to the time of the adoption of the Constitution, there is nothing in the legislation of the State indicating any change of opinion as to the relative rights and position of the white and black races in this country, or indicating that it meant to place the latter, when free, upon a level with its citizens; and certainly nothing which would have led the slave-holding States to suppose that Connecticut designed to claim for them, under the new Constitution, the equal rights and privileges and rank of citizens in every other State.

The first step taken by Connecticut upon this subject was as early as 1774, when it passed an act forbidding the further importation of slaves into the State. But the section containing the prohibition is introduced by the following preamble:

"And whereas the increase of slaves in this State is injurious to the poor, and inconvenient."

This recital would appear to have been carefully introduced in order to prevent any misunderstanding of the motive which induced the Legislature to pass the law, and place it distinctly upon the interest and convenience of the white population, excluding the inference that it might have been intended in any degree for the benefit of the other.

And in the Act of 1784, by which the issue of slaves, born after the time therein mentioned, were to be free at a certain age, the section is again introduced by a preamble assigning a similar motive for the act. It is in these words:

"Whereas sound policy requires that the abolition of slavery should be effected as soon as may be consistent with the rights of individuals, and the public safety and welfare," — showing that the right of property in the master was to be protected, and that the measure was one of policy, and to prevent the injury and inconvenience to the whites of a slave population in the State.

And still further pursuing its legislation, we find that in the same statute passed in 1774, which prohibited the further importation of slaves into the State, there is also a provision by which any negro, Indian, or mulatto servant, who was found wandering out of the town or place to which he belonged, without a written pass, such as is therein described, was made liable to be seized by any one, and taken before the next authority to be examined and delivered up to his master, who was required to pay the charge which had accrued thereby. And a subsequent section of the same law provides, that if any free negro shall travel without such a pass, and shall be stopped, seized, or taken up, he shall pay all charges arising thereby. And this law was in full operation when the Constitution of the United States was adopted, and was not repealed until 1797. So that up to that time, free negroes and mulattoes were associated with servants and slaves in the police regulations established by the laws of the State.

And again, in 1833, Connecticut passed another law which made it penal to set up or establish any school in that State for the instruction of persons of the African race not inhabitants of the State, or to instruct or teach in any such school or institution, or board or harbor for that purpose any such person, without the previous consent in writing of the civil authority of the town in which such school or institution might be.

And it appears by the case of Crandall *vs*. The State, reported in 10 Conn. Rep., 340, that upon an information filed against Prudence Crandall for a violation of this law, one of the points raised in the defence was, that the law was a violation of the Constitution of the United States, and that the persons instructed, although of the African race, were citizens of other States, and therefore entitled to the rights and privileges of citizens in the State of Connecticut. But Chief-Justice Daggett, before whom the case was tried, held that persons of that description were not citizens of a State within the meaning of the word "citizen" in the Constitution of the United States, and were not, therefore, entitled to the privileges and immunities of citizens in other States.

The case was carried up to the Supreme Court of Errors of the State, and the question fully argued there. But the case went off upon another point, and no opinion was expressed on this question.

We have made this particular examination into the legislative and judicial action of Connecticut, because, from the early hostility displayed to the slave-trade on the coast of Africa, we may expect to find the laws of that State as lenient and favorable to the subject race as those of any other State in the Union; and if we find that at the time the Constitution was adopted, they were not even there raised to the rank of citizens, but were still held and treated as property, and the laws relating to them passed with reference altogether to the interest and convenience of the white race, we shall hardly find them elevated to a higher rank anywhere else.

A brief notice of the laws of two other States, and we shall pass on to other considerations.

By the laws of New Hampshire, collected and finally passed in 1815, no one was permitted to be enrolled in the militia of the State but free white citizens; and the same provision is found in a subsequent collection of the laws made in 1855. Nothing could more strongly mark the entire repudiation of the African race. The alien is excluded, because, being born in a foreign country, he cannot be a member of the community until he is naturalized. But why are the African race, born in the State, not permitted to share in one of the highest duties of the citizen? The answer is obvious: he is not, by the institutions and laws of the State, numbered among its people. He forms no part of the sovereignty of the State, and is not therefore called on to uphold and defend it.

Again, in 1822, Rhode Island, in its revised code, passed a law forbidding persons who were authorized to join persons in marriage, from joining in marriage any white person with any negro, Indian, or mulatto, under the penalty of two hundred dollars, and declaring all such marriages absolutely null and void; and the same law was again re-enacted in its revised code of 1844. So that, down to the last-mentioned period, the strongest mark of inferiority and degradation was fastened upon the African race in that State.

It would be impossible to enumerate and compress in the space usually allotted to an opinion of a court, the various laws, marking the condition of this race, which were passed from time to time after the Revolution, and before and since the adoption of the Constitution of the United States. In addition to those already referred to, it is sufficient to say, that Chancellor Kent, whose accuracy and research no one will question, states in the sixth edition of his Commentaries, (published in 1848, 2d vol., 258, note *b*,) that in no part of the country, except Maine, did the African race, in point of fact, participate equally with the whites in the exercise of civil and political rights.

The legislation of the States therefore shows, in a manner not to be mistaken, the inferior and subject condition of that race at the time the Constitution was adopted, and long afterwards, throughout the thirteen States by which that instrument was framed; and it is hardly consistent with the respect due to these States, to suppose that they regarded at that time, as fellow-citizens and members of the sovereignty, a class of beings whom they had thus stigmatized; whom, as we are bound, out of respect to the State sovereignties, to assume they had deemed it just and necessary thus to stigmatize, and upon whom they had impressed such deep and enduring marks of inferiority and degradation ; or, that when they met in convention to form the Constitution, they looked upon them as a portion of their constituents, or designed to include them in the provisions so carefully inserted for the security and protection of the liberties and rights of their citizens. It cannot be supposed that they intended to secure to them rights, and privileges, and rank, in the new political body throughout the Union, which every one of them denied within the limits of its own dominion. More especially, it cannot be believed that the large slave-holding States regarded them as included in the word citizens, or would have consented to a Constitution which might compel them to receive them in that character from another State. For if they were so received, and entitled to the privileges and immunities of citizens, it would exempt them from the operation of the special laws and from the police regulations, which they considered to be necessary for their own safety. It would give to persons of the negro race, who were recognized as citizens in any one State of the Union, the right to enter every other State whenever they pleased, singly or in companies, without pass or passport, and without obstruction, to sojourn there as long as they pleased, to go where they pleased at every hour of the day or night without molestation, unless they committed some violation of law for which a white man would be punished ; and it would give them the full liberty of speech in public and in private upon all subjects upon which its own citizens might speak ; to hold public meetings upon political affairs, and to keep and carry arms wherever they went. And all of this would be done in the face of the subject race of the same color, both free and slaves, and inevitably producing discontent and insubordination among them, and endangering the peace and safety of the State.

It is impossible, it would seem, to believe that the great men of the slave-holding States, who took so large a share in framing the Constitution of the United States, and exercised so much influence in procuring its adoption, could have been so forgetful or regardless of their own safety and the safety of those who trusted and confided in them.

Besides, this want of foresight and care would have been utterly inconsistent with the caution displayed in providing for the admission of new members into this political family. For, when they gave to the citizens of each State the privileges and immunities of citizens in the several States, they, at the same time, took from the several States the power of naturalization, and confined that power exclusively to the Federal Government. No State was willing to permit another State to determine who should or should not be admitted as one of its citizens, and entitled to demand equal rights and privileges with their own people, within their own territories. The right of naturalization was, therefore, with one accord, surrendered by the States, and confided to the Federal Government. And this power granted to Congress to establish a uniform rule of *naturalization* is, by the well understood meaning of the word, confined to persons born in a foreign country, under a foreign government. It is not a power to raise to the rank of a citizen any one born in the United States, who, from birth or parentage, by the laws of the country, belongs to an inferior and subordinate class. And when we find the States guarding themselves from the indiscreet or improper admission by other States of emigrants from other countries, by giving the power exclusively to Congress, we cannot fail to see that they could never have left with the States a much more important power, — that is, the power of transforming into citizens a numerous class of persons who, in that character, would be much more dangerous to the peace and safety of a large portion of the Union than the few foreigners one of the States might improperly naturalize. The Constitution, upon its adoption, obviously took from the States all power by any subsequent legislation to introduce as a citizen into the political family of the United States any one, no matter where he was born, or what might be his character or condition ; and it gave to Congress the power to confer this character upon those only who were born outside of the dominions of the United States. And no law of a State, therefore, passed since the Constitution was adopted, can give any right of citizenship outside of its own territory.

A clause similar to the one in the Constitution, in relation to the rights and immunities of citizens of one State in the other States was contained in the Articles of Confederation. But there is a difference of language which is worthy of note. The provision in the Articles of Confederation was, "that the *free inhabitants* of each of the States (paupers, vagabonds, and fugitives from justice, excepted) should be entitled to all the privileges and immunities of free citizens in the several States."

It will be observed that under this Confederation each State had the right to decide for itself, and in its own tribunals, whom it would acknowledge as a free inhabitant of another State. The term *free* inhabitant, in the generality of its terms, would certainly include one of the African race who had been manumitted. But no example, we think, can be found of his admission to all the privileges of citizenship in any State of the Union after these Articles were formed, and while they continued in force. And, notwithstanding the generality of the words "free inhabitants," it is very clear that, according to their accepted meaning in that day, they did not include the African race, whether free or not; for the fifth section of the ninth article provides that Congress should have the power "to agree upon the number of land forces to be raised, and to make requisitions from each State for its quota in proportion to the number of *white* inhabitants in such State, which requisition should be binding."

Words could hardly be used which more strongly mark the line of distinction between the citizen and the subject; the free and the subjugated races. The latter were not even counted when the inhabitants of a State were to be embodied in proportion to its numbers for the general defence. And it cannot for a moment be supposed, that a class of persons thus separated and rejected from those who formed the sovereignty of the States, were yet intended to be included under the words "free inhabitants," in the preceding article, to whom privileges and immunities were so carefully secured in every State.

But although this clause of the Articles of Confederation is the same in principle with that inserted in the Constitution, yet the comprehensive word *inhabitant*, which might be construed to include an emancipated slave, is omitted; and the privilege is confined to *citizens* of the State. And this alteration in words would hardly have been made, unless a different meaning was intended to be conveyed, or a possible doubt removed. The just and fair inference is, that as this privilege was about to be placed under the protection of the general Government, and the words expounded by its tribunals, and all power in relation to it taken from the State and its courts, it was deemed prudent to describe with precision and caution the persons to whom this high privilege was given, and the word *citizen* was on that account substituted for the words *free inhabitant.* The word citizen excluded, and no doubt intended to exclude, foreigners who had not become citizens of some one of the States when the Constitution was adopted; and also every description of persons who were not fully recognized as citizens in the several States. This, upon any fair construction of the instruments to which we have referred, was evidently the object and purpose of this change of words.

To all this mass of proof we have still to add, that Congress has repeatedly legislated upon the same construction of the Constitution that we have given. Three laws, two of which were passed almost immediately after the Government went into operation, will be abundantly sufficient to show this. The first two are particularly worthy of notice, because many of the men who assisted in framing the Constitution, and took an active part in procuring its adoption, were then in the halls of legislation, and certainly understood what they meant when they used the words "people of the United States" and "citizens" in that well-considered instrument.

The first of these acts is the naturalization law, which was passed at the second session of the first Congress, March 26, 1790, and confines the right of becoming citizens "to aliens being free white persons."

Now the Constitution does not limit the power of Congress in this respect to white persons. And they may, if they think proper, authorize the naturalization of any one, of any color, who was born under allegiance to another Government. But the language of the law above quoted shows that citizenship at that time was perfectly understood to be confined to the white race; and that they alone constituted the sovereignty in the Government.

Congress might, as we before said, have authorized the naturalization of Indians, because they were aliens and foreigners. But, in their then untutored and savage state, no one would have thought of admitting them as citizens in a civilized community. And, moreover, the atrocities they had but recently committed, when they were the allies of Great Britain in the Revolutionary War, were yet fresh in the recollection of the people of the United States, and they were even then guarding themselves against the threatened renewal of Indian hostilities. No one supposed then that any Indian would ask for, or was capable of enjoying, the privileges of an American citizen, and the word *white* was not used with any particular reference to them.

Neither was it used with any reference to the African race imported into or born in this country; because Congress had no power to naturalize them, and therefore there was no necessity for using particular words to exclude them.

It would seem to have been used merely because it followed out the line of division which the Constitution has drawn between the citizen race, who formed and held the Government, and the African race, which they held in subjection and slavery, and governed at their own pleasure.

Another of the early laws of which we have spoken is the first militia law, which was passed in 1792, at the first session of the second Congress. The language of this law is equally plain and significant with the one just mentioned. It directs that every "free, able-bodied white male citizen" shall be enrolled in the militia. The word *white* is evidently used to exclude the African race, and the word "citizen" to exclude unnaturalized foreigners; the latter forming no part of the sovereignty, owing it no allegiance, and therefore under no obligation to defend it. The African race, however, born in the country, did owe allegiance to the Government, whether they were free or slave; but it is repudiated, and rejected from the duties and obligations of citizenship in marked language.

The third act to which we have alluded is even still more decisive; it was passed as late as 1813, (2 Stat., 809,) and it provides: "That from and after the termination of the war in which the United States are now engaged with Great Britain, it shall not be lawful to employ, on board of any public or private vessels of the United States, any person or persons except citizens of the United States, or persons of color, natives of the United States."

Here the line of distinction is drawn in express words. Persons of color, in the judgment of Congress, were not included in the word citizens, and they are described as another and different class of persons, and authorized to be employed, if born in the United States.

And even as late as 1820, (chap. 104, sec. 8,) in the charter to the city of Washington, the corporation is authorized "to restrain and prohibit the nightly and other disorderly meetings of slaves, free negroes, and mulattoes," thus associating them together in its legislation; and after prescribing the punishment that may be inflicted on the slaves, proceeds in the following words: "And to punish such free negroes and mulattoes by penalties not exceeding twenty dollars for any one offence; and in case of the inability of any such free negro or mulatto to pay any such penalty and cost thereon, to cause him or her to be confined to labor for any time not exceeding six calendar months." And in a subsequent part of the same section, the act authorizes the corporation " to prescribe the terms and conditions upon which free negroes and mulattoes may reside in the city."

This law, like the laws of the States, shows that this class of persons were governed by special legislation directed expressly to them, and always connected with provisions for the government of slaves, and not with those for the government of free white citizens. And after such an uniform course of legislation as we have stated, by the Colonies, by the States, and by Congress, running through a period of more than a century, it would seem that to call persons thus marked and stigmatized, " citizens " of the United States, " fellow-citizens," a constituent part of the sovereignty, would be an abuse of terms, and not calculated to exalt the character of an American citizen in the eyes of other nations.

The conduct of the Executive Department of the Government has been in perfect harmony upon this subject with this course of legislation. The question was brought officially before the late William Wirt, when he was the Attorney-General of the United States, in 1821, and he decided that the words "citizens of the United States" were used in the acts of Congress in the same sense as in the Constitution; and that free persons of color were not citizens within the meaning of the Constitution and laws; and this opinion has been confirmed by that of the late Attorney-General, Caleb Cushing, in a recent case, and acted upon by the Secretary of State, who refused to grant passports to them as " citizens of the United States."

But it is said that a person may be a citizen, and entitled to that character, although he does not possess all the rights which may belong to other citizens; as, for example, the right to vote, or to hold particular offices; and that yet, when he goes into another State, he is entitled to be recognized there as a citizen, although the State may measure his rights by the rights which it allows to persons of a like character or class resident in the State, and refuse to him the full rights of citizenship.

This argument overlooks the language of the provision in the Constitution of which we are speaking.

Undoubtedly, a person may be a citizen, that is, a member of the community, who form the sovereignty, although he exercises no share of the political power, and is incapacitated from holding particular offices. Women and minors, who form a part of the political family, cannot vote; and when a property qualification is required to vote or hold a particular office, those who have not the necessary qualification cannot vote or hold the office; yet they are citizens.

So, too, a person may be entitled to vote by the law of the State who is not a citizen even of the State itself. And in some of the States of the Union foreigners not naturalized are allowed to vote. And the State may give the right to free negroes and mulattoes, but that does not make them citizens of the State, and still less of the United States. And the provision in the Constitution giving privileges and immunities in other States does not apply to them.

Neither does it apply to a person who, being a citizen of a State, migrates to another State. For then he becomes subject to the laws of the State in which he lives, and he is no longer a citizen of the State from which he removed. And the State in which he resides may then, unquestionably, determine his *status* or condition, and place him among the class of persons who are not recognized as citizens, but belong to an inferior and subject race; and may deny him the privileges and immunities enjoyed by its citizens.

But so far as mere rights of person are concerned, the provision in question is confined to citizens of a State who are temporarily in another State without taking up their residence there. It gives them no political rights in the State, as to voting or holding office, or in any other respect. For a citizen of one State has no right to participate in the government of another. But if he ranks as a citizen in the State to which he belongs, within the meaning of the Constitution of the United States, then, whenever he goes into another State, the Constitution clothes him, as to the rights of person, with all the privileges and immunities which belong to citizens of the State. And if persons of the African race are citizens of a State, and of the United States, they would be entitled to all of these privileges and immunities in every State; and the State could not restrict them; for they would hold these privileges and immunities under the paramount authority of the Federal Government, and its courts would be bound to maintain and enforce them, the Constitution and laws of the State to the contrary notwithstanding. And if the States could limit or restrict them, or place the party in an inferior grade, this clause of the Constitution would be unmeaning, and could have no operation; and would give no rights to the citizen when in another State. He would have none but what the State itself chose to allow him. This is evidently not the construction or meaning of the clause in question. It guarantees rights to the citizen, and the State cannot withhold them. And these rights are of a character and would lead to consequences which make it absolutely certain that the African race was not included under the name of citizens of a State, and was not in the contemplation of the framers of the Constitution when these privileges and immunities were provided for the protection of the citizen in other States.

The case of Legrand *vs.* Darnall (2 Peters, 664) has been referred to for the purpose of showing that this Court has decided that the descendant of a slave may sue as a citizen in a court of the United States; but the case itself shows that the question did not arise and could not have arisen in the case.

It appears from the report, that Darnall was born in Maryland, and was the son of a white man by one of his slaves, and his father executed certain instruments to manumit him, and devised to him some landed property in the State. This property Darnall afterwards sold to Legrand, the appellant, who gave his notes for the purchase-money. But becoming afterwards apprehensive that the appellee had not been emancipated according to the laws of Maryland, he refused to pay the notes until he could be better satisfied as to Darnall's right to convey. Darnall, in the mean time, had taken up his residence in Pennsylvania, and brought suit on the notes, and recovered judgment in the Circuit Court for the District of Maryland.

The whole proceeding, as appears by the report, was an amicable one: Legrand being perfectly willing to pay the money, if he could obtain a title, and Darnall not wishing him to pay unless he could make him a good one. In point of fact, the whole proceeding was under the direction of the counsel who argued the case for the appellee, who was a mutual friend of the parties, and confided in by both of them, and whose only object was to have the rights of both parties established by judicial decision in the most speedy and least expensive manner.

Legrand, therefore, raised no objection to the jurisdiction of the court in the suit at law, because he was himself anxious to obtain the judgment of the court upon his title. Consequently, there was nothing in the record before the court to show that Darnall was of African descent, and the usual judgment and award of execution was entered. And Legrand thereupon filed his bill on the equity side of the Circuit Court, stating that Darnall was born a slave, and had not been legally emancipated, and could not therefore take the land devised to him, nor make Legrand a good title; and praying an injunction to restrain Darnall from proceeding to execution on the judgment, which was granted. Darnall answered, averring in his answer that he was a free man, and capable of conveying a good title. Testimony was taken on this point, and at the hearing the Circuit Court was of opinion that Darnall was a free man and his title good, and dissolved the injunction and dismissed the bill; and that decree was affirmed here, upon the appeal of Legrand.

Now, it is difficult to imagine how any question about the citizenship of Darnall, or his right to sue in that character, can be supposed to have arisen or been decided in that case. The fact that he was of African descent was first brought before the court upon the bill in equity. The suit at law had been passed into judgment and award of execution, and the Circuit Court as a court of law had no longer any authority over it. It was a valid and legal judgment, which the court that rendered it had not the power to reverse or set aside. And unless it had jurisdiction as a court of equity, to restrain him from using its process as a court of law, Darnall, if he thought proper, would have been at liberty to proceed on his judgment, and compel the payment of the money, although the allegations in the bill were true, and he was incapable of making a title. No other court could have enjoined him, for certainly no State equity court could interfere in that way with the judgment of the Circuit Court of the United States.

But the Circuit Court as a court of equity certainly had equity jurisdiction over its own judgment as a court of law, without regard to the character of the parties; and had not only the right, but it was its duty — no matter who were the parties in the judgment — to prevent them from proceeding to enforce it by execution, if the court was satisfied that the money was not justly and equitably due. The ability of Darnall to convey did not depend upon his citizenship, but upon his title to freedom. And if he was free, he could hold and convey property, by the laws of Maryland, although he was not a citizen. But if he was by law still a slave, he could not. It was therefore the duty of the court, sitting as a court of equity in the latter case, to prevent him from using its process, as a court of common law, to compel the payment of the purchase-money, when it was evident that the purchaser must lose the land. But if he was free, and could make a title, it was equally the duty of the court not to suffer Legrand to keep the land, and refuse the payment of the money, upon the ground that Darnall was incapable of suing or being sued as a citizen in a court of the United States. The character or citizenship of the parties had no connection with the question of jurisdiction, and the matter in dispute had no relation to the citizenship of Darnall. Nor is such a question alluded to in the opinion of the court.

Besides, we are by no means prepared to say that there are not many cases, civil as well as criminal, in which a Circuit Court of the United States may exercise jurisdiction, although one of the African race is a party; that broad question is not before the Court. The question with which we are now dealing is, whether a person of the African race can be a citizen of the United States, and become thereby entitled to a special privilege, by virtue of his title to that character, and which, under the Constitution, no one but a citizen can claim. It is manifest that the case of Legrand and Darnall has no bearing on that question, and can have no application to the case now before the Court.

This case, however, strikingly illustrates the consequences that would follow the construction of the Constitution which would give the power contended for to a State. It would, in effect, give it also to an individual. For if the father of young Darnall had manumitted him in his lifetime, and sent him to reside in a State which recognized him as a citizen, he might have visited and sojourned in Maryland when he pleased, and as long as he pleased, as a citizen of the United States; and the State officers and tribunals would be compelled, by the paramount authority of the Constitution, to receive him and treat him as one of its citizens, exempt from the laws and police of the State in relation to a person of that description, and allow him to enjoy all the rights and privileges of citizenship, without respect to the laws of Maryland, although such laws were deemed by it absolutely essential to its own safety.

The only two provisions which point to them and include them treat them as property, and make it the duty of the Government to protect it; no other power, in relation to this race, is to be found in the Constitution; and as it is a Government of special, delegated powers, no authority beyond these two provisions can be constitutionally exercised. The Government of the United States had no right to interfere for any other purpose but that of protecting the rights of the owner, leaving it altogether with the several States to deal with this race, whether emancipated or not, as each State may think justice, humanity, and the interests and safety of society require. The States evidently intended to reserve this power exclusively to themselves.

No one, we presume, supposes that any change in public opinion or feeling, in relation to this unfortunate race, in the civilized nations of Europe or in this country, should induce the Court to give to the words of the Constitution a more liberal construction in their favor than they were intended to bear when the instrument was framed and adopted. Such an argument would be altogether inadmissible in any tribunal called on to interpret it. If any of its provisions are deemed unjust, there is a mode prescribed in the instrument itself by which it may be amended; but while it remains unaltered, it must be construed now as it was understood at the time of its adoption. It is not only the same in words, but the same in meaning, and delegates the same powers to the Government, and reserves and secures the same rights and privileges to the citizens; and as long as it continues to exist in its present form, it speaks not only in the same words, but with the same

meaning and intent with which it spoke when it came from the
hands of its framers, and was voted on and adopted by the
people of the United States. Any other rule of construction would
abrogate the judicial character of this Court, and make it the
mere reflex of the popular opinion or passion of the day. This
Court was not created by the Constitution for such purposes.
Higher and graver trusts have been confided to it, and it must
not falter in the path of duty.

What the construction was at that time, we think can hardly
admit of doubt. We have the language of the Declaration of Independence and of the Articles of Confederation, in addition to
the plain words of the Constitution itself; we have the legislation
of the different States, before, about the time, and since, the Constitution was adopted; we have the legislation of Congress from
the time of its adoption to a recent period; and we have the constant and uniform action of the Executive Department, all concurring together and leading to the same result. And if anything
in relation to the construction of the Constitution can be regarded
as settled, it is that which we now give to the word " citizen " and
the word " people."

And upon a full and careful consideration of the subject, the
Court is of opinion, that, upon the facts stated in the plea in abatement, Dred Scott was not a citizen of Missouri within the meaning of the Constitution of the United States, and not entitled as
such to sue in its courts; and, consequently, that the Circuit Court
had no jurisdiction of the case, and that the judgment on the plea
in abatement is erroneous.

We are aware that doubts are entertained by some of the Court,
whether the plea in abatement is legally before the Court upon
this writ of error; but if that plea is regarded as waived, or out
of the case upon any other ground, yet the question as to the jurisdiction of the Circuit Court is presented on the face of the bill of
exception itself, taken by the plaintiff at the trial; for he admits
that he and his wife were born slaves, but endeavors to make out
his title to freedom and citizenship by showing that they were
taken by their owner to certain places, hereinafter mentioned,
where slavery could not by law exist, and that they thereby became free, and upon their return to Missouri became citizens of
that State.

Now, if the removal of which he speaks did not give them their freedom, then by his own admission he is still a slave; and whatever opinions may be entertained in favor of the citizenship of a free person of the African race, no one supposes that a slave is a citizen of the State or of the United States. If, therefore, the acts done by his owner did not make them free persons, he is still a slave, and certainly incapable of suing in the character of a citizen.

The principle of law is too well settled to be disputed, that a court can give no judgment for either party, where it has no jurisdiction; and if, upon the showing of Scott himself, it appeared that he was still a slave, the case ought to have been dismissed, and the judgment against him and in favor of the defendant for costs, is, like that on the plea in abatement, erroneous, and the suit ought to have been dismissed by the Circuit Court for want of jurisdiction in that court.

But before we proceed to examine this part of the case, it may be proper to notice an objection taken to the judicial authority of this Court to decide it; and it has been said, that as this Court has decided against the jurisdiction of the Circuit Court on the plea in abatement, it has no right to examine any question presented by the exception; and that anything it may say upon that part of the case will be extrajudicial, and mere *obiter dicta*.

This is a manifest mistake; there can be no doubt as to the jurisdiction of this Court to revise the judgment of the Circuit Court, and to reverse it for any error apparent on the record, whether it be the error of giving judgment in a case over which it had no jurisdiction, or any other material error; and this, too, whether there is a plea in abatement or not.

The objection appears to have arisen from confounding writs of error to a State court with writs of error to a Circuit Court of the United States. Undoubtedly, upon a writ of error to a State court, unless the record shows a case that gives jurisdiction, the case must be dismissed for want of jurisdiction in *this Court*. And if it is dismissed on that ground, we have no right to examine and decide upon any question presented by the bill of exceptions, or any other part of the record. But writs of error to a State court, and to a Circuit Court of the United States, are regulated by different laws, and stand upon entirely different principles. And in a writ of error to a Circuit Court of the United States, the whole record is before this Court for examination and decision; and, if the sum in controversy is large enough to give jurisdiction, it is not only the right, but it is the judicial duty, of the Court to examine the whole case as presented by the record; and if it appears upon its face that any material error or errors have been committed by the court below, it is the duty of this Court to reverse the judgment, and remand the case. And certainly an error in passing a judgment upon the merits in favor of either party, in a case which it was not authorized to try, and over which it had no jurisdiction, is as grave an error as a court can commit.

The plea in abatement is not a plea to the jurisdiction of this Court, but to the jurisdiction of the Circuit Court. And it appears by the record before us that the Circuit Court committed an error in deciding that it had jurisdiction upon the facts in the case, admitted by the pleadings. It is the duty of the appellate tribunal to correct this error; but that could not be done by dismissing the case for want of jurisdiction here, — for that would leave the erroneous judgment in full force, and the injured party without remedy. And the appellate court, therefore, exercises the power for which alone appellate courts are constituted, by reversing the judgment of the court below for this error. It exercises its proper and appropriate jurisdiction over the judgment and proceedings of the Circuit Court, as they appear upon the record brought up by the writ of error.

The correction of one error in the court below does not deprive the appellate court of the power of examining further into the record, and correcting any other material errors which may have been committed by the inferior court. There is certainly no rule of law, nor any practice, nor any decision of a court, which even questions this power in the appellate tribunal. On the contrary, it is the daily practice of this Court, and of all appellate courts where they reverse the judgment of an inferior court for error, to correct by its opinions whatever errors may appear on the record material to the case; and they have always held it to be their duty to do so where the silence of the court might lead to misconstruction or future controversy, and the point has been relied on by either side, and argued before the court.

In the case before us, we have already decided that the Circuit

Court erred in deciding that it had jurisdiction upon the facts admitted by the pleadings. And it appears that, in the further progress of the case, it acted upon the erroneous principle it had decided on the pleadings, and gave judgment for the defendant, where, upon the facts admitted in the exception, it had no jurisdiction.

We are at a loss to understand upon what principle of law, applicable to appellate jurisdiction, it can be supposed that this Court has not judicial authority to correct the last-mentioned error, because they had before corrected the former; or by what process of reasoning it can be made out, that the error of an inferior court in actually pronouncing judgment for one of the parties, in a case in which it had no jurisdiction, cannot be looked into or corrected by this Court, because we have decided a similar question presented in the pleadings. The last point is distinctly presented by the facts contained in the plaintiff's own bill of exceptions, which he himself brings here by this writ of error. It was the point which chiefly occupied the attention of the counsel on both sides in the argument, and the judgment which this Court must render upon both errors is precisely the same. It must, in each of them, exercise jurisdiction over the judgment, and reverse it for the errors committed by the court below; and issue a mandate to the Circuit Court to conform its judgment to the opinion pronounced by this Court, by dismissing the case for want of jurisdiction in the Circuit Court. This is the constant and invariable practice of this Court, where it reverses a judgment for want of jurisdiction in the Circuit Court.

It can scarcely be necessary to pursue such a question further. The want of jurisdiction in the court below may appear on the record without any plea in abatement. This is familiarly the case where a court of chancery has exercised jurisdiction in a case where the plaintiff had a plain and adequate remedy at law, and it so appears by the transcript when brought here by appeal. So, also, where it appears that a court of admiralty has exercised jurisdiction in a case belonging exclusively to a court of common law. In these cases there is no plea in abatement. And for the same reason, and upon the same principles, where the defect of jurisdiction is patent upon the record, this Court is bound to reverse the judgment, although the defendant has not pleaded in abatement to the jurisdiction of the inferior court.

The cases of Jackson *vs.* Ashton, and of Capron *vs.* Van Noorden, to which we have referred in a previous part of this opinion, are directly in point. In the last-mentioned case, Capron brought an action against Van Noorden in a Circuit Court of the United States, without showing, by the usual averments of citizenship, that the court had jurisdiction. There was no plea in abatement put in, and the parties went to trial upon the merits. The court gave judgment in favor of the defendant, with costs. The plaintiff thereupon brought his writ of error, and this Court reversed the judgment given in favor of the defendant, and remanded the case with directions to dismiss it, because it did not appear by the transcript that the Circuit Court had jurisdiction.

The case before us still more strongly imposes upon this Court the duty of examining whether the court below has not committed an error in taking jurisdiction and giving a judgment for costs in favor of the defendant; for in Capron *vs.* Van Noorden the judgment was reversed, because it *did not appear* that the parties were citizens of different States. They might or might not be. But in this case it *does appear* that the plaintiff was born a slave; and if the facts upon which he relies have not made him free, then it appears affirmatively on the record that he is not a citizen, and consequently his suit against Sandford was not a suit between citizens of different States, and the court had no authority to pass any judgment between the parties. The suit ought, in this view of it, to have been dismissed by the Circuit Court; and its judgment in favor of Sandford is erroneous, and must be reversed.

It is true that the result either way, by dismissal or by a judgment for the defendant, makes very little, if any, difference in a pecuniary or personal point of view to either party. But the fact that the result would be very nearly the same to the parties in either form of judgment, would not justify this court in sanctioning an error in the judgment which is patent on the record, and which, if sanctioned, might be drawn into precedent, and lead to serious mischief and injustice in some future suit.

We proceed, therefore, to inquire whether the facts relied on by the plaintiff entitle him to his freedom.

The case, as he himself states it on the record brought here by his writ of error, is this:

The plaintiff was a negro slave belonging to Dr. Emerson, who was a surgeon in the army of the United States. In the year 1834, he took the plaintiff from the State of Missouri to the military post at Rock Island, in the State of Illinois, and held him there as a slave until the month of April or May, 1836. At the time last mentioned, said Dr. Emerson removed the plaintiff from said military post at Rock Island to the military post at Fort Snelling, situate on the west bank of the Mississippi River, in the territory known as Upper Louisiana, acquired by the United States of France, and situate north of the latitude of thirty-six degrees thirty minutes north, and north of the State of Missouri. Said Dr. Emerson held the plaintiff in slavery, at said Fort Snelling, from said last-mentioned date until the year 1838.

In the year 1835, Harriet, who is named in the second count of the plaintiff's declaration, was the negro slave of Major Taliaferro, who belonged to the army of the United States. In that year, 1835, said Major Taliaferro took said Harriet to said Fort Snelling, a military post, situated as hereinbefore stated, and kept her there as a slave until the year 1836, and then sold and delivered her as a slave, at said Fort Snelling, unto the said Dr. Emerson hereinbefore named. Said Dr. Emerson held said Harriet in slavery at said Fort Snelling until the year 1838.

In the year 1836, the plaintiff and Harriet intermarried, at Fort Snelling, with the consent of Dr. Emerson, who then claimed to be their master and owner. Eliza and Lizzie, named in the third count of the plaintiff's declaration, are the fruit of that marriage. Eliza is about fourteen years old, and was born on board the steamboat Gipsey, north of the north line of the State of Missouri, and upon the river Mississippi. Lizzie is about seven years old, and was born in the State of Missouri, at the military post called Jefferson Barracks.

In the year 1838, said Dr. Emerson removed the plaintiff and said Harriet, and their said daughter Eliza, from said Fort Snelling to the State of Missouri, where they have ever since resided.

Before the commencement of this suit, said Dr. Emerson sold and conveyed the plaintiff, and Harriet, Eliza, and Lizzie, to the defendant, as slaves, and the defendant has ever since claimed to hold them, and each of them, as slaves.

In considering this part of the controversy, two questions arise : 1. Was he, together with his family, free in Missouri by reason of the stay in the territory of the United States hereinbefore mentioned? And, 2. If they were not, is Scott himself free by reason of his removal to Rock Island, in the State of Illinois, as stated in the above admissions?

We proceed to examine the first question.

The Act of Congress, upon which the plaintiff relies, declares that slavery and involuntary servitude, except as a punishment for crime, shall be forever prohibited in all that part of the territory ceded by France, under the name of Louisiana, which lies north of thirty-six degrees thirty minutes north latitude, and not included within the limits of Missouri. And the difficulty which meets us at the threshold of this part of the inquiry is, whether Congress was authorized to pass this law under any of the powers granted to it by the Constitution; for if the authority is not given by that instrument, it is the duty of this Court to declare it void and inoperative, and incapable of conferring freedom upon any one who is held as a slave under the laws of any one of the States.

The counsel for the plaintiff has laid much stress upon that article in the Constitution which confers on Congress the power " to dispose of and make all needful rules and regulations respecting the territory or other property belonging to the United States; " but, in the judgment of the Court, that provision has no bearing on the present controversy, and the power there given, whatever it may be, is confined, and was intended to be confined, to the territory which at that time belonged to or was claimed by the United States, and was within their boundaries as settled by the treaty with Great Britain, and can have no influence upon a territory afterwards acquired from a foreign Government. It was a special provision for a known and particular territory, and to meet a present emergency, and nothing more.

A brief summary of the history of the times, as well as the careful and measured terms in which the article is framed, will show the correctness of this proposition.

It will be remembered that, from the commencement of the Revolutionary war, serious difficulties existed between the States, in relation to the disposition of large and unsettled territories which were included in the chartered limits of some of the States. And some of the other States, and more especially Maryland, which had no unsettled lands, insisted that as the unoccupied lands, if wrested from Great Britain, would owe their preservation to the common purse and the common sword, the money arising from them ought to be applied in just proportion among the several States to pay the expenses of the war, and ought not to be appropriated to the use of the State in whose chartered limits they might happen to lie, to the exclusion of the other States, by whose combined efforts and common expense the territory was defended and preserved against the claim of the British Government.

These difficulties caused much uneasiness during the war, while the issue was in some degree doubtful, and the future boundaries of the United States yet to be defined by treaty, if we achieved our independence.

The majority of the Congress of the Confederation obviously concurred in opinion with the State of Maryland, and desired to obtain from the States which claimed it a cession of this territory, in order that Congress might raise money on this security to carry on the war. This appears by the resolution passed on the 6th of September, 1780, strongly urging the States to cede these lands to the United States, both for the sake of peace and union among themselves, and to maintain the public credit; and this was followed by the resolution of October 10th, 1780, by which Congress pledged itself, that if the lands were ceded, as recommended by the resolution above mentioned, they should be disposed of for the common benefit of the United States, and be settled and formed into distinct republican States, which should become members of the Federal Union, and have the same rights of sovereignty and freedom and independence as other States.

But these difficulties became much more serious after peace took place, and the boundaries of the United States were established. Every State, at that time, felt severely the pressure of its war debt; but in Virginia, and some other States, there were large territories of unsettled lands, the sale of which would enable them to discharge their obligations without much inconvenience; while other States, which had no such resource, saw before them many years of heavy and burdensome taxation; and the latter insisted, for the reasons before stated, that these unsettled lands should be treated as the common property of the States, and the proceeds applied to their common benefit.

The letters from the statesmen of that day will show how much this controversy occupied their thoughts, and the dangers that were apprehended from it. It was the disturbing element of the time, and fears were entertained that it might dissolve the Confederation by which the States were then united.

These fears and dangers were, however, at once removed, when the State of Virginia, in 1784, voluntarily ceded to the United States the immense tract of country lying northwest of the river Ohio, and was within the acknowledged limits of the State. The only object of the State in making this cession, was to put an end to the threatening and exciting controversy, and to enable the Congress of that time to dispose of the lands, and appropriate the proceeds as a common fund for the common benefit of the States. It was not ceded because it was inconvenient to the State to hold and govern it, nor from any expectation that it could be better or more conveniently governed by the United States.

The example of Virginia was soon afterwards followed by other States, and, at the time of the adoption of the Constitution, all of the States similarly situated had ceded their unappropriated lands, except North Carolina and Georgia. The main object for which these cessions were desired and made was on account of their money value, and to put an end to a dangerous controversy as to who was justly entitled to the proceeds when the lands should be sold. It is necessary to bring this part of the history of these cessions thus distinctly into view, because it will enable us the better to comprehend the phraseology of the article in the Constitution so often referred to in the argument.

Undoubtedly, the powers of sovereignty and the eminent domain were ceded with the land. This was essential, in order to make it effectual, and to accomplish its objects. But it must be remembered that, at that time, there was no Government of the United States in existence, with enumerated and limited powers; what was then called the United States were thirteen separate, sovereign, independent States, which had entered into a league or confederation for their mutual protection and advantage ; and the Congress of the United States was composed of the representatives of these separate sovereignties, meeting together as equals, to discuss and decide on certain measures which the States, by the Articles of Confederation, had agreed to submit to their decision. But this Confederation had none of the attributes of sovereignty in legislative, executive, or judicial power. It was little more than a Congress of ambassadors, authorized to represent separate nations in matters in which they had a common concern.

It was this Congress that accepted the cession from Virginia. They had no power to accept it under the Articles of Confederation. But they had an undoubted right, as independent sovereignties, to accept any cession of territory for their common benefit, which all of them assented to; and it is equally clear, that as their common property, and having no superior to control them, they had the right to exercise absolute dominion over it, subject only to the restrictions which Virginia had imposed in her act of cession. There was, as we have said, no Government of the United States then in existence with special enumerated and limited powers. The territory belonged to sovereignties, who, subject to the limitations above mentioned, had a right to establish any form of government they pleased, by compact or treaty among themselves, and to regulate rights of person and rights of property in the territory, as they might deem proper. It was by Congress, representing the authority of these several and separate sovereignties, and acting under their authority and command, (but not from any authority derived from the Articles of Confederation,) that the instrument usually called the ordinance of 1787 was adopted; regulating in much detail the principles and the laws by which this territory should be governed; and among other provisions slavery is prohibited in it. We do not question the power of the States, by agreement among themselves, to pass this ordinance, nor its obligatory force in the territory, while the confederation or league of the States in their separate sovereign character continued to exist.

This was the state of things when the Constitution of the United States was formed. The territory ceded by Virginia belonged to the several confederated States as common property, and they had united in establishing in it a system of government and jurisprudence, in order to prepare it for admission as States, according to the terms of the cession. They were about to dissolve this federative Union, and to surrender a portion of their independent sovereignty to a new Government, which, for certain purposes, would make the people of the several States one people, and which was to be supreme and controlling within its sphere of action throughout the United States; but this Government was to be carefully limited in its powers, and to exercise no authority beyond those expressly granted by the Constitution, or necessarily to be implied from the language of the instrument, and the objects it was intended to accomplish; and as this league of States would, upon the adoption of the new Government, cease to have any power over the territory, and the ordinance they had agreed upon be incapable of execution, and a mere nullity, it was obvious that some provision was necessary to give the new Government sufficient power to enable it to carry into effect the objects for which it was ceded, and the compacts and agreements which the States had made with each other in the exercise of their powers of sovereignty. It was necessary that the lands should be sold to pay the war debt; that a government and system of jurisprudence should be maintained in it, to protect the citizens of the United States who should migrate to the territory, in their rights of person and of property. It was also necessary that the new Government, about to be adopted, should be authorized to maintain the claim of the United States to the unappropriated lands in North Carolina and Georgia, which had not then been ceded, but the cession of which was confidently anticipated upon some terms that would be arranged between the general Government and these two States. And, moreover, there were many articles of value besides this property in land, such as arms, military stores, munitions, and ships of war, which were the common property of the States, when acting in their independent character as confederates, which neither the new Government nor any one else would have a right to take possession of, or control, without authority from them; and it was to place these things under the guardianship and protection of the new Government, and to clothe it with the necessary powers, that the clause was inserted in the Constitution which gives Congress the power " to dispose of and make all needful rules and regulations respecting the territory or other property belonging to the United States." It was intended for a specific purpose, to provide for the things we have mentioned. It was to transfer to the new Government the property then held in common by the States, and to give to that Government power to apply it to the objects for which it had been destined by mutual agreement among the States before their league was dissolved. It applied only to the property which the States held in common at that time, and has no reference whatever to any territory or other property which the new sovereignty might afterwards itself acquire.

The language used in the clause, the arrangement and combination of the powers, and the somewhat unusual phraseology it uses, when it speaks of the political power to be exercised in the government of the territory, all indicate the design and meaning of the clause to be such as we have mentioned. It does not speak of *any* territory, nor of *territories*, but uses language which, according to its legitimate meaning, points to a particular thing. The power is given in relation only to *the* territory of the United States, — that is, to a territory then in existence, and then known or claimed as the territory of the United States. It begins its enumeration of powers by that of disposing, in other words, making sale of the lands, or raising money from them, which, as we have already said, was the main object of the cession, and which is accordingly the first thing provided for in the article. It then gives the power which was necessarily associated with the disposition and sale of the lands, — that is, the power of making needful rules and regulations respecting the territory. And whatever construction may now be given to these words, every one, we think, must admit that they are not the words usually employed by statesmen in giving supreme power of legislation. They are certainly very unlike the words used in the power granted to legislate over territory which the new Government might afterwards itself obtain by cession from a State, either for its seat of government, or for forts, magazines, arsenals, dock-yards, and other needful buildings.

And the same power of making needful rules respecting the territory is, in precisely the same language, applied to the *other* property belonging to the United States, — associating the power over the territory in this respect with the power over movable or personal property, — that is, the ships, arms, and munitions of war, which then belonged in common to the State sovereignties. And it will hardly be said that this power, in relation to the last-mentioned objects, was deemed necessary to be thus specially given to the new Government in order to authorize it to make needful rules and regulations respecting the ships it might itself build, or arms and munitions of war it might itself manufacture or provide for the public service.

No one, it is believed, would think a moment of deriving the power of Congress to make needful rules and regulations in relation to property of this kind from this clause of the Constitution. Nor can it, upon any fair construction, be applied to any property but that which the new Government was about to receive from the confederated States. And if this be true as to this property, it must be equally true and limited as to the territory, which is so carefully and precisely limited with it, and, like it, referred to as property in the power granted. The concluding words of the clause appear to render this construction irresistible; for, after the provisions we have mentioned, it proceeds to say, "that nothing in the Constitution shall be so construed as to prejudice any claims of the United States, or of any particular State."

Now, as we have before said, all of the States, except North Carolina and Georgia, had made the cession before the Constitution was adopted, according to the resolution of Congress of October 10, 1780. The claims of other States, that the unappropriated lands in these two States should be applied to the common benefit, in like manner, was still insisted on, but refused by the States. And this member of the clause in question evidently applies to them, and can apply to nothing else. It was to exclude the conclusion that either party, by adopting the Constitution, would surrender what they deemed their rights. And when the latter provision relates so obviously to the unappropriated lands not yet ceded by the States, and the first clause makes provision for those then actually ceded, it is impossible, by any just rule of construction, to make the first provision general, and to extend to all territories which the Federal Government might in any way afterwards acquire, when the latter is plainly and unequivocally confined to a particular territory; which was a part of the same controversy, and involved in the same dispute, and depended upon the same principles. The union of the two provisions in the same clause shows that they were kindred subjects; and that the whole clause is local, and relates only to lands, within the limits of the United States, which had been or then were claimed by a State; and that no other territory was in the mind of the framers of the Constitution, or intended to be embraced in it. Upon any other construction it would be impossible to account for the insertion of the last provision in the place where it is found, or to comprehend why, or for what object, it was associated with the previous provision.

This view of the subject is confirmed by the manner in which the present Government of the United States dealt with the subject as soon as it came into existence. It must be borne in mind that the same States that formed the Confederation also formed and adopted the new Government, to which so large a portion of their former sovereign powers was surrendered. It must also be borne in mind that all of these same States which had then ratified the new Constitution were represented in the Congress which passed the first law for the government of this territory; and many of the members of that legislative body had been deputies from the States under the Confederation,— had united in adopting the ordinance of 1787, and assisted in forming the new Government under which they were then acting, and whose powers they were then exercising. And it is obvious, from the law they passed to carry into effect the principles and provisions of the ordinance, that they regarded it as the act of the States done in the exercise of their legitimate powers at the time. The new Government took the territory as it found it, and in the condition in which it was transferred, and did not attempt to undo anything that had been done. And among the earliest laws passed under the new Government is one reviving the ordinance of 1787, which had become inoperative and a nullity upon the adoption of the Constitution. This law introduces no new form or principles for its government, but recites, in the preamble, that it is passed in order that this ordinance may continue to have full effect, and proceeds to make only those rules and regulations which were needful to adapt it to the new Government into whose hands the power had fallen. It appears, therefore, that this Congress regarded the purposes to which the land in this territory was to be applied, and the form of government and principles of jurisprudence which were to prevail there, while it remained in the territorial state, as already determined on by the States when they had full power and right to make the decision; and that the new Government, having received it in this condition, ought to carry substantially into effect the plans and principles which had been previously adopted by the States, and which no doubt the States anticipated when they surrendered their power to the new Government. And if we regard this clause of the Constitution as pointing to this territory, with a territorial government already established in it, which had been ceded to the State for the purposes hereinbefore mentioned, every word in it is appropriate and easily understood, and the provisions it contains are in perfect harmony with the objects for which it was ceded, and with the condition of its government as a territory at the time. We can, then, easily account for the manner in which the first Congress legislated on the subject, and can also understand why this power over the territory was associated in the same clause with the other property of the United States, and subjected to the like power of making needful rules and regulations. But if the clause is construed in the expanded sense contended for, so as to embrace any territory acquired from a foreign nation by the present Government, and to give it in such territory a despotic and unlimited power over persons and property, such as the confederated States might exercise in their common property, it would be difficult to account for the phraseology used, when compared with other grants of power, — and also for its association with the other provisions in the same clause.

The Constitution has always been remarkable for the felicity of its arrangement of different subjects, and the perspicuity and appropriateness of the language it uses. But if this clause is construed to extend to territory acquired by the present Government from a foreign nation, outside of the limits of any charter from the British Government to a colony, it would be difficult to say why it was deemed necessary to give the Government power to sell any vacant lands belonging to the sovereignty which might be found within it; and if this was necessary, why the grant of this power should precede the power to legislate over it and establish a government there; and still more difficult to say why it was deemed necessary so specially and particularly to grant the power to make needful rules and regulations in relation to any personal or movable property it might acquire there. For the words *other property*, necessarily, by every known rule of interpretation, must mean property of a different description from territory or land. And the difficulty would perhaps be insurmountable in endeavoring to account for the last member of the sentence, which provides " that nothing in this Constitution shall be so construed as to prejudice any claims of the United States or any particular State," or to say how any particular State could have claims in or to a territory ceded by a foreign Government, or to account for associating this provision with the preceding provisions of the clause, with which it would appear to have no connection.

The words "needful rules and regulations" would seem, also, to have been cautiously used for some definite object. They are not the words usually employed by statesmen, when they mean to give the powers of sovereignty, or to establish a government, or to authorize its establishment. Thus, in the law to renew and keep alive the ordinance of 1787, and to re-establish the Government, the title of the law is: "An act to provide for the government of the territory northwest of the river Ohio." And in the Constitution, when granting the power to legislate over the territory that may be selected for the seat of Government independently of a State, it does not say Congress shall have power "to make all needful rules and regulations respecting the territory;" but it declares that "Congress shall have the power to exercise exclusive legislation in all cases whatsoever over such district (not exceeding ten miles square) as may, by cession of particular States and the acceptance of Congress, become the seat of the Government of the United States."

The words "rules and regulations" are usually employed in the Constitution in speaking of some particular specified power which it means to confer on the Government, and not, as we have seen, when granting general powers of legislation. As, for example, in the particular power to Congress "to make rules for the government and regulation of the land and naval forces, or the particular and specific power to regulate commerce;" "to establish an uniform *rule* of naturalization;" "to coin money and *regulate* the value thereof." And to construe the words of which we are speaking as a general and unlimited grant of sovereignty over territories which the government might afterwards acquire, is to use them in a sense and for a purpose for which they were not used in any other part of the instrument. But if confined to a particular territory, in which a Government and laws had already been established, but which would require some alterations to adapt it to the new Government, the words are peculiarly applicable and appropriate for that purpose.

The necessity of this special provision in relation to property, and the rights of property held in common by the confederated States, is illustrated by the first clause of the sixth article. This clause provides that "all debts, contracts, and engagements entered into before the adoption of this Constitution, shall be as valid against the United States under this Government as under the Confederation." This provision, like the one under consideration, was indispensable if the new Constitution was adopted. The new Government was not a mere change in a dynasty, or in a form of government, leaving the nation or sovereignty the same, and clothed with all the rights, and bound by all the obligations of the preceding one. But, when the present United States came into existence under the new Government, it was a new political body, a new nation, then for the first time taking its place in the family of nations. It took nothing by succession from the Confederation. It had no right, as its successor, to any property or rights of property which it had acquired, and was not liable for any of its obligations. It was evidently viewed in this light by the framers of the Constitution. And as the several States would cease to exist in their former confederated character upon the adoption of the Constitution, and could not, in that character, again assemble together, special provisions were indispensable to transfer to the new Government the property and rights which at that time they held in common; and at the same time to authorize it to lay taxes and appropriate money to pay the common debt which they had contracted; and this power could only be given to it by special provisions in the Constitution. The clause in relation to the territory and other property of the United States provided for the first, and the clause last quoted provided for the other. They have no connection with the general powers and rights of sovereignty delegated to the new Government, and can neither enlarge nor diminish them. They were inserted to meet a present emergency, and not to regulate its powers as a Government.

Indeed, a similar provision was deemed necessary, in relation to treaties made by the Confederation; and when, in the clause next succeeding the one of which we have last spoken, it is declared that treaties shall be the supreme law of the land, care is taken to include, by express words, the treaties made by the confederated States. The language is: "And all treaties made, or which shall be made, under the authority of the United States, shall be the supreme law of the land."

Whether, therefore, we take the particular clause in question by itself, or in connection with the other provisions of the Constitution, we think it clear that it applies only to the particular territory of which we have spoken, and cannot, by any just rule of interpretation, be extended to territory which the new Government might afterwards obtain from a foreign nation. Consequently, the power which Congress may have lawfully exercised in this territory, while it remained under a territorial government, and which may have been sanctioned by judicial decision, can furnish no justification and no argument to support a similar exercise of power over territory afterwards acquired by the Federal Government. We put aside, therefore, any argument, drawn from precedents, showing the extent of the power which the general Government exercised over slavery in this territory, as altogether inapplicable to the case before us.

But the case of the American and Ocean Insurance Companies *vs.* Canter (1 Pet. 511,) has been quoted as establishing a different construction of this clause of the Constitution. There is, however, not the slightest conflict between the opinion now given and the one referred to ; and it is only by taking a single sentence out of the latter, and separating it from the context, that even an appearance of conflict can be shown. We need not comment on such a mode of expounding an opinion of the Court. Indeed, it most commonly misrepresents instead of expounding it. And this is fully exemplified in the case referred to, where, if one sentence is taken by itself, the opinion would appear to be in direct conflict with that now given ; but the words which immediately follow that sentence show that the Court did not mean to decide the point, but merely affirmed the power of Congress to establish a government in the territory ; leaving it an open question, whether that power was derived from this clause in the Constitution, or was to be necessarily inferred from a power to acquire territory by cession from a foreign government. The opinion on this part of the case is short, and we give the whole of it to show how well the selection of a single sentence is calculated to mislead.

The passage referred to is in page 542, in which the Court, in speaking of the power of Congress to establish a territorial government in Florida until it should become a State, uses the following language:

"In the mean time, Florida continues to be a territory of the United States, governed by that clause of the Constitution which empowers Congress to make all needful rules and regulations respecting the territory or other property of the United States. Perhaps the power of governing a territory belonging to the United States, which has not, by becoming a State, acquired the means of self-government, may result, necessarily, from the fact that it is not within the jurisdiction of any particular State, and is within the power and jurisdiction of the United States. The right to govern may be the inevitable consequence of the right to acquire territory. *Whichever may be the source from which the power is derived, the possession of it is unquestionable.*"

It is thus clear, from the whole opinion on this point, that the Court did not mean to decide whether the power was derived from the clause in the Constitution, or was the necessary consequence of the right to acquire. They do decide that the power in Congress is unquestionable, and in this we entirely concur, and nothing will be found in this opinion to the contrary. The power stands firmly on the latter alternative put by the Court,— that is, as "*the inevitable consequence of the right to acquire territory.*"

And what still more clearly demonstrates that the Court did not mean to decide the question, but leave it open for future consideration, is the fact that the case was decided in the Circuit Court by Mr. Justice Johnson, and his decision was affirmed by the Supreme Court. His opinion at the circuit is given in full in a note to the case, and in that opinion he states, in explicit terms, that the clause of the Constitution applies only to the territory then within the limits of the United States, and not to Florida, which had been acquired by cession from Spain. This part of his opinion will be found in the note in page 517 of the report. But he does not dissent from the opinion of the Supreme Court; thereby showing that, in his judgment, as well as that of the Court, the case before them did not call for a decision on that particular point, and the Court abstained from deciding it. And in a part of its opinion subsequent to the passage we have quoted, where the Court speak of the legislative power of Congress in Florida, they still speak with the same reserve. And in page 546, speaking of the power of Congress to authorize the territorial Legislature to establish courts there, the Court say : "They are legislative courts, created in virtue of the general right of sovereignty which exists in the Government, or in virtue of that clause which enables Congress to make all needful rules and regulations respecting the territory belonging to the United States."

It has been said that the construction given to this clause is new, and now for the first time brought forward. The case of which we are speaking, and which has been so much discussed, shows that the fact is otherwise. It shows that precisely the same question came before Mr. Justice Johnson, at his circuit, thirty years ago ; was fully considered by him, and the same construction given to the clause in the Constitution which is now given by this Court. And that, upon an appeal from his decision, the same question was brought before this Court, but was not decided because a decision upon it was not required by the case before the Court.

There is another sentence in the opinion which has been commented on, which even in a still more striking manner shows how one may mislead or be misled by taking out a single sentence from the opinion of a court, and leaving out of view what precedes and follows. It is in page 546, near the close of the opinion, in which the Court say : "In legislating for them" (the territories of the United States), "Congress exercises the combined powers of the general and of a State Government." And it is said, that as a State may unquestionably prohibit slavery within its territory, this sentence decides in effect that Congress may do the same in a territory of the United States, exercising there the powers of a State, as well as the power of the general Government.

The examination of this passage, in the case referred to, would be more appropriate when we come to consider, in another part of this opinion, what power Congress can constitutionally exercise in a territory over the rights of person or rights of property of a citizen. But, as it is in the same case with the passage we have before commented on, we dispose of it now, as it will save the Court from the necessity of referring again to the case. And it will be seen, upon reading the page in which this sentence is found, that it has no reference whatever to the power of Congress over rights of person or rights of property, but relates altogether to the power of establishing judicial tribunals to administer the laws constitutionally passed, and defining the jurisdiction they may exercise.

The law of Congress establishing a territorial government in Florida, provided that the Legislature of the territory should have legislative powers over " all rightful objects of legislation; but no law should be valid which was inconsistent with the laws and Constitution of the United States."

Under the power thus conferred, the Legislature of Florida passed an act erecting a tribunal at Key West to decide cases of salvage. And in the case of which we are speaking, the question arose whether the territorial Legislature could be authorized by Congress to establish such a tribunal with such powers; and one of the parties, among other objections, insisted that Congress could not, under the Constitution, authorize the Legislature of the territory to establish such a tribunal with such powers, but that it must be established by Congress itself; and that a sale of cargo made under its order, to pay salvors, was void, as made without legal authority, and passed no property to the purchaser.

It is in disposing of this objection that the sentence relied on occurs, and the Court begin that part of the opinion by stating with great precision the point which they are about to decide.

They say : " It has been contended that, by the Constitution of the United States, the judicial power of the United States extends to all cases of admiralty and maritime jurisdiction ; and that the whole of the judicial must be vested 'in one Supreme Court, and in such inferior courts as Congress shall from time to time ordain and establish.' Hence it has been argued that Congress cannot vest admiralty jurisdiction in courts created by the territorial Legislature."

And after thus clearly stating the point before them, and which they were about to decide, they proceed to show that these territorial tribunals were not constitutional courts, but merely legislative, and that Congress might, therefore, delegate the power to the territorial government to establish the court in question; and they conclude that part of the opinion in the following words : " Although admiralty jurisdiction can be exercised in the States in those courts only which are established in pursuance of the

third article of the Constitution, the same limitation does not
extend to the territories. In legislating for them, Congress exercises the combined powers of the general and State Governments."

Thus it will be seen by these quotations from the opinion, that
the Court, after stating the question it was about to decide in a
manner too plain to be misunderstood, proceeded to decide it, and
announced as the opinion of the tribunal, that in organizing the
judicial department of the government in a territory of the United
States, Congress does not act under, and is not restricted by,
the third article in the Constitution, and is not bound, in a territory, to ordain and establish courts in which the judges hold their
offices during good behavior, but may exercise the discretionary
power which a State exercises in establishing its judicial department, and regulating the jurisdiction of its courts, and may authorize the territorial government to establish, or may itself
establish, courts in which the judges hold their offices for a term
of years only, and may vest in them judicial power upon subjects
confided to the judiciary of the United States. And in doing this,
Congress undoubtedly exercises the combined power of the general
and a State Government. It exercises the discretionary power of
a State Government in authorizing the establishment of a court
in which the judges hold their appointments for a term of years
only, and not during good behavior; and it exercises the power
of the general Government in investing that court with admiralty
jurisdiction, over which the general Government had exclusive
jurisdiction in the territory.

No one, we presume, will question the correctness of that opinion;
nor is there anything in conflict with it in the opinion now given.
The point decided in the case cited has no relation to the question
now before the Court. That depended on the construction of the
third article of the Constitution, in relation to the judiciary of the
United States, and the power which Congress might exercise in a
territory in organizing the judicial department of the Government.
The case before us depends upon other and different provisions
of the Constitution altogether separate and apart from the one
above mentioned. The question as to what courts Congress may
ordain or establish in a territory to administer laws which the
Constitution authorizes it to pass, and what laws it is or is not

authorized to pass, are widely different — are regulated by different and separate articles of the Constitution, and stand upon different principles. And we are satisfied that no one who reads attentively the page in Peters's Reports, to which we have referred, can suppose that the attention of the Court was drawn for a moment to the question now before this Court, or that it meant in that case to say that Congress had a right to prohibit a citizen of the United States from taking any property which he lawfully held into a territory of the United States.

This brings us to examine by what provision of the Constitution the present Federal Government, under its delegated and restricted powers, is authorized to acquire territory outside of the original limits of the United States, and what powers it may exercise therein over the person or property of a citizen of the United States, while it remains a territory, and until it shall be admitted as one of the States of the Union.

There is certainly no power given by the Constitution to the Federal Government to establish or maintain colonies, bordering on the United States or at a distance, to be ruled and governed at its own pleasure; nor to enlarge its territorial limits in any way, except by the admission of new States. That power is plainly given; and if a new State is admitted, it needs no further legislation by Congress, because the Constitution itself defines the relative rights and powers and duties of the State, and the citizens of the State and the Federal Government. But no power is given to acquire a territory to be held and governed permanently in that character.

And, indeed, the power exercised by Congress to acquire territory and establish a government there, according to its own unlimited discretion, was viewed with great jealousy by the leading statesmen of the day. And in The Federalist, (No. 38,) written by Mr. Madison, he speaks of the acquisition of the northwestern territory by the confederated States, by the cession from Virginia, and the establishment of a government there, as an exercise of power not warranted by the Articles of Confederation, and dangerous to the liberties of the people. And he urges the adoption of the Constitution as a security and safeguard against such an exercise of power.

We do not mean, however, to question the power of Congress in this respect. The power to expand the territory of the United States by the admission of new States is plainly given; and in the construction of this power by all the departments of the Government, it has been held to authorize the acquisition of territory not fit for admission at the time, but to be admitted as soon as its population and situation would entitle it to admission. It is acquired to become a State, and not to be held as a colony, and governed by Congress with absolute authority; and as the propriety of admitting a new State is committed to the sound discretion of Congress, the power to acquire territory for that purpose, to be held by the United States until it is in a suitable condition to become a State upon an equal footing with the other States, must rest upon the same discretion. It is a question for the political department of the Government, and not the judicial; and whatever the political department of the Government shall recognize as within the limits of the United States, the judicial department is also bound to recognize, and to administer in it the laws of the United States, so far as they apply, and to maintain in the territory the authority and rights of the Government, and also the personal rights and rights of property of individual citizens, as secured by the Constitution. All we mean to say on this point is, that, as there is no express regulation in the Constitution defining the power which the general Government may exercise over the person or property of a citizen in a territory thus acquired, the Court must necessarily look to the provisions and principles of the Constitution, and its distribution of powers, for the rules and principles by which its decision must be governed.

Taking this rule to guide us, it may be safely assumed that citizens of the United States who migrated to a territory belonging to the people of the United States, cannot be ruled as mere colonists, dependent upon the will of the general Government, and to be governed by any laws it may think proper to impose. The principle upon which our Governments rest, and upon which alone they continue to exist, is the union of States, sovereign and independent within their own limits in their internal and domestic concerns, and bound together as one people by a general Government, possessing certain enumerated and restricted powers, delegated to it by the people of the several States, and exercising supreme authority within the scope of the powers granted to it, throughout the dominion of the United States. A power, therefore, in the general Government to obtain and hold colonies, and dependent territories, over which they might legislate without restriction, would be inconsistent with its own existence in its present form. Whatever it acquires, it acquires for the benefit of the people of the several States who created it. It is their trustee acting for them, and charged with the duty of promoting the interests of the whole people of the Union in the exercise of the powers specifically granted.

At the time when the territory in question was obtained by cession from France, it contained no population fit to be associated together and admitted as a State; and it therefore was absolutely necessary to hold possession of it, as a territory belonging to the United States, until it was settled and inhabited by a civilized community capable of self-government, and in a condition to be admitted on equal terms with the other States as a member of the Union. But, as we have before said, it was acquired by the general Government, as the representative and trustee of the people of the United States, and it must therefore be held in that character for their common and equal benefit; for it was the people of the several States, acting through their agent and representative, the Federal Government, who in fact acquired the territory in question, and the Government holds it for their common use until it shall be associated with the other States as a member of the Union.

But until that time arrives, it is undoubtedly necessary that some government should be established, in order to organize society, and to protect the inhabitants in their persons and property; and as the people of the United States could act in this matter only through the government which represented them, and through which they spoke and acted when the territory was obtained, it was not only within the scope of its powers, but it was its duty to pass such laws and establish such a government as would enable those by whose authority they acted to reap the advantages anticipated from its acquisition, and to gather there a population which would enable it to assume the position to which it was destined among the States of the Union. The power to acquire necessarily carries with it the power to preserve and apply to the purposes for which it was acquired. The form of government to be established necessarily rested in the discretion of Congress. It was their duty to establish the one that would be best suited for the protection and security of the citizens of the United States, and other inhabitants who might be authorized to take up their abode there, and that must always depend upon the existing condition of the territory, as to the number and character of its inhabitants, and their situation in the territory. In some cases a government consisting of persons appointed by the Federal Government, would best subserve the interests of the territory, when the inhabitants were few and scattered, and new to one another. In other instances, it would be more advisable to commit the powers of self-government to the people who had settled in the territory, as being the most competent to determine what was best for their own interests. But some form of civil authority would be absolutely necessary to organize and preserve civilized society, and prepare it to become a State; and what is the best form must always depend on the condition of the territory at the time, and the choice of the mode must depend upon the exercise of a discretionary power by Congress, acting within the scope of its constitutional authority, and not infringing upon the rights of person or rights of property of the citizen who might go there to reside, or for any other lawful purpose. It was acquired by the exercise of this discretion, and it must be held and governed in like manner, until it is fitted to be a State.

But the power of Congress over the person or property of a citizen can never be a mere discretionary power under our Constitution and form of government. The powers of the Government and the rights and privileges of the citizen are regulated and plainly defined by the Constitution itself. And when the territory becomes a part of the United States, the Federal Government enters into possession in the character impressed upon it by those who created it. It enters upon it with its powers over the citizen strictly defined and limited by the Constitution, from which it derives its own existence, and by virtue of which alone it continues to exist and act as a government and sovereignty. It has no power of any kind beyond it; and it cannot, when it enters a territory of the United States, put off its character, and assume discretionary or despotic powers which the Constitution has denied to it. It cannot create for itself a new character separated from the citizens of the United States, and the duties it owes them under the provisions of the Constitution. The territory being a part of the United States, the Government and the citizen both enter it under the authority of the Constitution, with their respective rights defined and marked out; and the Federal Government can exercise no power over his person or property beyond what that instrument confers, nor lawfully deny any right which it has reserved.

A reference to a few of the provisions of the Constitution will illustrate this proposition.

For example, no one, we presume, will contend that Congress can make any law in a territory respecting the establishment of religion or the free exercise thereof, or abridging the freedom of speech or of the press, or the right of the people of the territory peaceably to assemble and to petition the Government for the redress of grievances.

Nor can Congress deny to the people the right to keep and bear arms, nor the right to trial by jury, nor compel any one to be a witness against himself in a criminal proceeding.

These powers, and others, in relation to rights of person, which if not necessary here to enumerate, are, in express and positive terms, denied to the general Government; and the rights of private property have been guarded with equal care. Thus the rights of property are united with the rights of person, and placed on the same ground by the fifth amendment to the Constitution, which provides that no person shall be deprived of life, liberty, and property, without due process of law. And an act of Congress which deprives a citizen of the United States of his liberty or property, merely because he came himself or brought his property into a particular territory of the United States, and who had committed no offence against the laws, could hardly be dignified with the name of due process of law.

So, too, it will hardly be contended that Congress could by law quarter a soldier in a house in a territory without the consent of the owner, in time of peace; nor in time of war, but in a manner prescribed by law. Nor could they by law forfeit the property of a citizen in a territory, who was convicted of treason, for a longer period than the life of the person convicted; nor take private property for public use without just compensation.

The powers over person and property of which we speak are not only not granted to Congress, but are in express terms denied, and they are forbidden to exercise them. And this prohibition is not confined to the States, but the words are general, and extend to the whole territory over which the Constitution gives it power to legislate, including those portions of it remaining under territorial government, as well as that covered by States. It is a total absence of power everywhere within the dominion of the United States, and places the citizens of a territory, so far as these rights are concerned, on the same footing with citizens of the States, and guards them as firmly and plainly against any inroads which the general Government might attempt, under the plea of implied or incidental powers. And if Congress itself cannot do this, — if it is beyond the powers conferred on the Federal Government, — it will be admitted, we presume, that it could not authorize a territorial government to exercise them. It could confer no power on any local government, established by its authority, to violate the provisions of the Constitution.

It seems, however, to be supposed, that there is a difference between property in a slave and other property, and that different rules may be applied to it in expounding the Constitution of the United States. And the laws and usages of nations, and the writings of eminent jurists upon the relation of master and slave and their mutual rights and duties, and the powers which Governments may exercise over it, have been dwelt upon in the argument.

But in considering the question before us, it must be borne in mind that there is no law of nations standing between the people of the United States and their Government, and interfering with their relation to each other. The powers of the Government, and the rights of the citizen under it, are positive and practical regulations plainly written down. The people of the United States have delegated to it certain enumerated powers, and forbidden it to exercise others. It has no power over the person or property of a citizen but what the citizens of the United States have granted. And no laws or usages of other nations, or reasoning of statesmen or jurists upon the relations of master and slave, can enlarge the powers of the Government, or take from the citizens the rights they have reserved. And if the Constitution recognizes the right of property of the master in a slave, and makes no distinction between that description of property and other property owned by a citizen, no tribunal, acting under the authority of the United States, whether it be legislative, executive, or judicial, has a right to draw such a distinction, or deny to it the benefit of the provisions and guarantees which have been provided for the protection of private property against the encroachments of the Government.

Now, as we have already said in an earlier part of this opinion, upon a different point, the right of property in a slave is distinctly and expressly affirmed in the Constitution. The right to traffic in it, like an ordinary article of merchandise and property, was guaranteed to the citizens of the United States, in every State that might desire it, for twenty years. And the Government in express terms is pledged to protect it in all future time, if the slave escapes from his owner. This is done in plain words — too plain to be misunderstood. And no word can be found in the Constitution which gives Congress a greater power over slave property, or which entitles property of that kind to less protection than property of any other description. The only power conferred is the power coupled with the duty of guarding and protecting the owner in his rights.

Upon these considerations, it is the opinion of the Court that the act of Congress which prohibited a citizen from holding and owning property of this kind in the territory of the United States north of the line therein mentioned, is not warranted by the Constitution, and is therefore void; and that neither Dred Scott himself, nor any of his family, were made free by being carried into this territory; even if they had been carried there by the owner, with the intention of becoming a permanent resident.

We have so far examined the case, as it stands under the Constitution of the United States, and the powers thereby delegated to the Federal Government.

But there is another point in the case which depends on State power and State law. And it is contended, on the part of the plaintiff, that he is made free by being taken to Rock Island, in the State of Illinois, independently of his residence in the territory of the United States; and being so made free, he was not again reduced to a state of slavery by being brought back to Missouri.

Our notice of this part of the case will be very brief; for the principle on which it depends was decided in this Court, upon much consideration, in the case of Strader et al. *vs.* Graham, reported in 10th Howard, 82. In that case, the slaves had been taken from Kentucky to Ohio, with the consent of the owner, and afterwards brought back to Kentucky. And this Court held that their *status* or condition, as free or slave, depended upon the laws of Kentucky, when they were brought back into that State, and not of Ohio; and that this Court had no jurisdiction to revise the judgment of a State court upon its own laws. This was the point directly before the Court, and the decision that this Court had not jurisdiction turned upon it, as will be seen by the report of the case.

So in this case. As Scott was a slave when taken into the State of Illinois by his owner, and was there held as such, and brought back in that character, his *status*, as free or slave, depended on the laws of Missouri, and not of Illinois.

It has, however, been urged in the argument, that by the laws of Missouri he was free on his return, and that this case, therefore, cannot be governed by the case of Strader et al. *vs.* Graham, where it appeared, by the laws of Kentucky, that the plaintiffs continued to be slaves on their return from Ohio. But whatever doubts or opinions may, at one time, have been entertained on this subject, we are satisfied, upon a careful examination of all the cases decided in the State courts of Missouri referred to, that it is now firmly settled by the decisions of the highest court in the State, that Scott and his family upon their return were not free, but were, by the laws of Missouri, the property of the defendant; and that the Circuit Court of the United States had no jurisdiction, when, by the laws of the State, the plaintiff was a slave, and not a citizen.

Moreover, the plaintiff, it appears, brought a similar action against the defendant in the State court of Missouri, claiming the freedom of himself and his family upon the same grounds and the same evidence upon which he relies in the case before the Court. The case was carried before the Supreme Court of the State; was fully argued there; and that court decided that neither the plaintiff nor his family were entitled to freedom, and were still the slaves of the defendant; and reversed the judgment of the inferior State court, which had given a different decision. If the plaintiff supposed that this judgment of the Supreme Court of the State was erroneous, and that this Court had jurisdiction to revise and reverse it, the only mode by which he could legally bring it before this Court was by a writ of error directed to the Supreme Court of the State, requiring it to transmit the record to this Court. If this had been done, it is too plain for argument that the writ must have been dismissed for want of jurisdiction in this Court. The case of Strader and Others *vs.* Graham is directly in point; and, indeed, independent of any decision, the language of the 25th section of the Act of 1789 is too clear and precise to admit of controversy.

But the plaintiff did not pursue the mode prescribed by law for bringing the judgment of a State court before this Court for revision, but suffered the case to be remanded to the inferior State court; where it is still continued, and is, by agreement of parties, to await the judgment of this Court on the point. All of this appears on the record before us, and by the printed report of the case.

And while the case is yet open and pending in the inferior State court, the plaintiff goes into the Circuit Court of the United States, upon the same case and the same evidence, and against the same party, and proceeds to judgment, and then brings here the same case from the Circuit Court, which the law would not have permitted him to bring directly from the State court. And if this Court takes jurisdiction in this form, the result, so far as the rights of the respective parties are concerned, is in every respect substantially the same as if it had, in open violation of law, entertained jurisdiction over the judgment of the State court upon a writ of error, and revised and reversed its judgment upon the ground that its opinion upon the question of law was erroneous. It would ill become this Court to sanction such an attempt to evade the law, or to exercise an appellate power in this circuitous way, which it is forbidden to exercise in the direct and regular and invariable forms of judicial proceedings.

Upon the whole, therefore, it is the judgment of this Court, that it appears by the record before us that the plaintiff in error is not a citizen of Missouri, in the sense in which that word is used in the Constitution; and that the Circuit Court of the United States, for that reason, had no jurisdiction in the case, and could give no judgment in it. Its judgment for the defendant must, consequently, be reversed, and a mandate issued, directing the suit to be dismissed for want of jurisdiction.

SUPPLEMENT TO THE DRED SCOTT OPINION.

WASHINGTON, D. C., September, 1858.

The decision in the case of Dred Scott is among the most important in the judicial history of the Supreme Court. And as the subject is still fresh in my mind, I have prepared this statement in order to prove the truth of the historical fact stated in the opinion in relation to England, and the principle decided by the Court. If the questions come before 'the Court again in my lifetime, it will save the trouble of again investigating and annexing the proofs.

I have learned from publications in the newspapers that, since the decision of the Supreme Court in the case of Dred Scott, the Circuit Court of the United States for the District of Indiana have decided that a negro of the African race born in the United States, whose ancestors had not been brought here as slaves, is a citizen of the United States within the meaning of the Constitution, and entitled as such to sue in its courts. The opinion has not, I believe, been published; and I do not therefore know upon what ground the Circuit Court distinguished the case before it from the one decided by the Supreme Court.

It is true, that in the case of Dred Scott the decision is in express terms confined to the case of a person of the African race whose ancestors had been brought to this country as slaves. It was admitted by the pleadings that this was the case in relation to Dred Scott. And the Court deemed it to be its duty to confine the decision to the case before it, and says so in the opinion delivered.

But there is no difference in principle between the case in the Supreme Court and the case at the Circuit. The Supreme Court did not decide the case upon the ground that the slavery of the ancestor affixed a mark of inferiority upon the issue which degraded them below the rank of citizens. It stated the enslaved condition of the whole negro race at the time the Constitution was formed, as a well-known historical fact, in order to show the meaning of the words used in that instrument. The argument in the opinion rests, not upon the actual condition of the ancestors of the plaintiff as to freedom or slavery, but is placed altogether upon the condition of the race to which he belonged, and upon the opinions then entertained by the white race universally, in the civilized portions of Europe and in this country, in relation to the powers and rights which they might justly and morally exercise over the African or negro race.

The part of the opinion to which I allude is in 19th How., 457, in the following words:

" They (the negroes) had for more than a century before been regarded as beings of an inferior order, and altogether unfit to associate with the white race either in social or political relations, and so far inferior that they had no rights which the white man was bound to respect, and that the negro might justly and lawfully be reduced to slavery for his benefit. He was bought and sold and treated as an ordinary article of merchandise and traffic whenever a profit could be made by it."

And as the Constitution of the United States was framed and adopted in that state of public opinion and of public law, the Court held that it must be construed with reference to the description of persons by whom and for whom it was made, and with reference also to the principles and opinions upon which they at that time habitually acted in all the relations and duties of life, public and private; and consequently, that the provisions contained in it for the security and protection of individual liberty, and conferring special rights and privileges in certain cases upon citizens of different States, could not fairly be construed to embrace a description or class of persons whom they regarded as inferior and subordinate to the white race, and in the order of nature made subject to their dominion and will, and whom they were accustomed to buy and sell like any other property.

It will be seen by this summary statement of the opinion on this point that it authorizes no distinction between persons of the negro race, whether their ancestors were held in slavery or not. The historical fact as stated by the Court, and upon which the decision rests, applies equally to the whole race.

When the opinion of the Court was prepared, it was supposed that the doctrine and public opinion in England at the time spoken of were so well known to every one conversant with English history, that no one would question the statement of the Court. For that reason it was not thought necessary to refer to public documents and official acts of the Government in order to prove it. But, as it was suggested that a change had taken place in some of the colonies before the Revolution, and that the barriers which had so long divided the black race from the white had in one or more of them been broken down, the Court felt it to be its duty to show by public and official documents what was in fact the established doctrine and opinion in every one of the thirteen colonies which united in the Declaration of Independence, and to prove that they remained the same with the doctrines and opinions originally imbibed from the mother country; upon that point I do not desire to add to the proofs set forth in the opinion. But the historical fact as relates to England itself has been denied, and that too by persons whose pursuits and position in society are calculated to give weight to their assertions. It is therefore due to truth and to the Court, to show by indisputable testimony that the statement made by the Court is literally correct to its full extent. And I now proceed to do so by authentic public documents beginning as far back as 1689, and coming down to the year when the Constitution of the United States was formed.

I begin with the period above mentioned because the English colonies on this continent were then rapidly filling up, and the emigrants of course brought with them the English opinions of the time. And I select it also because it was a period when the English mind was greatly excited by encroachments upon their own individual liberty, and were placing safeguards about it in order more effectually to protect and preserve it for the people of England, and when the measures of the Government were controlled by the popular opinion. There was at that time, it appears, a large demand for negro slaves in the American dominions of the King of Spain. And contracts were made by the Spanish Government with individuals, and the Guinea Company in France, authorizing the introduction and sale of negroes in these American possessions, and specifying the terms and conditions upon which the permission was granted. A contract of this description was called " el assiento de negres," and was generally and familiarly known by that name. All of this will appear from the opinions of English jurists, and English treaties with Spain, to which I shall presently refer. The same documents will also show that the English Royal African Company desired to share in this profitable trade, and addressed a memorial to their own Government upon the subject in 1688. This was the year after William and Mary ascended the English throne, and negotiations were accordingly opened with the Spanish Government to effect this object. But it appears that Spain required that the right which the English African Company sought to obtain, should, if granted, be reciprocal; and that Spanish ships should have the same right to import negroes into British colonies. And the British ministry, it seems, were willing to treat on this basis, if they had the power to do so under the existing laws of England. But the Navigation Act of Charles II. was then in force, and that statute provided that "*no goods or commodities*" whatever should be imported into or exported from any plantation except in British vessels. And if negroes were by the laws of England "goods or commodities," the British ministry could not by treaty grant the reciprocal privilege required by Spain. For they had no power to dispense with a statute, nor to enter into any treaty stipulation, inconsistent with its provisions.

The question upon the construction of the statute was therefore referred to Treby the Attorney and Somers the Solicitor-General, the then law officers of the Crown; and for greater security, according to the practice of the day, the opinions of all the Judges of the higher courts were called for by an order of the King and Queen in council. These opinions will be found at length in Chalmer's Opinions of Eminent Lawyers, 2d vol., 263, and the next succeeding pages. The opinion of the Judges is also given in full in 1st Burge's Com. on Colonial and Foreign Laws, 736.

It is proper to say that neither the memorial of the African Company, nor the correspondence between the two Governments, nor the order of the King and Queen in council, are within my reach. But the facts above stated in relation to them are evident from the language of the opinions. There is no date to the opinion of the Attorney and Solicitor-General as published in Chalmers. But it was obviously given at the same time with that of the Judges, and their opinion, it appears, was given in 1689. Indeed, the opinion of the law officers must have been given between 1688 and 1692. And in 1692 Treby was appointed Chief Justice of the Court of Common Pleas, and Somers succeeded him as Attorney-General; so that Treby was not Attorney-General nor Somers Solicitor-General after 1692.

I transcribe these opinions at large as they appear in Chalmers, beginning with that of the Attorney and Solicitor-General, 2d vol., 264.

"*The opinion of the Attorney and Solicitor-General Treby and Somers on the Spanish trade to the West Indies.*

"Most of the privileges and permissions proposed by the Spanish Commissioner cannot be granted without dispensing with the Act of Navigation, 12 Car. 2, ch. 18, wherein, besides the matters of law, there is a great consideration of policy:

"1st. The Act requires that no goods or commodities whatsoever shall be imported to or exported from any plantation but in English vessels. But this must have a reasonable construction, and must be understood of such goods and commodities as are to be traded with, and not of provisions for present sustenance, or tackle for refitting a ship, or such like necessaries for incidental occasions.

"2d. To disburden a ship for careening may be lawful, so it be *bona fide;* but it is dangerous to make such an article, lest, under the umbrage of that, a secret trade be covered and carried on contrary to the Act.

"3d. Negroes are merchandise, and can no more be exported by the Act than any other goods. Bullion is allowed by the Act to be imported.

"4th. The Act makes a forfeiture of the ship as well as of the goods, and does not distinguish whether the goods belonged to the owners or merchants, or to the officers or seamen; and it is difficult to render any such distinction practicable.

"5th. The laws and customs of the place must be observed; but in the proceedings there, due regard will be had to the King of Spain's orders and his subjects' contracts.

"6th. The private exercise of religion will not be gainsaid.

GEO. TREBY,
J. SOMERS."

The opinion of the Judges is as follows, 2 Chal. 263:

"The report of the whole Judges upon the memorial of the African Company touching the *assiento* in 1689.

"In pursuance of his Majesty's order in council, hereunto annexed, we do humbly certify our opinions to be '*that negroes are merchandise;*' that it is against the statute for navigation made for the general good and preservation of the shipping and trade of this kingdom, to give liberty to any alien, not made denizen, to trade in Jamaica or other of his Majesty's plantations, or for any shipping belonging to aliens, to trade there, or export thence

negroes, provisions for shipping, or aliens trading there; that for
ships that shall happen by tempest, or in case of peril and distress,
to come into the plantations for preservation, and to amend, or
take in necessary provisions, or repair there in such case, it is not
against the Act of Navigation, or any other law."

J. HOLT,	R. LECHMERE,
H. POLLEXFEN,	THOMAS ROKEBY,
ED. NEVILL,	GYLES EYRE,
J. POWELL,	PEYTON VENTRIO,
H. GREGORY,	JOHN TURTON.

These opinions show too plainly to be mistaken the condition
of the African race in 1689, according to the English doctrines
and usages of that day. They were regarded and dealt with as
"*goods and commodities*," and are classed in these opinions with
ordinary articles of commerce and property, in which the owner
has an absolute and unqualified right, and may dispose of as he
pleases. And it will be observed that the opinions are not confined to "*slaves or negro slaves*," but use general words which embrace the whole negro race, without qualification or limitation.
They say, "*negroes are merchandise*."

The Solicitor-General who gave this opinion, it will be seen,
was Somers, afterwards Lord-Chancellor of England, and one of
the leading statesmen of the time. And at the head of the Judges
stands the name of Lord Holt. I need hardly say of names so
familiar to every reader of English history, that no two men have
been more distinguished in the annals of English jurisprudence;
and that even at this day they are regarded in England as eminently distinguished for their love of liberty, and for their bold-
ness in asserting and defending it. The proofs I am about to ad-
duce will prove most conclusively, that the opinions they gave in
1689 were entertained and acted on by the Government and people
of England until and after this country declared its independence,
and formed and adopted its Constitution.

The proposal for this *assiento* failed on account of obstacles
stated in these opinions. But the desire of the Government and
of the African Company to share in this profitable trade was
unabated.

And in the reign of Queen Anne, when the victories of the

Duke of Marlborough enabled the English Government to take a higher stand in its negotiations with Spain, it demanded and secured not only a share of this trade, but the exclusive right to it, thereby shutting out all competition from other nations or individuals, and not permitting even the subjects of the King of Spain to trade in this merchandise with his own colonies.

This treaty was made at Utrecht in 1713. The treaties of peace made at Utrecht at that time closed a long and desolating war, in which all the leading nations of Europe had been involved. But amid the great European interests which were then negotiated and adjusted, the English Government did not lose sight of the profits that might be derived from trading in negroes; and by the 12th Article of the treaty of peace between Great Britain and the King of Spain, the king granted to her Britannic Majesty, and to the company of her subjects, appointed for that purpose, as well as the subjects of Spain, as all others being excluded, the contract for introducing negroes into several ports of the dominions of his Catholic Majesty in America, commonly called "*el pacto de el assiento de negres*," for the space of thirty years successively, beginning from the 1st day of May, 1713.

After making this grant in the words above stated, the article proceeds to make some general provisions to guard the privileges of the company, and also to prevent them from abusing them to the injury of Spain. And in order to carry out the intent and meaning of this article, a contract or *assiento*, dated on the 26th of March, 1713, (referred to in some of the subsequent treaties as dated on the 26th of May, 1713,) was entered into between the King of Spain and the English African Company.

It is necessary to refer particularly to a few of the articles, and insert them in full, in order to show how completely and entirely the *assiento* carried out practically the doctrine that "negroes are merchandise," as announced by the law authorities of England in 1689. The *assiento* is in the 1st volume, page 83, of the collection of treaties between Great Britain and other powers, published in London in 1772, and the 12th Article of the treaty of peace, to which the *assiento* refers, in 175 of the same volume.

The *assiento* begins with a preamble which recites that the contract with the Guinea Company of France had determined, and that the Queen of Great Britain was desirous of coming into the commerce, and in her name the English Company, as stipulated in the preliminaries of the treaty of peace; and recites also that this *assiento* was to continue for the space of thirty years; and after stating the negotiations which had taken place on the subject, it sets forth in forty-two separate articles the terms and conditions which the parties had finally agreed to.

The First Article is in the following words:

" 1. First, then, to procure by this means, a mutual and reciprocal advantage to the sovereigns and subjects of both crowns, her British Majesty does offer and undertake for the persons whom she shall name and appoint, that they shall oblige and charge themselves with the bringing into the West Indies of America, belonging to his Catholic Majesty, in the space of the said thirty years, to commence on the first day of May, one thousand seven hundred and thirteen, and to determine on the like day, which shall be in the year one thousand seven hundred and forty-three, viz., one hundred and forty-four thousand negroes, *Piezas de India*, of both sexes and of all ages, at the rate of four thousand and eight hundred negroes, *Piezas de India*, in each of the said thirty years, with this condition, that the persons who shall go to the West Indies to take care of the concerns of the *assiento* shall avoid giving any offence; for in such case they shall be prosecuted and punished in the same manner as they would have been in Spain, if the like misdemeanors had been committed there."

The 19th section provides the assientists, their factors and agents, should have power to navigate and import their negro slaves, according to that contract, to all the northern ports of his Catholic Majesty's West Indies, including the river *Platte*, with prohibition to all others, whether subjects of the crown or strangers, to carry on or introduce thither any negroes under the penalties established by the laws that relate to this contract of trade.

The 27th Article declares, that if any of the ships of the *assiento* should be fitted out as ships of war, and should take any prizes from the enemies of either crown, or from pirates, they may bring them into any port belonging to his Catholic Majesty, where they are to be admitted, and the prizes being declared good and lawful, the captors shall not be obliged to pay greater duties upon the entry of their prizes than what are established and payable by the natural born subjects of his Majesty; and it is declared that if there should be any negroes on board such prizes they may sell them in part of the number they have engaged to furnish.

The 28th Article provides, that whereas in establishing and adjusting this *assiento* a particular regard is had to the advantage that may thence accrue to their British and Catholic Majesties and to their revenues, it is agreed and stipulated that both their Majesties shall be concerned for one-half of this trade, each of them a quarter part, which is to belong to them pursuant to this agreement.

And by the 29th Article, the assientists are to give an account of their profits at the end of the first four years, upon oath with proper vouchers, which accounts are to be first examined and settled by her Britannic Majesty's ministers employed in that service in regard to the share she is to have, and then to be examined in the like manner and for the like purpose at the Spanish court.

Here, then, is a treaty between two of the leading nations of Europe, in which the one coolly, and as an ordinary matter of business and trade, engages to furnish the other with one hundred and forty-four thousand negroes to be held by them as slaves; no mention is made of any right in the negro, either before or after his sale as a slave, no stipulation as to the manner in which he is to be obtained and transported to the Spanish possessions, nor for his treatment after he is brought there. He and his posterity were to be the property of the purchaser, and at his absolute control and disposal like any other property. And the sovereigns themselves do not deem it derogatory to their dignity to become partners in this gigantic traffic, and actually by this *assiento* enter into partnership with a company of private individuals, each of the crowned heads to have one-fourth share of the profits. And their ministers are to supervise and settle the accounts of this trade in all its details, in order to secure to them respectively their portion of the gains. And this treaty is made publicly in the face of the civilized world, in an enlightened period of the public mind, and when a free press was already firmly established in England, and yet it brought no reproach upon the parties, nor did it lessen the affection, respect, and reverence of their own subjects. The reason of all this is plain Negroes were then regarded as an inferior order of beings unfit for any association with the whites, and having no rights which the white man was bound to respect. They were *merchandise* in which it was supposed to be as just, and lawful, and morally right to trade, as in any other goods and commodities.

The 27th Article of the *assiento* above referred to marks the distinction then made between the two races in the most emphatic manner. The assientists, by this article, are authorized to fit out ships of war, and take prizes, pirates, or the ships of the enemy of either of the contracting nations. And there is an express stipulation that any negroes found on board the prize may be sold as slaves in part fulfilment of their contract. The *whites* on board the prizes taken from an enemy, who was at war with England and Spain, would, of course, be prisoners of war. But negroes, no matter where born, whether in Africa, or in the colonies of France, or Portugal, or the States General, no matter whether they or their ancestors had been slaves or not, were yet to be sold like the other goods found on board. They might have shipped voluntarily as a part of the crew of the captured ship. But they were by this treaty not to be recognized as such. They were cargo, and to be dealt with accordingly.

I have said that the interest which the English Government and English people took in this trade in 1713, is manifested by its insertion as one of the articles in the treaty of Utrecht, when questions of such magnitude were to be adjusted, and in which almost every part of the civilized world had a deep stake. The same opinions evidently continued, and were constantly acted upon, until the thirty years were out. And indeed this monopoly appears to have been watched over, and guarded with peculiar care, by a succession of treaties in the same and subsequent reigns; and great care is taken in them all to prevent any possible implication that this exclusive right was impaired either in duration or the number of negroes which the Company were entitled to introduce under the *assiento*.

Thus, for example, in 1716, near the close of the reign of Queen Anne, some inconvenience was alleged by the English Company to have arisen from certain regulations of the trade contained in the original contract. These regulations were modified by treaty in that year, and in a manner greatly to the advantage of the Company, and the last clause takes care to provide that the original treaty of *assiento* shall remain in force, with the exception only of these new modifications (*see volume of treaties before referred to, page* 286). Again, in the treaty of peace made at Madrid in 1721 (*same volume, page* 366), it was stipulated that the *assiento*, with the modifications made in 1716, should remain in full force, and that the ships employed for the traffic of negroes by the Royal Company of Great Britain, established at London, may be admitted without hindrance to trade, freely and in the same manner as they did before the last rupture between the two crowns. This last-mentioned treaty, it will be observed, was in the reign of George I.

Again, in the reign of George II., in the treaty of peace, union, and friendship, and mutual defence between Great Britain, France, and Spain, concluded at Seville in 1729, it was deemed advisable, for greater exactness (as it is said in the treaty), to introduce in a separate article a provision declaring that this *assiento*, as modified in 1716, "*should remain in force, virtue, and full vigor*," (see 2d volume of the same collection of treaties, page 11.)

The thirty years for which the *assiento* was granted expired in 1743. But the traffic had been interrupted for four years before its expiration by the war between England and Spain. And when peace was restored by the treaty of *Aix-la-Chapelle* in 1748, the profits which the African Company and the King of England himself, as one of the partners, might have made in this trade during these four years, were, it seems, too important to be forgotten, and the 16th Article of the treaty of peace of 1748 is in the following words:

"The treaty of *assiento* for the trade of negroes, signed at Madrid on the 26th of March, 1713, and the article of the annual ship making part of the said treaty, are particularly confirmed by the present treaty for the four years during which the enjoyment thereof has been interrupted since the commencement of the present war, and shall be executed on the same footing, and under the same conditions, as they have or ought to have been executed before the said war." (See 2d volume same collection of treaties, page 82.)

It seems, however, that there was an understanding at the time of the treaty of Aix-La-Chapelle, between the ambassadors of Great Britain and Spain, that an equivalent in money should be paid to Spain for the loss of these four years, the amount to be ascertained by ministers named on each side for that purpose. This was accordingly done by a treaty signed at Madrid, October 5th, 1750. By the 1st, 2d, and 3d Articles of this treaty, his Britannic Majesty yielded his right to the enjoyment of the *assiento* for these four years. In consideration whereof, the King of Spain agreed to pay, either at Madrid or London, to the Royal Assiento Company one hundred thousand pounds sterling within three months from the signing of that treaty; his Britannic Majesty yielding also to the King of Spain all that might be due to the said Company for the balance of accounts arising in any manner from the *assiento*, and the King of Spain in like manner all his pretensions and demands in consequence of the *assiento* and annual ship.

Thus ended the *assiento*, a contract in which three of the sovereigns of England — Queen Anne, George I., and George II. — in an enlightened period of English history, were partners, and reaped a large share of its profits.

It is impossible to read these treaties, and not feel convinced that down to 1750 at least, the English Government and people acknowledged no rights in the negro race which they were bound to respect. Such most obviously must have been the opinion of Queen Anne, George I., and George II. For each of them knew how these one hundred and forty-four thousand negroes, consisting of men, women, and children, were to be obtained on the coast of Africa, and transported to the Spanish colonies, and there sold as ordinary merchandise in the market. They were sovereigns of a rich and powerful nation; they were provided for munificently from the public treasury; they were elevated far above the pursuits of commerce, and far above the temptations of want or the ambition to be individually rich; yet they were, each of them, eager (as is proved by the treaties I have quoted) to descend from their royal state to the level of an ordinary individual trader, and to become partners in a slave-trading company and share in its profits.

It is, however, but just to these monarchs to say, that they undoubtedly acted upon the established doctrines of the age in which they lived. For nobody reproached them for it. It did not lessen in any degree the respect and reverence of their subjects. The whole people of England concurred in opinion with them, and Queen Anne, who organized this Company, and was one of the original partners, is still called the good Queen Anne.

The monopoly of the traffic to the Spanish colonies having

ended, the mercantile community of England insisted upon its right to share in the trade to the British colonies and plantations. And their claims were pressed with so much force, that by the stat. of 23 Geo. II., ch. 31, (1749,) the trade in negroes was opened to every British subject that might choose to engage in it. The language and provisions of this statute sufficiently indicate the doctrine and opinion of the time, if there was even no other proof. It contains thirty-nine sections, makes provisions for a new Company to be formed, and designates the description of persons who would have the right to be admitted as members, and in what manner. The preamble recites that, "whereas the trade to and from Africa is very advantageous to Great Britain, and necessary for the supplying of the plantations with a sufficient number of negroes at reasonable rates, and for that purpose the said trade ought to be free and open to all his Majesty's subjects." The first section proceeds to declare it open.

The 3d section authorizes the Company which the 2d section creates, to erect and keep forts, settlements, and factories on the coast, and vests in them all the forts, castles, and military stores, canoe-men, and castle slaves of the former African Company, "*to the intent and purpose (as it says) that the said forts, settlements, and premises shall be employed at all times hereafter only for the protection, encouragement, and defence of the said trade.*"

And the 29th Section enacts that no commander or master of any ship trading to Africa shall, by force or violence or by any other indirect practice whatever, take on board or carry away from the coast of Africa any negro or native of the said country, or commit or suffer to be committed any violence to the natives to the prejudice of the said trade; and the section then proceeds to inflict a penalty of one hundred pounds for every such offence, one-half to the support of the forts, and the other to the informer.

An act of violence or fraud by means of which a native was carried into slavery, it thus appears, was not regarded as an offence unless it was an injury to the slave-trade. The negro carried away was not to be restored to his country or his freedom, but to remain a slave. The fine was for the injury done to the trade; and it would seem that these law makers supposed that no wrong was done to the African of which he had a right to complain or to ask redress.

With this statute in force, opening the trade to the activity and enterprise of individual cupidity, the importations into the British plantations and colonies soon became exceedingly heavy. And the supply so far exceeded the demand, that the colonies in which slave labor was deemed most profitable, and in which they were held in the greatest numbers, began to feel this great influx of untutored savages a serious inconvenience. They were unaccustomed to labor of any kind, and ignorant and inexperienced in the cultivation of the land, and their association by no means likely to improve the intelligence or moral habits of the slaves they already possessed. Influenced by these considerations, the Colony of South Carolina in 1760 passed an Act prohibiting the further importation. But the English Government disallowed the Act, reprimanded the Governor of the Colony for assenting to it, and sent a circular order to the Governors of all the colonies on this continent and in the West India Islands, forbidding them to give their assent to any similar act of a colonial assembly. (1 Colquhoun on Roman and Civil Law, 423. 1 Burges's Commentaries on Colonial and Foreign Laws, 736, 737, and in the following pages, and in the notes.)

Notwithstanding this rebuke, the evil of this over-importation was felt so sensibly in the colonies where the negroes were most numerous, that five years afterwards (1765) a bill was brought into the provincial Assembly of Jamaica to restrain it. But before it was passed, the Governor informed the Assembly that, consistently with his instructions, he could not give his assent to the bill, and it was thereupon dropped. This it will be remembered was in the reign of George III.

The colonists, however, were unwilling to rest under this increasing grievance without making another effort to prevent it, and endeavored to accomplish the object by increasing the duty on negroes. Two acts increasing the duty were accordingly passed by the Colonial Assembly of Jamaica.

But the merchants of Bristol and Liverpool petitioned against their allowance. The board of trade made a report against them. The Agent of Jamaica was heard against that report, but, upon the recommendation of the Privy Council, the acts were disallowed, and the disallowance was accompanied by an instruction to the Governor, dated the 28th of February, 1775, by which he was prohibited, "upon pain of being removed from his government," from giving his assent to any act by which the duties on the importation of slaves should be augmented, upon the ground, as the instruction states, "that such duties were to the injury and oppression of the merchants of this Kingdom, and the obstruction of its commerce."

The documents and public acts in relation to these colonial laws will be found stated or referred to in 1st Burges's Commentaries on Colonial and Foreign Laws, pages 736, 737, and 738, printed at London in 1838; and in 1st Colquhoun on Roman and Civil Law, pages 422, 423, and 424, printed at London in 1849.

These proceedings were upon the eve of our Declaration of Independence, and nearly contemporaneous with it, and four years after the decision of Lord Mansfield in Somerset's case, of which I shall hereafter speak more particularly. They were followed by the statute of 27 George III., ch. 27, (passed in 1787,) granting certain privileges of trade to certain ports in the British West Indies. This statute, like all of the other documents I have hereinbefore referred to, still treats negroes as ordinary articles of property and commerce. The language of the 4th section conveys this idea in language not to be mistaken. It is in the following words:

" 4. And it is hereby further enacted by the authority aforesaid, that it shall and may be lawful, from and after the 1st day of September, to export from any of the said ports to any of the colonies or plantations in America belonging to or under the dominion of any foreign European sovereign or State, in any sloop, schooner, or other vessel whatever owned and navigated by the subjects of any foreign European sovereign or State, not having more than one deck and not exceeding the burthen of seventy tons, rum of the produce of any British island, and also negroes which shall have been brought into said islands, respectively, in British built ships owned, and registered, and navigated according to law, and all manner of goods, wares, and merchandise which shall have been legally imported into the said islands, respectively, except masts, yards, or bowsprits, pitch, tar, turpentine, and tobacco, and except also such iron as shall have been brought from the British colonies or plantations in America, any law, custom, or usage to the contrary, notwithstanding."

It will be observed that *negroes* are in this section associated in general and unqualified terms with *rum* and other articles of commerce in which the owner has the absolute property. And the statute includes in its provisions all negroes brought into the islands in British vessels, without any inquiry or qualification as to their previous condition. If they were *negroes*, and brought in by a British vessel, the British law regarded them as absolute property, to be traded in like any other merchandise.

This statute brings me down to the period when the Constitution was formed. For it happens that this last-mentioned statute was passed in the same year (1787) in which the Constitution of the United States was framed by the Convention, and promulgated for the consideration of the people.

It would be foreign therefore to the question I am now considering, to proceed further with English legislation and doctrines upon this subject, for the purpose of showing when the change of public opinion took place which finally resulted in the emancipation of the whole African race under British dominion; my only object in this historical review is to show the point of view in which the African race was regarded in England at the time when the declaration of rights was framed, and the Constitution of the United States was adopted.

The public documents to which I have referred show one fixed, unvarying opinion from 1689 to 1787, and that, according to that opinion, the relation between the white man and the negro was in the order of nature that of master and slave, and that the white man exercised nothing more than his just rights when he made the negro his property. There is not a word in these documents that indicates any doubt upon the subject. Every word and provision in every one of them shows that they were never thought of or spoken of but as articles of commerce, of the growth and production of Africa, to be traded in and appropriated to the use of the white man, like any other property.

These opinions were carried out to their full extent by the English Company, in which the monarchs were partners, as well as the English traders who succeeded them. The negroes were seized in their native country by the agents of the traders or the native chiefs employed for the purpose, brought to the coast, stowed away and packed together on board the ships like bales of merchandise, and without the slightest regard to their sufferings or to age or sex or the common decencies of human life. The documents and reports laid before the British Parliament during the discussions upon the abolition of the slave-trade prove past doubt that this was the ordinary course of traffic. These discussions are of such recent date that it is unnecessary to refer particularly to the documents then produced and laid before the English Parliament. I allude to them and rely upon them to show that the doctrines and opinions so plainly indicated in the official acts of the Government were not merely speculative theories or political principles upon which there might be different opinions at the time, but had been adopted by the people of England as a part of their code of morals, and acted upon for a century as undoubted truths. What right in the negro was respected by the white man, who thus dealt with him without scruple from generation to generation?

Nor indeed were these opinions confined to England. They prevailed to the same extent and were acted upon in like manner in Spain, in France, in Holland, in Denmark, and in Sweden, in proportion to their commercial enterprise and power. It was the unwavering opinion of the civilized world during the period of which I am speaking.

Two English cases have been mentioned which are supposed to indicate a different doctrine in England. But they have no relation to the point in question.

The first is the case of Smith *vs.* Brown, 2 Salk. 667, in which Lord Holt is reported to have said that "as soon as a negro comes into England he becomes free." But this expression is in no degree in conflict with the opinion he gave in 1689, in conjunction with the other Judges. He obviously could not have intended to recall it, for he does not even allude to it, as he would have done, if he had supposed it had any bearing upon the question then before him. And the evident result of these two opinions taken together is, that although negroes were merchandise, it was not lawful to import it into England, and if brought there the right of the owner was forfeited. But it was not forfeited upon the ground that the negroes were not property, or had any claim to freedom in their own right, but because it was unlawful to import such property into England. The opinion does not assign to the negro any higher position in his relation to the white man than he assigned to him in 1689; and when the expressions of Lord Holt in Smith *vs.* Brown are quoted, without calling attention at the same time to his former opinion, the quotation is calculated, and perhaps intended, to mislead and deceive, and to impute to Lord Holt opinions which he evidently never entertained.

The point upon which Lord Holt expressed this opinion was not in truth before the Court. The action under trial was trover for a negro, and the declaration did not allege that he was the property of the plaintiff; and it is well settled that an action of trover cannot be maintained unless the plaintiff shows that he has a right of property, general or special, in the thing sued for; and as the declaration did not aver property in the plaintiff, it is clear that the action could not be maintained, even if the full right of property in point of fact still remained in him. The opinion relied on therefore was merely a dictum thrown out in deciding the case, nor was it afterwards followed or regarded as the law by the English courts, even limited as it was to the condition of the negro, when he was brought into England. For in Jelly *vs.* Cline, 1 Lord Raymond, 147, it was decided that trover would lie for a negro, and the same doctrine was maintained in Pearne *vs.* Lisle, 1 Amb., 75, which was decided in 1749. The language of Lord Hardwicke in the last-mentioned case is so clear and explicit upon this subject that I give the decision in his own words. He says, " 1st. As to the nature of the demand. It is for the use of negroes. A man may hire the servant of another, whether he be a slave or not, and will be bound to satisfy the master for the use of him. I have no doubt but trover will lie for a negro slave; it is as much property as anything. The case in Salk. 666 was determined on the want of proper description. It was trover *pro uno Ethiope vocat negro*, without saying slave; and the being negro did not necessarily imply slave. The reason said at the Bar to have been given by Lord Chief-Justice Holt in that case, as the cause of his doubt, viz., that the moment a slave sets foot in England he becomes free, has no weight in it, nor can any reason be found why they should not be equally so when they set foot in Jamaica or any other English plantation. All our colonies are subject to the laws of England, although, as to some purposes, they have laws of their own."

And acting under these decisions and this high authority the

English colonists were accustomed to bring their negroes with them, when they came to England, and to sell them there as slaves when they did not desire to take or send them back. And as personal intercourse between the mother country and the colonies increased, the introduction and sale of negroes became more frequent, and in 1774, when the case of Somerset was decided by Lord Mansfield, there were about fourteen thousand negro slaves held in London. The fact that they were sold as above stated, and the number held in London at the time above mentioned will be found stated in the pages 1 Colquhoun, and 1st Burges, to which I have referred in other parts of this opinion.

Negroes were therefore not only merchandise according to the laws and the decisions of the English courts, but merchandise in which it was lawful to trade in England as well as in the colonies, until the decision of Lord Mansfield in the case of Somerset. It was otherwise in the other European nations who held colonies and engaged in the slave-trade. Serfdom had been finally abolished in most if not all of them. And as all of them had abundance of labor for the wants of agriculture and the mechanic arts as known and practised at the time, it was not deemed advisable to reinstate domestic slavery, nor to introduce among them a body of ignorant and uncivilized Africans unsuited to the climate, and altogether unacquainted with and unfit for the labors of the farm or the workshop. The French edict which authorized the traffic in negroes spoke of the colonies only. And the French courts held that it did not authorize their introduction into France itself, and that a negro brought there became thereby emancipated and free. This rule of the French law, as decided by its courts, was afterwards qualified in some degree by a subsequent edict, which allowed them to be brought from their own colonies for temporary purposes under certain regulations, but which at the same time provided that if these regulations were not complied with his owner forfeited his right of property, and the negro became free. 1 Burges, 740, &c., &c.

This was the state of the law upon this subject in the civilized nations of Europe when the case of Somerset came before the Court. In England, according to the decisions above referred to, the right of property remained in the master even in England itself as well as in its colonies, and was acknowledged and enforced there by its courts. In France, and the other continental nations which had engaged in the traffic, the owner forfeited his right, if the negro was brought into the European dominions of the State or Kingdom; and the question presented in Somerset's case was whether the Court of King's Bench would adhere to the previous decisions of its own courts, or adopt the principles of the Civil Law Courts on the continent. In its social condition, England had the same inducements with the other nations to prevent the introduction of uncivilized savages as laborers in England itself. For villenage had very nearly worn out, and the nation had already sufficient labor, and a population sufficiently dense, for the wants and customs of the age. It was under these circumstances that Lord Mansfield overruled the decisions and opinions of the high judicial authorities which had preceded him, and followed the decisions of the continental Cival Law Courts in order to conform the law to what he obviously deemed the established policy of England; and the introduction of negro slavery would have been altogether repugnant to the policy which was gradually but steadily putting an end to the slavery of *villenage*. But Lord Mansfield did not in that opinion deny, and indeed, could not deny, that by the laws of England negroes were merchandise. For the statute of Geo. II., putting an end to the monopoly of the Royal African Company, and opening the traffic to the traders of England generally, was then in full force. He could in this case overrule former judicial decisions, as he often did, where he thought they had mistaken the principle of law upon which the case turned, or were inconsistent with the existing state of things and established national policy. But he could not repeal or dispense with the provisions of a statute, and certainly never intended to do so. And what he says of breathing the air of England, so far as the rights of the negro race are concerned, he might have said with as much truth of the air of France or Spain, or of any other European State engaged in the slave-trade. For, as I have already said, all of them as a matter of policy excluded African slavery from their European dominions, not because they supposed the trade to be unjust or immoral, or that the negroes had any right to complain of it, but because they supposed the introduction of such a race of slaves would be injurious to their own interests. The decision of Lord Mansfield goes no further, and, like the dictum of Lord Holt, is confined to the negro when brought into England, adopts principles pre-viously decided by the French courts, and does not go beyond them.

It is evident that this opinion was so understood at the time it was given. For the strong rebuke to the Governor of Jamaica in 1775, and the statute of Geo. III., passed in 1787, (herein-before referred to,) affirm the rights of the white man over the negro as clearly and broadly as they were affirmed in the opinions of the Judges and law officers of the Crown in 1689, or as they were affirmed in the *assiento del negres* in 1713, which practically carried these principles into full operation.

It is also worthy of remark, that the opinions of Lord Holt and Lord Mansfield, even narrowed down to the condition of the negro in England, were each of them overruled and denied to be law by Judges who were at least equally eminent with the jurists by whom they were given. I have already quoted the opinion of Lord Hardwicke upon the dictum imputed to Lord Holt. And in the case of the slave Grace, 2 Hag., Admr. Rep., 94, Lord Stowell in emphatic terms denies the doctrine of Lord Mansfield in the case of Somerset, and maintains that a negro brought into England was not thereby emancipated, nor the right of property in the owner thereby forfeited; and that although the right of the master could not be enforced against the negro in England, because there was no law authorizing process there for that purpose, yet the right of property was not forfeited, but remained in the master, and might be enforced if the negro returned to the colonies, or to any country where the law of the place provided a remedy. It is not, however, material to the point in question, in the case of Dred Scott, which of these opinions was right. They turn entirely upon the local policy and institutions in England itself, and have no connection whatever with the relative position of the African and white races, nor with the unlimited power of appropriation which the latter claimed the right to exercise over the former whenever it suited their interest, as appears in the statutes and treaties of England.

The cases above mentioned are the only English cases which can be supposed to have any bearing upon the question I am con-sidering. I am not aware of any other worth notice. And it appears to me that the unbroken chain of testimony which I have adduced from 1689 down to 1787 proves, past doubt, that the public opinion in England when our Constitution was formed is correctly stated in the case of Dred Scott, and that no one capable of comprehending the force of testimony, and whose mind is in a condition to give it its just weight, will question the statement.

There have undoubtedly in all ages of the world been persons, even among the educated and intelligent, who were capable of shutting their eyes against the plainest proofs, if they were unwilling to believe the fact they established. Such persons may exist at the present day, and with them it would be useless to reason or produce testimony. I have collected and arranged these proofs for the consideration of those who are in search of truth, and are willing to admit and acknowledge it when found, although it may come in conflict with previous cherished opinions or prejudices. I leave these proofs to their judgment without further comment.

I do not think it necessary to go again into an examination of documentary evidence to show that the doctrines and fixed opinions in this country at the time of which I am speaking corresponded with those of England. The proofs set forth in the Dred Scott case are abundantly sufficient for that purpose. But if there were no proofs upon the subject, no intelligent mind could for a moment persuade itself that the colonial opinions were more favorable to the rights of the African race than those of the mother country. The colonists brought with them the laws of England, and the rights, duties, and privileges of Englishmen, as far as they were applicable in their new homes; and they naturally also and certainly brought with them English opinions upon political and personal rights, English morals and English prejudices. And with them the inferior and subject condition of the African race must have been more deeply and firmly rooted (if that were possible) than even among the English people. For with the colonists this inferiority and degradation was not merely an admitted axiom upon which it was morally lawful to act, and upon which they acted without reproach in distant countries, but it was habitually and daily acted upon by themselves in their domestic and social relations or under their own eyes. For negroes were bought and sold by them like any other stock on their plantations. They saw them brought into their ports by the ships of the mother country in cargoes, in their native, ignorant, degraded, and savage state, packed like bales of merchandise, and sold in the market like bales of woollen goods or puncheons of rum. And can any one seriously believe that the men who framed the Declaration of Independence, and who had grown up amid these scenes, and who were themselves holding and dealing with the negro merely as property, could have intended to embrace these unfortunate beings among the men whom they pronounced to be their equals, or to say in that instrument that those whom they held as slaves had an inalienable right to freedom. If such had been the construction of the Declaration of Independence at the time of its adoption, it would have emancipated the slaves in every colony as soon as this Declaration was adopted and sanctioned by the people of the colony. Yet no one supposed that it impaired any right of property in the colonies, or cast any reproach upon those who were actively engaged in the African slave-trade.

The American Revolution was not the offspring of fanaticism, nor was it produced by the wild theories of political dreamers. It was not designed to subvert the established order of society and social relations, nor to sweep away traditional usages and established opinions. On the contrary, it was undertaken to maintain ancient and established rights which had been invaded by the British Government. The colonists claimed the rights of Englishmen, as secured by *magna charta* and the principles upon which the British Government was founded. They did nothing more. And when this claim was disregarded, they remonstrated, and calmly, but at the same time earnestly and firmly, argued the questions, and did not resort to the Declaration of Independence until they lost all hope of redress by any other means. The Declaration of Independence was intended to preserve their ancient and established rights and privileges, and not to upturn their own social institutions and domestic relations. It was in fact intended as a conservative measure, and not as revolutionary, nor was it adopted in passion, but carefully, calmly, and deliberately considered. And they certainly did not mean by a few brief words in the preamble to the instrument to annihilate in a moment long established social relations, to admit their slave population to be their equals, and the African race, whom they were daily transporting from their native country and selling as slaves in the open market, to have an "*inalienable right to liberty*," and equal in the order of nature to themselves. Every honest mind of every country, acquainted with the history of the American Revolution and the character of the men who signed the Declaration of Independence, will at once reject indignantly such an imputation upon such men. And the history of the times, taken in connection with the language of the instrument, makes it obvious that rights in the African race were not in their minds nor thought of at the time; nor were the negroes supposed to have the slightest interest in the controversy when the colonists proclaimed their undoubted rights, and enumerated the wrongs they had received from England, nor indeed could it well have been otherwise in the ordinary operations of the human mind. For almost every man who signed the Declaration of Independence was born, educated, and had grown into manhood in the reign of George II., and had naturally imbibed the opinions of that age in regard to the negro race. They had seen the monarch whom they were taught to love, honor, and reverence for his virtues, openly engaged in the trafficking in negroes as if they were ordinary merchandise; and that, too, in its worst and most revolting form, that is, seizing them in their own country, and selling them to whoever would buy. With such examples and teachings of the mother country and their king, the opinions of the colonies of England can hardly, I suppose, be doubted.

Indeed, so deep was this impression made on the white race in this country, that it appears to be indelible. For, amid all the changes in public opinion and legislation which have since taken place, the line of division between the two races, marking the superiority of the one and the inferiority of the other, is as plain now as it was in the days of the *assiento*. There is not a State in the Union where this distinction is not recognized by public opinion, and daily acted upon. There is not one in which the intermarriage of a white person with a negro is not still deemed unnatural; not one in which it does not degrade the white man or woman who forms the connection, and exclude them from the social position to which they were before entitled. The few persons who, in certain localities, have endeavored to obliterate the line of division, and to amalgamate the races, are hardly sufficient in number or in weight of character to be noticed as an exception to the overwhelming current of public opinion and feeling upon this subject.

And such being the public opinion and laws which universally prevailed in the Colonies when the Declaration of Independence was framed, and when the Constitution was adopted, it would be a palpable perversion of this meaning to expound these instruments as if made at the present day, and under existing circumstances and laws.

The Navigation Act of Charles II., of which I have before spoken, shows the absurdity and injustice of interpreting an ancient instrument without regard to the times and circumstances under which it was made. All the law authorities of that period held that negroes were *merchandise*, and could not, for that reason, be brought into a British colony except in British vessels. But who supposes that a statute passed at the present day, in the very same words by the English Parliament, would embrace negroes, or that they would be included by the words "goods or commodities." It is true that negroes are not now merchandise by the English law, subsequent statutes having changed the law in that respect have repealed it. But that does not alter the meaning of the statute, or make the opinions given at the time erroneous. Its true construction then is its true construction now; what it meant then it means now; and it is not in force merely because subsequent legislation has repealed it and changed the law. But there is no alteration or change in the Constitution of the United States in relation to the African race since it was adopted. It is still in full force according to its original meaning.

There are some judicial decisions in the American courts which were casually omitted, and which it is proper here to notice, as my attention has again been called to the subject. The case of Hobbs and Others *vs.* Fogg, decided in the Supreme Court of Pennsylvania, and reported in 6 Watts, 553, is particularly worthy of attention, from the just weight and authority of the Court by which the opinion was given. This case was decided twenty years ago, and so far as the condition of the African race in this country is concerned, and the rule of interpretation which must be applied to public instruments, it maintains precisely the same principles which this Court affirmed in the case of Dred Scott.

The case before the State court was this: the Constitution of Pennsylvania provided, "that in elections by the citizens, every freeman of the age of twenty-one years, having resided in the

State two years before the election, and having within that time paid a State or County tax," should enjoy the rights of an elector. The question before the Court was whether a free colored man was a "freeman" in the sense in which that word was used in the Constitution. The Court held that he was not. The point is fully and ably argued by the Court, and was evidently carefully considered. I quote a single passage in which the Court states the result of its reasoning. "But (says the Court), in addition to interpretation from usage, this antecedent legislation furnishes other proofs that no colored race was party to our social compact. As was justly remarked by President Fox, in the matter of the late contested election, our ancestors settled the province as a community of white men, and the blacks were introduced into it as a race of slaves; whence an unconquerable prejudice of *caste* which has come down to our day, insomuch that a suspicion of taint still has the unjust effect of sinking the subject of it below the common level. Consistently with this prejudice, is it to be credited that parity of rank would be allowed to such a race?"

It will be observed that the Constitution of Pennsylvania, which the Court was expounding, was adopted in 1790, and that the Constitution of the United States had been previously framed and adopted, and was at that time in actual operation. The decision of the Court, defining the meaning of the word "*freeman*" in the State Constitution, was made in 1837, long after the disturbing question of slavery had been raised upon the admission of the State of Missouri, and when the public opinion of the civilized world had undergone a change as to the justice and morality of the African slave-trade, and when that traffic had been made piracy by act of Congress. It must also be remembered that Pennsylvania, when the colony was first planted, objected to the introduction of negro slavery, and was the first State in the Union which passed a law to put an end to it within its limits, and none of her citizens or ships before the Revolution, as far as I can ascertain, ever engaged in the traffic.

Another case was referred to and not noticed in the opinion of the Court, but which appears to have been much relied on in the dissenting opinions. I allude to the case of the State *vs.* Manuel, decided in the Supreme Court of North Carolina, and reported in Dev. and Bat. Rep. 20, in which the Court held that every person born in North Carolina, who would before the Revolution have been a British subject, was after the Revolution a citizen of the State, and consequently that free negroes born in the State were by birthright citizens of the State; and this doctrine was reaffirmed in the case of the State *vs.* Newcomb, 5 Dev. and Bat., 253.

It is proper, from the high character of the State court by which these decisions were given, and the importance attached to them in the dissenting opinions in this Court, to examine the principles upon which they were determined.

In the case of the State *vs.* Manuel, in which the question first came before the State court, the opinion was delivered by the late Judge Gaston. But with every respect for that learned jurist, I must say that the principle he assumes, and upon which his whole reasoning is founded, is evidently erroneous.

In speaking of allegiance arising from birth according to the principles of the English law, he defines British subjects to be all *free persons* born within the dominions of the King of Great Britain. This certainly is not the definition of Coke and Blackstone. They say "natural allegiance is such as is due from *all men* born within the King's dominions immediately upon their birth." See 7 Rep., and 1 Black. Com., 369. They do not limit this natural allegiance to *free persons* only, nor do I know upon what authority it is so limited by the learned Judge. *All persons*, say the high English authorities to which I have referred, born within the King's dominions owe this allegiance on their birth, and consequently are British subjects. Negro slaves, therefore, born within the British colonies were British subjects, and owed allegiance to the British Crown. They were his subjects, and if they levied war against him, or murdered him, they would be guilty of treason. They were *persons* as well as *property*, and are so regarded in every nation or State in which slavery exists. Yet it is upon this mistaken definition of natural allegiance, and of a British subject, that the State court rests altogether its decision. Upon the true definition as given by Coke and Blackstone, the argument of the Court would not stand a moment's examination. For if it be true, that all persons born within the dominions of the King, and who were on that ground his subjects, became citizens of the State upon the change of sovereignty, then the negro slaves who had been so born, and who were his subjects, became citizens of the State, and consequently, like other citizens, were entitled to equal rights, and placed upon the same level with their masters. Undoubtedly they became subjects to the new sovereignty, as they had before been subjects to the Crown, and owed it allegiance. But whether, under the new government, they were elevated above the rank of subjects, and became citizens and members of the new community, is a very different question. Certainly the State court did not mean to say that the Revolution produced this effect. Yet it would be the necessary and inevitable result, if, according to the argument of the Court, every one who was a native-born subject of the British Crown in one of the colonies became a citizen of the State when the colony became sovereign and independent.

But even if the definition of natural allegiance as adopted by the State court were the true one, yet the argument founded upon it cannot be maintained. For sovereignty in England and sovereignty in a State stand upon principles which are essentially and radically different.

In England, the sovereignty resides exclusively in the person or individual who is king. All Englishmen are his subjects. And the highest peer in the realm, whatever may be his rights and privileges as a subject, has no share in the sovereignty. Their statutes profess to be passed by the King, by and with the advice and consent of the Parliament, treating the Parliament as advisers and not as the makers of the law. The monarch always speaks of the people as " my people," that is, as persons subject to his dominion, and not sharing in his sovereignty. All offences are charged in indictments to be committed " against his peace and dignity," and the crime of treason can be committed against the King only, and not against the Parliament or people of England.

But, according to our institutions, the sovereignty does not reside in any one individual, but in the whole people, who form the political body called the State. Every one who is a member of this social compact is a citizen, and a component part of the sovereignty. Persons who are not citizens, not members of the sovereignty, may yet owe it allegiance, may be subject to it; and certainly every one, whether free or slave, who was the subject of Great Britain before the Revolution, and was within the territorial limits of the new government, became subject to the State when the new government was formed. But it does not by any means follow that every one of these subjects was elevated to the rank of citizen, and permitted to share in the sovereignty.

Those who displaced the sovereignty of the English monarch, and associated themselves in a new political body, retaining the sovereignty in their own hands, had the power and the right to determine who should, and who should not, be admitted as members of this association, and share equally with themselves the sovereignty they had established and retained in their own hands. They might, if they had chosen to do so, admit as members, or, in other words, as citizens, persons who never had been British subjects, and who could not become so by the laws of England, or they might reject and exclude those who had been British subjects, or would become such if the old government continued. And the simple question to be decided is, who formed this association, and what have they done? Did they admit the negro race as members of the political body, and allow them, when they became free, to share equally with the white race in the sovereignty reserved to the citizens of the Republic, and in the rights and privileges reserved to them individually? The condition of subject and sovereign, therefore, as it existed under the English Government, has no analogy to the present question, and any argument founded upon any such supposed analogy must necessarily lead to erroneous conclusions; no such question as that decided in the case of Dred Scott could have arisen in England or under English law. It is purely an American question, and depends entirely upon our own institutions, and upon the construction and meaning of the constitutions we have established. And in that point of view the subject was fully considered and discussed in the opinion delivered by this Court. The argument of the State court would be correct if the Revolution had been a mere change of dynasty, still leaving the sovereignty of the State in a single individual. But it is altogether untenable, when applied to the American constitutions, and to citizenship under them.

The case of Williams *vs.* Ash, reported in 1 How. 1, was mentioned in the argument, but it was not suggested that it had any bearing upon the case, and was not, therefore, noticed in the opinion. The case was this: A suit for freedom was brought by Ash, who was a negro, against Williams, who claimed him as his slave. The suit was in the Circuit Court of the United States for the District of Columbia. Ash claimed his freedom under the will of his former owner. The Circuit Court decided that he was entitled to his freedom under the will, and the Supreme Court affirmed the decision.

Undoubtedly, by affirming that judgment, the Supreme Court decided that the Circuit Court of the District of Columbia had jurisdiction in a suit brought in that Court by one of the African race to assert his title to freedom, nor has any one ever questioned the correctness of that decision. I mention the case now only for the purpose of stating that it was a suit in the Circuit Court of the United States in the District of Columbia, and not in a Circuit Court of the United States sitting in a State. The statement of this fact is in itself a sufficient answer to the inferences attempted to be drawn from it, as if it were inconsistent with the recent decision. No one, who has read the Constitution, supposes that the jurisdiction of a Circuit Court of the United States sitting in a territory is limited to the same persons or description of persons as a Circuit Court of the United States sitting in a State. Indeed, if the courts of a territory were so limited by the Constitution, citizens of a territory could not sue one another anywhere in a court of the United States, and would be without remedy against each other upon matters of contract, or for injuries to person or property. But it is useless to pursue the argument upon a question upon which no one can doubt who reads the Constitution. The case has no application whatever to the points decided in the case of Dred Scott.

I have seen and heard of various comments and reviews of the opinion, published since its delivery, adverse to the decision of the Court. But I have seen none that I think it worth while to reply to, for they are founded upon misrepresentations and perversions of the points decided by the Court. It would be a waste of time to expose these perversions and misrepresentations. For if they were exposed, they would nevertheless be repeated, and new ones invented to support them. They are for the most part carefully and elaborately put together in a volume published at Boston soon after the opinion appeared in the report, and which from the beginning to the end is a disingenuous perversion and misrepresentation of what passed in conference, and also of what the Court has decided. They cannot mislead the judgment of any one who is in search of truth, and will read the opinion; and I have no desire to waste time and throw away arguments upon those who evidently act upon the principle that the end will justify the means.

Supreme Court of the United States, December Term, 1858.
21 Howard R., 506.

Stephen V. R. Ableman, Plaintiff in Error, *vs.* Sherman M. Booth ; and the United States, Plaintiff in Error, *vs.* Sherman M. Booth

Mr. Chief-Justice Taney delivered the opinion of the Court.

The plaintiff in error in the first of these cases is the Marshal of the United States for the District of Wisconsin, and the two cases have arisen out of the same transaction, and depend, to some extent, upon the same principles. On that account, they have been argued and considered together; and the following are the facts as they appear in the transcripts before us :

Sherman M. Booth was charged before Winfield Smith, a commissioner duly appointed by the District Court of the United States for the District of Wisconsin, with having, on the 11th day of March, 1854, aided and abetted, at Milwaukee, in the said district, the escape of a fugitive slave from the deputy marshal, who had him in custody under a warrant issued by the District Judge of the United States for that district, under the Act of Congress of September 18, 1850.

Upon the examination before the commissioner, he was satisfied that an offence had been committed as charged, and that there was probable cause to believe that Booth had been guilty of it; and thereupon held him to bail to appear and answer before the District Court of the United States for the District of Wisconsin, on the first Monday in July then next ensuing. But on the 26th of May his bail, or surety in the recognizance, delivered him to the marshal, in the presence of the commissioner, and requested the commissioner to recommit Booth to the custody of the marshal; and he having failed to recognize again for his appearance before the District Court, the commissioner committed him to the custody of the marshal, to be delivered to the keeper of the jail until he should be discharged by due course of law.

Booth made application on the next day, the 27th of May, to A. D. Smith, one of the Justices of the Supreme Court of the State of Wisconsin, for a writ of habeas corpus, stating that he was restrained of his liberty by Stephen V. R. Ableman, Marshal of the United States for that district, under the warrant of commitment hereinbefore mentioned; and alleging that his imprisonment was illegal, because the Act of Congress of September 18, 1850, was unconstitutional and void; and also that the warrant was defective, and did not describe the offence created by that act, even if the act were valid.

Upon this application, the Justice, on the same day, issued the writ of habeas corpus, directed to the marshal, requiring him forthwith to have the body of Booth before him, (the said Justice,) together with the time and cause of his imprisonment. The marshal thereupon, on the day above mentioned, produced Booth, and made his return, stating that he was received into his custody as marshal on the day before, and held in custody by virtue of the warrant of the commissioner above mentioned, a copy of which he annexed and returned with the writ.

To this return Booth demurred, as not sufficient in law to justify his detention. And upon the hearing the Justice decided that his detention was illegal, and ordered the marshal to discharge him and set him at liberty, which was accordingly done.

Afterwards, on the 9th of June, in the same year, the marshal applied to the Supreme Court of the State for a *certiorari*, setting forth in his application the proceedings hereinbefore mentioned, and charging that the release of Booth by the Justice was erroneous and unlawful, and praying that his proceedings might be brought before the Supreme Court of the State for revision.

The *certiorari* was allowed on the same day; and the writ was accordingly issued on the 12th of the same month, and returnable on the third Tuesday of the month; and on the 20th the return was made by the Justice, stating the proceedings, as hereinbefore mentioned.

The case was argued before the Supreme Court of the State; and on the 19th of July it pronounced its judgment, affirming the decision of the Associate Justice discharging Booth from imprisonment, with costs against Ableman, the marshal.

Afterwards, on the 26th of October, the marshal sued out a writ of error, returnable to this Court on the first Monday of December, 1854, in order to bring the judgment here for revision; and the defendant in error was regularly cited to appear on that day; and the record and proceedings were certified to this Court by the clerk of the State court in the usual form, in obedience to the writ of error. And on the 4th of December, Booth, the defendant in error, filed a memorandum in writing in this Court, stating that he had been cited to appear here in this case, and that he submitted it to the judgment of this Court on the reasoning in the argument and opinions in the printed pamphlets therewith sent.

After the judgment was entered in the Supreme Court of Wisconsin, and before the writ of error was sued out, the State court entered on its record, that, in the final judgment it had rendered, the validity of the Act of Congress of September 18, 1850, and of February 12, 1793, and the authority of the marshal to hold the defendant in his custody, under the process mentioned in his return to the writ of habeas corpus, were respectively drawn in question, and the decision of the Court in the final judgment was against their validity, respectively.

This certificate was not necessary to give this Court jurisdiction, because the proceedings upon their face show that these questions arose, and how they were decided; but it shows that at that time the Supreme Court of Wisconsin did not question their obligation to obey the writ of error, nor the authority of this Court to re-examine their judgment in the cases specified. And the certificate is given for the purpose of placing distinctly on the record the points that were raised and decided in that Court, in order that this Court might have no difficulty in exercising its appellate power, and pronouncing its judgment upon all of them.

We come now to the second case. At the January term of the District Court of the United States for the District of Wisconsin, after Booth had been set at liberty, and after the transcript of the proceedings in the case above mentioned had been returned to and filed in this Court, the grand jury found a bill of indictment against Booth for the offence with which he was charged before the commissioner, and from which the State court had discharged him. The indictment was found on the 4th January, 1855. On the 9th a motion was made, by counsel on behalf of the accused, to quash the indictment; which was overruled by the Court; and he thereupon pleaded not guilty, upon which issue was joined. On the 10th a jury was called and appeared in court, when he challenged the array; but the challenge was overruled and the jury empanelled. The trial, it appears, continued from day to day, until the 13th, when the jury found him guilty in the manner and form in which he stood indicted in the fourth and fifth counts. On the 16th he moved for a new trial and in arrest of judgment; which motions were argued on the 20th, and on the 23d the Court overruled the motions, and sentenced the prisoner to be imprisoned for one month, and to pay a fine of $1000 and the costs of prosecution, and that he remain in custody until the sentence was complied with.

We have stated more particularly these proceedings, from a sense of justice to the District Court, as they show that every opportunity of making his defence was afforded him, and that his case was fully heard and considered.

On the 26th of January, three days after the sentence was passed, the prisoner, by his counsel, filed his petition in the Supreme Court of the State, and with his petition filed a copy of the proceedings in the District Court, and also affidavits from the foreman and one other member of the jury who tried him, stating that their verdict was, guilty on the fourth and fifth counts, and not guilty on the other three; and stated in his petition that his imprisonment was illegal, because the fugitive slave law was unconstitutional; that the District Court had no jurisdiction to try or punish him for the matter charged against him, and that the proceedings and sentence of that Court were absolute nullities in law. Various other objections to the proceedings are alleged, which are unimportant in the questions now before the Court, and need not, therefore, be particularly stated. On the next day, the 27th, the Court directed two writs of *habeas corpus* to be issued — one to the marshal, and one to the sheriff of Milwaukee, to whose actual keeping the prisoner was committed by the marshal, by order of the District Court. The *habeas corpus* directed each of them to produce the body of the prisoner, and make known the cause of his imprisonment, immediately after the receipt of the writ.

On the 30th January the marshal made his return, not acknowledging the jurisdiction, but stating the sentence of the District Court as his authority; that the prisoner was delivered to and was then in the actual keeping of the sheriff of Milwaukee County, by order of the Court, and he therefore had no control of the body of the prisoner; and if the sheriff had not received him, he should have so reported to the District Court, and should have conveyed him to some other place or prison, as the Court should command.

On the same day the sheriff produced the body of Booth before the State court, and returned that he had been committed to his custody by the marshal, by virtue of a transcript, a true copy of which was annexed to his return, and which was the only process or authority by which he detained him.

This transcript was a full copy of the proceedings and sentence in the District Court of the United States, as hereinbefore stated. To this return the accused, by his counsel, filed a general demurrer.

The Court ordered the hearing to be postponed until the 2d of February, and notice to be given to the District Attorney of the United States. It was accordingly heard on that day, and on the next, (February 3d,) the Court decided that the imprisonment was illegal, and ordered and adjudged that Booth be, and he was by that judgment, forever discharged from that imprisonment and restraint; and he was accordingly set at liberty.

On the 21st of April next following, the Attorney-General of the United States presented a petition to the Chief Justice of the Supreme Court, stating briefly the facts in the case, and at the same time presenting an exemplification of the proceedings hereinbefore stated, duly certified by the clerk of the State court, and averring in his petition that the State court had no jurisdiction in the case, and praying that a writ of error might issue to bring its judgment before this Court to correct the error. The writ of error was allowed and issued, and, according to the rules and practice of the Court, was returnable on the first Monday of December, 1855, and a citation for the defendant in error to appear on that day was issued by the Chief Justice at the same time.

No return having been made to this writ, the Attorney-General, on the 1st of February, 1856, filed affidavits, showing that the writ of error had been duly served on the clerk of the Supreme Court of Wisconsin, at his office, on the 30th of May, 1855, and the citation served on the defendant in error on the 28th of June, in the same year. And also the affidavit of the district attorney of the United States for the District of Wisconsin, setting forth that when he served the writ of error upon the clerk, as above mentioned, he was informed by the clerk, and has also been informed by one of the Justices of the Supreme Court which released Booth, "*that the Court had directed the clerk to make no return to the writ of error, and to enter no order upon the journals or records of the Court concerning the same.*" And, upon these proofs, the Attorney-General moved the Court for an order upon the clerk to make return to the writ of error, on or before the first day of the next ensuing term of this Court. The rule was accordingly laid, and on the 22d of July, 1856, the Attorney-General filed with the clerk of this Court the affidavit of the marshal of the District of Wisconsin, that he had served the rule on the clerk on the 7th of the month above mentioned; and no return having been made, the Attorney-General, on the 27th of February, 1857, moved for leave to file the certified copy of the record of the Supreme Court of Wisconsin, which he had produced with his application for the writ of error, and to docket the case in this Court, in conformity with a motion to that effect made at the last term. And the Court thereupon, on the 6th of March, 1857, ordered the copy of the record filed by the Attorney-General to be received and entered on the docket of this Court, to have the same effect and legal operation as if returned by the clerk with the writ of error, and that the case stand for argument at the next ensuing term, without further notice to either party.

The case was accordingly docketed, but was not reached for argument in the regular order and practice of the Court until the present term.

This detailed statement of the proceedings in the different courts has appeared to be necessary in order to form a just estimate of the action of the different tribunals in which it has been heard, and to account for the delay in the final decision of a case which, from its character, would seem to have demanded prompt action. The first case, indeed, was reached for trial two terms ago. But as the two cases are different portions of the same prosecution for the same offence, they unavoidably, to some extent, involve the same principles of law, and it would hardly have been proper to hear and decide the first before the other was ready for hearing and decision. They have accordingly been argued together, by the Attorney-General of the United States, at the present term. No counsel has in either case appeared for the defendant in error. But we have the pamphlet arguments filed and referred to by Booth in the first case, as hereinbefore mentioned; also the opinions and arguments of the Supreme Court of Wisconsin, and of the Judges who compose it, in full, and are enabled, therefore, to see the grounds on which they rely to support their decisions.

It will be seen, from the foregoing statement of facts, that a Judge of the Supreme Court of the State of Wisconsin, in the first of these cases, claimed and exercised the right to supervise and annul the proceedings of a commissioner of the United States, and to discharge a prisoner who had been committed by the commissioner for an offence against the laws of this Government, and that this exercise of power by the Judge was afterwards sanctioned and affirmed by the Supreme Court of the State.

In the second case, the State court has gone a step further, and claimed and exercised jurisdiction over the proceedings and judgment of a District Court of the United States; and upon a summary and collateral proceeding, by *habeas corpus*, has set aside and annulled its judgment, and discharged a prisoner who had been tried and found guilty of an offence against the laws of the United States, and sentenced to imprisonment by the District Court.

And it further appears, that the State court have not only claimed and exercised this jurisdiction, but have also determined that their decision is final and conclusive upon all the courts of the United States, and ordered their clerk to disregard and refuse obedience to the writ of error issued by this Court, pursuant to the Act of Congress of 1789, to bring here for examination and revision the judgment of the State court.

These propositions are new in the jurisprudence of the United States, as well as of the States; and the supremacy of the State courts over the courts of the United States, in cases arising under the Constitution and laws of the United States, is now for the first time asserted and acted upon in the Supreme Court of a State.

The supremacy is not, indeed, set forth distinctly and broadly, in so many words, in the printed opinions of the Judges. It is intermixed with elaborate discussions of different provisions in the fugitive slave law, and of the privileges and power of the writ of *habeas corpus*. But the paramount power of the State court lies at the foundation of these decisions; for their commentaries upon the provisions of that law, and upon the privileges and power of the writ of *habeas corpus*, were out of place, and their judicial action upon them without authority of law, unless they had the power to revise and control the proceedings in the criminal case of which they were speaking; and their judgments, releasing the prisoner, and disregarding the writ of error from this Court, can rest upon no other foundation.

If the judicial power exercised in this instance has been reserved to the States, no offence against the laws of the United States can be punished by their own courts, without the permission and according to the judgment of the courts of the State in which the party happens to be imprisoned; for, if the Supreme Court of Wisconsin possessed the power it has exercised in relation to offences against the act of Congress in question, it necessarily follows that they must have the same judicial authority in relation to any other law of the United States; and, consequently, their supervising and controlling power would embrace the whole criminal code of the United States, and extend to offences against our revenue laws, or any other law intended to guard the different departments of the general Government from fraud or violence. And it would embrace all crimes from the highest to the lowest; including felonies, which are punished with death, as well as misdemeanors, which are punished by imprisonment. And, moreover, if the power is possessed by the Supreme Court of the State of Wisconsin, it must belong equally to every other State in the Union, when the prisoner is within its territorial limits; and it is very certain that the State courts would not always agree in opinion; and it would often happen that an act, which was admitted to be an offence, and justly punished, in one State, would be regarded as innocent, and, indeed, as praiseworthy in another.

It would seem to be hardly necessary to do more than state the result to which these decisions of the State courts must inevitably lead. It is, of itself, a sufficient and conclusive answer; for no one will suppose that a Government which has now lasted nearly seventy years, enforcing its laws by its own tribunals, and preserving the union of the States, could have lasted a single year, or fulfilled the high trusts committed to it, if offences against its laws could not have been punished without the consent of the State in which the culprit was found.

The Judges of the Supreme Court of Wisconsin do not distinctly state from what source they suppose they have derived this judicial power. There can be no such thing as judicial authority, unless it is conferred by a government or sovereignty; and if the judges and courts of Wisconsin possess the jurisdiction they claim, they must derive it either from the United States or the State. It certainly has not been conferred on them by the United States; and it is equally clear it was not in the power of the State to confer it, even if it had attempted to do so; for no State can authorize one of its judges or courts to exercise judicial power, by *habeas corpus* or otherwise, within the jurisdiction of another and independent government. And although the State of Wisconsin is sovereign within its territorial limits to a certain extent, yet that sovereignty is limited and restricted by the Constitution of the United States. And the powers of the general Government, and of the State, although both exist and are exercised within the same territorial limits, are yet separate and distinct sovereignties, acting separately and independently of each other, within their respective spheres. And the sphere of action appropriated to the United States is as far beyond the reach of the judicial process issued by a State judge or a State court, as if the line of division was traced by landmarks and monuments visible to the eye. And the State of Wisconsin had no more power to authorize these proceedings of its judges and courts, than it would have had if the prisoner had been confined in Michigan, or in any other State of the Union, for an offence against the laws of the State in which he was imprisoned.

It is, however, due to the State to say, that we do not find this claim of paramount jurisdiction in the State courts over the courts of the United States asserted or countenanced by the Constitution or laws of the State. We find it only in the decisions of the Judges of the Supreme Court. Indeed, at the very time these decisions were made, there was a statute of the State which declares that a person brought up on a *habeas corpus* shall be remanded, if it appears that he is confined :

" 1st. By virtue of process, by any court or judge of the United States, in a case where such court or judge has exclusive jurisdiction; or,

" 2d. By virtue of the final judgment or decree of any competent court of civil or criminal jurisdiction." (Revised Statutes of the State of Wisconsin, 1849, ch. 124, page 629.)

Even, therefore, if these cases depended upon the laws of Wisconsin, it would be difficult to find in these provisions such a grant of judicial power as the Supreme Court claims to have derived from the State.

But, as we have already said, questions of this kind must always depend upon the Constitution and laws of the United States, and not of a State. The Constitution was not formed merely to guard the States against danger from foreign nations, but mainly to secure union and harmony at home; for if this object could be attained, there would be but little danger from abroad; and to accomplish this purpose, it was felt by the statesmen who framed the Constitution, and by the people who adopted it, that it was necessary that many of the rights of sovereignty which the States then possessed should be ceded to the general Government; and that in the sphere of action assigned to it, it should be supreme, and strong enough to execute its own laws by its own tribunals, without interruption from a State or from State authorities. And it was evident that anything short of this would be inadequate to the main objects for which the Government was established; and that local interests, local passions or prejudices, incited and fostered by individuals for sinister purposes, would lead to acts of aggression and injustice by one State upon the rights of another, which would ultimately terminate in violence and force, unless there was a common arbiter between them, armed with power enough to protect and guard the rights of all, by appropriate laws, to be carried into execution peacefully by its judicial tribunals.

The language of the Constitution, by which this power is granted, is too plain to admit of doubt or to need comment. It declares that " this Constitution, and the laws of the United States which shall be passed in pursuance thereof, and all treaties made, or which shall be made, under the authority of the United States, shall be the supreme law of the land, and the Judges in every State shall be bound thereby, anything in the Constitution or laws of any State to the contrary notwithstanding."

But the supremacy thus conferred on this Government could not peacefully be maintained, unless it was clothed with judicial power, equally paramount in authority to carry it into execution; for if left to the courts of justice of the several States, conflicting decisions would unavoidably take place, and the local tribunals could hardly be expected to be always free from the local influences of which we have spoken. And the Constitution and laws and treaties of the United States, and the powers granted to the Federal Government, would soon receive different interpretations in different States, and the Government of the United States would soon become one thing in one State and another thing in another. It was essential, therefore, to its very existence as a Government, that it should have the power of establishing courts of justice, altogether independent of State power, to carry into effect its own laws; and that a tribunal should be established in which all cases which might arise under the Constitution and laws and treaties of the United States, whether in a State court or a court of the United States, should be finally and conclusively decided. Without such a tribunal, it is obvious that there would be no uniformity of judicial decision; and that the supremacy, (which is but another name for independence,) so carefully provided in the clause of the Constitution above referred to, could not possibly be maintained peacefully, unless it was associated with this paramount judicial authority.

Accordingly, it was conferred on the general Government, in clear, precise, and comprehensive terms. It is declared that its judicial power shall (among other subjects enumerated) extend to all cases in law and in equity arising under the Constitution and laws of the United States, and that in such cases, as well as the others there enumerated, this Court shall have appellate jurisdiction both as to law and fact, with such exceptions and under such regulations as Congress shall make. The appellate power, it will be observed, is conferred on this Court in all cases or suits in which such a question shall arise. It is not confined to suits in the inferior courts of the United States, but extends to all cases where such a question arises, whether it be in a judicial tribunal of a State or of the United States. And it is manifest that this ultimate appellate power in a tribunal created by the Constitution itself was deemed essential to secure the independence and supremacy of the general Government in the sphere of action assigned to it; to make the Constitution and laws of the United States uniform, and the same in every State; and to guard against evils which would inevitably arise from conflicting opinions between the courts of a State and the United States, if there was no common arbiter authorized to decide between them.

The importance which the framers of the Constitution attached to such a tribunal, for the purpose of preserving internal tranquillity, is strikingly manifested by the clause which gives this Court jurisdiction over the sovereign States which compose this Union, when a controversy arises between them. Instead of reserving the right to seek redress for injustice from another State by their sovereign powers, they have bound themselves to submit to the decision of this Court, and to abide by its judgment. And it is not out of place to say here, that experience has demonstrated that this power was not unwisely surrendered by the States; for in the time that has already elapsed since this Government came into existence, several irritating and angry controversies have taken place between adjoining States, in relation to their respective boundaries, and which have sometimes threatened to end in force and violence, but for the power vested in this Court to hear them and decide between them.

The same purposes are clearly indicated by the different language employed when conferring supremacy upon the laws of the United States, and jurisdiction upon its courts. In the first case, it provides that " this Constitution, and the laws of the United States *which shall be made in pursuance thereof*, shall be the supreme law of the land, and obligatory upon the judges in every State." The words in italics show the precision and foresight which mark every clause in the instrument. The sovereignty to be created was to be limited in its powers of legislation; and if it passed a law not authorized by its enumerated powers, it was not to be regarded as the supreme law of the land, nor were the State judges bound to carry it into execution. And as the courts of a State, and the courts of the United States, might, and indeed certainly would, often differ as to the extent of the powers conferred by the general Government, it was manifest that serious controversies would arise between the authorities of the United States and of the States, which must be settled by force of arms, unless some tribunal was created to decide between them finally and without appeal.

The Constitution has accordingly provided, as far as human foresight could provide, against this danger. And in conferring judicial power upon the Federal Government, it declares that the jurisdiction of its courts shall extend to all cases arising under " this Constitution " and the laws of the United States — leaving out the words of restriction contained in the grant of legislative power which we have above noticed. The judicial power covers every legislative act of Congress, whether it be made within the limits of its delegated powers, or be an assumption of power beyond the grants in the Constitution.

This judicial power was justly regarded as indispensable, not merely to maintain the supremacy of the laws of the United States, but also to guard the States from any encroachment upon their reserved rights by the general Government. And as the Constitution is the fundamental and supreme law, if it appears that an act of Congress is not pursuant to, and within the limits of, the power assigned to the Federal Government, it is the duty of the courts of the United States to declare it unconstitutional and void. The grant of judicial power is not confined to the administration of laws passed in pursuance to the provisions of the Constitution, nor confined to the interpretation of such laws; but, by the very terms of the grant, the Constitution is under their view, when any act of Congress is brought before them, and it is their duty to declare the law void, and refuse to execute it, if it is not pursuant to the legislative powers conferred upon Congress. And as the final appellate power in all such questions is given to this Court, controversies as to the respective powers of the United States and the States, instead of being determined by military and physical force, are heard, investigated, and finally settled, with the calmness and deliberation of judicial inquiry. And no one can fail to see, that if such an arbiter had not been provided, in our complicated system of government, internal tranquillity could not have been preserved; and if such controversies were left to arbitrament of physical force, our governments, State and National, would soon cease to be governments of laws, and revolutions by force of arms would take the place of courts of justice and judicial decisions.

In organizing such a tribunal, it is evident that every precaution was taken, which human wisdom could devise, to fit it for the high duty with which it was intrusted. It was not left to Congress to create it by law; for the States could hardly be expected to confide in the impartiality of a tribunal created exclusively by the general Government, without any participation on their part. And as the performance of its duty would sometimes come in conflict with individual ambition or interests, and powerful political combinations, an act of Congress establishing such a tribunal might be repealed, in order to establish another more subservient to the predominant political influences or excited passions of the day. This tribunal, therefore, was erected, and the powers of which we have spoken conferred upon it, not by the Federal Government, but by the people of the States, who formed and adopted that Government, and conferred upon it all the powers, legislative, executive, and judicial, which it now possesses. And in order to secure its independence, and enable it faithfully and firmly to perform its duty, it engrafted it upon the Constitution itself, and declared that this Court should have appellate power in all cases arising under the Constitution and laws of the United States. So long, therefore, as this Constitution shall endure, this tribunal must exist with it; deciding, in the peaceful forms of judicial proceeding, the angry and irritating controversies between sovereignties, which, in other countries, have been determined by the arbitrament of force.

These principles of constitutional law are confirmed and illustrated by the clause which confers legislative power upon Congress. That power is specifically given in Article I., Section 8, paragraph 18, in the following words:

" To make all laws which shall be necessary and proper to carry into execution the foregoing powers, and all other powers vested by this Constitution in the Government of the United States, or in any department or officer thereof."

Under this clause of the Constitution, it became the duty of Congress to pass such laws as were necessary and proper to carry into execution the powers vested in the judicial department. And in the performance of this duty, the first Congress, at its first session, passed the Act of 1789, ch. 20, entitled " An act to establish the judicial courts of the United States." It will be remembered that many of the members of the Convention were also members of this Congress, and it cannot be supposed that they did not understand the meaning and intention of the great instrument which they had so anxiously and deliberately considered, clause by clause, and assisted to frame. And the law they passed to carry into execution the powers vested in the judicial department of the Government proves, past doubt, that their interpretation of the appellate powers conferred on this Court was the same with that which we have now given; for by the 25th section of the Act of 1789, Congress authorized writs of error to be issued from this Court to a State court, whenever a right had been claimed under the Constitution or laws of the United States, and the decision of the State court was against it. And to make this appellate power effectual, and altogether independent of the action of State tribunals, this act further provides, that upon writs of error to a State court, instead of remanding the cause for a final decision in the State court, this Court may at their discretion, if the cause shall have been once remanded before, proceed to a final decision of the same, and award execution.

These provisions in the Act of 1789 tell us, in language not to be mistaken, the great importance which the patriots and statesmen of the first Congress attached to this appellate power, and the foresight and care with which they guarded its free and independent exercise against interference or obstruction by States or State tribunals.

In the case before the Supreme Court of Wisconsin, a right was claimed under the Constitution and laws of the United States, and the decision was against the right claimed; and it refuses obedience to the writ of error, and regards its own judgment as final. It has not only reversed and annulled the judgment of the District Court of the United States, but it has reversed and annulled the provisions of the Constitution itself, and the Act of Congress of 1789, and made the superior and appellate tribunal the inferior and subordinate one.

We do not question the authority of a State court, or Judge who is authorized by the laws of the State to issue the writ of *habeas corpus*, to issue it in any case where the party is imprisoned within its territorial limits, provided it does not appear, when the application is made, that the person imprisoned is in custody under the authority of the United States. The Court or Judge has a right to inquire, in this mode of proceeding, for what cause, and by what authority, the prisoner is confined within the territorial limits of the state sovereignty. And it is the duty of the marshal, or other person having the custody of the prisoner, to make known to the Judge or Court, by a proper return, the authority by which he holds him in custody. This right to inquire by process of *habeas corpus*, and the duty of the officer to make a return, grows, necessarily, out of the complex character of our Government, and the existence of two distinct and separate sovereignties within the same territorial space, each of them restricted in its powers, and each within its sphere of action, prescribed by the Constitution of the United States, independent of the other. But, after the return is made, and the State judge or court judicially apprized that the party is in custody under the authority of the United States, they can proceed no further. They then know that the prisoner is within the dominion and jurisdiction of another Government, and that neither the writ of *habeas corpus*, nor any other process issued under State authority, can pass over the line of division between the two sovereignties. He is then within the dominion and exclusive jurisdiction of the United States. If he has committed an offence against their laws, their tribunals alone can punish him. If he is wrongfully imprisoned, their judicial tribunals can release him, and afford him redress. And, although, as we have said, it is the duty of the marshal, or other person holding him, to make known, by a proper return, the authority under which he detains him, it is at the same time imperatively his duty to obey the process of the United States, to hold the prisoner in custody under it, and to refuse obedience to the mandate or process of any other Government. And, consequently, it is his duty not to take the prisoner, nor suffer him to be taken, before a State judge or court upon a *habeas corpus* issued under State authority. No State judge or court, after they are judicially informed that the party is imprisoned under the authority of the United States, has any right to interfere with him, or to require him to be brought before them. And if the authority of a State, in the form of judicial process or otherwise, should attempt to control the marshal or other authorized officer or agent of the United States, in any respect, in the custody of his prisoner, it would be his duty to resist it, and to call to his aid any force that might be necessary to maintain the authority of law against illegal interference. No judicial process, whatever form it may assume, can have any lawful authority outside of the limits of the jurisdiction of the Court or Judge by whom it is issued; and an attempt to enforce beyond these boundaries is nothing less than lawless violence.

Nor is there anything in this supremacy of the general Government, or the jurisdiction of its judicial tribunals, to awaken the jealousy, or offend the natural and just pride of State sovereignty. Neither this Government, nor the powers of which we were speaking, were forced upon the States. The Constitution of the United States, with all the powers conferred by it upon the general Government, and surrendered by the States, was the voluntary act of the people of the several States, deliberately done, for their own protection and safety against injustice from one another. And their anxiety to preserve it in full force, in all its powers, and to guard against resistance to or evasion of its authority, on the part of a State, is proved by the clause which requires that the members of the State Legislatures, and all executive and judicial officers of the several States, (as well as those of the general Government,) shall be bound, by oath or affirmation, to support this Constitution. This is the last and closing clause of the Constitution, and inserted, when the whole frame of Government, with the powers hereinbefore specified, had been adopted by the Convention; and it was in that form, and with these powers, that the Constitution was submitted to the people of the several States for their consideration and decision.

Now, it certainly can be no humiliation to the citizen of a republic to yield a ready obedience to the laws as administered by the constituted authorities. On the contrary, it is among his first and highest duties as a citizen, because free government cannot exist without it. Nor can it be inconsistent with the dignity of a sovereign State to observe faithfully, and in the spirit of sincerity and truth, the compact into which it voluntarily entered when it became a State of this Union. On the contrary, the highest honor of sovereignty is untarnished faith. And certainly no faith could be more deliberately and solemnly pledged than that which every State has plighted to the other States to support the Constitution as it is, in all its provisions, until they shall be altered in the manner which the Constitution itself prescribes. In the emphatic language of the pledge required, it is *to support this Constitution.* And no power is more clearly conferred by the Constitution and laws of the United States, than the power of this Court to decide, ultimately and finally, all cases arising under such Constitution and laws; and for that purpose to bring here for revision, by writ of error, the judgment of a State court, where such questions have arisen, and the right claimed under them denied by the highest judicial tribunal in the State.

We are sensible that we have extended the examination of these decisions beyond the limits required by any intrinsic difficulty in the question. But the decisions in question were made by the supreme judicial tribunal of the State; and when a court so elevated in its position has pronounced a judgment which, if it could be maintained, would subvert the very foundations of this Government, it seemed to be the duty of this Court, when exercising its appellate power, to show plainly the grave errors into which the State court has fallen, and the consequences to which they would inevitably lead.

But it can hardly be necessary to point out the errors which followed their mistaken· view of the jurisdiction they might lawfully exercise; because, if there was any defect of power in the commissioner, or in his mode of proceeding, it was for the tribunals of the United States to revise and correct it, and not for a State court. And as regards the decision of the District Court, it had exclusive and final jurisdiction by the laws of the United States; and neither the regularity of its proceedings nor the validity of its sentence could be called in question in any other court, either of a State or the United States, by *habeas corpus*, or any other process.

But although we think it unnecessary to discuss these questions, yet, as they have been decided by the State court, and are before us on the record, and we are not willing to be misunderstood, it is proper to say that, in the judgment of this Court, the Act of·Congress commonly called the fugitive slave law is, in all its provisions, fully authorized by the Constitution of the United States; that the commissioner had lawful authority to issue the warrant and commit the party, and that his proceedings were regular and conformable to law. We have already stated the opinion and judgment of the Court as to the exclusive jurisdiction of the District Court, and the appellate powers which this Court is authorized and required to exercise. And if any argument was needed to show the wisdom and necessity of this appellate power, the cases before us sufficiently prove it, and at the same time emphatically call for its exercise.

The judgment of the Supreme Court of Wisconsin must therefore be reversed in each of the cases now before the Court.

Supreme Court of the United States, December Term, 1860.

Howard's Reports, Vol. 24, p. 66.

Ex parte. In the Matter of the Commonwealth of Kentucky, one of the United States of America, by Beriah Magoffin, Governor, and the Executive Authority thereof, Petitioner, *vs.* William Dennison, Governor and Executive Authority of the State of Ohio.

A motion was made in behalf of the State of Kentucky, against the Governor of Ohio, to show cause why a *mandamus* should not be issued by the Supreme Court of the United States, commanding him to cause Willis Lago, a fugitive from justice, to be delivered up, to be removed to the State of Kentucky, having jurisdiction of the crime with which he was charged. The facts on which this motion was made are as follows:

The grand jury of Woodford County, in the State of Kentucky, indicted Willis Lago, a free man of color, for seducing and enticing a slave to leave her owner and possessor, and aiding and assisting said slave in an attempt to make her escape from her owner and possessor.

A copy of this indictment, properly authenticated, was presented by an authorized agent of the Governor of Kentucky to the Governor of Ohio, and the arrest and delivery of the fugitive demanded.

The Governor of Ohio refused to comply with the demand.

Mr. Chief-Justice Taney delivered the opinion of the Court.

The Court is sensible of the importance of this case, and of the great interest and gravity of the questions involved in it, and which have been raised and fully argued at the bar.

Some of them, however, are not now for the first time brought to the attention of this Court; and the objections made to the jurisdiction, and the form and nature of the process to be issued, and upon whom it is to be served, have all been heretofore considered and decided, and cannot now be regarded as open to further dispute.

As early as 1792, in the case of Georgia *vs.* Brailsford, the Court exercised the original jurisdiction conferred by the Constitution, without any further legislation by Congress, to regulate it, than the Act of 1789. And no question was then made, nor any doubt then expressed, as to the authority of the Court. The same power was again exercised without objection in the case of Oswold *vs.* the State of Georgia, in which the Court regulated the form and nature of the process against the State, and directed it to be served on the Governor and Attorney-General. But in the case of Chisholm's Executors *vs.* the State of Georgia, at February Term, 1793, reported in 2 Dall., 419, the authority of the Court in this respect was questioned, and brought to its attention in the argument of counsel; and the report shows how carefully and thoroughly the subject was considered. Each of the Judges delivered a separate opinion, in which these questions, as to the jurisdiction of the Court, and the mode of exercising it, are elaborately examined.

Mr. Chief-Justice Jay, Mr. Justice Cushing, Mr. Justice Wilson, and Mr. Justice Blair, decided in favor of the jurisdiction, and held that process served on the Governor and Attorney-General was sufficient. Mr. Justice Iredell differed, and thought that further legislation by Congress was necessary to give the jurisdiction, and regulate the manner in which it should be exercised. But the opinion of the majority of the Court upon these points has always been since followed. And in the case of New Jersey *vs.* New York, in 1831, 5 Pet., 284, Chief-Justice Marshall, in delivering the opinion of the Court, refers to the case of Chisholm *vs.* the State of Georgia, and to the opinions then delivered, and the judgment pronounced, in terms of high respect; and after enumerating the various cases in which that decision had been acted on, reaffirms it in the following words:

" It has been settled by our predecessors, on great deliberation, that this Court may exercise its original jurisdiction in suits against a State, under the authority conferred by the Constitution and existing acts of Congress. The rule respecting the process, the persons on whom it is to be served, and the time of service are fixed. The course of the Court, on the failure of the State to appear after due service of process, has been also prescribed."

And in the same case, page 289, he states in full the process which had been established by the Court as a rule of practice in the case of Grayson *vs.* the State of Virginia, 3 Dall., 320, and ever since followed. This rule directs, "that when process at common law, or in equity, shall issue against a State, the same shall be served upon the Governor or chief executive magistrate and the Attorney-General of such State."

It is equally well settled, that a mandamus in modern practice is nothing more than an action at law between the parties, and is not now regarded as a prerogative writ. It undoubtedly came into use by virtue of the prerogative power of the English Crown, and was subject to regulations and rules which have long since been disused. But the right to the writ, and the power to issue it, has ceased to depend upon any prerogative power, and it is now regarded as an ordinary process in cases to which it is applicable. It was so held by this Court in the cases of Kendall *vs.* United States, 12 Pet., 615; Kendall *vs.* Stokes and Others, 3 How., 100.

So, also, as to the process in the name of the Governor, in his official capacity, in behalf of the State.

In the case of Madraso *vs.* the Governor of Georgia, 1 Pet., 110, it was decided, that in a case where the chief magistrate of a State is sued, not by his name as an individual, but by his style of office, and the claim made upon him is entirely in his official character, the State itself may be considered a party on the record. This was a case where the State was the defendant; the practice, where it is plaintiff, has been frequently adopted of suing in the name of the Governor, in behalf of the State, and was indeed the form originally used, and always recognized as the suit of the State.

Thus, in the first case to be found in our reports, in which a suit was brought by a State, it was entitled, and set forth in the bill, as the suit of "the State of Georgia, by Edward Tellfair, Governor of the said State, complainant, against Samuel Brailsford and Others;" and the second case, which was as early as 1793, was entitled, and set forth in the pleadings, as the suit of "His Excellency, Edward Tellfair, Esquire, Governor and Commander-in-chief in and over the State of Georgia, in behalf of the said State, complainant, against Samuel Brailsford and Others, defendants."

The cases referred to leave no question open to controversy, as to the jurisdiction of the Court. They show that it has been the established doctrine upon this subject ever since the Act of 1789, that in all cases where original jurisdiction is given by the Constitution, this Court has authority to exercise it without any further act of Congress to regulate its process, or confer jurisdiction, and that the Court may regulate and mould the process it uses, in such manner as in its judgment will best promote the purposes of justice. And that it has also been settled, that where the State is a party, plaintiff or defendant, the Governor represents the State, and the suit may be, in form, a suit by him as Governor in behalf of the State, where the State is plaintiff, and he must be summoned or notified as the officer representing the State, where the State is defendant. And further, that the writ of mandamus does not issue from or by any prerogative power, and is nothing more than the ordinary process of a court of justice, to which every one is entitled, where it is the appropriate process for asserting the right he claims.

We may therefore dismiss the question of jurisdiction without further comment, as it is very clear, that if the right claimed by Kentucky can be enforced by judicial process, the proceeding by mandamus is the only mode in which the object can be accomplished.

This brings us to the examination of the provision of the Constitution which has given rise to this controversy. It is in the following words:

"A person charged in any State with treason, felony, or other crime, who shall flee from justice, and be found in another State, shall, on demand of the executive authority of the State from which he fled, be delivered up, to be removed to the State having jurisdiction of the crime."

Looking to the language of the clause, it is difficult to comprehend how any doubt could have arisen as to its meaning and construction. The words, "treason, felony, or other crime," in their plain and obvious import, as well as in their legal and technical sense, embrace every act forbidden and made punishable by a law of the State. The word "crime" of itself includes every offence, from the highest to the lowest, in the grade of offences, and includes what are called "misdemeanors," as well as treason and felony. 4 Bl. Com., 5, 6, and note 3, Wendall's edition.

But as the word crime would have included treason and felony, without specially mentioning those offences, it seems to be supposed that the natural and legal import of the word, by associating it with those offences, must be restricted and confined to offences already known to the common law, and to the usage of nations, and regarded as offences in every civilized community, and that they do not extend to acts made offences by local statutes growing out of local circumstances, nor to offences against ordinary police regulations. This is one of the grounds upon which the Governor of Ohio refused to deliver Lago, under the advice of the Attorney-General of that State.

But this inference is founded upon an obvious mistake as to the purposes for which the words " treason and felony" were introduced. They were introduced for the purpose of guarding against any restriction of the word " crime," and to prevent this provision from being construed by the rules and usages of independent nations in compacts for delivering up fugitives from justice. According to these usages, even where they admitted the obligation to deliver the fugitive, persons who fled on account of political offences were almost always excepted, and the nation upon which the demand is made also uniformly claims and exercises a discretion in weighing the evidence of the crime, and the character of the offence. The policy of different nations, in this respect, with the opinions of eminent writers upon public law, are collected in Wheaton on the Law of Nations, 171 ; Fœlix, 312 ; and Martin, Verge's edition, 182. And the English Government, from which we .have borrowed our general system of law and jurisprudence, has always refused to deliver up political offenders who had sought an asylum within its dominions. And as the States of this Union, although united as one nation for certain specified purposes, are yet, so far as concerns their internal government, separate sovereignties, independent of each other, it was obviously deemed necessary to show, by the terms used, that this compact was not to be regarded or construed as an ordinary treaty for extradition between nations altogether independent of each other, but was intended to embrace political offences against the sovereignty of the State, as well as all other crimes. And as treason was also a " felony," (4 Bl. Com., 94,) it was necessary to insert those words, to show, in language that could not be mistaken, that political offenders were included in it. For this was not a compact of peace and comity between separate nations who had no claim on each other for mutual support, but a compact binding them to give aid and assistance to each other in executing their laws, and to support each other in preserving order and law within its confines, whenever such aid was needed and required; for it is manifest that the statesmen who framed the Constitution were fully sensible, that from the complex character of the Government, it must fail unless the States mutually supported each other and the general Government; and that nothing would be more likely to disturb its peace, and end in discord, than permitting an offender against the laws of a State, by passing over a mathematical line which divides it from another, to defy its process, and stand ready, under the protection of the State, to repeat the offence as soon as another opportunity offered.

Indeed, the necessity of this policy of mutual support, in bringing offenders to justice, without any exception as to the character and nature of the crime, seems to have been first recognized and acted on by the American colonies; for we find, by Winthrop's History of Massachusetts, vol. 2, pages 121 and 126, that as early as 1643, by "Articles of Confederation between the plantations under the Government of Massachusetts, the plantation under the Government of New Plymouth, the plantations under the Government of Connecticut, and the Government of New Haven, with the plantations in combination therewith," these plantations pledged themselves to each other, that, upon the escape of any prisoner or fugitive for any criminal cause, whether by breaking prison, or getting from the officer, or otherwise escaping, upon the certificate of two magistrates of the jurisdiction out of which the escape was made that he was a prisoner or such an offender at the time of the escape, the magistrate, or some of them, of the jurisdiction where, for the present, the said prisoner or fugitive abideth, shall forthwith grant such a warrant as the case will bear, for the apprehending of any such person, and the delivery of him into the hands of the officer or other person who pursueth him; and if there be help required for the safe returning of any such offender, then it shall be granted unto him that craves the same, he paying the charges thereof." It will be seen that this agreement gave no discretion to the magistrate of the Government where the offender was found; but he was bound to arrest and deliver, upon the production of the certificate under which he was demanded.

When the thirteen colonies formed a Confederation for mutual support, a similar provision was introduced, most probably suggested by the advantages which the plantations had derived from their compact with one another. But, as these colonies had then, by the Declaration of Independence, become separate and independent sovereignties, against which treason might be committed, their compact is carefully worded, so as to include treason and felony — that is, political offences — as well as crimes of an inferior grade. It is in the following words:

"If any person, guilty of or charged with treason, felony, or other high misdemeanor, in any State, shall flee from justice, and be found in any other of the United States, he shall, upon demand of the Governor or executive power of the State from which he fled, be delivered up and removed to the State having jurisdiction of his offence."

And when these colonies were about to form a still closer union by the present Constitution, but yet preserving their sovereignty, they had learned from experience the necessity of this provision for the internal safety of each of them, and to promote concord and harmony among all their members; and it is introduced in the Constitution substantially in the same words, but substituting the word "crime" for the words "high misdemeanor," and thereby showing the deliberate purpose to include every offence known to the law of the State from which the party charged had fled.

The argument on behalf of the Governor of Ohio, which insists upon excluding from this clause new offences created by a statute of the State, and growing out of its local institutions, and which are not admitted to be offences in the State where the fugitive is found, nor so regarded by the general usage of civilized nations, would render the clause useless for any practical purpose. For where can the line of division be drawn with anything like certainty? Who is to mark it? The Governor of the demanding State would probably draw one line, and the Governor of the other State another. And, if they differed, who is to decide between them? Under such a vague and indefinite construction, the article would not be a bond of peace and union, but a constant source of controversy and irritating discussion. It would have been far better to omit it altogether, and to have left it to the comity of the States, and their own sense of their respective interests, than to have inserted it as conferring a right, and yet defining that right so loosely as to make it a never-failing subject of dispute and ill-will.

The clause in question, like the clause in the Confederation, authorizes the demand to be made by the executive authority of the State where the crime was committed, but does not in so many words specify the officer of the State upon whom the demand is to be made, and whose duty it is to have the fugitive delivered and removed to the State having jurisdiction of the crime. But, under the Confederation, it is plain that the demand was to be made on the Governor or executive authority of the State, and could be made on no other department or officer; for the Confederation was only a league of separate sovereignties, in which each State, within its own limits, held and exercised all the powers of sovereignty; and the Confederation had no officer, either executive, judicial, or ministerial, through whom it could exercise an authority within the limits of a State. In the present Constitution, however, these powers, to a limited extent, have been conferred on the general Government within the territories of the several States. But the part of the clause in relation to the mode of demanding and surrendering the fugitive is (with the exception of an unimportant word or two) a literal copy of the article of the Confederation; and it is plain that the mode of the demand, and the official authority by and to whom it was addressed, under the Confederation, must have been in the minds of the members of the Convention when this article was introduced, and that, in adopting the same words, they manifestly intended to sanction the mode of proceeding practised under the Confederation — that is, of demanding the fugitive from the executive authority, and making it his duty to cause him to be delivered up.

Looking, therefore, to the words of the Constitution — to the obvious policy and necessity of this provision to preserve harmony between States, and order and law within their respective borders, and to its early adoption by the colonies, and then by the Confederated States, whose mutual interest it was to give each other aid and support whenever it was needed — the conclusion is irresistible, that this compact engrafted in the Constitution included, and was intended to include, every offence made punishable by the law of the State in which it was committed, and that it gives the right to the executive authority of the State to demand the fugitive from the executive authority of the State in which he is found; that the right given to "demand" implies that it is an absolute right; and it follows that there must be a correlative obligation to deliver, without any reference to the character of the crime charged, or to the policy or laws of the State to which the fugitive has fled.

This is evidently the construction put upon this article in the Act of Congress of 1793, under which the proceedings now before us are instituted. It is therefore the construction put upon it almost contemporaneously with the commencement of the Government itself, and when Washington was still at its head, and many of those who had assisted in framing it were members of the Congress which enacted the law.

The Constitution having established the right on one part, and the obligation on the other, it became necessary to provide by law the mode of carrying it into execution. The Governor of the State could not, upon a charge made before him, demand the fugitive; for, according to the principles upon which all of our institutions are founded, the Executive Department can act only in subordination to the Judicial Department, where rights of person or property are concerned, and its duty in those cases consists only in aiding to support the judicial process, and enforcing its authority, when its interposition for that purpose becomes necessary, and is called for by the Judicial Department. The executive authority of the State, therefore, was not authorized by this article to make the demand, unless the party was charged in the regular course of judicial proceedings. And it was equally necessary that the executive authority of the State upon which the demand was made, when called on to render his aid, should be satisfied by competent proof that the party was so charged. This proceeding, when duly authenticated, is his authority for arresting the offender.

This duty of providing by law the regulations necessary to carry this compact into execution, from the nature of the duty and the object in view, was manifestly devolved upon Congress; for if it was left to the States, each State might require different proof to authenticate the judicial proceeding upon which the demand was founded; and as the duty of the Governor of the State where the fugitive was found is in such cases merely ministerial, without the right to exercise either executive or judicial discretion, he could not lawfully issue a warrant to arrest an individual without a law of the State or of Congress to authorize it. These difficulties presented themselves as early as 1791, in a demand made by the Governor of Pennsylvania upon the Governor of Virginia, and both of them admitted the propriety of bringing the subject before the President, who immediately submitted the matter to the consideration of Congress. And this led to the Act of 1793, of which we are now speaking. All difficulty as to the mode of authenticating the judicial proceeding was removed by the article in the Constitution which declares "that full faith and credit shall be given in each State to the public acts, records, and judicial proceedings of every other State; and the Congress may by general laws prescribe the manner in which acts, records, and proceedings shall be proved, and the effect thereof." And without doubt the provision of which we are now speaking — that is, for the delivery of a fugitive, which requires official communications between States, and the authentication of official documents — was in the minds of the framers of the Constitution, and had its influence in inducing them to give this power to Congress. And acting upon this authority, and the clause of the Constitution, which is the subject of the present controversy, Congress passed the Act of 1793, February 12th, which, as far as relates to this subject, is in the following words:

"Section 1. That whenever the executive authority of any State in the Union, or of either of the Territories northwest or south of the river Ohio, shall demand any person as a fugitive from justice of the executive authority of any such State or Territory to which such person shall have fled, and shall, moreover, produce the copy of an indictment found, or an affidavit made before a magistrate of any State or Territory as aforesaid, charging the person so demanded with having committed treason, felony, or other crime, certified as authentic by the Governor or chief magistrate of the State or Territory from whence the person so charged fled, it shall be the duty of the executive authority of the State or Territory to which such person shall have fled to cause him or her to be arrested and secured, and notice of the arrest to be given to the executive authority making such demand, or to the agent of such authority appointed to receive the fugitive, and to cause the fugitive to be delivered to such agent when he shall appear; but if no such agent shall appear within six months from the time of the arrest, the prisoner may be discharged. And all costs or expenses incurred in the apprehending, securing, and transmitting such fugitive to the State or Territory making such demand shall be paid by such State or Territory.

"Section 2. And be it further enacted, That any agent, appointed as aforesaid, who shall receive the fugitive into his custody, shall be empowered to transport him or her to the State or Territory from which he or she shall have fled; and if any person or persons shall by force set at liberty or rescue the fugitive from such agent while transporting as aforesaid, the person or persons so offending shall, on conviction, be fined not exceeding five hundred dollars, and be imprisoned not exceeding one year."

It will be observed, that the judicial acts which are necessary to authorize the demand are plainly specified in the act of Congress; and the certificate of the executive authority is made conclusive as to their verity when presented to the executive of the State where the fugitive is found. He has no right to look behind them, or to question them, or to look into the character of the crime specified in this judicial proceeding. The duty which he is to perform is, as we have already said, merely ministerial — that is, to cause the party to be arrested, and delivered to the agent or authority of the State where the crime was committed. It is said in the argument, that the executive officer upon whom this demand is made must have a discretionary executive power, because he must inquire and decide who is the person demanded. But this certainly is not a discretionary duty upon which he is to exercise any judgment, but is a mere ministerial duty — that is, to do the act required to be done by him, and such as every marshal and sheriff must perform when process, either criminal or civil, is placed in his hands to be served on the person named in it. And it never has been supposed that this duty involved any discretionary power, or made him anything more than a mere ministerial officer; and such is the position and character of the executive of the State under this law, when the demand is made upon him, and the requisite evidence produced. The Governor has only to issue his warrant to an agent or officer, to arrest the party named in the demand.

The question which remains to be examined is a grave and important one. When the demand was made, the proofs required by the Act of 1793 to support it were exhibited to the Governor of Ohio, duly certified and authenticated; and the objection made to the validity of the indictment is altogether untenable. Kentucky has an undoubted right to regulate the forms of pleading and process in her own Courts, in criminal as well as civil cases, and is not bound to conform to those of any other State. And whether the charge against Lago is legally and sufficiently laid in this indictment, according to the laws of Kentucky, is a judicial question to be decided by the Courts of the State, and not by the executive authority of the State of Ohio.

The demand being thus made, the act of Congress declares that "it shall be the duty of the executive authority of the State" to cause the fugitive to be arrested and secured, and delivered to the agent of the demanding State. The words, "it shall be the duty," in ordinary legislation, imply the assertion of the power to command and to coerce obedience. But looking to the subject-matter of this law, and the relations which the United States and the several States bear to each other, the Court is of opinion the words, "it shall be the duty," were not used as mandatory and compulsory, but as declaratory of the moral duty which this compact created when Congress had provided the mode of carrying it into execution. The act does not provide any means to compel the execution of this duty, nor inflict any punishment for neglect or refusal on the part of the executive of the State; nor is there any clause or provision in the Constitution which arms the Government of the United States with this power. Indeed, such a power would place every State under the control and dominion of the general Government, even in the administration of its internal concerns and reserved rights. And we think it clear that the Federal Government, under the Constitution, has no power to impose on a State officer, as such, any duty whatever, and compel him to perform it; for if it possessed this power, it might overload the officer with duties which would fill up all his time, and disable him from performing his obligations to the State, and might impose on him duties of a character incompatible with the rank and dignity to which he was elevated by the State.

It is true that Congress may authorize a particular State officer to perform a particular duty; but if he declines to do so, it does not follow that he may be coerced, or punished for his refusal. And we are very far from supposing that, in using this word "duty," the statesmen who framed and passed the law, or the President who approved and signed it, intended to exercise a coercive power over State officers not warranted by the Constitution. But the general Government having in that law fulfilled the duty devolved upon it, by prescribing the proof and mode of authentication upon which the State authorities were bound to deliver the fugitive, the word "duty" in the law points to the obligation on the State to carry it into execution.

It is true that in the early days of the Government, Congress relied with confidence upon the co-operation and support of the States, when exercising the legitimate powers of the general Government, and were accustomed to receive it upon principles of comity, and from a sense of mutual and common interest, where no such duty was imposed by the Constitution. And laws were passed authorizing State courts to entertain jurisdiction in proceedings by the United States to recover penalties and forfeitures incurred by breaches of their revenue laws, and giving to the State courts the same authority with the District Court of the United States to enforce such penalties and forfeitures, and also the power to hear the allegations of parties, and to take proofs, if an application for a remission of the penalty or forfeiture should be made, according to the provisions of the acts of Congress. And these powers were for some years exercised by State tribunals, readily, and without objection, until in some of the States it was declined because it interfered with and retarded the performance of duties which properly belonged to them as State courts; and in other States doubts appear to have arisen as to the power of the Courts, acting under the authority of the State, to inflict these penalties and forfeitures for offences against the general Government, unless especially authorized to do so by the State.

And in these cases the co-operation of the States was a matter of comity, which the several sovereignties extended to one another for their mutual benefit. It was not regarded by either party as an obligation imposed by the Constitution. And the acts of Congress conferring the jurisdiction merely give the power to the State tribunals, but do not purport to regard it as a duty, and they leave it to the States to exercise it or not, as might best comport with their own sense of justice and their own interest and convenience.

But the language of the Act of 1793 is very different. It does not purport to give authority to the State executive to arrest and deliver the fugitive, but requires it to be done; and the language of the law implies an absolute obligation which the State authority is bound to perform. And when it speaks of the duty of the Governor, it evidently points to the duty imposed by the Constitution in the clause we are now considering. The performance of this duty, however, is left to depend on the fidelity of the State executive to the compact entered into with the other States when it adopted the Constitution of the United States, and became a member of the Union. It was so left by the Constitution, and necessarily so left by the Act of 1793.

And it would seem that when the Constitution was framed, and when this law was passed, it was confidently believed that a sense of justice and of mutual interest would insure a faithful execution of this constitutional provision by the executive of every State, for every State had an equal interest in the execution of a compact absolutely essential to their peace and well-being in their internal concerns, as well as members of the Union. Hence, the use of the words ordinarily employed when an undoubted obligation is required to be performed, " it shall be his duty."

But if the Governor of Ohio refuses to discharge this duty, there is no power delegated to the general Government, either through the judicial department, or any other department, to use any coercive means to compel him.

And upon this ground the motion for the mandamus must be overruled.

HABEAS CORPUS.

STATEMENT OF THE CASE.

On the 26th May, A. D. 1861, the following sworn petition was presented to the Chief Justice of the Supreme Court of the United States on behalf of John Merryman, he being at the time in confinement in Fort McHenry.

To the HON. ROGER B. TANEY,

 Chief Justice of the Supreme Court of the United States.

The petition of John Merryman, of Baltimore County, and State of Maryland, respectfully shows, that being at home, in his own domicil, he was, about the hour of two o'clock, A. M., on the 25th of May, A. D. 1861, aroused from his bed by an armed force pretending to act under military orders from some person to your petitioner unknown. That he was by said armed force deprived of his liberty by being taken into custody, and removed from his said home to Fort McHenry, near to the city of Baltimore, and in the district aforesaid, and where your petitioner now is in close custody.

That he has been so imprisoned without any process or color of law whatsoever, and that none such is pretended by those who are thus detaining him ; and that no warrant from any court, magistrate, or other person having legal authority to issue the same, exists to justify such arrest ; but, to the contrary, the same, as above stated, hath been done without color of law, and in violation of the Constitution and laws of the United States, of which he is a citizen. That since his arrest he has been informed that some order purporting to come from one General Keim, of Pennsylvania, to the petitioner unknown, directing the arrest of the captain of some company in Baltimore County, of which company the petitioner never was and is not captain, was the pretended ground of his arrest, and is the sole ground, as he believes, on which he is detained.

That the person now so detaining him at said Fort is Brigadier-General George Cadwalader, the military commander of said post, professing to act in the premises under or by color of the authority of the United States. Your petitioner therefore prays that the writ of *habeas corpus* may issue, to be directed to the said George Cadwalader, commanding him to produce your petitioner before you, Judge as aforesaid, with the cause, if any, for his arrest and detention, to the end that your petitioner be discharged and restored to liberty, and as in duty, &c.

JOHN MERRYMAN.

Fort McHenry, 25th May, 1861.

United States of America, District of Maryland, to wit:

Before the subscriber, a Commissioner appointed by the Circuit Court of the United States, in and for the fourth circuit and district of Maryland, to take affidavits, &c., personally appeared, the 25th day of May, A. D. 1861, Geo. H. Williams, of the city of Baltimore and district aforesaid, and made oath on the Holy Evangely of Almighty God that the matters and facts stated in the foregoing petition are true, to the best of his knowledge, information and belief, and that the said petition was signed in his presence by the petitioner, and would have been sworn to by him, said petitioner, but that he was at the time and still is in close custody, and all access to him denied, except to his counsel and his brother-in-law — this deponent being one of said counsel.

Sworn to before me, this 25th day of May, A. D. 1861.

JOHN HANAN, *U. S. Commissioner.*

United States of America, District of Maryland, to wit:

Before the subscriber, a Commissioner appointed by the Circuit Court of the United States, in and for the fourth circuit and district of Maryland, to take affidavits, &c., personally appeared this 26th day of May, 1861, George H. Williams, of the city of Baltimore and district aforesaid, and made oath on the Holy Evangely of Almighty God that on the 26th day of May he went to Fort McHenry, in the preceding affidavit mentioned, and obtained an interview with Gen. Geo. Cadwalader, then and there in command, and deponent, one of the counsel of said John Merryman, in the foregoing petition named, and at his request, and declaring himself to be such counsel, requested and demanded that he might be permitted to see the written papers, and to be permitted to make copies thereof, under and by which he, the said General, detained the said Merryman in custody, and that to said demand the said Gen. Cadwalader replied that he would neither permit the deponent, though officially requesting and demanding, as such counsel, to read the said papers, nor to have or make copies thereof. Sworn to this 26th day of May, A. D. 1861, before me.

JOHN HANAN,
U. S. Commissioner for Maryland.

Upon this petition the Chief Justice passed the following order:

In the matter of the petition of John Merryman for a writ of *habeas corpus:*

Ordered, this 26th day of May, A. D. 1861, that the writ of *habeas corpus* issued in this case, as prayed, and that the same be directed to General George Cadwalader, and be issued in the usual form, by Thomas Spicer, clerk of the Circuit Court of the United States in and for the District of Maryland, and that the said writ of *habeas corpus* be returnable at eleven o'clock, on Monday, the 27th of May, 1861, at the Circuit Court room, in the Masonic Hall, in the city of Baltimore, before me, Chief Justice of the Supreme Court of the United States.

R. B. TANEY.

In obedience to this order, Mr. Spicer issued the following writ:

District of Maryland, to wit: the United States of America:

To GENERAL GEORGE CADWALADER, *Greeting:*

You are hereby commanded to be and appear before the Honorable ROGER B. TANEY, Chief Justice of the Supreme Court of the United States, at the United States Court room, in the Masonic Hall, in the city of Baltimore, on Monday, the 27th day of May, 1861, at eleven o'clock in the morning, and that you have with you the body of John Merryman, of Baltimore County, and now in your custody, and that you certify and make known the day and cause of the caption and detention of the said John Merryman, and that you then and there do submit it to, and receive whatsoever the said Chief Justice shall determine upon concerning you on this behalf, according to law, and have you then and there this writ.

Witness, the Honorable R. B. TANEY, Chief Justice of our Supreme Court, &c., &c., &c.

THOS. SPICER, *Clerk.*

Issued 26th May, 1861.

The Marshal made his return that he had served the writ on General Cadwalader on the same day on which it issued, and filed that return on the 27th May, 1861, on which day, at eleven o'clock precisely, the Chief Justice took his seat on the bench. In a few minutes Colonel Lee, a military officer, appeared with General Cadwalader's return to the writ, which is as follows:

HEADQUARTERS, DEPARTMENT OF ANNAPOLIS,

Fort McHenry, May 26, 1861.

To the HON. ROGER B. TANEY,

Chief Justice of the Supreme Court of the United States, Baltimore, Md.

SIR — The undersigned, to whom the annexed writ of this date, signed by Thomas Spicer, clerk of the Supreme Court of the United States, is directed, most respectfully states that the arrest of Mr. John Merryman, in the said writ named, was not made with his knowledge or by his order or direction, but was made by Col. Samuel Yohe, acting under the orders of Major-General Wm. H. Keim, both of said officers being in the military service of the United States, but not within the limits of his command.

The prisoner was brought to this post on the 20th inst. by Adjutant James Wittimore and Lieut. Wm. H. Abel, by order of Col. Yohe, and is charged with various acts of treason, and with being publicly associated with and holding a commission as lieutenant in a company having in their possession arms belonging to the United States, and avowing his purpose of armed hostility against the Government. He is also informed that it can be clearly established that the prisoner has made often and unreserved declarations of his association with this organized force as being in avowed hostility to the Government, and in readiness to co-operate with those engaged in the present rebellion against the Government of the United States. He has further to inform you that he is duly authorized by the President of the United States in such cases to suspend the writ of *habeas corpus* for public safety.

This is a high and delicate trust, and it has been enjoined upon him that it should be executed with judgment and discretion, but he is nevertheless also instructed that in times of civil strife, errors, if any, should be on the side of the safety of the country. He most respectfully submits for your consideration that those who should co-operate in the present trying and painful position in which our country is placed, should not, by any unnecessary want of confidence in each other, increase our embarrassments.

He therefore respectfully requests that you will postpone further action upon this case until he can receive instructions from the President of the United States, when you shall hear further from him.

I have the honor to be, with high respect, your obedient servant,

GEORGE CADWALADER,

Brevet Major-General U. S. A. Commanding.

The Chief Justice then inquired of the officer whether he had brought with him the body of John Merryman, and on being answered that he had no instructions but to deliver the return, the Chief Justice then said:

Gen. Cadwalader was commanded to produce the body of Mr. Merryman before me this morning, that the case might be heard, and the petitioner be either remanded to custody or set at liberty if held on insufficient grounds; but he has acted in disobedience to the writ, and I therefore direct that an attachment be at once issued against him, returnable before me here at twelve o'clock to-morrow. The order was then passed as follows:

Ordered, That an attachment forthwith issue against General George Cadwalader for a contempt in refusing to produce the body of John Merryman according to the command of the writ of *habeas corpus* returnable and returned before me to-day, and that said attachment be returned before me at twelve o'clock to-morrow, at the room of the Circuit Court.

R. B. TANEY.

Monday, May 27th, 1861.

The Clerk then issued the writ of attachment as directed.

At twelve o'clock on the 28th May, 1861, the Chief Justice again took his seat on the bench, and called for the Marshal's return to the writ of attachment. It was as follows:

I hereby certify to the Honorable ROGER B. TANEY, Chief Justice of the Supreme Court of the United States, that by virtue of the within writ of attachment to me directed on the 27th day of May, 1861, I proceeded on this 28th day of May, 1861, to Fort McHenry for the purpose of serving the said writ. I sent in my name at the outer gate; the messenger returned with the reply "that there was no answer to my card," and therefore could not serve the writ as I was commanded. I was not permitted to enter the gate. So answers

WASHINGTON BONIFANT,
U. S. Marshal for the District of Maryland.

After it was read, the Chief Justice said that the Marshal had the power to summon the *posse comitatus* to aid him in seizing and bringing before the Court the party named in the attachment, who would, when so brought in, be liable to punishment by fine and imprisonment. But where, as in this case, the power refusing obedience was so notoriously superior to any the Marshal could command, he held that officer excused from doing anything more than he had done. The Chief Justice then proceeded as follows:

"I ordered this attachment yesterday, because, upon the face of the return, the detention of the prisoner was unlawful upon the grounds:

"First — That the President, under the Constitution of the United States, *cannot suspend the privilege of the writ of habeas corpus*, nor authorize a military officer to do it.

"Second — A military officer has no right to arrest and detain a person not subject to the rules and articles of war for an offence against the laws of the United States, except in aid of the judicial authority, and subject to its control; and if the party is arrested by the military, it is the duty of the officer to deliver him over immediately to the civil authority to be dealt with according to law.

"It is therefore very clear that John Merryman, the petitioner, is entitled to be set at liberty, and discharged immediately from imprisonment.

"I forbore yesterday to state orally the provisions of the Constitution of the United States which make those principles the fundamental law of the Union, because an oral statement might be misunderstood in some portions of it, and I shall therefore put my opinion in writing, and file it in the office of the Clerk of the Circuit Court in the course of this week."

He concluded by saying that he should cause his opinion, when filed, and all the proceedings to be laid before the President, in order that he might perform his constitutional duty, to enforce the laws by securing obedience to the process of the United States.

ACCORDINGLY ON THE 1ST JUNE, 1861, THE CHIEF JUSTICE
FILED THE FOLLOWING

OPINION.

EX PARTE JOHN MERRYMAN.

*Before the Chief Justice of the Supreme Court of the United States,
at Chambers.*

The application in this case for a writ of *habeas corpus* is made
to me under the 14th Section of the Judiciary Act of 1789, which
renders effectual for the citizen the constitutional privilege of the
writ of *habeas corpus.* That act gives to the Courts of the United
States, as well as to each Justice of the Supreme Court, and to
every District Judge, power to grant writs of *habeas corpus* for the
purpose of an inquiry into the cause of commitment. The petition
was presented to me at Washington, under the impression that I
would order the prisoner to be brought before me there; but as he
was confined in Fort McHenry, at the city of Baltimore, which is
in my circuit, I resolved to hear it in the latter city, as obedience
to the writ, under such circumstances, would not withdraw General
Cadwalader, who had him in charge, from the limits of his military command.

The petition presents the following case: The petitioner resides
in Maryland, in Baltimore County. While peaceably in his own
house, with his family, it was at two o'clock, on the morning of the
25th of May, 1861, entered by an armed force, professing to act
under military orders. He was then compelled to rise from his
bed, taken into custody, and conveyed to Fort McHenry, where
he is imprisoned by the commanding officer, without warrant from
any lawful authority.

The Commander of the Fort, General George Cadwalader, by
whom he is detained in confinement, in his return to the writ, does
not deny any of the facts alleged in the petition. He states that
the prisoner was arrested by order of General Keim, of Pennsylvania, and conducted as aforesaid to Fort McHenry by his order,
and placed in his (General Cadwalader's) custody, to be there detained by him as a prisoner.

A copy of the warrant or order under which the prisoner was
arrested was demanded by his counsel, and refused: And it is not

alleged in the return that any specific act, constituting any offence against the laws of the United States, has been charged against him upon oath, but he appears to have been arrested upon general charges of treason and rebellion, without proof, and without giving the names of the witnesses, or specifying the acts which, in the judgment of the military officer, constituted these crimes. And having the prisoner thus in custody upon these vague and unsupported accusations, he refuses to obey the writ of *habeas corpus*, upon the ground that he is duly authorized by the President to suspend it.

The case, then, is simply this : — A military officer, residing in Pennsylvania, issues an order to arrest a citizen of Maryland, upon vague and indefinite charges, without any proof, so far as appears. Under this order, his house is entered in the night, he is seized as a prisoner, and conveyed to Fort McHenry, and there kept in close confinement. And when a *habeas corpus* is served on the commanding officer, requiring him to produce the prisoner before a Justice of the Supreme Court, in order that he may examine into the legality of the imprisonment, the answer of the officer is that he is authorized by the President to suspend the writ of *habeas corpus* at his discretion, and, in the exercise of that discretion, suspends it in this case, and on that ground refuses obedience to the writ.

As the case comes before me, therefore, I understand that the President not only claims the right to suspend the writ of *habeas corpus* himself, at his discretion, but to delegate that discretionary power to a military officer, and to leave it to him to determine whether he will or will not obey judicial process that may be served upon him.

No official notice has been given to the courts of justice, or to the public, by proclamation or otherwise, that the President claimed this power, and had exercised it in the manner stated in the return. And I certainly listened to it with some surprise, for I had supposed it to be one of those points of constitutional law upon which there was no difference of opinion, and that it was admitted on all hands that the privilege of the writ could not be suspended, except by act of Congress.

When the conspiracy of which Aaron Burr was the head became so formidable, and was so extensively ramified as to justify, in Mr. Jefferson's opinion, the suspension of the writ, he claimed, on his part, no power to suspend it, but communicated his opinion to Congress, with all the proofs in his possession, in order that Congress might exercise its discretion upon the subject, and determine whether the public safety required it. And in the debate which took place upon the subject, no one suggested that Mr. Jefferson might exercise the power himself if, in his opinion, the public safety demanded it.

Having, therefore, regarded the question as too plain and too well settled to be open to dispute, if the commanding officer had stated that upon his own responsibility, and in the exercise of his own discretion, he refused obedience to the writ, I should have contented myself with referring to the clause in the Constitution, and to the construction it received from every jurist and statesman of that day, when the case of Burr was before them. But being thus officially notified that the privilege of the writ has been suspended under the orders, and by the authority, of the President, and believing, as I do, that the President has exercised a power which he does not possess under the Constitution, a proper respect for the high office he fills requires me to state plainly and fully the grounds of my opinion, in order to show that I have not ventured to question the legality of his act without a careful and deliberate examination of the whole subject.

The clause of the Constitution, which authorizes the suspension of the privilege of the writ of *habeas corpus*, is in the 9th section of the first article.

This article is devoted to the legislative department of the United States, and has not the slightest reference to the executive department. It begins by providing "that all legislative powers therein granted shall be vested in a Congress of the United States, which shall consist of a Senate and House of Representatives." And after prescribing the manner in which these two branches of the legislative department shall be chosen, it proceeds to enumerate specifically the legislative powers which it thereby grants; and, at the conclusion of this specification, a clause is inserted giving Congress "the power to make all laws which may be necessary and proper for carrying into execution the foregoing powers, and all other powers vested by this Constitution in the Government of the United States, or in any department or office thereof."

The power of legislation granted by this latter clause is by its words carefully confined to the specific objects before enumerated. But as this limitation was unavoidably somewhat indefinite, it was deemed necessary to guard more effectually certain great cardinal principles essential to the liberty of the citizen, and to the rights and equality of the States, by denying to Congress, in express terms, any power of legislation over them. It was apprehended, it seems, that such legislation might be attempted under the pretext that it was necessary and proper to carry into execution the powers granted; and it was determined that there should be no room to doubt, where rights of such vital importance were concerned, and accordingly, this clause is immediately followed by an enumeration of certain subjects, to which the powers of legislation shall not extend; and the great importance which the framers of the Constitution attached to the privilege of the writ of *habeas corpus* to protect the liberty of the citizen is proved by the fact that its suspension, except in cases of invasion and rebellion, is first in the list of prohibited powers — and even in these cases the power is denied, and its exercise prohibited, unless the public safety shall require it.

It is true that in the cases mentioned, Congress is of necessity the judge of whether the public safety does or does not require it; and their judgment is conclusive. But the introduction of these words is a standing admonition to the legislative body of the danger of suspending it, and of the extreme caution they should exercise before they give the Government of the United States such power over the liberty of a citizen.

It is the second article of the Constitution that provides for the organization of the executive department, and enumerates the powers conferred on it, and prescribes its duties. And if the high power over the liberty of the citizen now claimed was intended to be conferred on the President, it would undoubtedly be found in plain words in this article. But there is not a word in it that can furnish the slightest ground to justify the exercise of the power.

The article begins by declaring that the executive power shall be vested in a President of the United States of America, to hold his office during the term of four years — and then proceeds to prescribe the mode of election, and to specify in precise and plain words the powers delegated to him, and the duties imposed upon him. And the short term for which he is elected, and the narrow limits to which his power is confined, show the jealousy and apprehensions of future danger which the framers of the Constitution felt in relation to that department of the Government, and how carefully they withheld from it many of the powers belonging to the executive branch of the English Government, which were considered as dangerous to the liberty of the subject — and conferred (and that in clear and specific terms) those powers only which were deemed essential to secure the successful operation of the Government.

He is elected, as I have already said, for the brief term of four years, and is made personally responsible, by impeachment, for malfeasance in office. He is from necessity and the nature of his duties the commander-in-chief of the army and navy, and of the militia, when called into actual service. But no appropriation for the support of the army can be made by Congress for a longer term than two years, so that it is in the power of the succeeding House of Representatives to withhold the appropriation for its support, and thus disband it, if, in their judgment, the President used or designed to use it for improper purposes. And although the militia, when in actual service, are under his command, yet the appointment of the officers is reserved to the States as a security against the use of the military power for purposes dangerous to the liberties of the people or the rights of the States.

So, too, his powers in relation to the civil duties and authority necessarily conferred on him are carefully restricted, as well as those belonging to his military character. He cannot appoint the ordinary officers of Government, nor make a treaty with a foreign nation or Indian tribe, without the advice and consent of the Senate, and cannot appoint even inferior officers, unless he is authorized by an act of Congress to do so. He is not empowered to arrest any one charged with an offence against the United States, and whom he may, from the evidence before him, believe to be guilty; nor can he authorize any officer, civil or military, to exercise this power, for the 5th article of the Amendments to the Constitution expressly provides that no person "shall be deprived of life, liberty, or property, without due process of law" — that is, judicial process.

And even if the privilege of the writ of *habeas corpus* were suspended by act of Congress, and a party not subject to the rules and articles of war was afterwards arrested and imprisoned by regular judicial process, he could not be detained in prison, or brought to trial before a military tribunal, for the article in the Amendments to the Constitution immediately following the one above referred to — that is, the 6th article — provides that " in all criminal prosecutions the accused shall enjoy the right to a speedy and public trial by an impartial jury of the State and district wherein the crime shall have been committed, which district shall have been previously ascertained by law, and to be informed of the nature and cause of the accusation; to be confronted with the witnesses against him; to have compulsory process for obtaining witnesses in his favor, and to have the assistance of counsel for his defence."

And the only power, therefore, which the President possesses, where the " life, liberty, or property " of a private citizen are concerned, is the power and duty prescribed in the third section of the second article, which requires " that he shall take care that the laws shall be faithfully executed." He is not authorized to execute them himself, or through agents or officers, civil or military, appointed by himself, but he is to take care that they be faithfully carried into execution, as they are expounded and adjudged by the co-ordinate branch of the Government to which that duty is assigned by the Constitution. It is thus made his duty to come in aid of the judicial authority, if it shall be resisted by a force too strong to be overcome without the assistance of the Executive arm. But in exercising this power he acts in subordination to judicial authority, assisting it to execute its process and enforce its judgments.

With such provisions in the Constitution, expressed in language too clear to be misunderstood by any one, I can see no ground whatever for supposing that the President, in any emergency or in any state of things, can authorize the suspension of the privileges of the writ of *habeas corpus*, or arrest a citizen, except in aid of the judicial power. He certainly does not faithfully execute the laws if he takes upon himself legislative power by suspending the writ of *habeas corpus*, and the judicial power also, by arresting and imprisoning a person without due process of law. Nor can any argument be drawn from the nature of sovereignty, or the necessity of government, for self-defence in times of tumult and danger. The Government of the United States is one of delegated and limited powers. It derives its existence and authority altogether from the Constitution, and neither of its branches, Executive, Legislative, or Judicial, can exercise any of the powers of government beyond those specified and granted. For the 10th article of the Amendments to the Constitution in express terms provides that "the powers not delegated to the United States by the Constitution, nor prohibited by it to the States, are reserved to the States respectively, or to the people."

Indeed, the security against imprisonment by executive authority, provided for in the fifth article of the Amendments to the Constitution, which I have before quoted, is nothing more than a copy of the like provision in the English Constitution, which had been firmly established before the Declaration of Independence.

Blackstone, in his Commentaries (1st vol., page 137), states it in the following words:

"To make imprisonment lawful, it must be either by process of law from the Courts of Judicature or by warrant from some legal officer having authority to commit to prison." And the people of the United Colonies, who had themselves lived under its protection while they were British subjects, were well aware of the necessity of this safeguard for their personal liberty. And no one can believe that in framing a government intended to guard still more efficiently the rights and liberties of the citizen against executive encroachment and oppression, they would have conferred on the President a power which the history of England had proved to be dangerous and oppressive in the hands of the Crown, and which the people of England had compelled it to surrender after a long and obstinate struggle on the part of the English Executive to usurp and retain it.

The right of the subject to the benefit of the writ of *habeas corpus*, it must be recollected, was one of the great points in controversy during the long struggle in England between arbitrary government and free institutions, and must therefore have strongly attracted the attention of the statesmen engaged in framing a new and, as they supposed, a freer Government than the one which they had thrown off by the Revolution. For from the earliest history of the common law, if a person were imprisoned, no matter by what authority, he had a right to the writ of *habeas corpus* to bring his case before the King's Bench; and if no specific offence was charged against him in the warrant of commitment, he was entitled to be forthwith discharged; and if an offence was charged which was bailable in its character, the Court was bound to set him at liberty on bail. And the most exciting contests between the Crown and the people of England from the time of Magna Charta were in relation to the privilege of this writ, and they continued until the passage of the statute of 31st Charles II., commonly known as the great *habeas corpus* act.

This statute put an end to the struggle, and finally and firmly secured the liberty of the subject against the usurpation and oppression of the Executive branch of the Government. It nevertheless conferred no new right upon the subject, but only secured a right already existing. For, although the right could not justly be denied, there was often no effectual remedy against its violation. Until the statute of 13th William III., the judges held their offices at the pleasure of the King, and the influence which he exercised over timid, time-serving, and partisan judges often induced them, upon some pretext or other, to refuse to discharge the party, although entitled by law to his discharge, or delayed their decisions from time to time, so as to prolong the imprisonment of persons who were obnoxious to the King for their political opinions, or had incurred his resentment in any other way.

The great and inestimable value of the *habeas corpus* act of the 31st Charles II. is that it contains provisions which compel courts and judges, and all parties concerned, to perform their duties promptly, in the manner specified in the statute.

A passage in Blackstone's Commentaries, showing the ancient state of the law on this subject, and the abuses which were practised through the power and influence of the Crown, and a short extract from Hallam's Constitutional History, stating the circumstances which gave rise to the passage of this statute, explain briefly, but fully, all that is material to this subject.

Blackstone, in his Commentaries on the Laws of England (3d vol., pages 133, 134), says:

"To assert an absolute exemption from imprisonment in all cases is inconsistent with every idea of law and political society, and in the end would destroy all civil liberty by rendering its protection impossible.

"But the glory of the English law consists in clearly defining the times, the causes, and the extent, when, wherefore, and to what degree the imprisonment of the subject may be lawful. This it is which induces the absolute necessity of expressing upon every commitment the reason for which it is made, that the Court upon a *habeas corpus* may examine into its validity, and according to the circumstances of the case may discharge, admit to bail or remand the prisoner.

"And yet early in the reign of Charles I. the Court of King's Bench, relying on some arbitrary precedents (and those perhaps misunderstood), determined that they would not, upon a *habeas corpus*, either bail or deliver a prisoner, though committed without any cause assigned, in case he was committed by the special command of the King or by the Lords of the Privy Council. This drew on a Parliamentary inquiry and produced the *Petition of Right* — 3 Charles I. — which recites this illegal judgment, and enacts that no freeman hereafter shall be so imprisoned or detained. But when in the following year Mr. Selden and others were committed by the Lords of the Council in pursuance of his Majesty's special command, under a general charge of 'notable contempts, and stirring up sedition against the King and the Government,' the judges delayed for two terms (including also the long vacation) to deliver an opinion how far such a charge was bailable. And when at length they agreed that it was, they however annexed a condition of finding sureties for their good behavior, which still protracted their imprisonment, the Chief Justice, Sir Nicholas Hyde, at the same time declaring that 'if they were again remanded for that cause, perhaps the Court would not afterwards grant a *habeas corpus*, being already made acquainted with the cause of the imprisonment.' But this was heard with indignation and astonishment by every lawyer present, according to Mr. Selden's own account of the matter, whose resentment was not cooled at the distance of four and twenty years."

It is worthy of remark that the offences charged against the prisoner in this case, and relied on as a justification for his arrest and imprisonment, in their nature and character, and in the loose and vague manner in which they are stated, bear a striking resemblance to those assigned in the warrant for the arrest of Mr. Selden. And yet, even at that day, the warrant was regarded as such a flagrant violation of the rights of the subject that the delay of the time-serving judges to set him at liberty upon the *habeas corpus* issued in his behalf excited the universal indignation of the bar. The extract from Hallam's Constitutional History is equally impressive, and equally in point. (It is in vol. 4, p. 9, and is also cited at length in the note to pp. 136, 137, of the 3d volume of Wendell's edition of Blackstone.)

" It is a very common mistake, and not only among foreigners, but many from whom some knowledge of our constitutional laws might be expected, to suppose that this statute of Charles II. enlarged in a great degree our liberties, and forms a sort of epoch in their history. But though a very beneficial enactment, and eminently remedial in many cases of illegal imprisonment, it introduced no new principle, nor conferred any right upon the subject. From the earliest records of the English law, no freeman could be detained in prison, except upon a criminal charge or conviction, or for a civil debt. In the former case it was always in his power to demand of the Court of King's Bench a writ of *habeas corpus ad subjiciendum*, directed to the person detaining him in custody, by which he was enjoined to bring up the body of the prisoner with the warrant of commitment that the Court might judge of its sufficiency and remand the party, admit him to bail, or discharge him, according to the nature of the charge. This writ issued of right, and could not be refused by the Court. It was not to bestow an immunity from arbitrary imprisonment, which is abundantly provided for in Magna Charta, (if, indeed, it is not more ancient,) that the statute of Charles II. was enacted, but to cut off the abuses by which the Government's lust of power, and the servile subtlety of Crown lawyers, had impaired so fundamental a privilege."

While the value set upon this writ in England has been so great that the removal of the abuses which embarrassed its enjoyment have been looked upon as almost a new grant of liberty to the subject, it is not to be wondered at that the continuance of the writ thus made effective should have been the object of the most jealous care. Accordingly, no power in England, short of that of Parliament, can suspend or authorize the suspension of the writ of *habeas corpus*. I quote again from Blackstone (1 Comm., 136) : " But the happiness of our Constitution is that it is not left to the Executive power to determine when the danger of the State is so great as to render this measure expedient. It is the Parliament only or legislative power that, whenever it sees proper, can authorize the Crown, by suspending the *habeas corpus* for a short and limited time, to imprison suspected persons without giving any reason for so doing." And if the President of the United States may suspend the writ, then the Constitution of the United States has conferred upon him more regal and absolute power over the liberty of the citizen than the people of England have thought it safe to entrust to the Crown — a power which the Queen of England cannot exercise at this day, and which could not have been lawfully exercised by the sovereign even in the reign of Charles the First.

But I am not left to form my judgment upon this great question from analogies between the English Government and our own, or the commentaries of English jurists, or the decisions of English courts, although upon this subject they are entitled to the highest respect, and are justly regarded and received as authoritative by our courts of justice. To guide me to a right conclusion, I have the commentaries on the Constitution of the United States of the late Mr. Justice Story, not only one of the most eminent jurists of the age, but for a long time one of the brightest ornaments of the Supreme Court of the United States, and also the clear and authoritative decision of that Court itself, given more than half a century since, and conclusively establishing the principles I have above stated.

Mr. Justice Story, speaking in his Commentaries of the *habeas corpus* clause in the Constitution, says:

"It is obvious that cases of a peculiar emergency may arise, which may justify, nay, even require, the temporary suspension of any right to the writ. But as it has frequently happened in foreign countries, and even in England, that the writ has, upon various pretexts and occasions, been suspended, whereby persons apprehended upon suspicion have suffered a long imprisonment, sometimes from design, and sometimes because they were forgotten, the right to suspend it is expressly confined to cases of rebellion or invasion, where the public safety may require it. A very just and wholesome restraint, which cuts down at a blow a fruitful means of oppression, capable of being abused in bad times to the worst of purposes. Hitherto no suspension of the writ has ever been authorized by Congress since the establishment of the Constitution. It would seem, as the power is given to Congress to suspend the writ of *habeas corpus* in cases of rebellion or invasion, that the right to judge whether the exigency had arisen must exclusively belong to that body." 3 Story's Comm. on the Constitution, section 1336.

And Chief-Justice Marshall, in delivering the opinion of the Supreme Court in the case of *ex parte* Bollman and Swartwout, uses this decisive language in 4 Cranch, 95 : " It may be worthy of remark that this act (speaking of the one under which I am proceeding) was passed by the first Congress of the United States, sitting under a Constitution which had declared ' that the privilege of the writ of *habeas corpus* should not be suspended unless when, in cases of rebellion or invasion, the public safety might require it.' Acting under the immediate influence of this injunction, they must have felt, with peculiar force, the obligation of providing efficient means by which this great constitutional privilege should receive life and activity ; for if the means be not in existence, the privilege itself would be lost, although no law for its suspension should be enacted. Under the impression of this obligation they give to all the Courts the power of awarding writs of *habeas corpus.*"

And again, in page 101 :

" If at any time the public safety should require the suspension of the powers vested by this act in the Courts of the United States, it is for the Legislature to say so. That question depends on political considerations, on which the Legislature is to decide. Until the Legislative will be expressed, this Court can only see its duty, and must obey the laws."

I can add nothing to these clear and emphatic words of my great predecessor.

But the documents before me show that the military authority in this case has gone far beyond the mere suspension of the privilege of the writ of *habeas corpus.* It has, by force of arms, thrust aside the judicial authorities and officers to whom the Constitution has confided the power and duty of interpreting and administering the laws, and substituted a military government in its place, to be administered and executed by military officers. For at the time these proceedings were had against John Merryman, the District Judge of Maryland, the Commissioner appointed under the act of Congress, the District Attorney, and the Marshal, all resided in the city of Baltimore, a few miles only from the home of the prisoner. Up to that time there had never been the slightest resistance or obstruction to the process of any Court or judicial officer of the United States in Maryland, except by the military authority. And if a military officer, or any other person, had reason to believe that the prisoner had committed any offence against the laws of the United States, it was his duty to give information of the fact, and the evidence to support it, to the District Attorney; and it would then have become the duty of that officer to bring the matter before the District Judge or Commissioner, and if there was sufficient legal evidence to justify his arrest, the Judge or Commissioner would have issued his warrant to the Marshal to arrest him; and upon the hearing of the case would have held him to bail, or committed him for trial, according to the character of the offence as it appeared in the testimony, or would have discharged him immediately, if there was not sufficient evidence to support the accusation. There was no danger of any obstruction or resistance to the action of the civil authorities, and therefore no reason whatever for the interposition of the military.

And yet, under these circumstances, a military officer, stationed in Pennsylvania, without giving any information to the District Attorney, and without any application to the judicial authorities, assumes to himself the judicial power in the District of Maryland; undertakes to decide what constitutes the crime of treason or rebellion; what evidence (if, indeed, he required any) is sufficient to support the accusation and justify the commitment; and commits the party, without a hearing even before himself, to close custody in a strongly garrisoned fort, to be there held, it would seem, during the pleasure of those who committed him.

The Constitution provides, as I have before said, that "no person shall be deprived of life, liberty, or property without due process of law." It declares that "the right of the people to be secure in their persons, houses, papers, and effects, against unreasonable searches and seizures, shall not be violated, and no warrant shall issue, but upon probable cause, supported by oath or affirmation, and particularly describing the place to be searched, and the persons or things to be seized." It provides that the party accused shall be entitled to a speedy trial in a court of justice.

And these great and fundamental laws, which Congress itself could not suspend, have been disregarded and suspended, like the writ of *habeas corpus*, by a military order, supported by force of arms. Such is the case now before me, and I can only say that if the authority which the Constitution has confided to the judiciary department and judicial officers may thus upon any pretext or under any circumstances be usurped by the military power at its discretion, the people of the United States are no longer living under a government of laws, but every citizen holds life, liberty, and property at the will and pleasure of the army officer in whose military district he may happen to be found.*

In such a case my duty was too plain to be mistaken. I have exercised all the power which the Constitution and laws confer upon me, but that power has been resisted by a force too strong for me to overcome. It is possible that the officer who has incurred this grave responsibility may have misunderstood his instructions, and exceeded the authority intended to be given him. I shall, therefore, order all the proceedings in this case, with my opinion, to be filed and recorded in the Circuit Court of the United States for the District of Maryland, and direct the Clerk to transmit a copy, under seal, to the President of the United States. It will then remain for that high officer, in fulfilment of his constitutional obligation, to "take care that the laws be faithfully executed," to determine what measures he will take to cause the civil process of the United States to be respected and enforced.

R. B. TANEY,
Chief Justice of the Supreme Court of the United States.

* See letter to Conway Robinson, p. 460.

THE END.